WONDER WOMAN
Odyssey

volume two

J. MICHAEL STRACZYNSKI
PHIL HESTER
Writers

DON KRAMER
EDUARDO PANSICA
GERALDO BORGES
TRAVIS MOORE
LEE GARBETT
Pencillers

ANDY OWENS
SEAN PARSONS
EBER FERREIRA
MARLO ALQUIZA
WAYNE FAUCHER
WALDEN WONG
DREW GERACI
ROBIN RIGGS
TREVOR SCOTT
Inkers

ALEX SINCLAIR
PETE PANTAZIS
Colorist

TRAVIS LANHAM
Letterer

ALEX GARNER
Collection Cover Artist

Special thanks to MATTHEW WAITE

Wonder Woman created by
William Moulton Marston

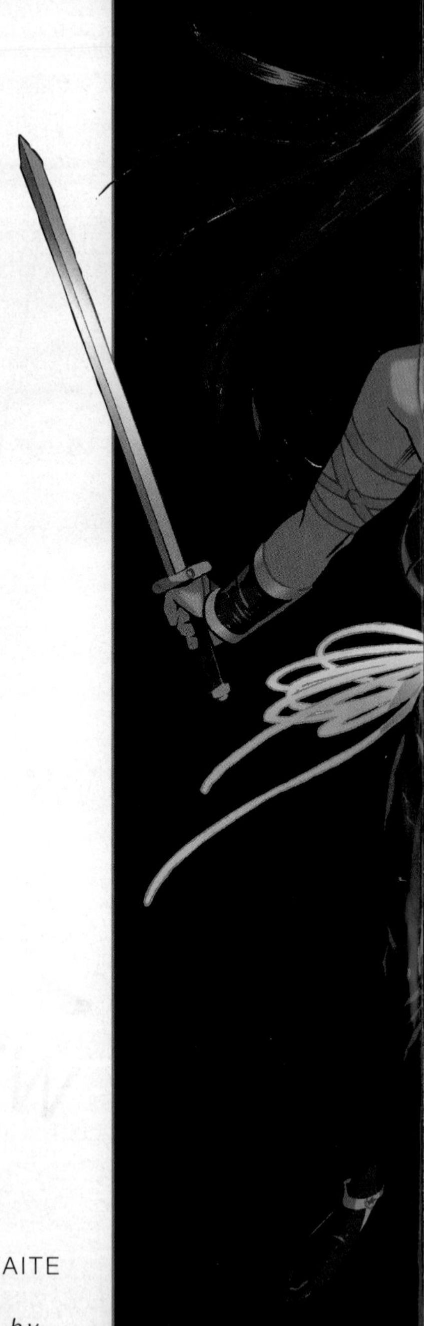

Wonder Woman Odyssey

volume two

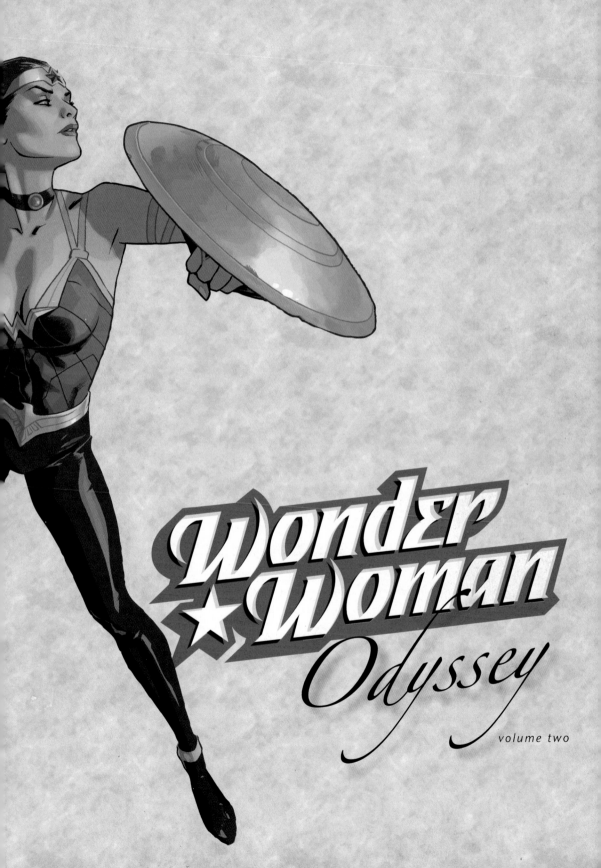

Brian Cunningham Matt Idelson Editors-original series
Chris Conroy Sean Ryan Associate Editors-original series
Darren Shan Assistant Editor-original series
Peter Hamboussi Editor
Robbin Brosterman Design Director-Books

Bob Harras VP-Editor-in-Chief

Diane Nelson President
Dan DiDio and Jim Lee Co-Publishers
Geoff Johns Chief Creative Officer
John Rood Executive VP-Sales, Marketing and Business Development
Amy Genkins Senior VP-Business and Legal Affairs
Nairi Gardiner Senior VP-Finance
Jeff Boison VP-Publishing Operations
Mark Chiarello VP-Art Direction and Design
John Cunningham VP-Marketing
Terri Cunningham VP-Talent Relations and Services
Alison Gill Senior VP-Manufacturing and Operations
Hank Kanalz Senior VP-Digital
Jay Kogan VP-Business and Legal Affairs, Publishing
Jack Mahan VP-Business Affairs, Talent
Nick Napolitano VP-Manufacturing Administration
Sue Pohja VP-Book Sales
Courtney Simmons Senior VP-Publicity
Bob Wayne Senior VP-Sales

WONDER WOMAN: ODYSSEY VOLUME TWO

DC Comics, 1700 Broadway, New York, NY 10019
A Warner Bros. Entertainment Company.
Printed by RR Donnelley, Salem, VA, USA. 1/4/13. First Printing

ISBN: 978-1-4012-3432-4

Library of Congress Cataloging-in-Publication Data

Straczynski, J. Michael.
Wonder Woman. Vol. 2, Odyssey / Phil Hester, Don Kramer, Andy Owens.
p. cm.
"Originally published in single magazine form in Wonder Woman #607-61."
ISBN 978-1-4012-3431-7
1. Graphic novels. I. Hester, Phil. II. Kramer, Don. III. Title: Wonder woman: odyssey volume 2.
PN6728.W6 S78 2012
741.5'973 – dc23
                                            2012376558

SUSTAINABLE
FORESTRY
INITIATIVE
Certified Chain of Custody
At Least 20% Certified Forest Content
www.sfiprogram.org
SFI-01042
APPLIES TO TEXT STOCK ONLY

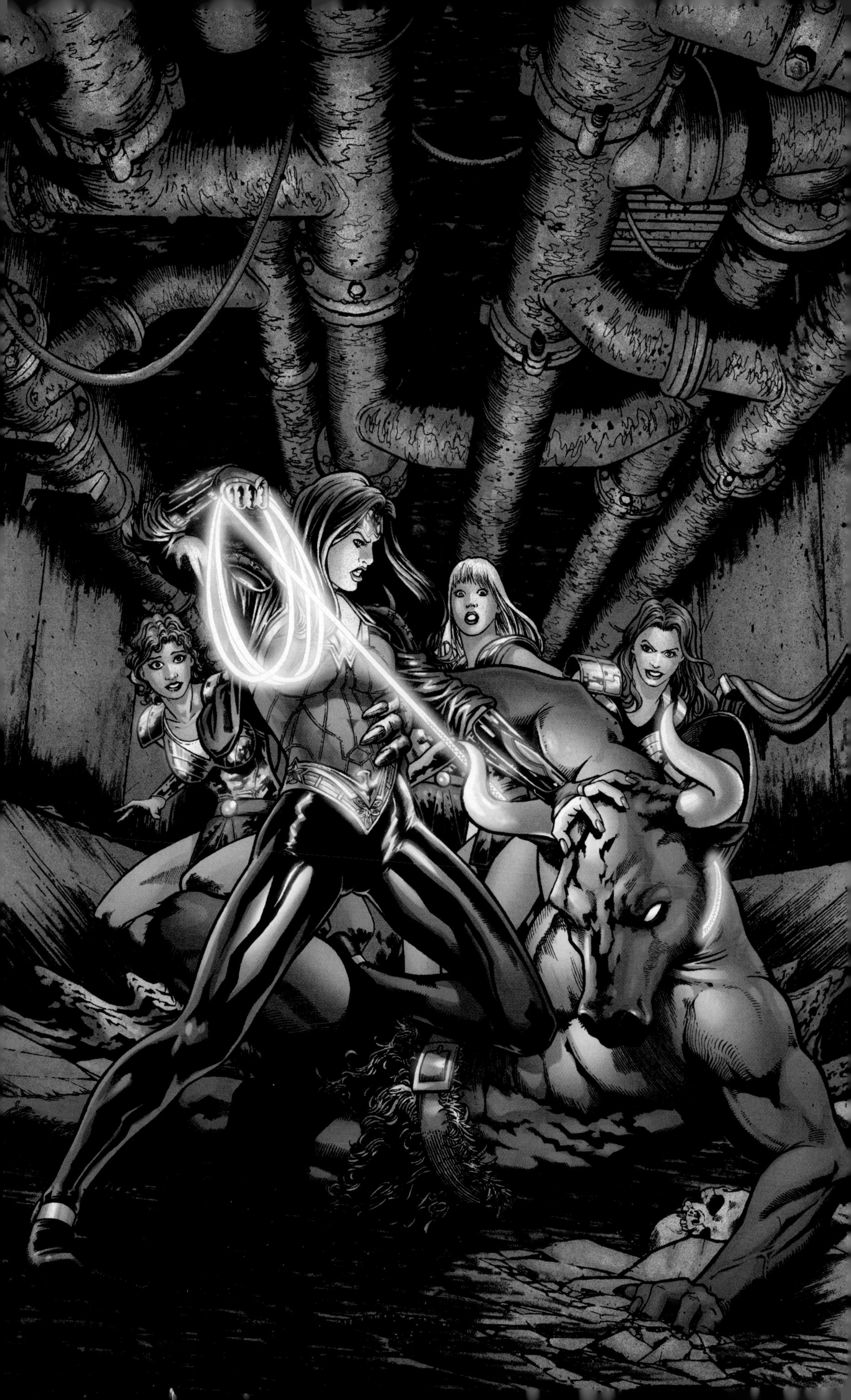

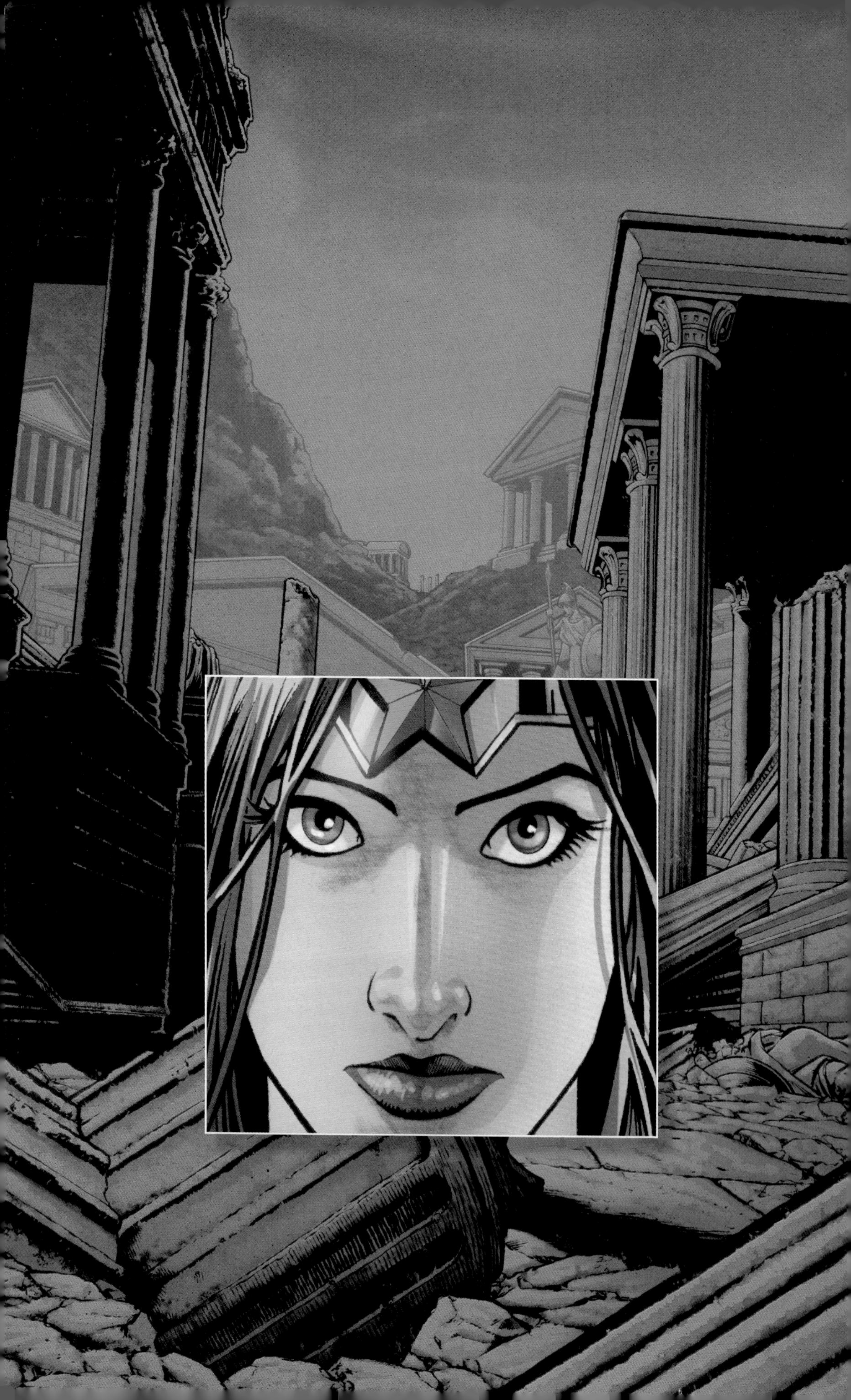

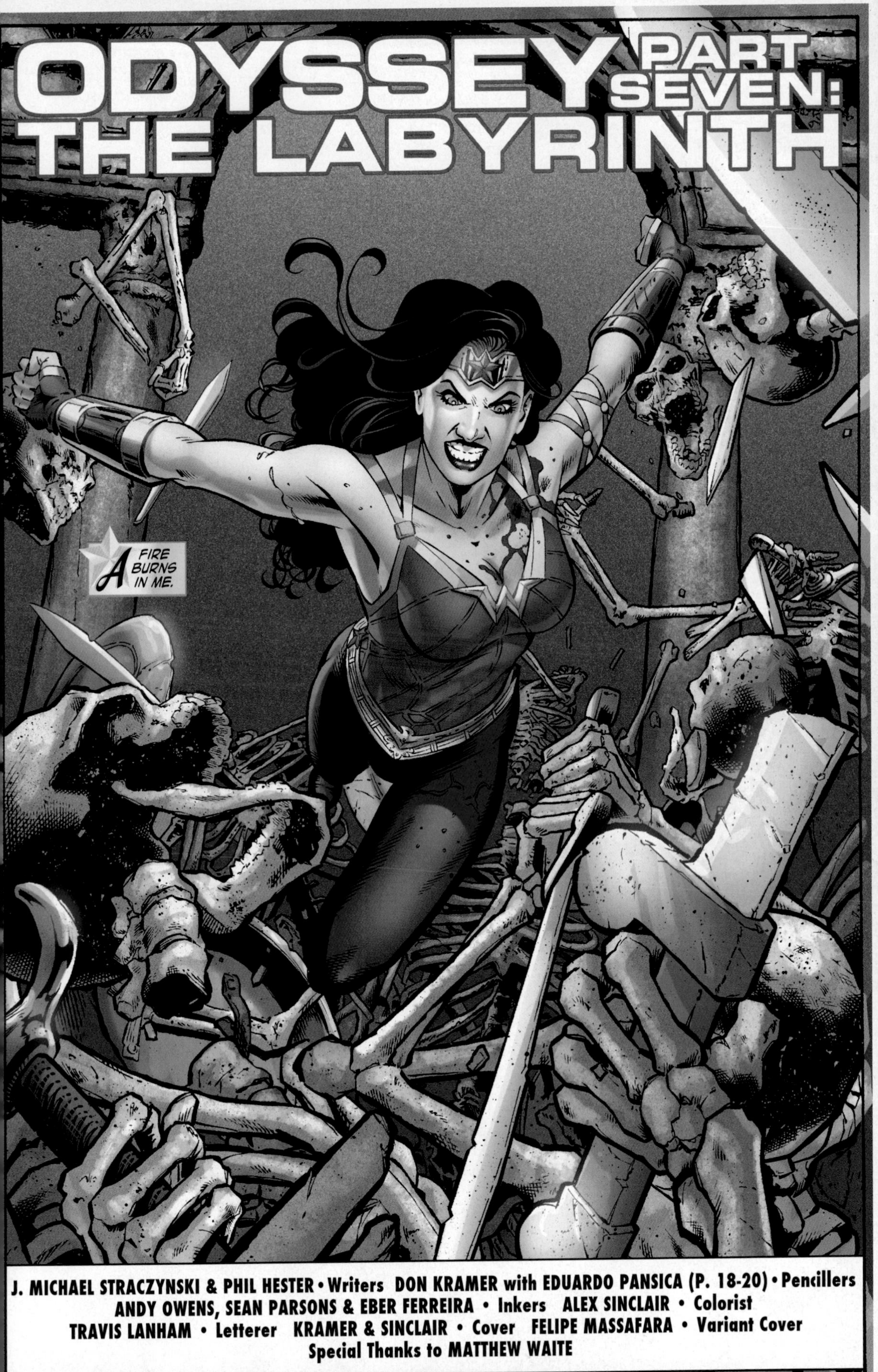
ODYSSEY PART SEVEN: THE LABYRINTH
A FIRE BURNS IN ME.

J. MICHAEL STRACZYNSKI & PHIL HESTER • Writers DON KRAMER with EDUARDO PANSICA (P. 18-20) • Pencillers
ANDY OWENS, SEAN PARSONS & EBER FERREIRA • Inkers ALEX SINCLAIR • Colorist
TRAVIS LANHAM • Letterer KRAMER & SINCLAIR • Cover FELIPE MASSAFARA • Variant Cover
Special Thanks to MATTHEW WAITE

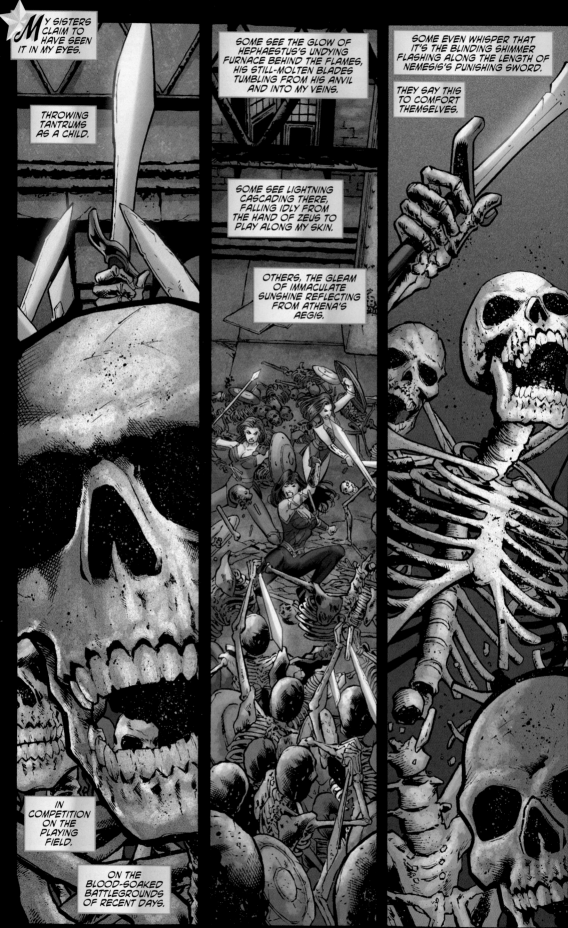

MY SISTERS CLAIM TO HAVE SEEN IT IN MY EYES.

THROWING TANTRUMS AS A CHILD.

IN COMPETITION ON THE PLAYING FIELD.

ON THE BLOOD-SOAKED BATTLEGROUNDS OF RECENT DAYS.

SOME SEE THE GLOW OF HEPHAESTUS'S UNDYING FURNACE BEHIND THE FLAMES, HIS STILL-MOLTEN BLADES TUMBLING FROM HIS ANVIL AND INTO MY VEINS.

SOME SEE LIGHTNING CASCADING THERE, FALLING IDLY FROM THE HAND OF ZEUS TO PLAY ALONG MY SKIN.

OTHERS, THE GLEAM OF IMMACULATE SUNSHINE REFLECTING FROM ATHENA'S AEGIS.

SOME EVEN WHISPER THAT IT'S THE BLINDING SHIMMER FLASHING ALONG THE LENGTH OF NEMESIS'S PUNISHING SWORD.

THEY SAY THIS TO COMFORT THEMSELVES.

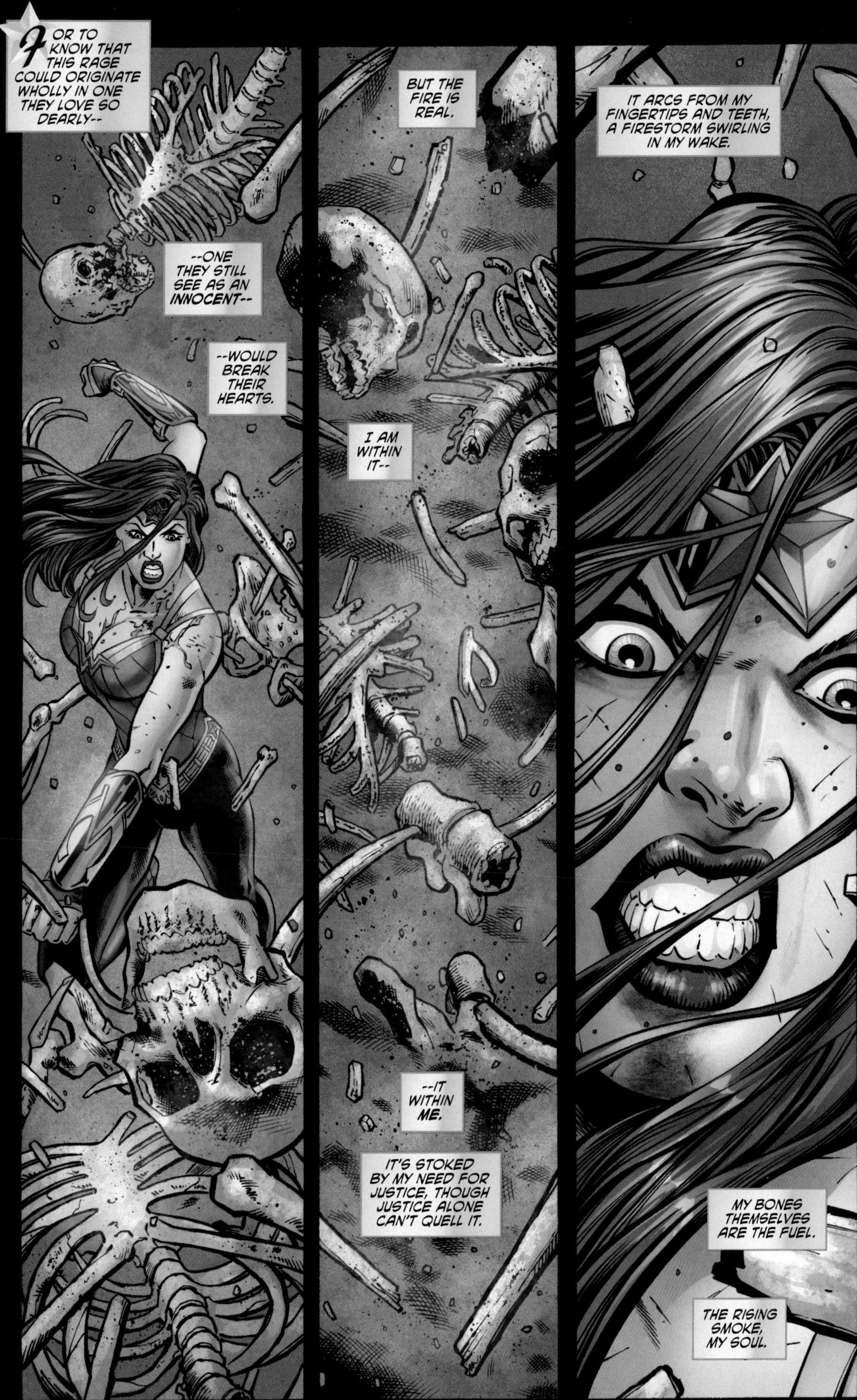
FOR TO KNOW THAT THIS RAGE COULD ORIGINATE WHOLLY IN ONE THEY LOVE SO DEARLY--
--ONE THEY STILL SEE AS AN INNOCENT--
--WOULD BREAK THEIR HEARTS.
BUT THE FIRE IS REAL.
I AM WITHIN IT--
--IT WITHIN ME.
IT'S STOKED BY MY NEED FOR JUSTICE, THOUGH JUSTICE ALONE CAN'T QUELL IT.
IT ARCS FROM MY FINGERTIPS AND TEETH, A FIRESTORM SWIRLING IN MY WAKE.
MY BONES THEMSELVES ARE THE FUEL.
THE RISING SMOKE, MY SOUL.

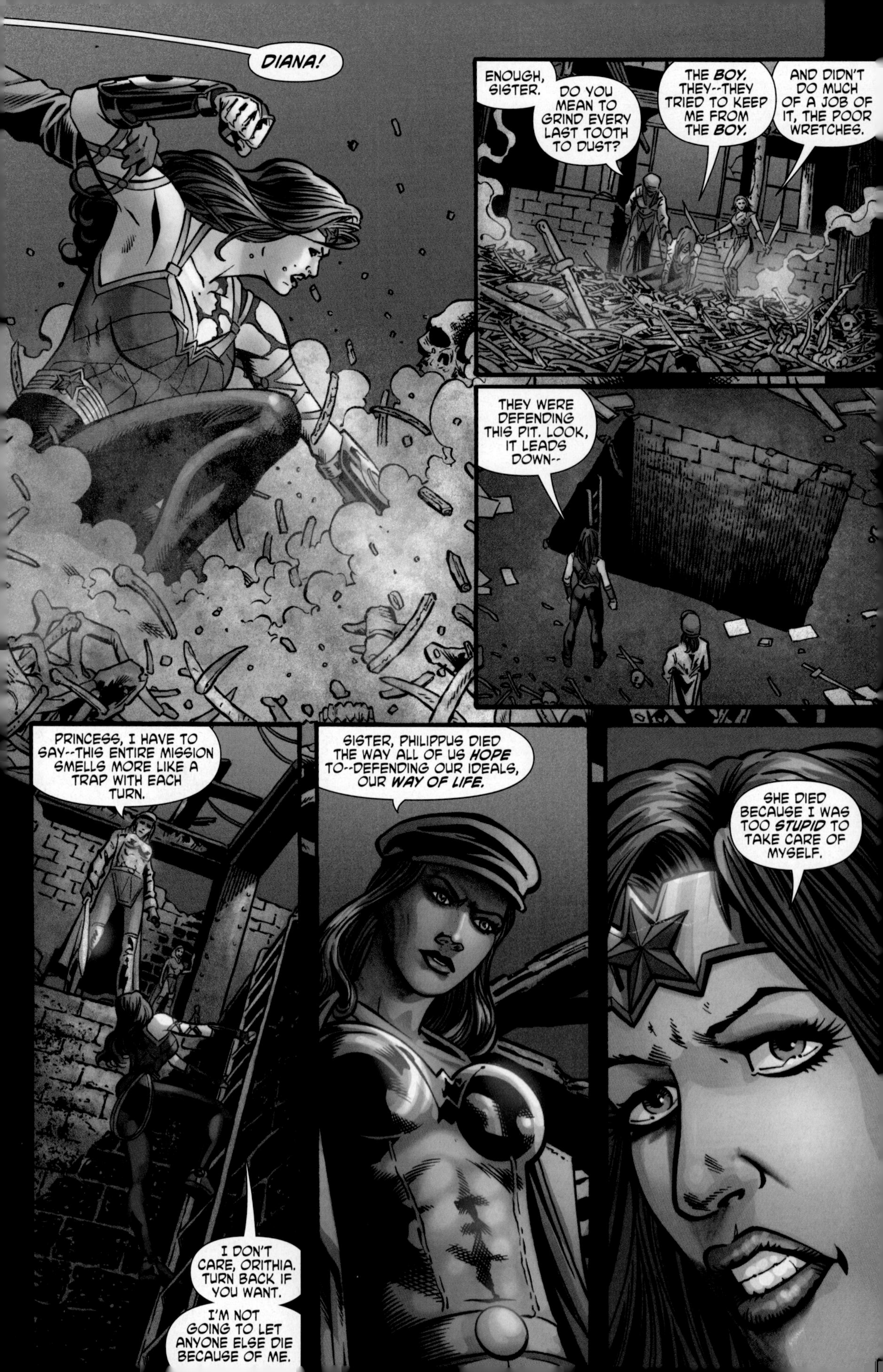
DIANA!
ENOUGH, SISTER.
DO YOU MEAN TO GRIND EVERY LAST TOOTH TO DUST?
THE BOY. THEY--THEY TRIED TO KEEP ME FROM THE BOY.
AND DIDN'T DO MUCH OF A JOB OF IT, THE POOR WRETCHES.
THEY WERE DEFENDING THIS PIT. LOOK, IT LEADS DOWN--
PRINCESS, I HAVE TO SAY--THIS ENTIRE MISSION SMELLS MORE LIKE A TRAP WITH EACH TURN.
I DON'T CARE, ORITHIA. TURN BACK IF YOU WANT.
I'M NOT GOING TO LET ANYONE ELSE DIE BECAUSE OF ME.
SISTER, PHILIPPUS DIED THE WAY ALL OF US HOPE TO--DEFENDING OUR IDEALS, OUR WAY OF LIFE.
SHE DIED BECAUSE I WAS TOO STUPID TO TAKE CARE OF MYSELF.

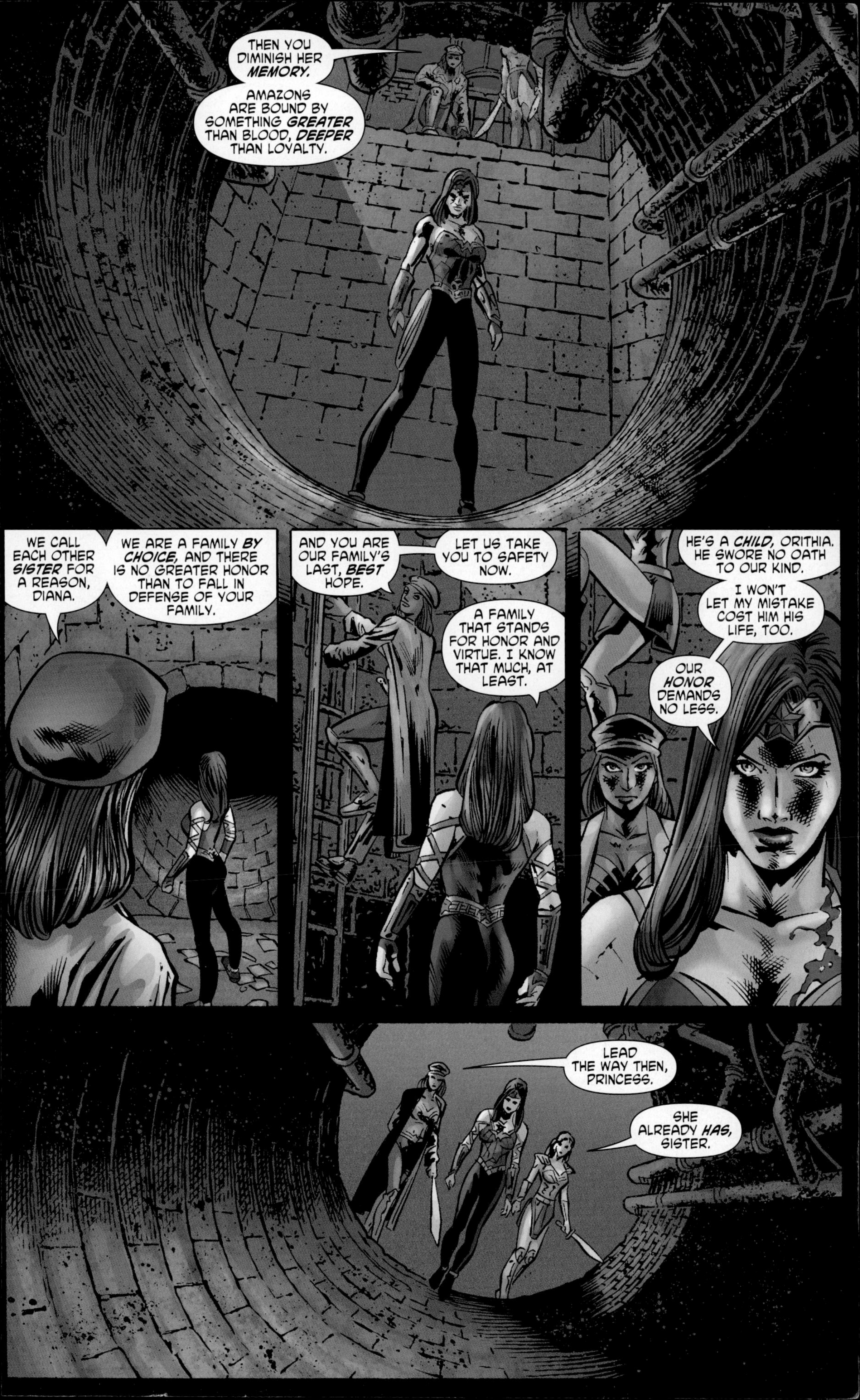
THEN YOU DIMINISH HER MEMORY.
AMAZONS ARE BOUND BY SOMETHING GREATER THAN BLOOD, DEEPER THAN LOYALTY.
WE CALL EACH OTHER SISTER FOR A REASON, DIANA.
WE ARE A FAMILY BY CHOICE, AND THERE IS NO GREATER HONOR THAN TO FALL IN DEFENSE OF YOUR FAMILY.
AND YOU ARE OUR FAMILY'S LAST, BEST HOPE.
LET US TAKE YOU TO SAFETY NOW.
A FAMILY THAT STANDS FOR HONOR AND VIRTUE. I KNOW THAT MUCH, AT LEAST.
HE'S A CHILD, ORITHIA. HE SWORE NO OATH TO OUR KIND.
I WON'T LET MY MISTAKE COST HIM HIS LIFE, TOO.
OUR HONOR DEMANDS NO LESS.
LEAD THE WAY THEN, PRINCESS.
SHE ALREADY HAS, SISTER.

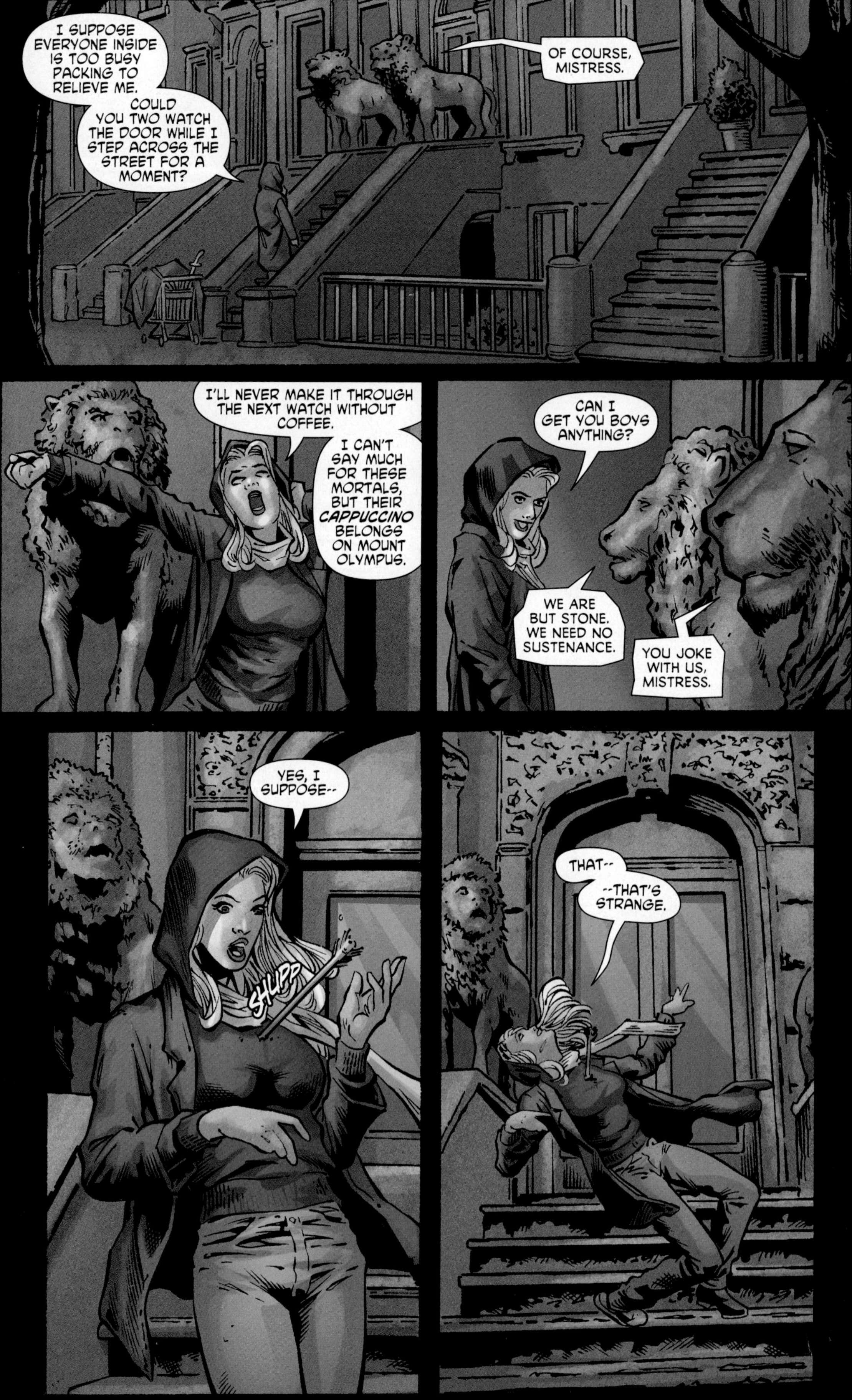
I SUPPOSE EVERYONE INSIDE IS TOO BUSY PACKING TO RELIEVE ME.
COULD YOU TWO WATCH THE DOOR WHILE I STEP ACROSS THE STREET FOR A MOMENT?
OF COURSE, MISTRESS.
I'LL NEVER MAKE IT THROUGH THE NEXT WATCH WITHOUT COFFEE.
I CAN'T SAY MUCH FOR THESE MORTALS, BUT THEIR CAPPUCCINO BELONGS ON MOUNT OLYMPUS.
CAN I GET YOU BOYS ANYTHING?
WE ARE BUT STONE. WE NEED NO SUSTENANCE.
YOU JOKE WITH US, MISTRESS.
YES, I SUPPOSE--
SHUPP
THAT--
--THAT'S STRANGE.

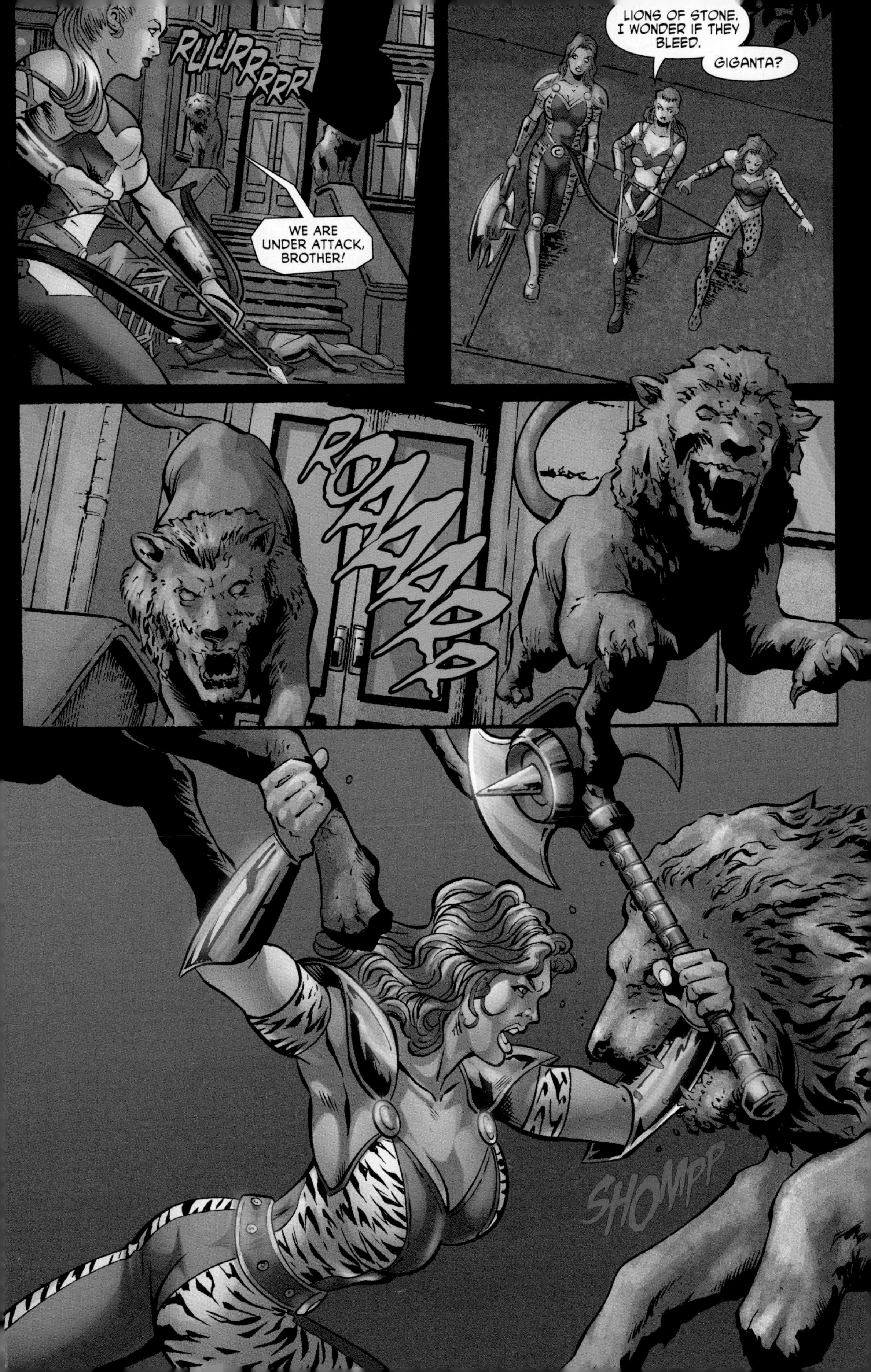
RUURRRRRR
WE ARE UNDER ATTACK, BROTHER!
LIONS OF STONE. I WONDER IF THEY BLEED.
GIGANTA?
ROAAAARR
SHOMPP

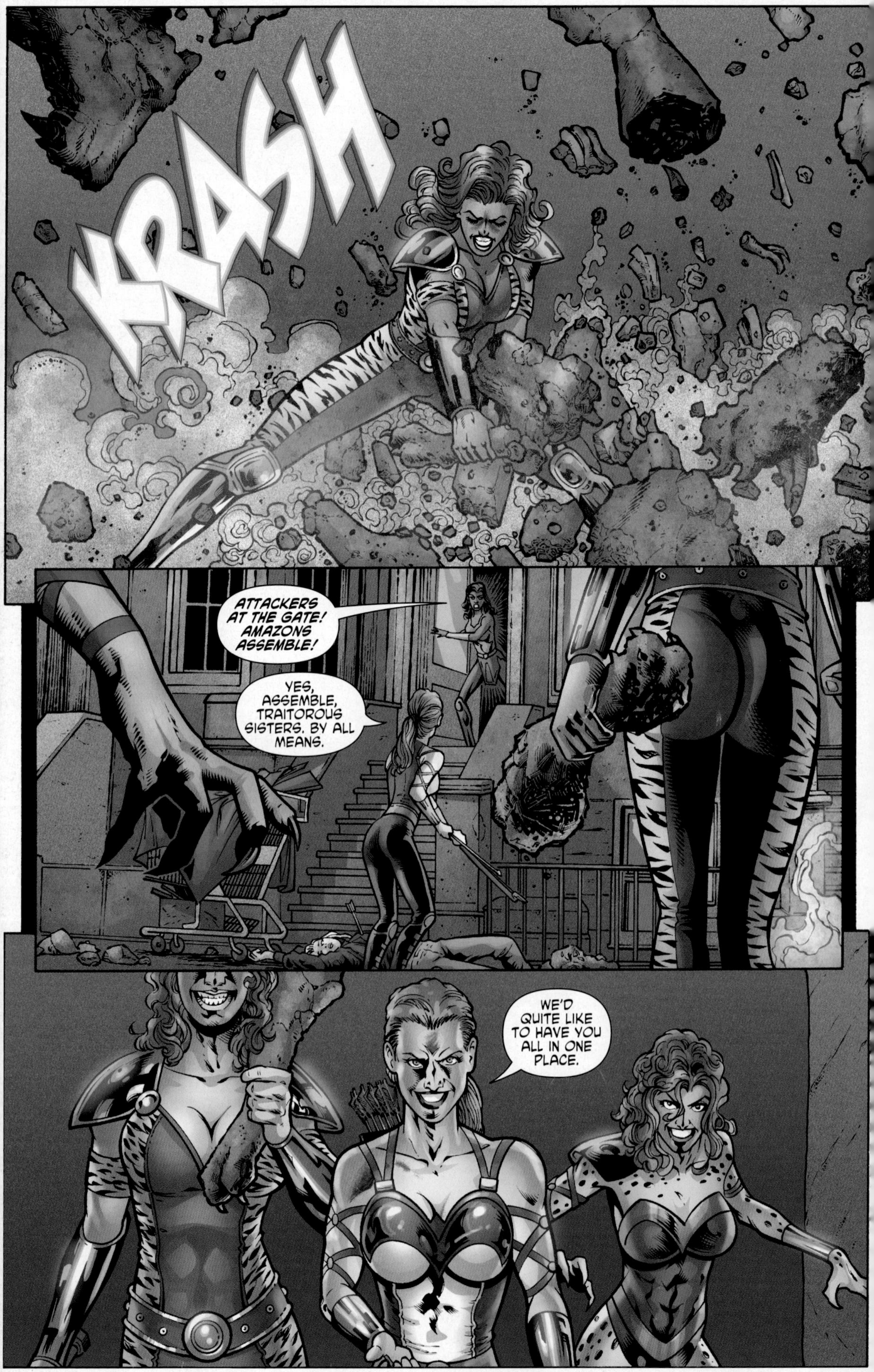
KRASH
ATTACKERS AT THE GATE! AMAZONS ASSEMBLE!
YES, ASSEMBLE, TRAITOROUS SISTERS. BY ALL MEANS.
WE'D QUITE LIKE TO HAVE YOU ALL IN ONE PLACE.

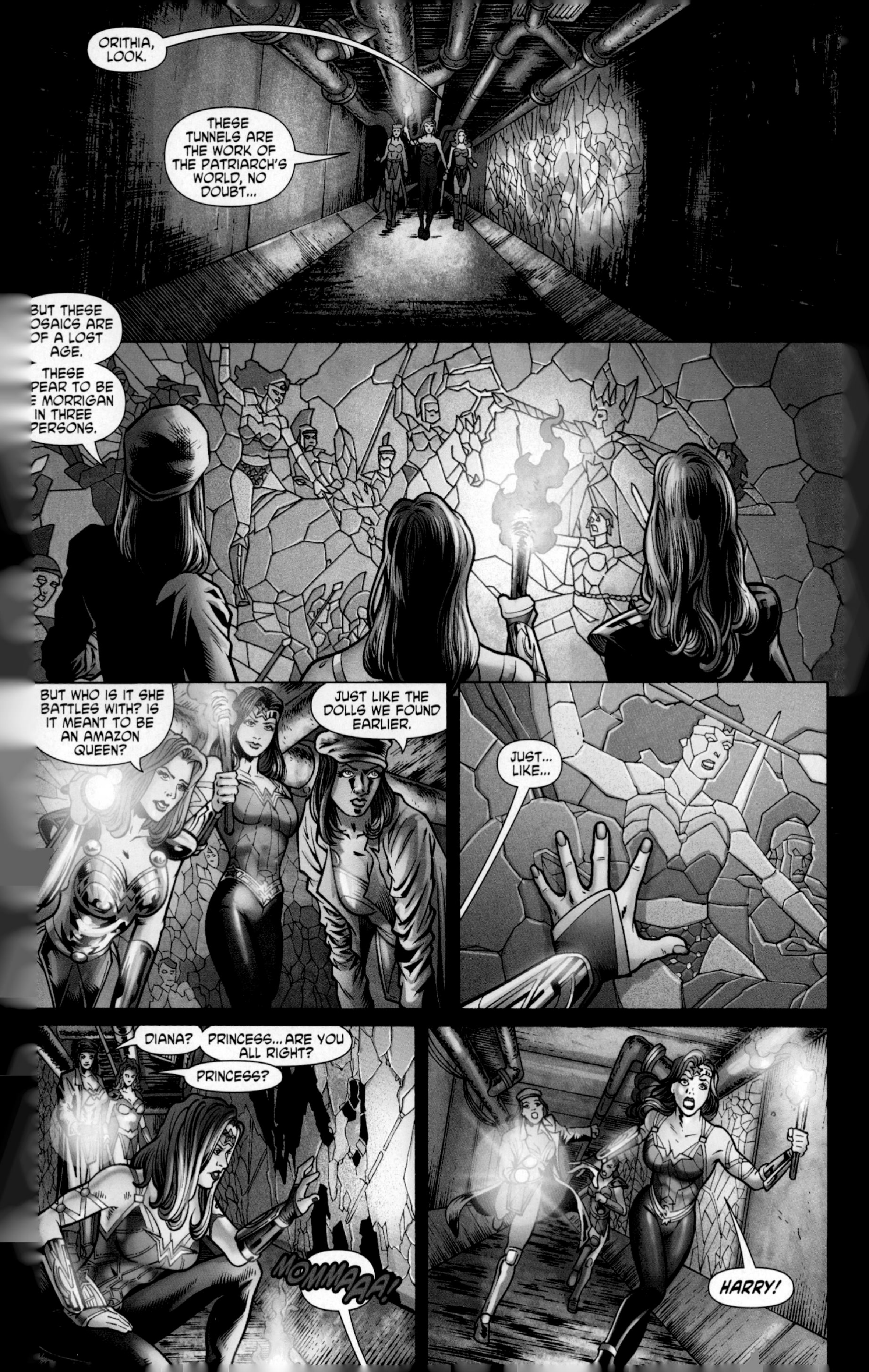
ORITHIA, LOOK.
THESE TUNNELS ARE THE WORK OF THE PATRIARCH'S WORLD, NO DOUBT...
BUT THESE OSAICS ARE OF A LOST AGE.
THESE PEAR TO BE E MORRIGAN IN THREE PERSONS.
BUT WHO IS IT SHE BATTLES WITH? IS IT MEANT TO BE AN AMAZON QUEEN?
JUST LIKE THE DOLLS WE FOUND EARLIER.
JUST... LIKE...
DIANA?
PRINCESS... ARE YOU ALL RIGHT?
PRINCESS?
MOMMAAA!
HARRY!

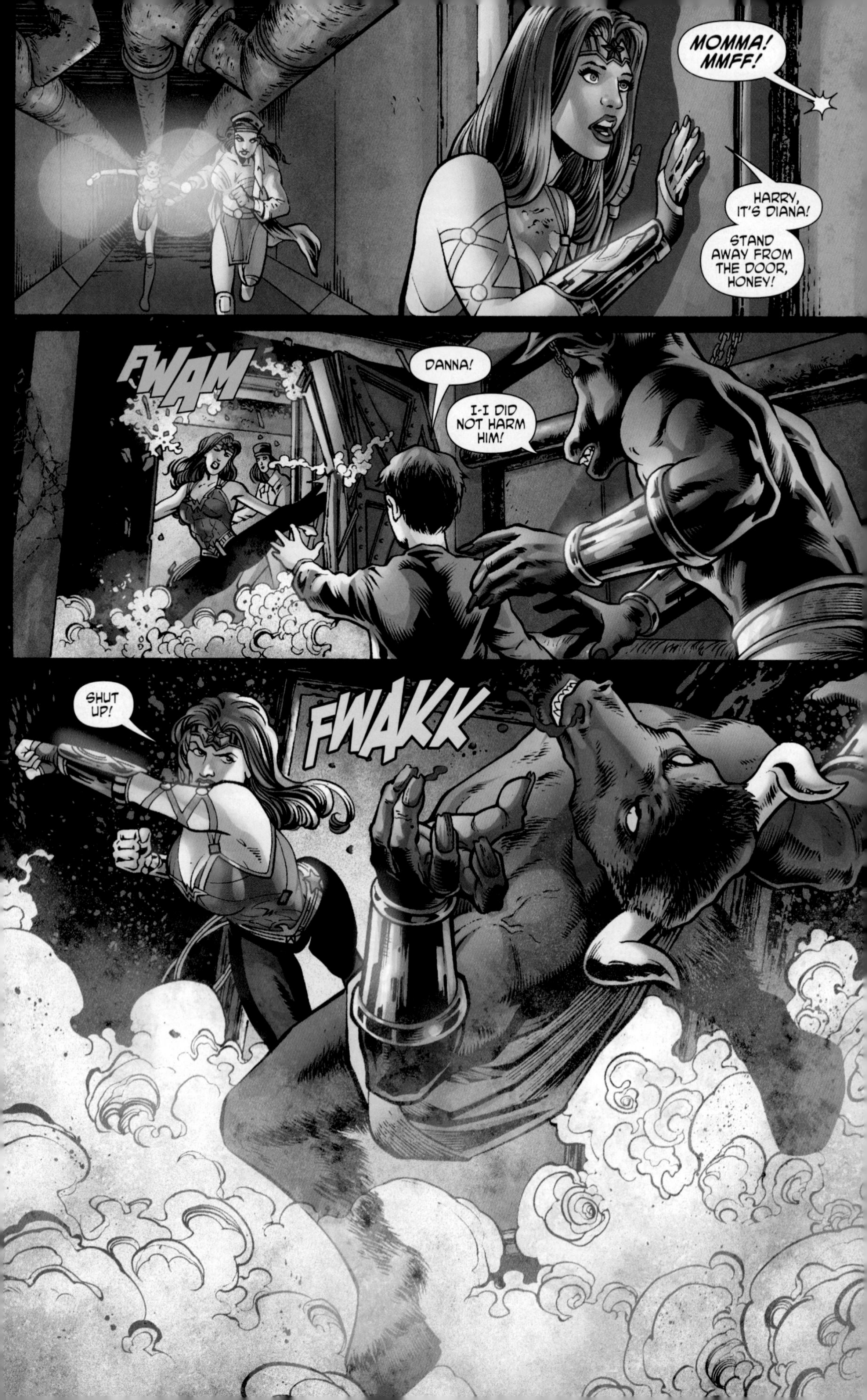
MOMMA! MMFF!
HARRY, IT'S DIANA!
STAND AWAY FROM THE DOOR, HONEY!
FWAM
DANNA!
I-I DID NOT HARM HIM!
SHUT UP!
FWAKK

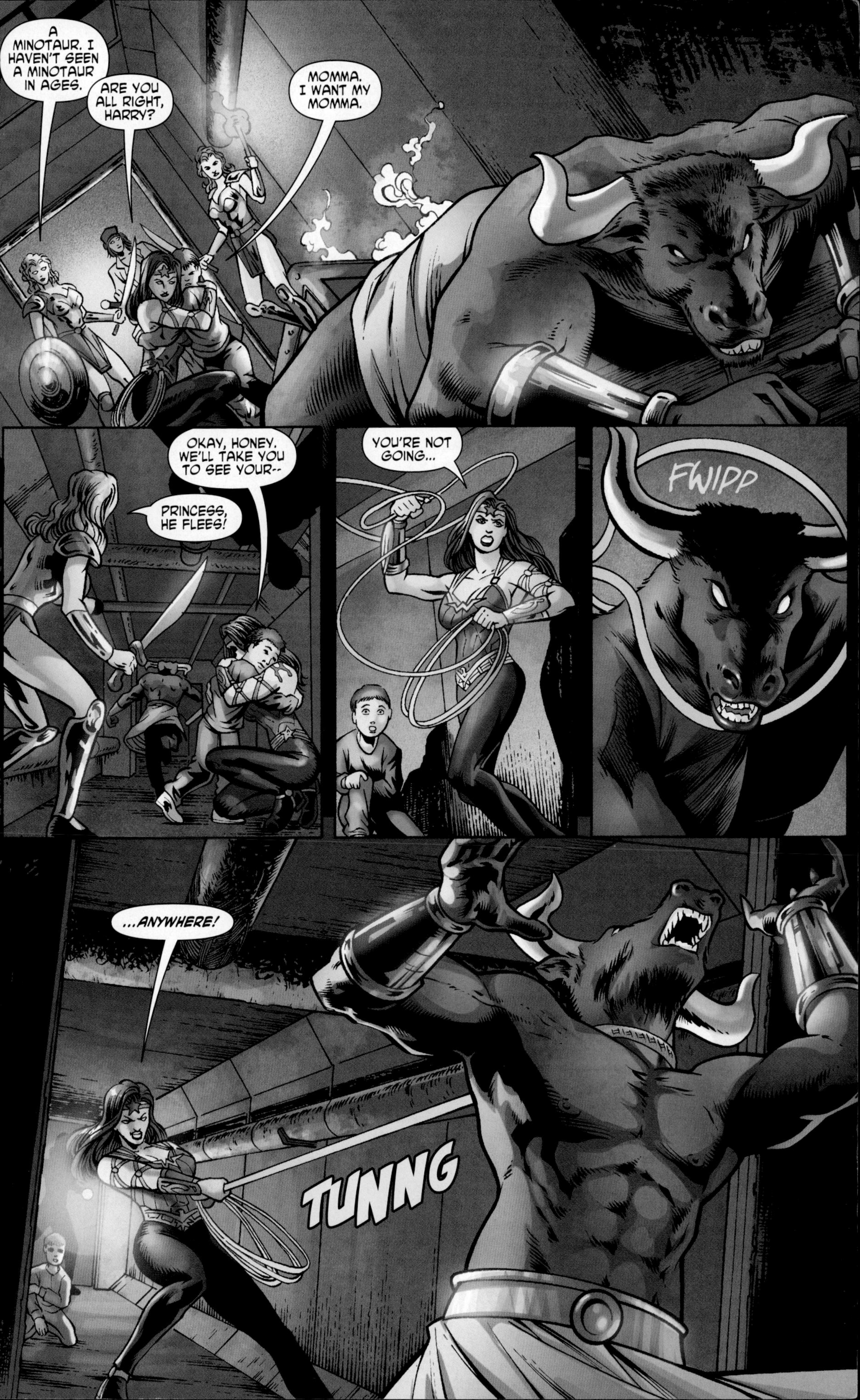
A MINOTAUR. I HAVEN'T SEEN A MINOTAUR IN AGES.
ARE YOU ALL RIGHT, HARRY?
MOMMA. I WANT MY MOMMA.
OKAY, HONEY. WE'LL TAKE YOU TO SEE YOUR--
PRINCESS, HE FLEES!
YOU'RE NOT GOING...
FWIPP
...ANYWHERE!
TUNNG

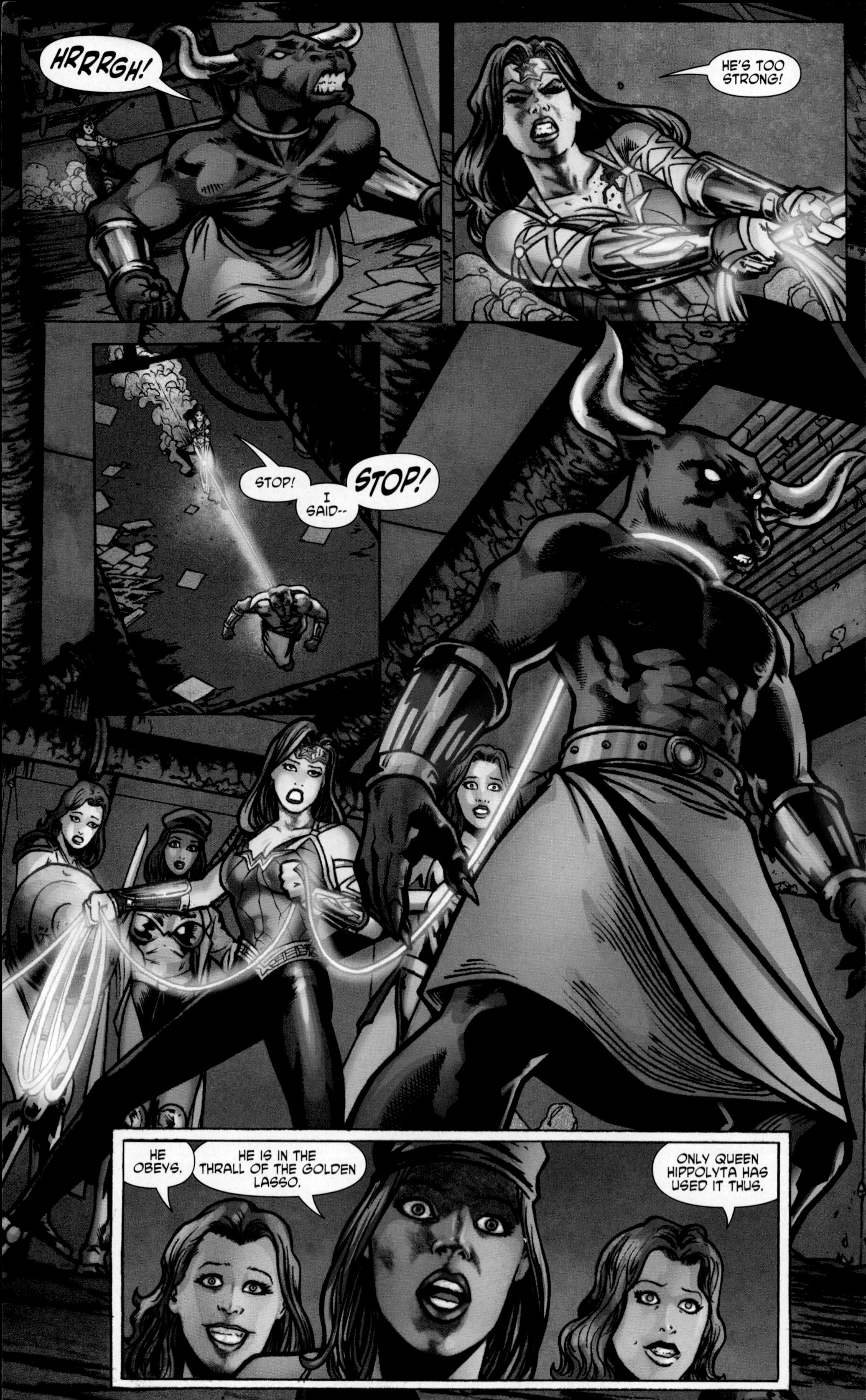
HRRRGH!
HE'S TOO STRONG!
STOP!
I SAID--
STOP!
HE OBEYS.
HE IS IN THE THRALL OF THE GOLDEN LASSO.
ONLY QUEEN HIPPOLYTA HAS USED IT THUS.

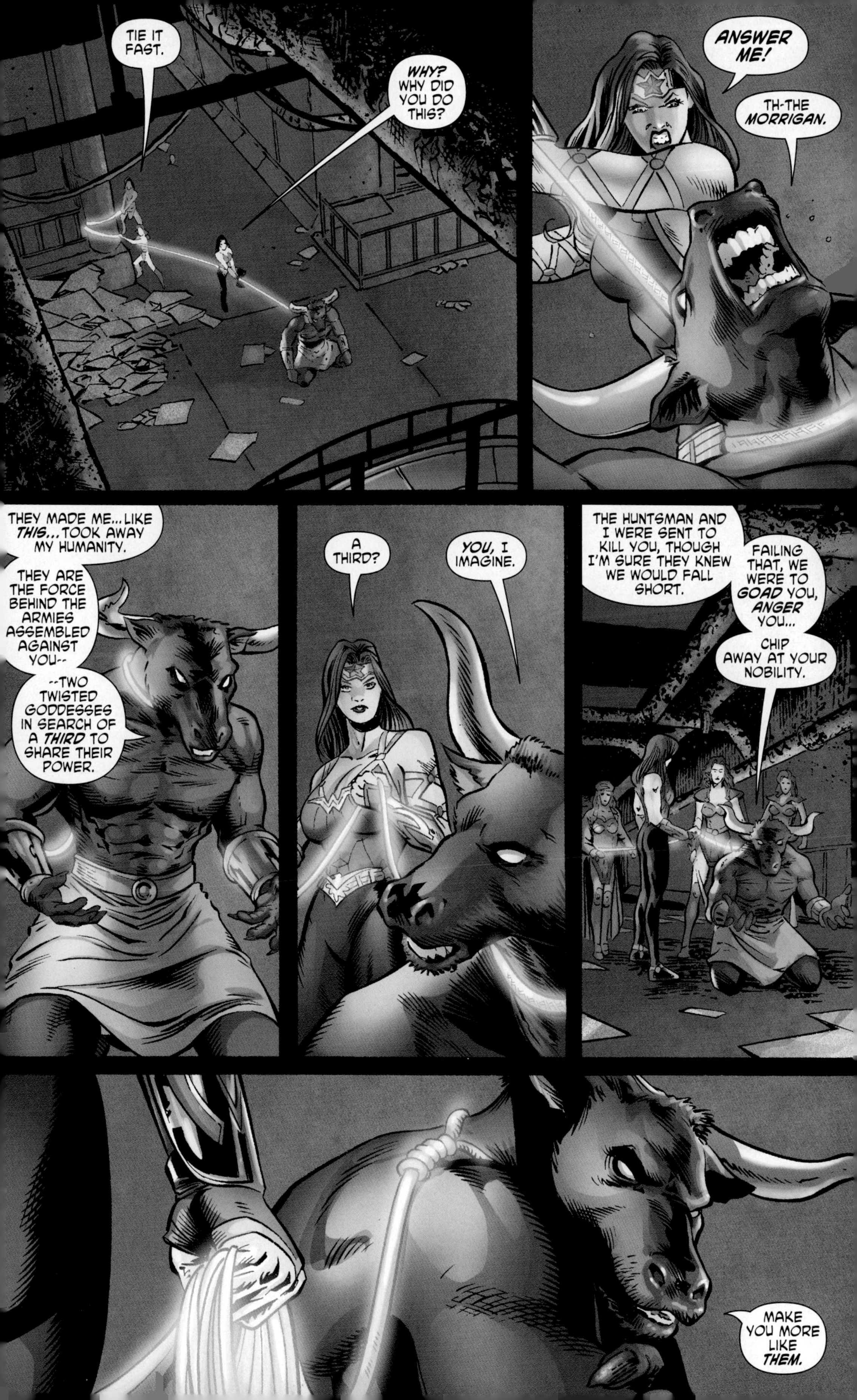
TIE IT FAST.
WHY? WHY DID YOU DO THIS?
ANSWER ME!
TH-THE MORRIGAN.
THEY MADE ME...LIKE THIS...TOOK AWAY MY HUMANITY.
THEY ARE THE FORCE BEHIND THE ARMIES ASSEMBLED AGAINST YOU--
--TWO TWISTED GODDESSES IN SEARCH OF A THIRD TO SHARE THEIR POWER.
A THIRD?
YOU, I IMAGINE.
THE HUNTSMAN AND I WERE SENT TO KILL YOU, THOUGH I'M SURE THEY KNEW WE WOULD FALL SHORT.
FAILING THAT, WE WERE TO GOAD YOU, ANGER YOU...
CHIP AWAY AT YOUR NOBILITY.
MAKE YOU MORE LIKE THEM.

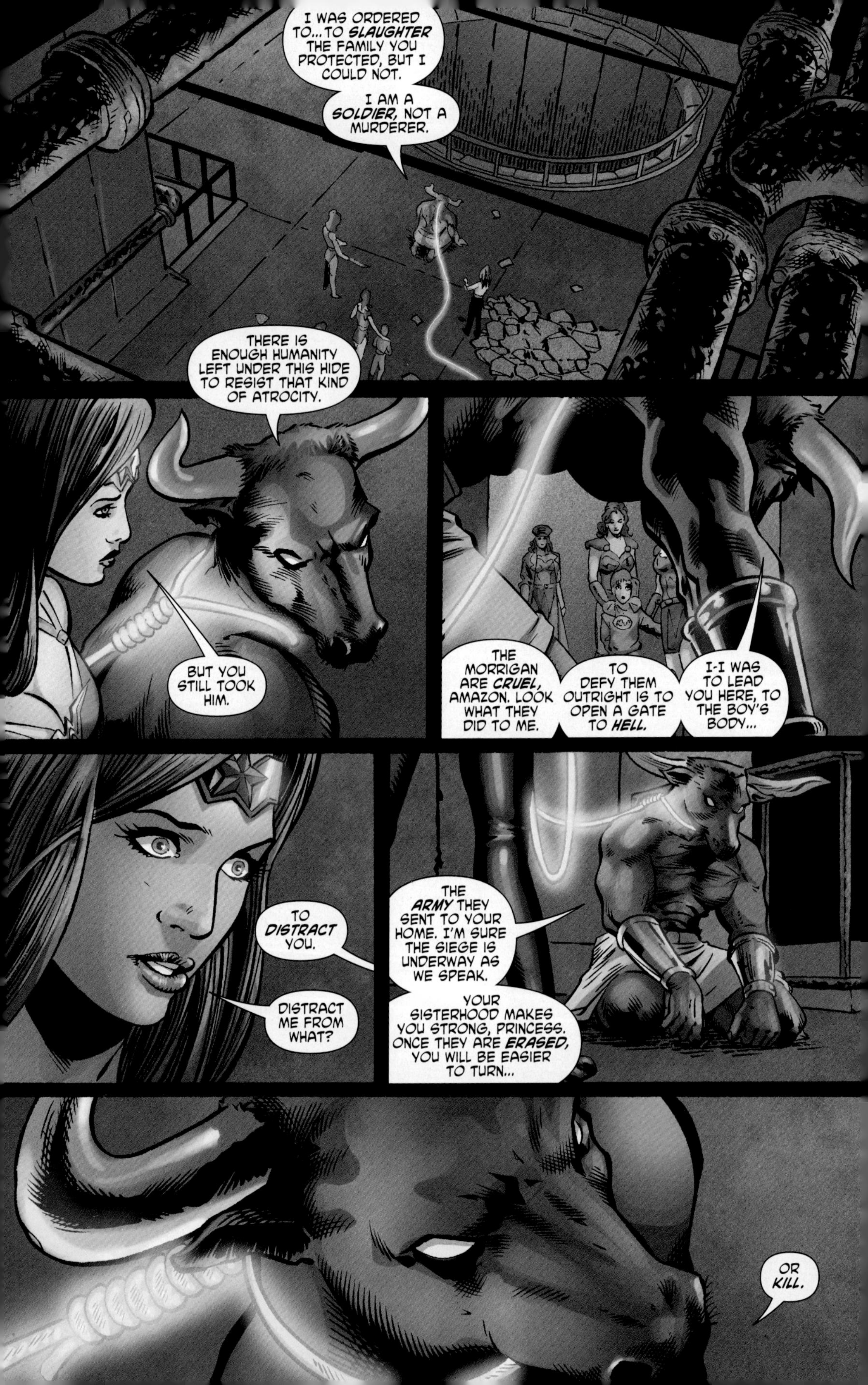
I WAS ORDERED TO...TO SLAUGHTER THE FAMILY YOU PROTECTED, BUT I COULD NOT.
I AM A SOLDIER, NOT A MURDERER.
THERE IS ENOUGH HUMANITY LEFT UNDER THIS HIDE TO RESIST THAT KIND OF ATROCITY.
BUT YOU STILL TOOK HIM.
THE MORRIGAN ARE CRUEL, AMAZON. LOOK WHAT THEY DID TO ME.
TO DEFY THEM OUTRIGHT IS TO OPEN A GATE TO HELL.
I-I WAS TO LEAD YOU HERE, TO THE BOY'S BODY...
TO DISTRACT YOU.
DISTRACT ME FROM WHAT?
THE ARMY THEY SENT TO YOUR HOME. I'M SURE THE SIEGE IS UNDERWAY AS WE SPEAK.
YOUR SISTERHOOD MAKES YOU STRONG, PRINCESS. ONCE THEY ARE ERASED, YOU WILL BE EASIER TO TURN...
OR KILL.

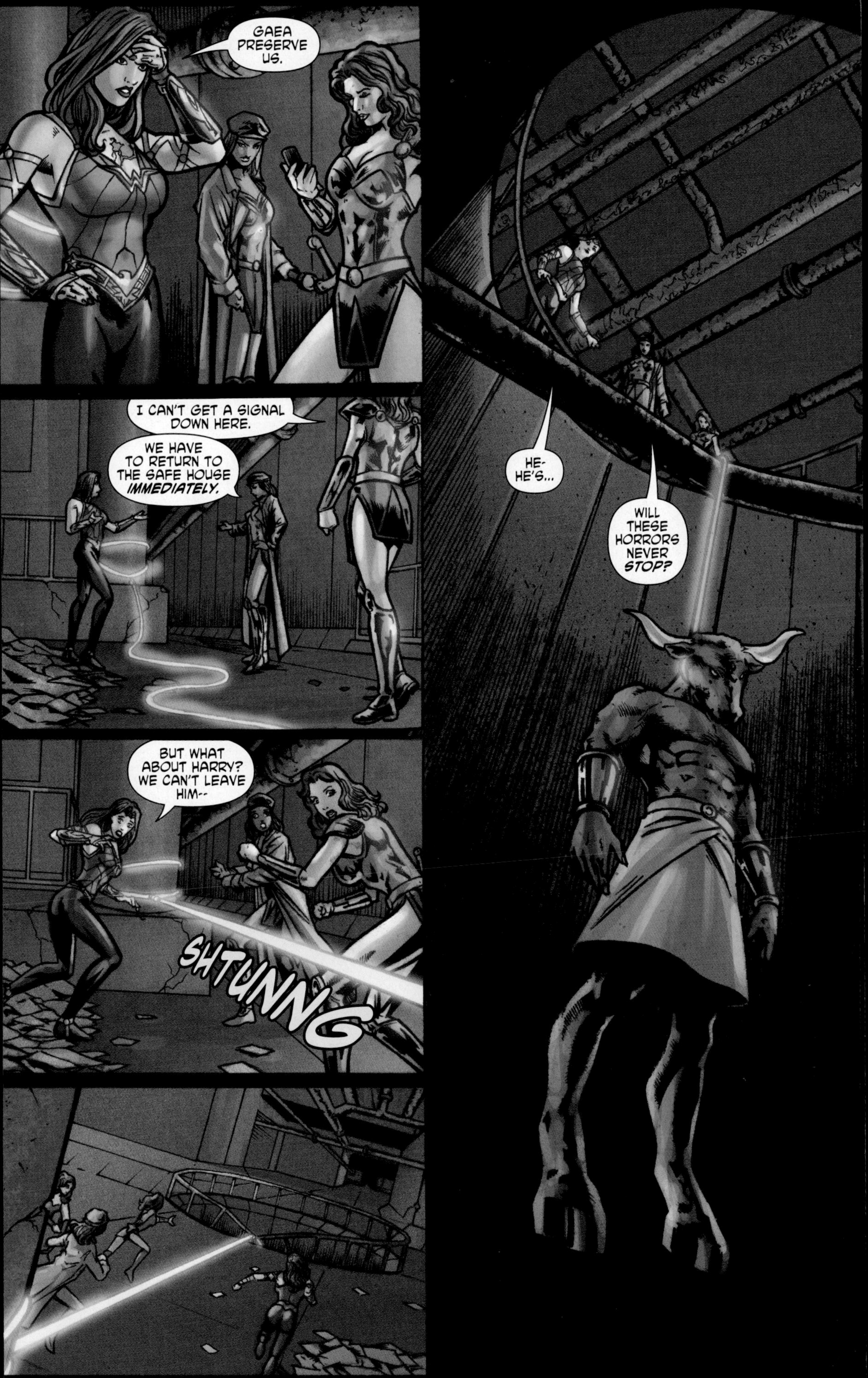
GAEA PRESERVE US.
I CAN'T GET A SIGNAL DOWN HERE.
WE HAVE TO RETURN TO THE SAFE HOUSE IMMEDIATELY.
BUT WHAT ABOUT HARRY? WE CAN'T LEAVE HIM--
SHTUNNG
HE- HE'S...
WILL THESE HORRORS NEVER STOP?

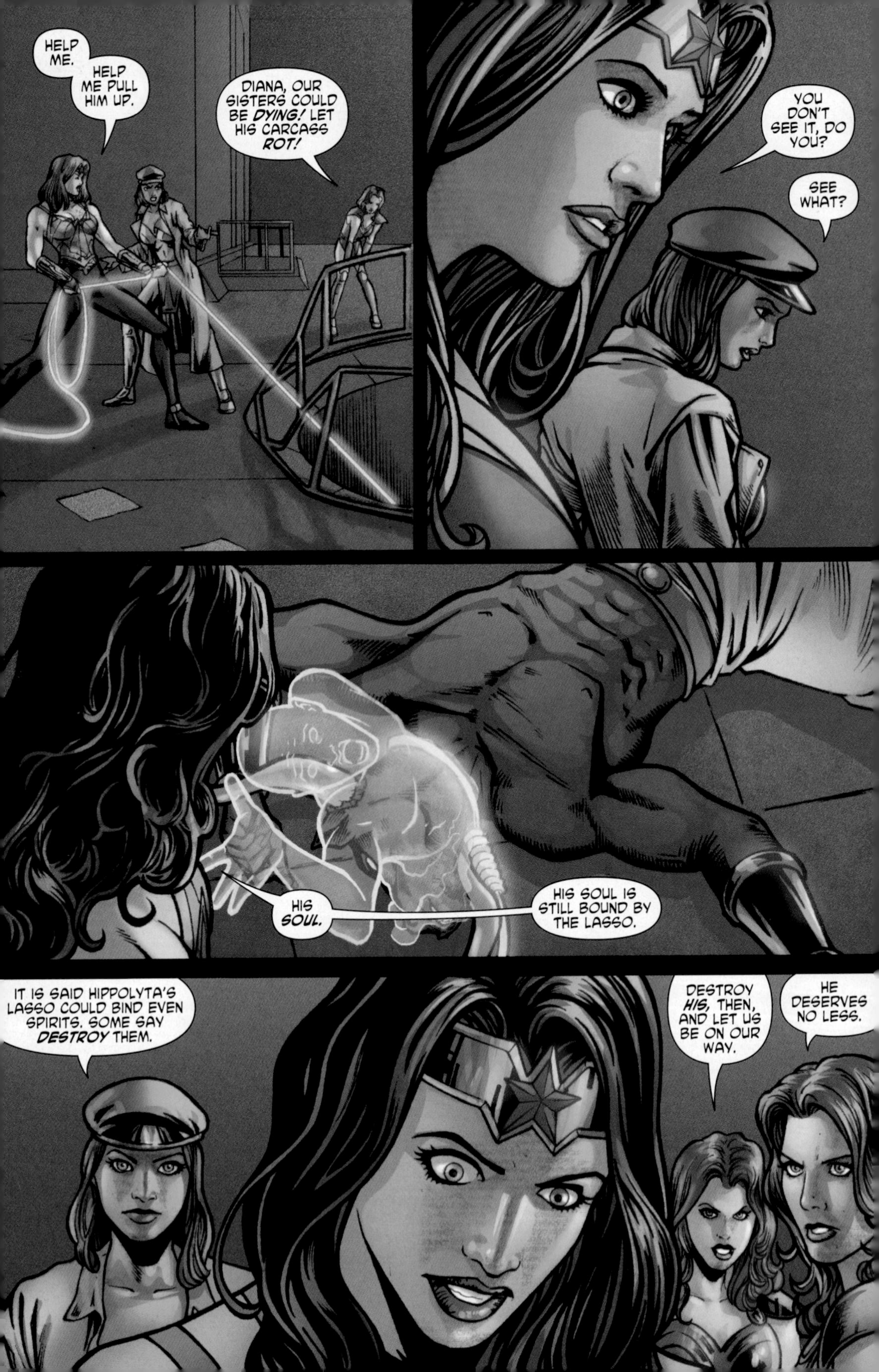
HELP ME.
HELP ME PULL HIM UP.
DIANA, OUR SISTERS COULD BE *DYING!* LET HIS CARCASS *ROT!*
YOU DON'T SEE IT, DO YOU?
SEE WHAT?
HIS *SOUL.*
HIS SOUL IS STILL BOUND BY THE LASSO.
IT IS SAID HIPPOLYTA'S LASSO COULD BIND EVEN SPIRITS. SOME SAY *DESTROY* THEM.
DESTROY *HIS,* THEN, AND LET US BE ON OUR WAY.
HE DESERVES NO LESS.

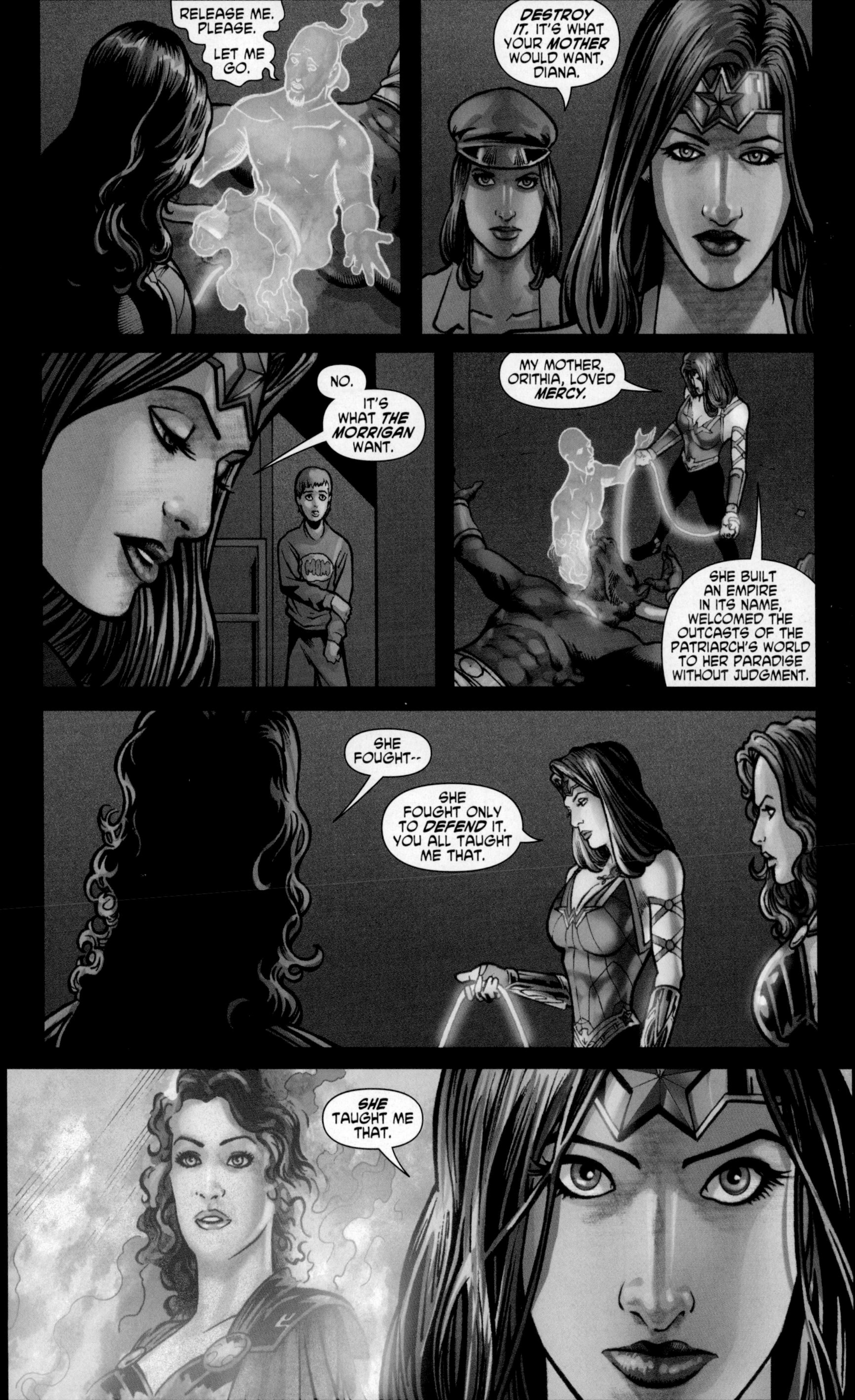
RELEASE ME. PLEASE.
LET ME GO.
DESTROY IT. IT'S WHAT YOUR MOTHER WOULD WANT, DIANA.
NO.
IT'S WHAT THE MORRIGAN WANT.
MY MOTHER, ORITHIA, LOVED MERCY.
SHE BUILT AN EMPIRE IN ITS NAME, WELCOMED THE OUTCASTS OF THE PATRIARCH'S WORLD TO HER PARADISE WITHOUT JUDGMENT.
SHE FOUGHT--
SHE FOUGHT ONLY TO DEFEND IT. YOU ALL TAUGHT ME THAT.
SHE TAUGHT ME THAT.

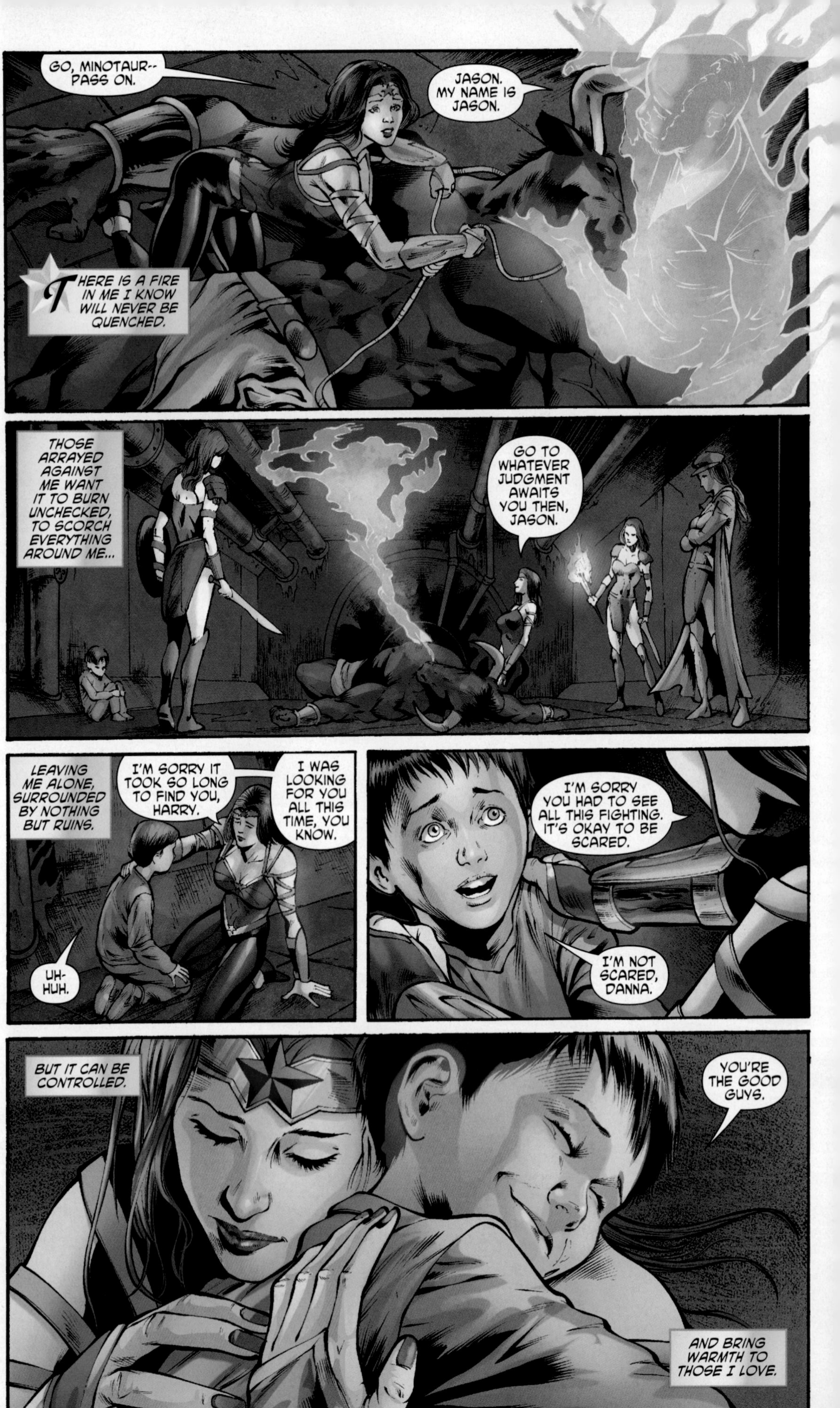
GO, MINOTAUR--
PASS ON.
JASON.
MY NAME IS
JASON.
THERE IS A FIRE IN ME I KNOW WILL NEVER BE QUENCHED.
THOSE ARRAYED AGAINST ME WANT IT TO BURN UNCHECKED, TO SCORCH EVERYTHING AROUND ME...
GO TO WHATEVER JUDGMENT AWAITS YOU THEN, JASON.
LEAVING ME ALONE, SURROUNDED BY NOTHING BUT RUINS.
I'M SORRY IT TOOK SO LONG TO FIND YOU, HARRY.
I WAS LOOKING FOR YOU ALL THIS TIME, YOU KNOW.
UH-HUH.
I'M SORRY YOU HAD TO SEE ALL THIS FIGHTING. IT'S OKAY TO BE SCARED.
I'M NOT SCARED, DANNA.
BUT IT CAN BE CONTROLLED.
YOU'RE THE GOOD GUYS.
AND BRING WARMTH TO THOSE I LOVE.

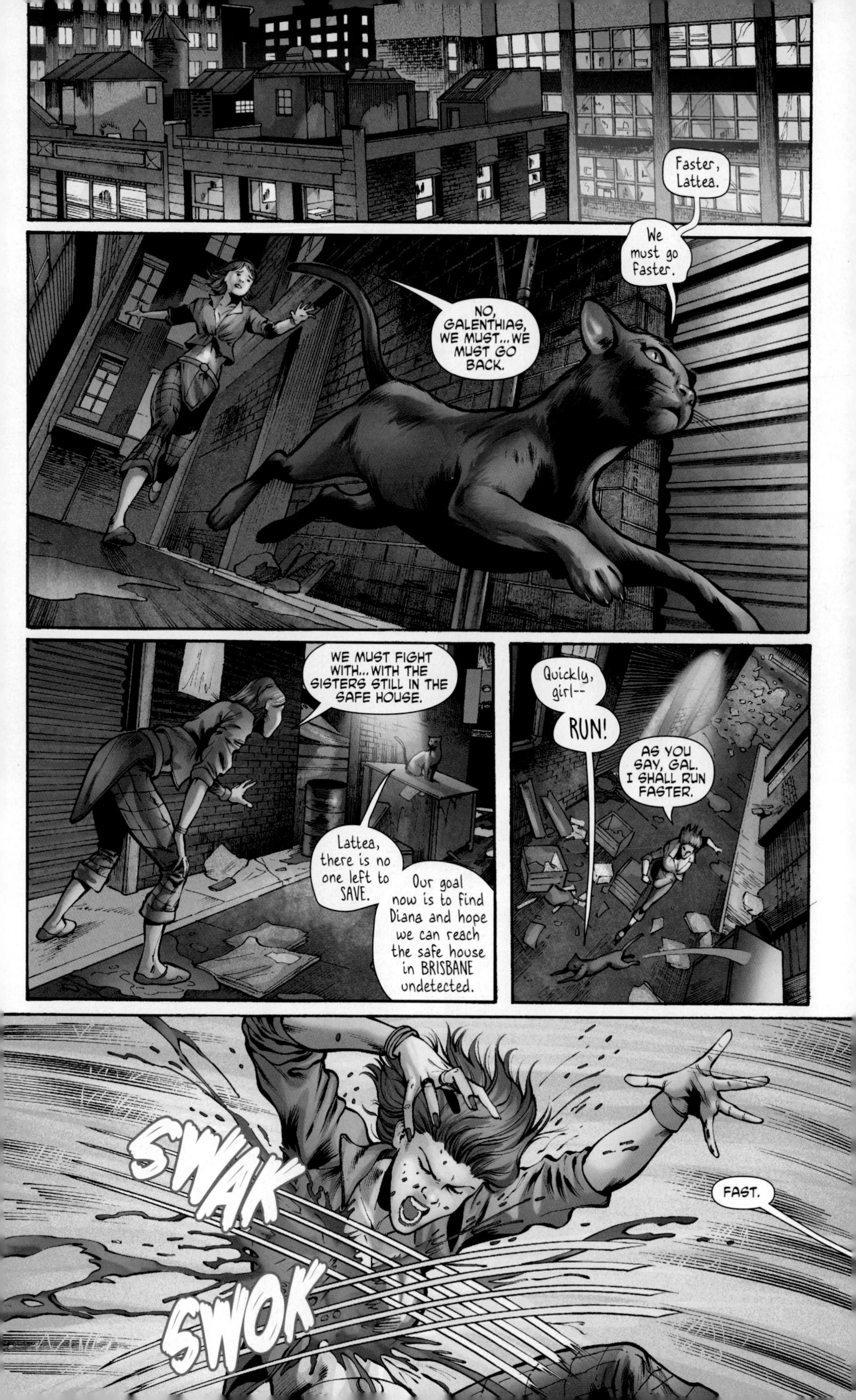

Faster, Lattea.
We must go Faster.
NO, GALENTHIAS, WE MUST... WE MUST GO BACK.
WE MUST FIGHT WITH... WITH THE SISTERS STILL IN THE SAFE HOUSE.
Lattea, there is no one left to SAVE.
Our goal now is to find Diana and hope we can reach the safe house in BRISBANE undetected.
Quickly, girl--
RUN!
AS YOU SAY, GAL. I SHALL RUN FASTER.
SWAK
FAST.
SWOK

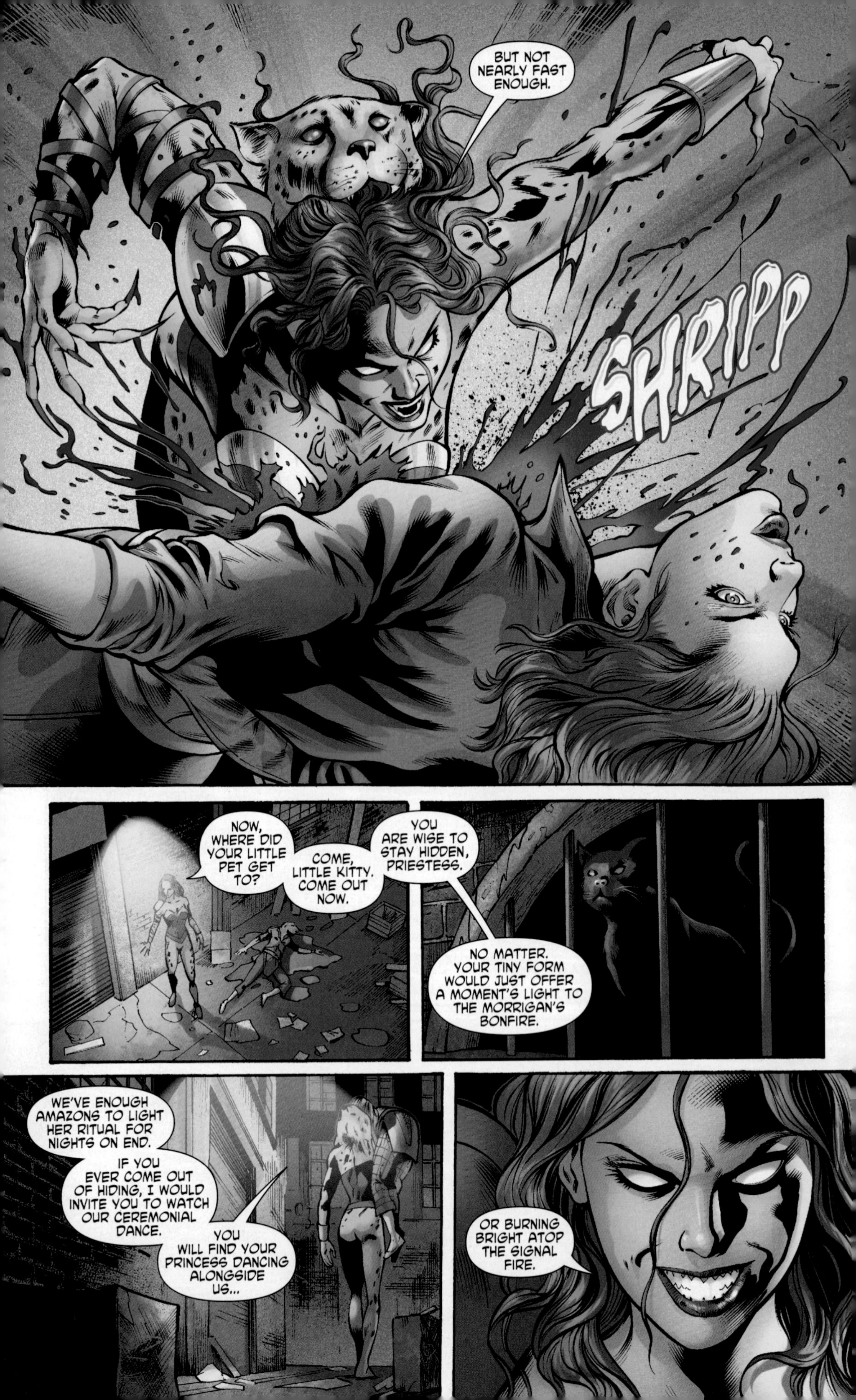
BUT NOT NEARLY FAST ENOUGH.
SHRIPP
NOW, WHERE DID YOUR LITTLE PET GET TO?
COME, LITTLE KITTY. COME OUT NOW.
YOU ARE WISE TO STAY HIDDEN, PRIESTESS.
NO MATTER. YOUR TINY FORM WOULD JUST OFFER A MOMENT'S LIGHT TO THE MORRIGAN'S BONFIRE.
WE'VE ENOUGH AMAZONS TO LIGHT HER RITUAL FOR NIGHTS ON END.
IF YOU EVER COME OUT OF HIDING, I WOULD INVITE YOU TO WATCH OUR CEREMONIAL DANCE.
YOU WILL FIND YOUR PRINCESS DANCING ALONGSIDE US...
OR BURNING BRIGHT ATOP THE SIGNAL FIRE.

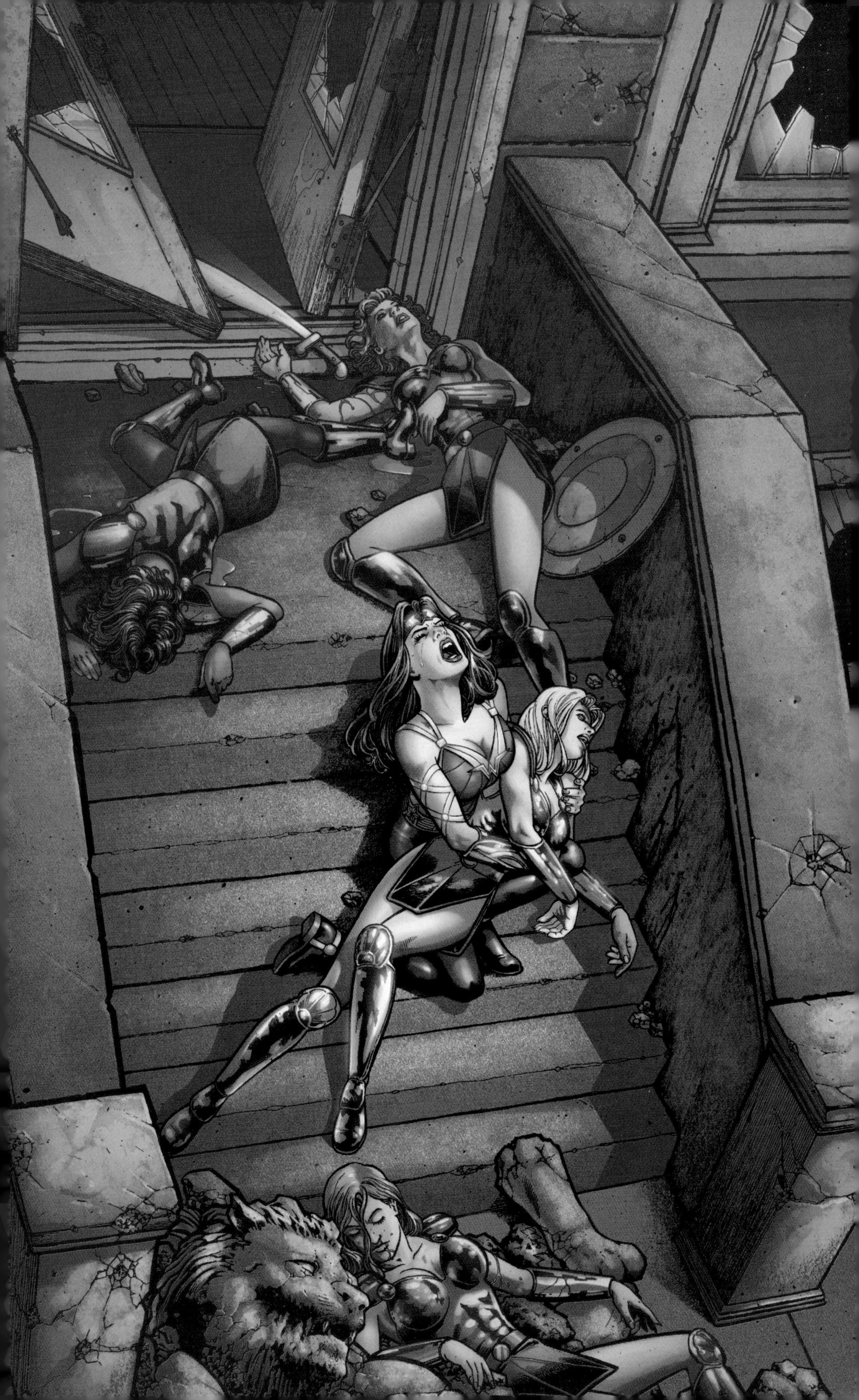

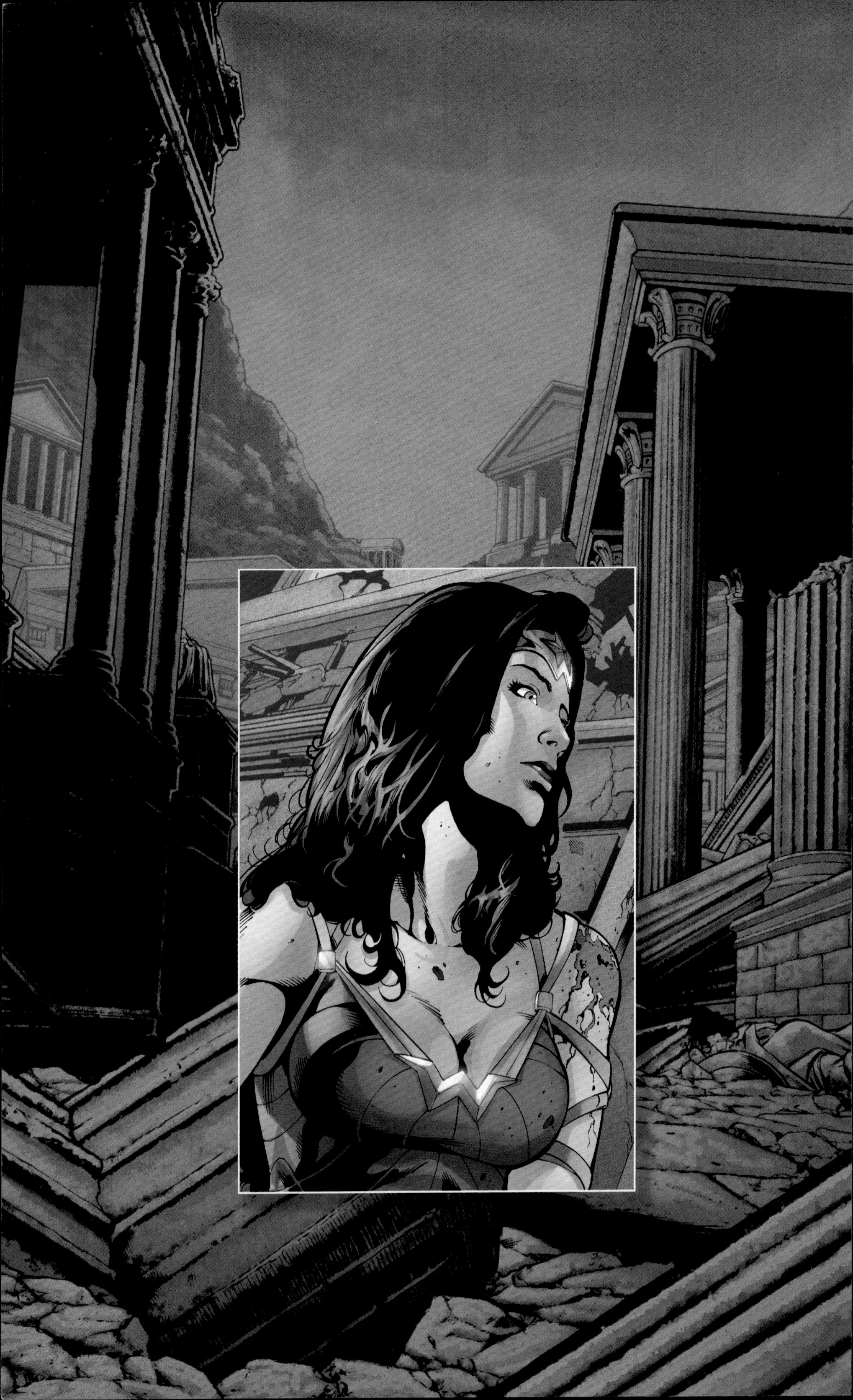

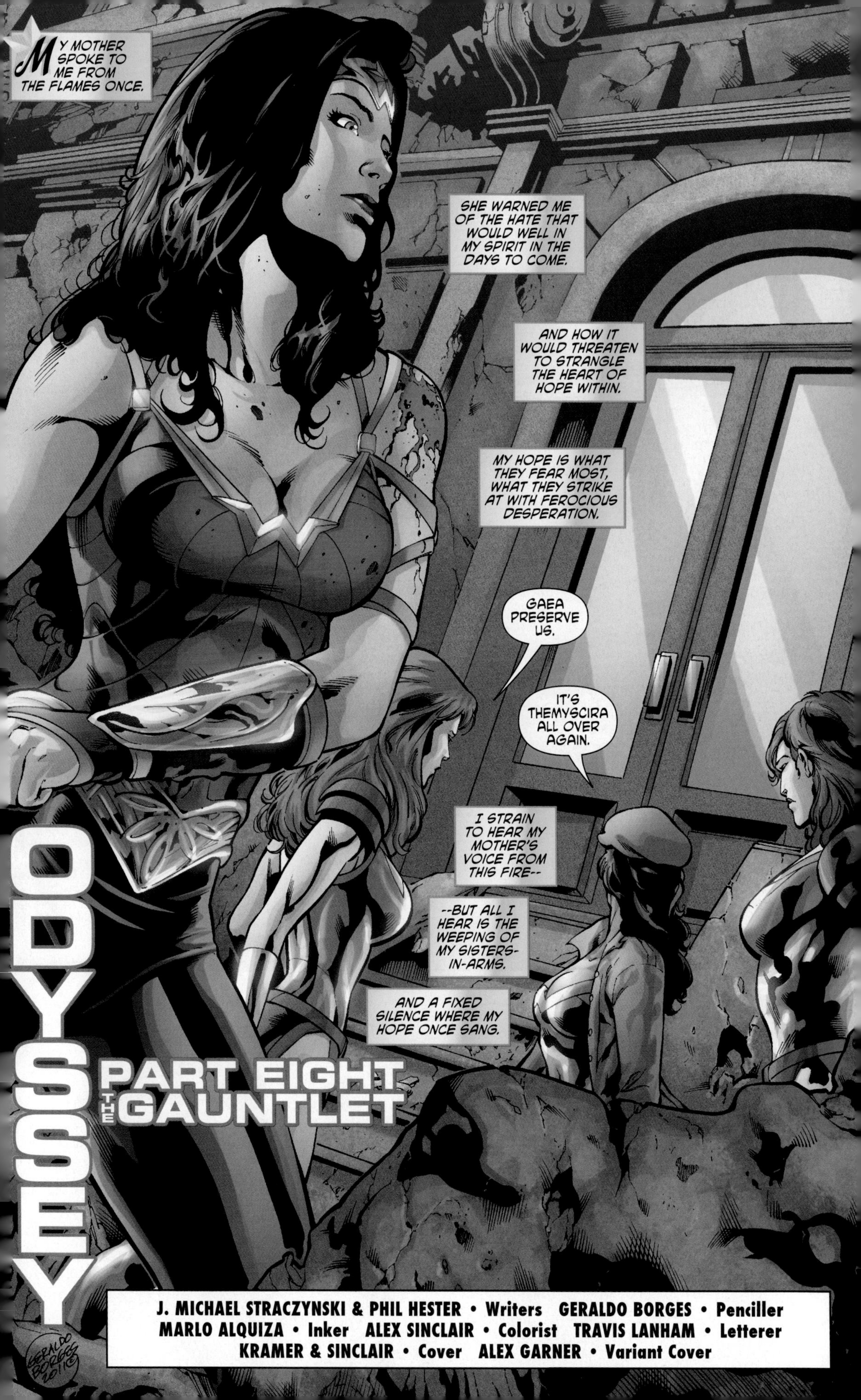
MY MOTHER SPOKE TO ME FROM THE FLAMES ONCE.
SHE WARNED ME OF THE HATE THAT WOULD WELL IN MY SPIRIT IN THE DAYS TO COME.
AND HOW IT WOULD THREATEN TO STRANGLE THE HEART OF HOPE WITHIN.
MY HOPE IS WHAT THEY FEAR MOST, WHAT THEY STRIKE AT WITH FEROCIOUS DESPERATION.
GAEA PRESERVE US.
IT'S THEMYSCIRA ALL OVER AGAIN.
I STRAIN TO HEAR MY MOTHER'S VOICE FROM THIS FIRE--
--BUT ALL I HEAR IS THE WEEPING OF MY SISTERS-IN-ARMS.
AND A FIXED SILENCE WHERE MY HOPE ONCE SANG.
ODYSSEY
PART EIGHT THE GAUNTLET
J. MICHAEL STRACZYNSKI & PHIL HESTER • Writers GERALDO BORGES • Penciller
MARLO ALQUIZA • Inker ALEX SINCLAIR • Colorist TRAVIS LANHAM • Letterer
KRAMER & SINCLAIR • Cover ALEX GARNER • Variant Cover
GERALDO BORGES 2011©

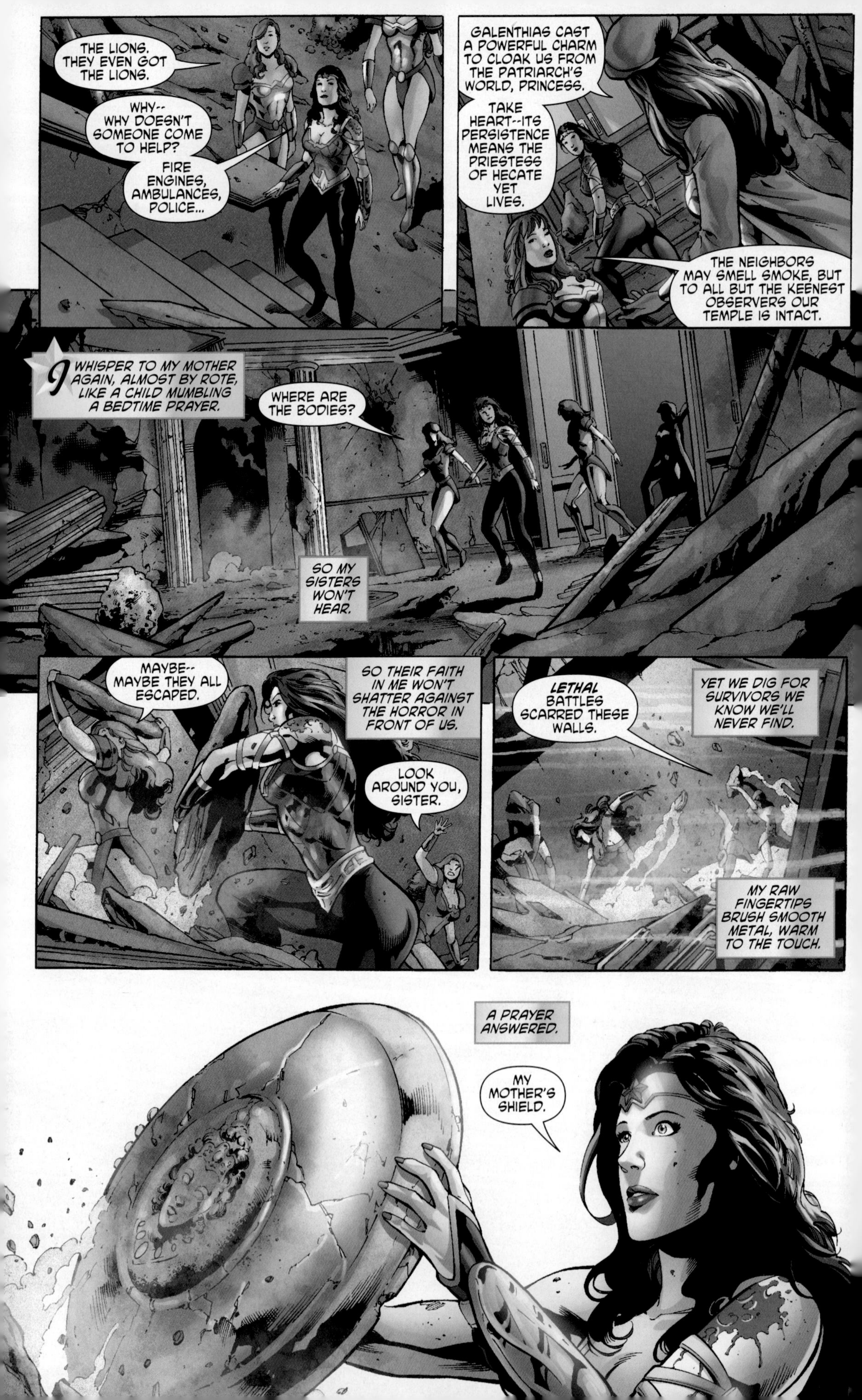
THE LIONS. THEY EVEN GOT THE LIONS.
WHY-- WHY DOESN'T SOMEONE COME TO HELP?
FIRE ENGINES, AMBULANCES, POLICE...
GALENTHIAS CAST A POWERFUL CHARM TO CLOAK US FROM THE PATRIARCH'S WORLD, PRINCESS.
TAKE HEART--ITS PERSISTENCE MEANS THE PRIESTESS OF HECATE YET LIVES.
THE NEIGHBORS MAY SMELL SMOKE, BUT TO ALL BUT THE KEENEST OBSERVERS OUR TEMPLE IS INTACT.
I WHISPER TO MY MOTHER AGAIN, ALMOST BY ROTE, LIKE A CHILD MUMBLING A BEDTIME PRAYER.
WHERE ARE THE BODIES?
SO MY SISTERS WON'T HEAR.
MAYBE-- MAYBE THEY ALL ESCAPED.
SO THEIR FAITH IN ME WON'T SHATTER AGAINST THE HORROR IN FRONT OF US.
LOOK AROUND YOU, SISTER.
LETHAL BATTLES SCARRED THESE WALLS.
YET WE DIG FOR SURVIVORS WE KNOW WE'LL NEVER FIND.
MY RAW FINGERTIPS BRUSH SMOOTH METAL, WARM TO THE TOUCH.
A PRAYER ANSWERED.
MY MOTHER'S SHIELD.

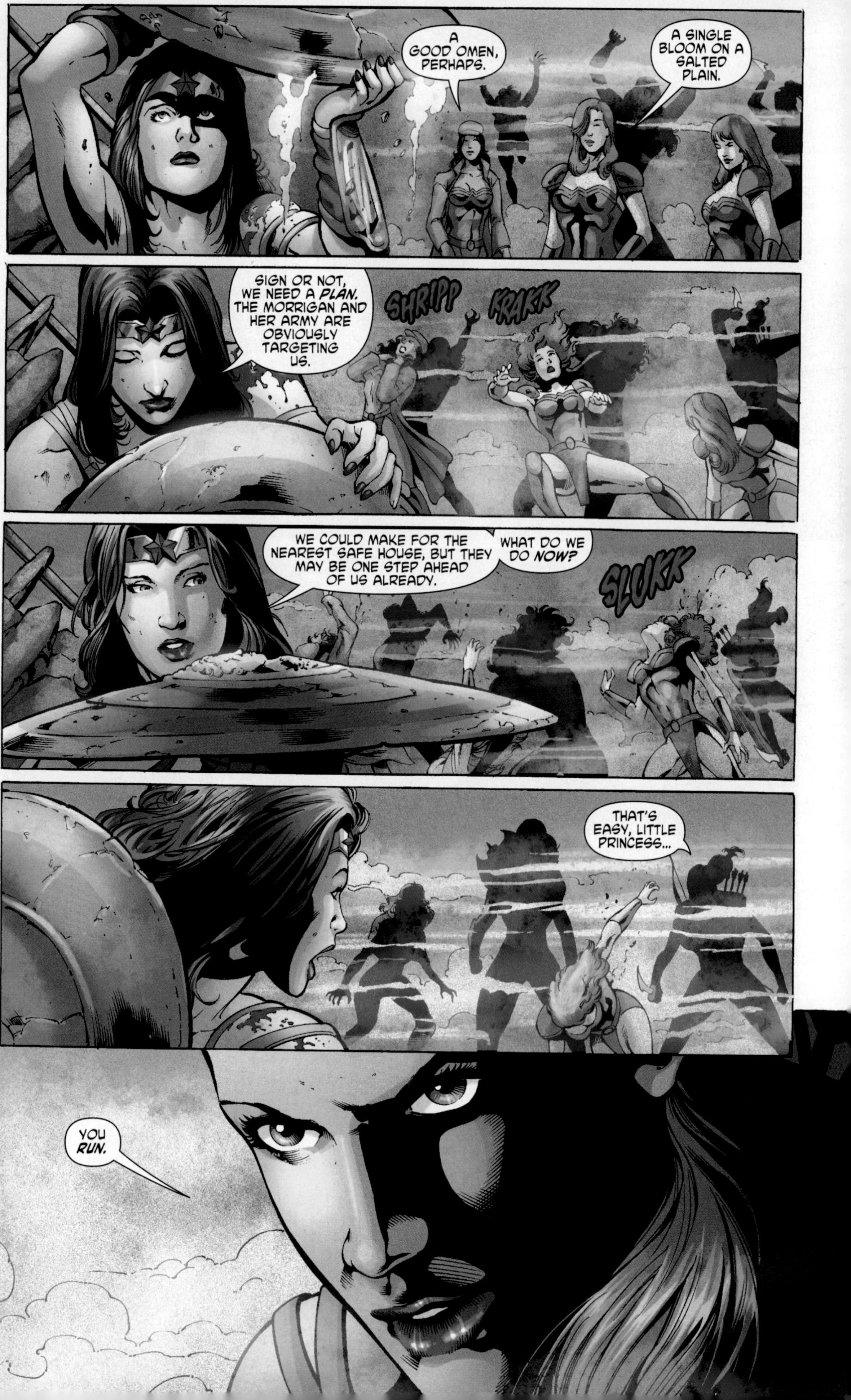
A GOOD OMEN, PERHAPS.
A SINGLE BLOOM ON A SALTED PLAIN.
SIGN OR NOT, WE NEED A PLAN. THE MORRIGAN AND HER ARMY ARE OBVIOUSLY TARGETING US.
SHRIPP
KRAKK
WE COULD MAKE FOR THE NEAREST SAFE HOUSE, BUT THEY MAY BE ONE STEP AHEAD OF US ALREADY.
WHAT DO WE DO NOW?
SLUKK
THAT'S EASY, LITTLE PRINCESS...
YOU RUN.

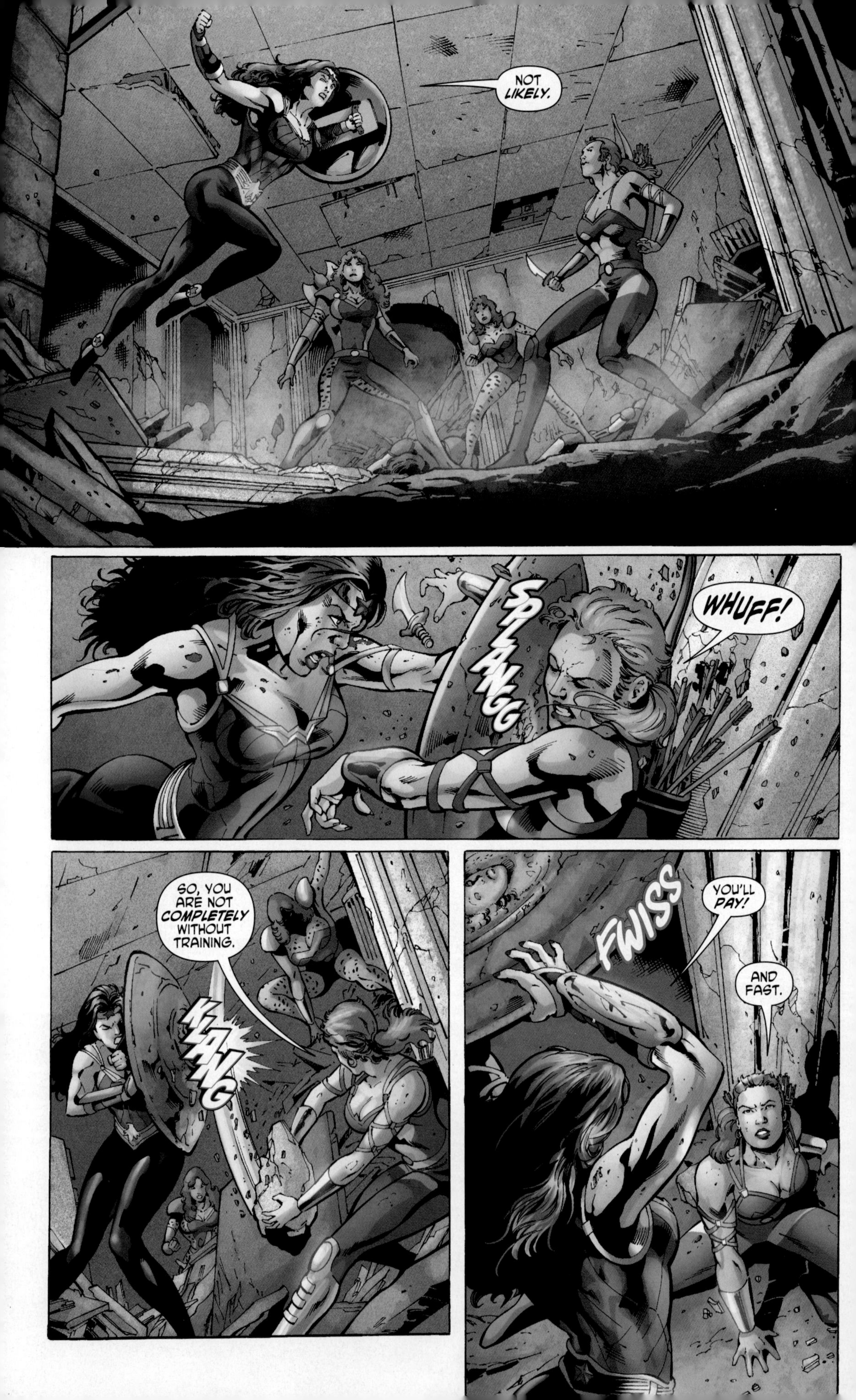
NOT LIKELY.
SPLANGG
WHUFF!
SO, YOU ARE NOT COMPLETELY WITHOUT TRAINING.
KLANG
FWISS
YOU'LL PAY!
AND FAST.

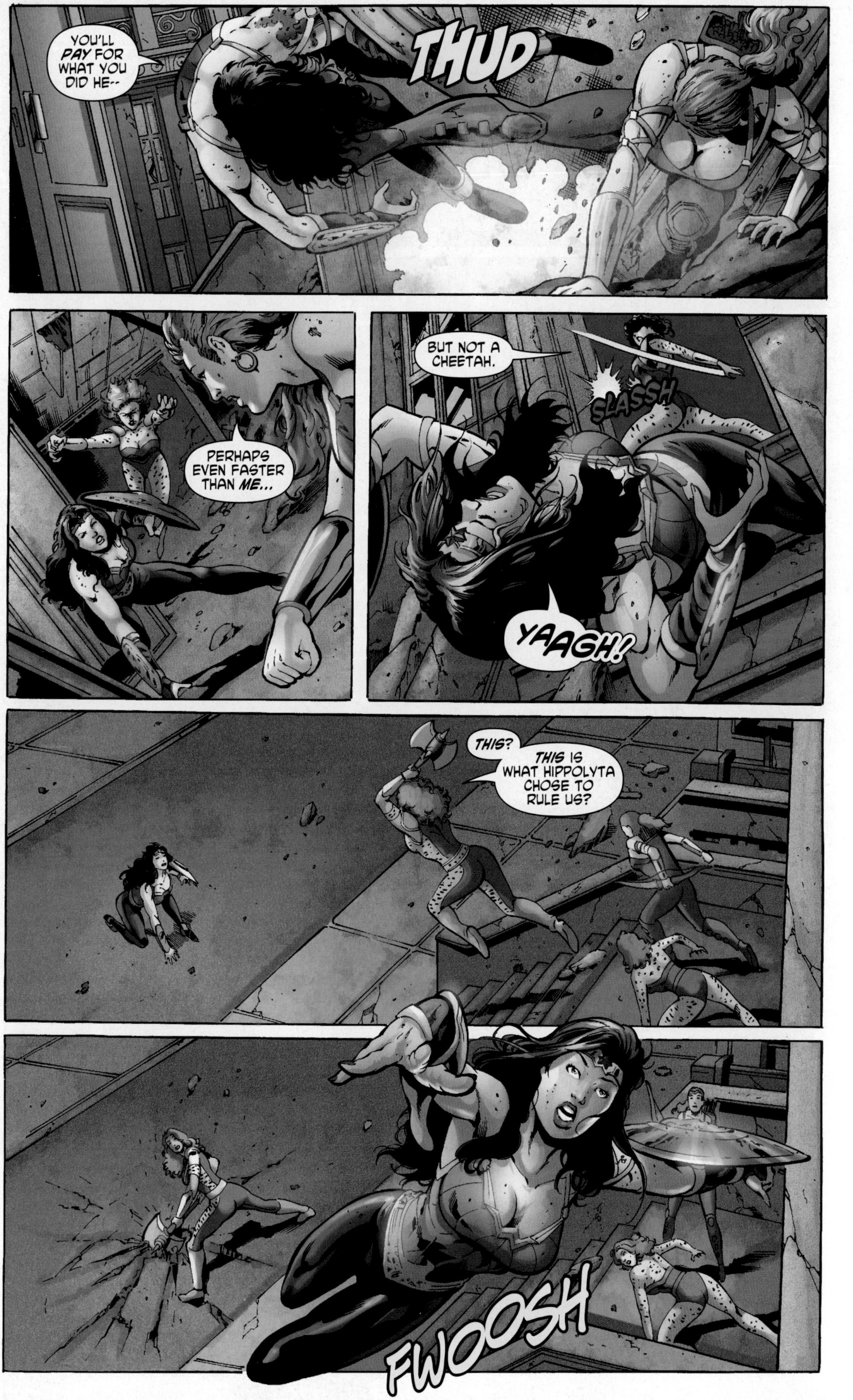
YOU'LL PAY FOR WHAT YOU DID HE--
THUD
PERHAPS EVEN FASTER THAN ME...
BUT NOT A CHEETAH.
SLASSH
YAAGH!
THIS? THIS IS WHAT HIPPOLYTA CHOSE TO RULE US?
FWOOSH

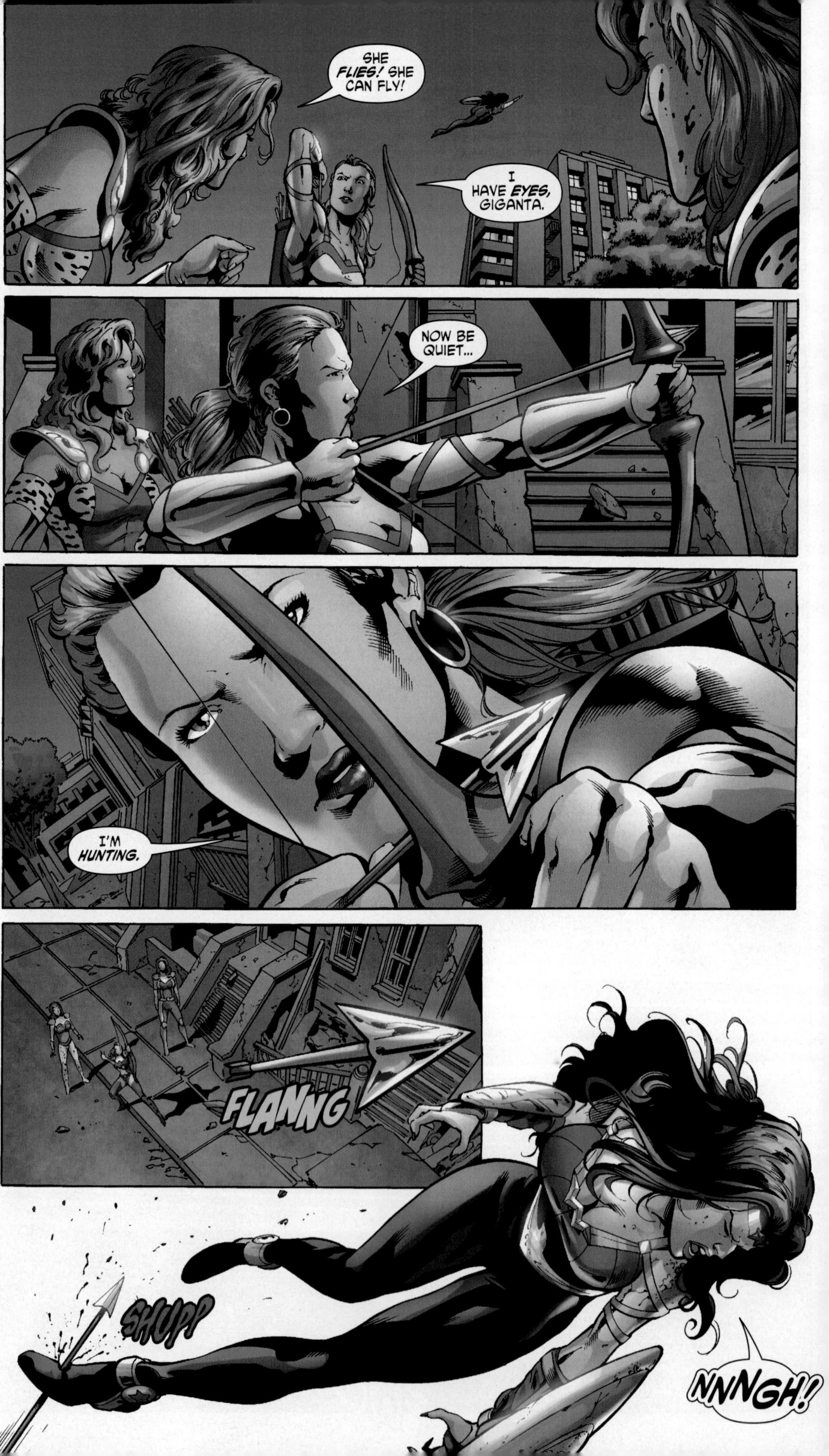
SHE FLIES! SHE CAN FLY!
I HAVE EYES, GIGANTA.
NOW BE QUIET...
I'M HUNTING.
FLANNG
SHUPP
NNNGH!

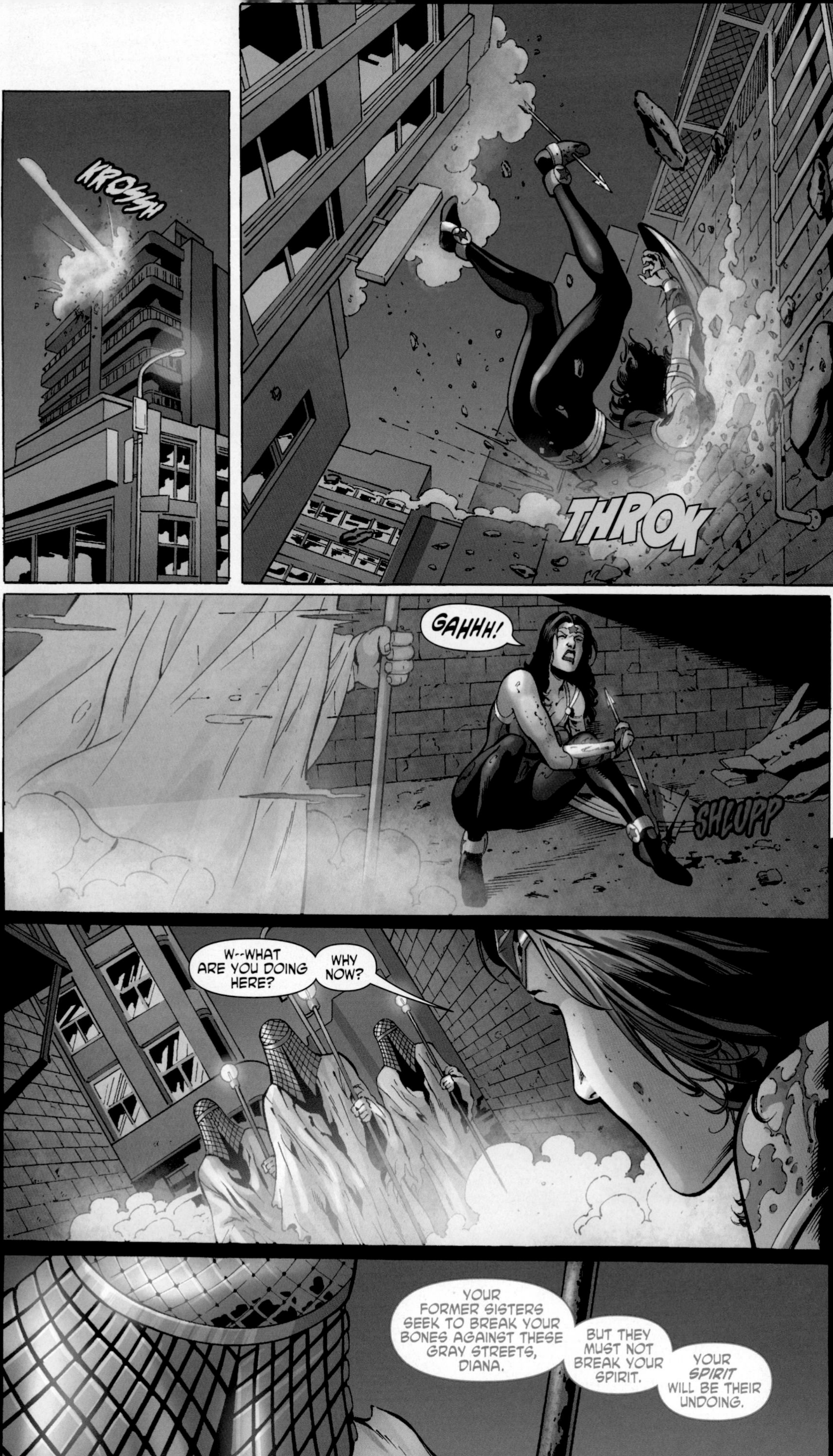
KROSSH
THROK
GAHHH!
SHLUPP
W--WHAT ARE YOU DOING HERE?
WHY NOW?
YOUR FORMER SISTERS SEEK TO BREAK YOUR BONES AGAINST THESE GRAY STREETS, DIANA.
BUT THEY MUST NOT BREAK YOUR SPIRIT.
YOUR *SPIRIT* WILL BE THEIR UNDOING.

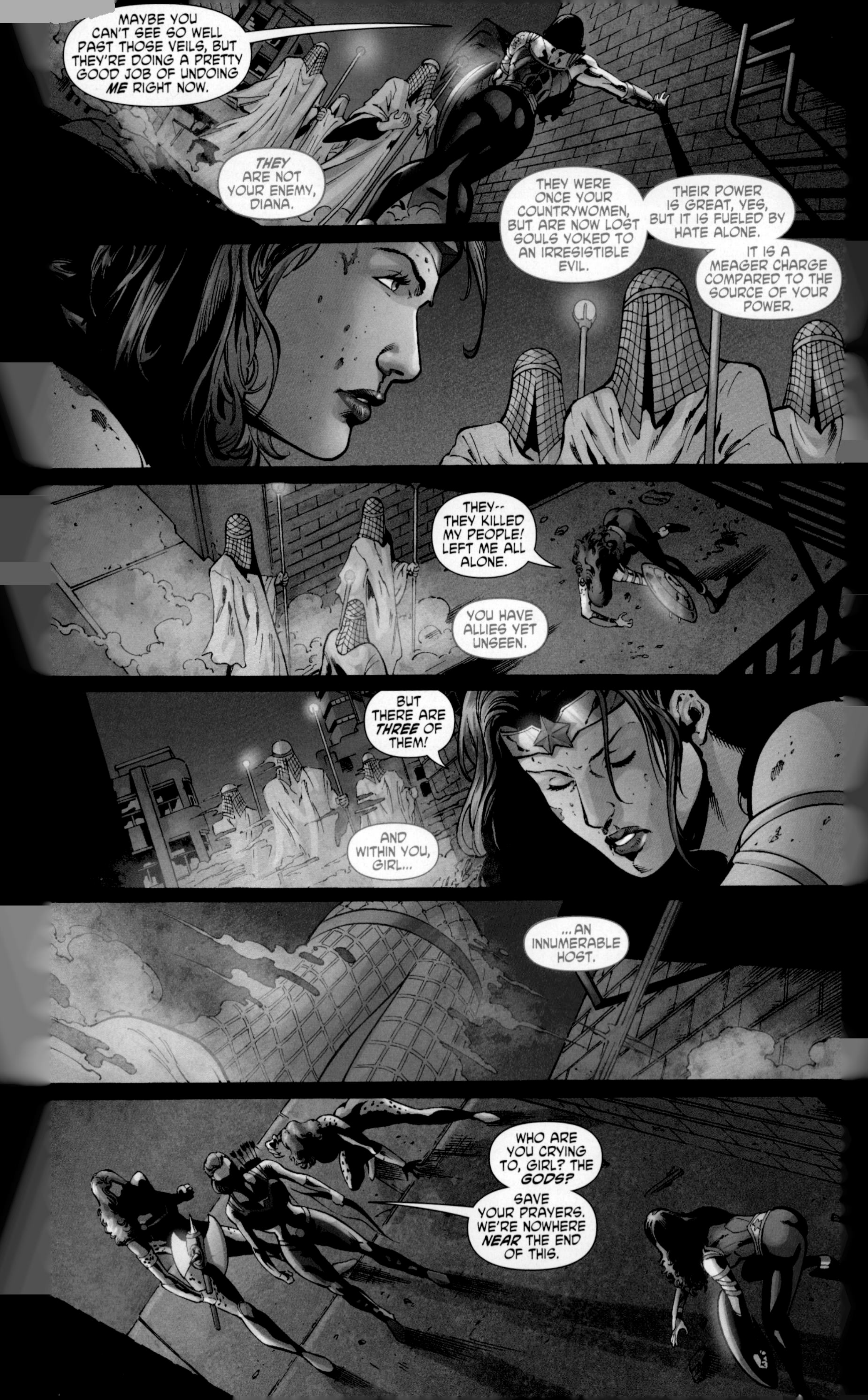
MAYBE YOU CAN'T SEE SO WELL PAST THOSE VEILS, BUT THEY'RE DOING A PRETTY GOOD JOB OF UNDOING *ME* RIGHT NOW.
THEY ARE NOT YOUR ENEMY, DIANA.
THEY WERE ONCE YOUR COUNTRYWOMEN, BUT ARE NOW LOST SOULS YOKED TO AN IRRESISTIBLE EVIL.
THEIR POWER IS GREAT, YES, BUT IT IS FUELED BY HATE ALONE.
IT IS A MEAGER CHARGE COMPARED TO THE SOURCE OF YOUR POWER.
THEY-- THEY KILLED MY PEOPLE! LEFT ME ALL ALONE.
YOU HAVE ALLIES YET UNSEEN.
BUT THERE ARE *THREE* OF THEM!
AND WITHIN YOU, GIRL...
...AN INNUMERABLE HOST.
WHO ARE YOU CRYING TO, GIRL? THE *GODS*?
SAVE YOUR PRAYERS. WE'RE NOWHERE *NEAR* THE END OF THIS.

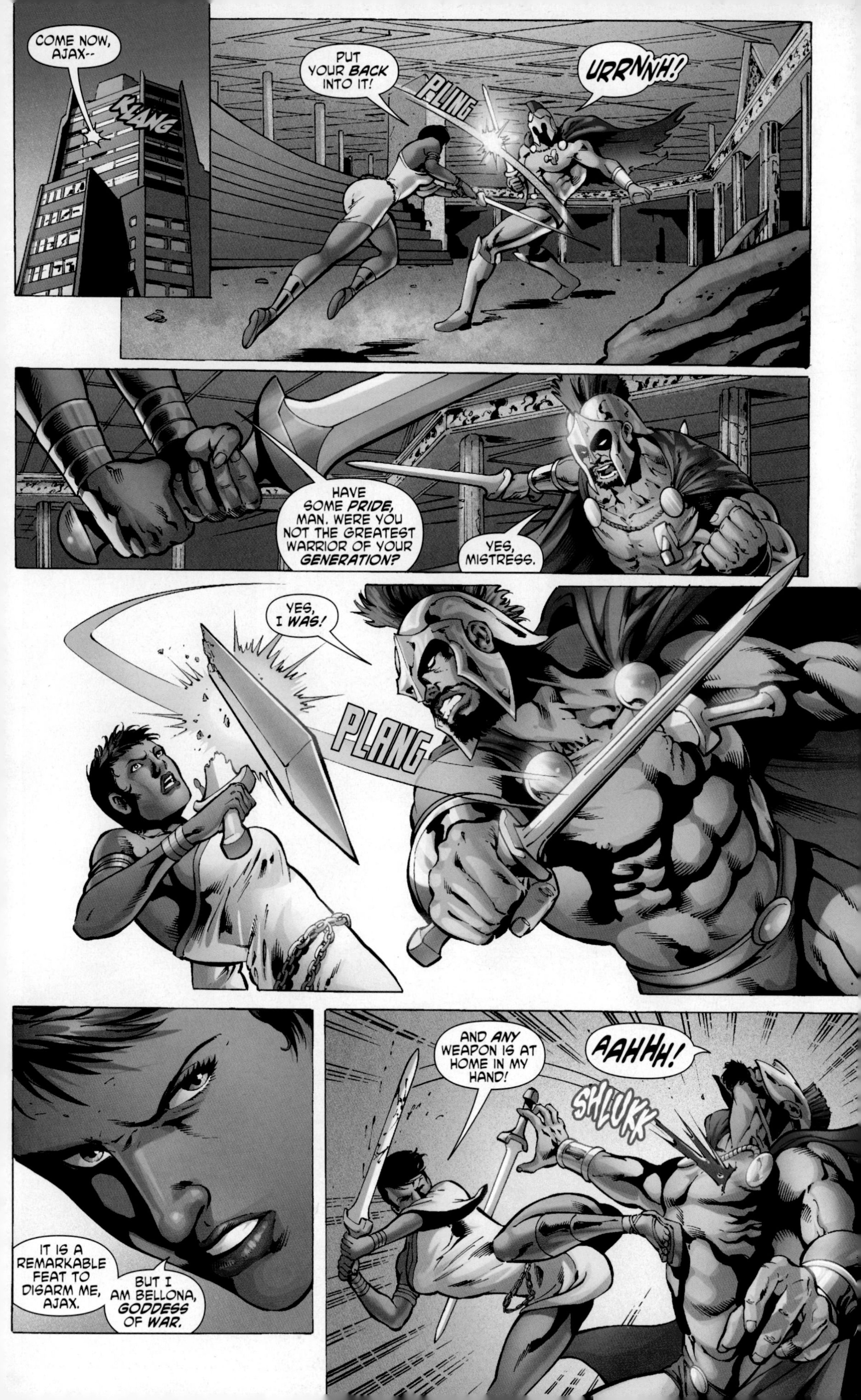
COME NOW, AJAX--
KLANG
PUT YOUR BACK INTO IT!
PLING
URRNNH!
HAVE SOME PRIDE, MAN. WERE YOU NOT THE GREATEST WARRIOR OF YOUR GENERATION?
YES, MISTRESS.
YES, I WAS!
PLANG
IT IS A REMARKABLE FEAT TO DISARM ME, AJAX.
BUT I AM BELLONA, GODDESS OF WAR.
AND ANY WEAPON IS AT HOME IN MY HAND!
AAHHH!
SHLUKK

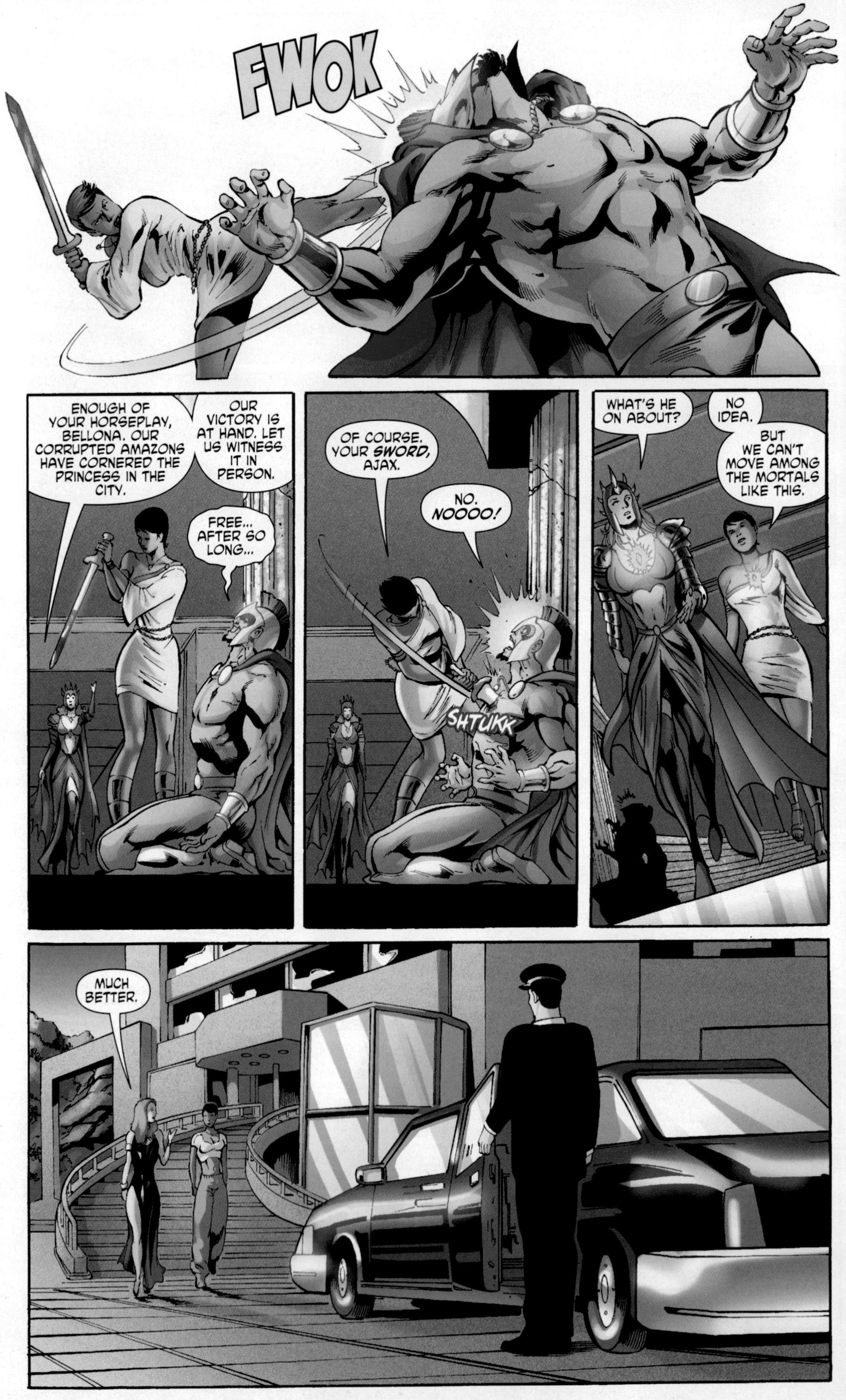
FWOK
ENOUGH OF YOUR HORSEPLAY, BELLONA. OUR CORRUPTED AMAZONS HAVE CORNERED THE PRINCESS IN THE CITY.
OUR VICTORY IS AT HAND. LET US WITNESS IT IN PERSON.
FREE... AFTER SO LONG...
OF COURSE. YOUR SWORD, AJAX.
NO. NOOOO!
SHTUKK
WHAT'S HE ON ABOUT?
NO IDEA.
BUT WE CAN'T MOVE AMONG THE MORTALS LIKE THIS.
MUCH BETTER.

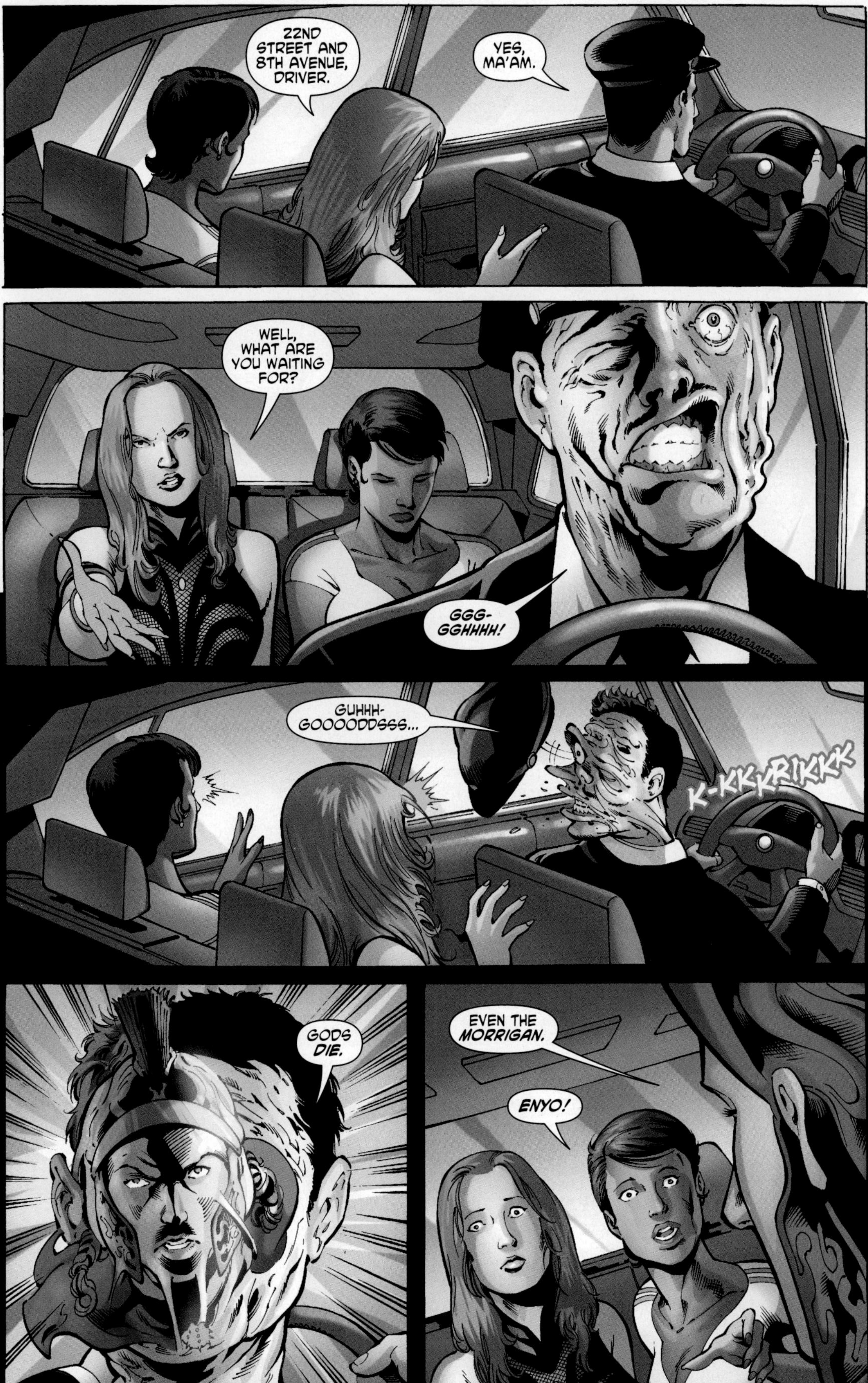

22ND STREET AND 8TH AVENUE, DRIVER.
YES, MA'AM.
WELL, WHAT ARE YOU WAITING FOR?
GGG-GGHHHH!
GUHHH-GOOOODDSSS...
K-KKKRIKKK
GODS DIE.
EVEN THE MORRIGAN.
ENYO!

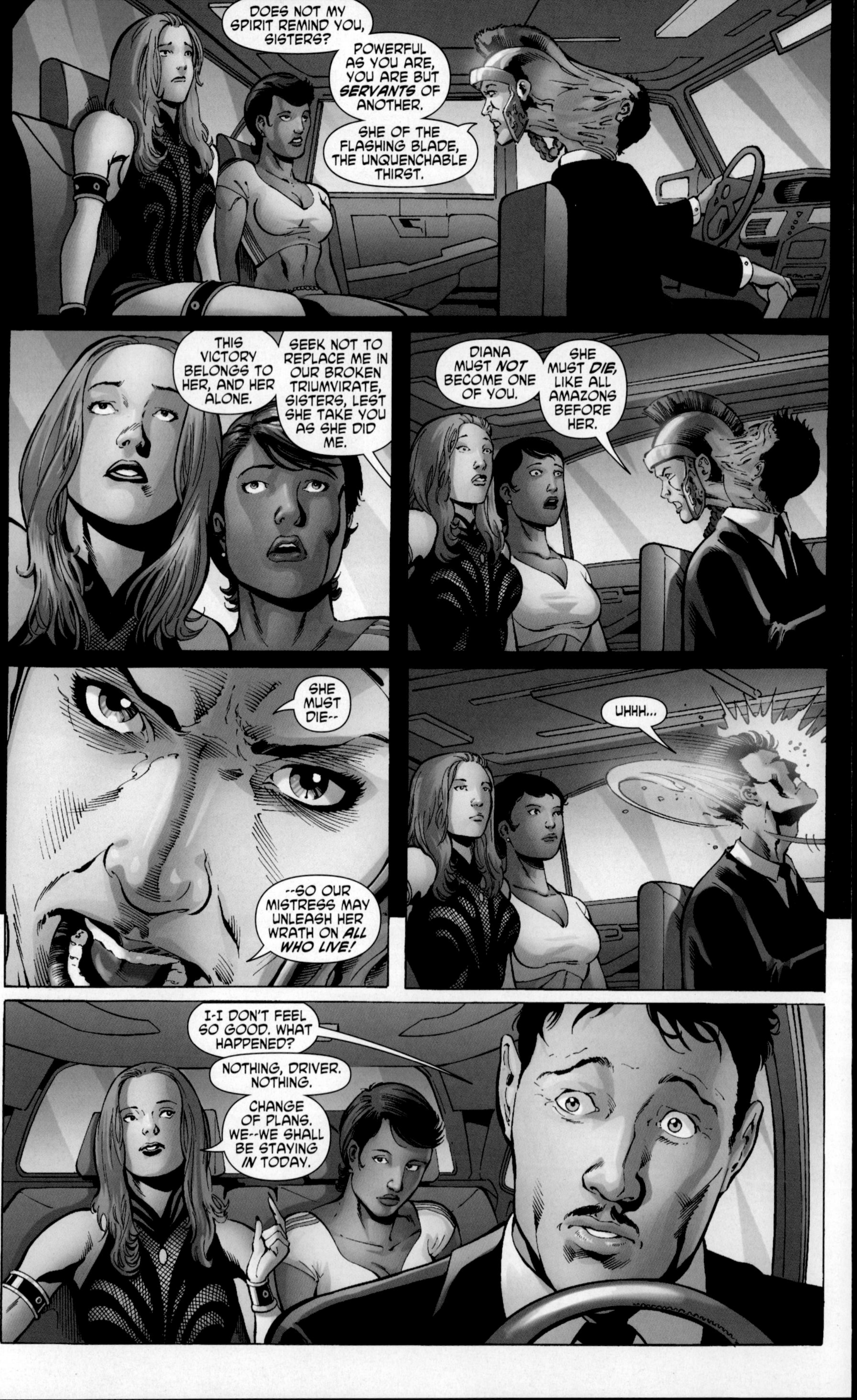
DOES NOT MY SPIRIT REMIND YOU, SISTERS?
POWERFUL AS YOU ARE, YOU ARE BUT SERVANTS OF ANOTHER.
SHE OF THE FLASHING BLADE, THE UNQUENCHABLE THIRST.
THIS VICTORY BELONGS TO HER, AND HER ALONE.
SEEK NOT TO REPLACE ME IN OUR BROKEN TRIUMVIRATE, SISTERS, LEST SHE TAKE YOU AS SHE DID ME.
DIANA MUST NOT BECOME ONE OF YOU.
SHE MUST DIE, LIKE ALL AMAZONS BEFORE HER.
SHE MUST DIE--
--SO OUR MISTRESS MAY UNLEASH HER WRATH ON ALL WHO LIVE!
UHHH...
I-I DON'T FEEL SO GOOD. WHAT HAPPENED?
NOTHING, DRIVER. NOTHING.
CHANGE OF PLANS. WE--WE SHALL BE STAYING IN TODAY.

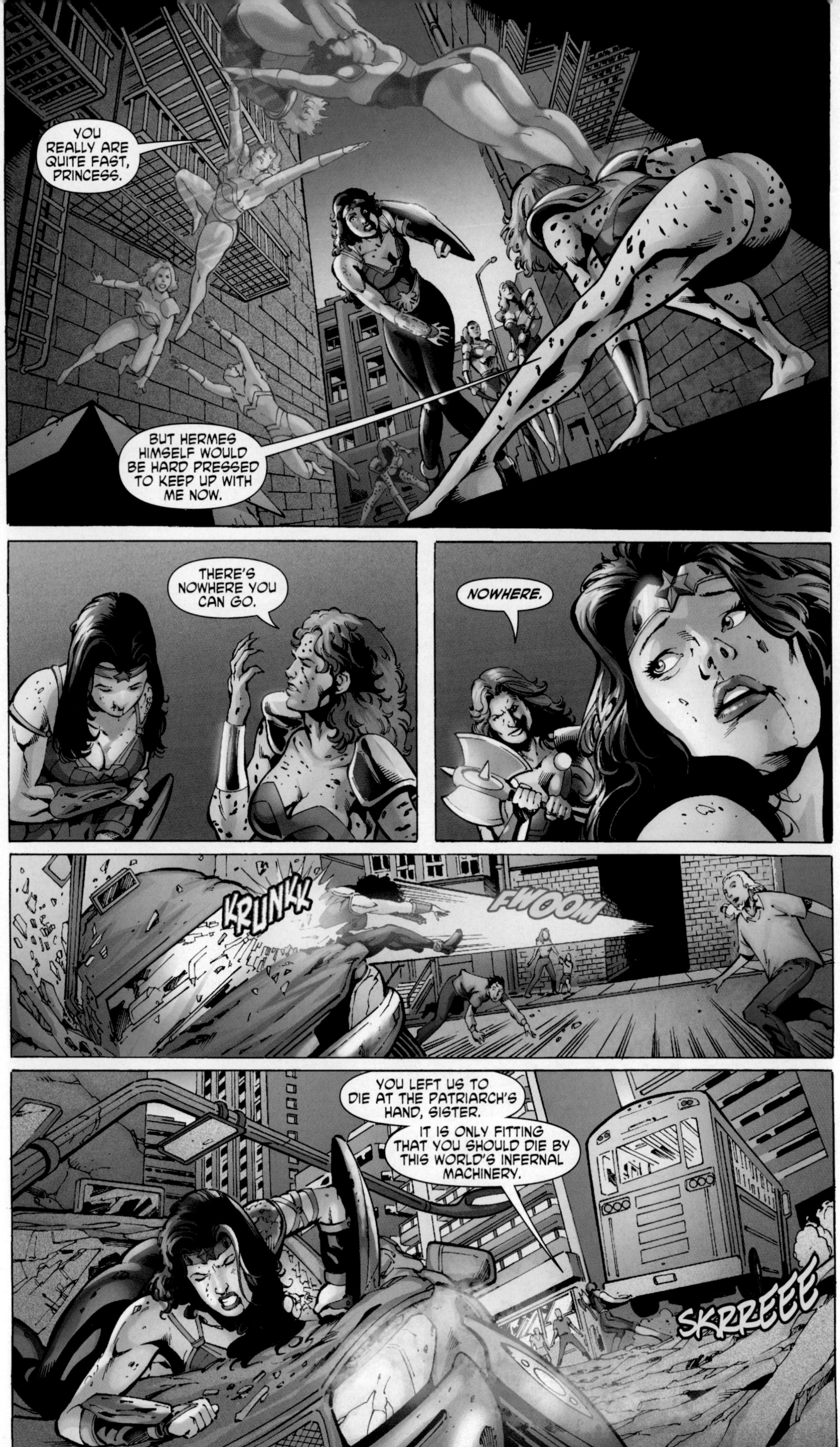
YOU REALLY ARE QUITE FAST, PRINCESS.
BUT HERMES HIMSELF WOULD BE HARD PRESSED TO KEEP UP WITH ME NOW.
THERE'S NOWHERE YOU CAN GO.
NOWHERE.
KRUNKK
FWOOM
YOU LEFT US TO DIE AT THE PATRIARCH'S HAND, SISTER.
IT IS ONLY FITTING THAT YOU SHOULD DIE BY THIS WORLD'S INFERNAL MACHINERY.
SKRREEE

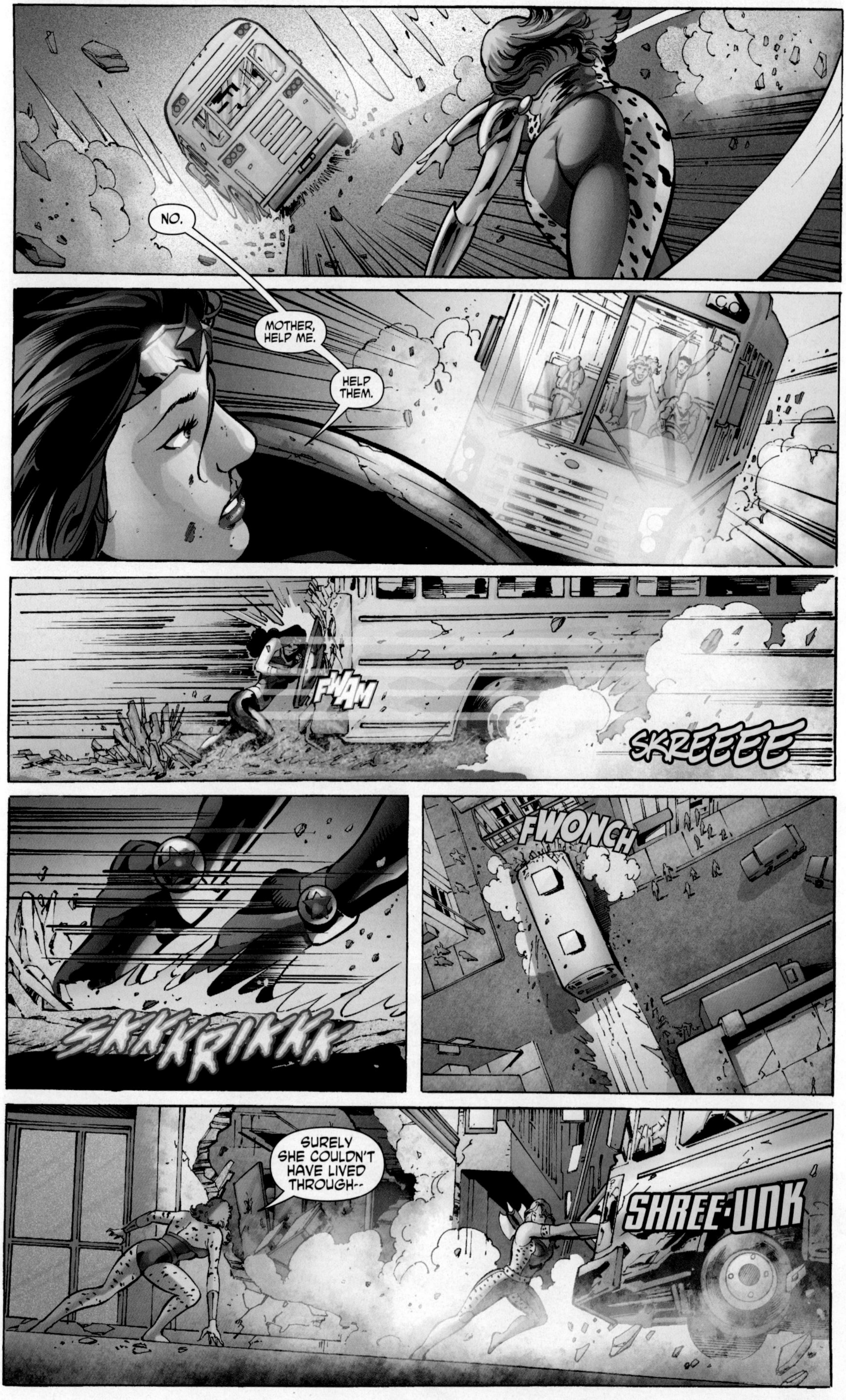
NO.
MOTHER, HELP ME.
HELP THEM.
FWAM
SKREEEE
SKKKRIKKK
FWONCH
SURELY SHE COULDN'T HAVE LIVED THROUGH--
SHREE-UNK

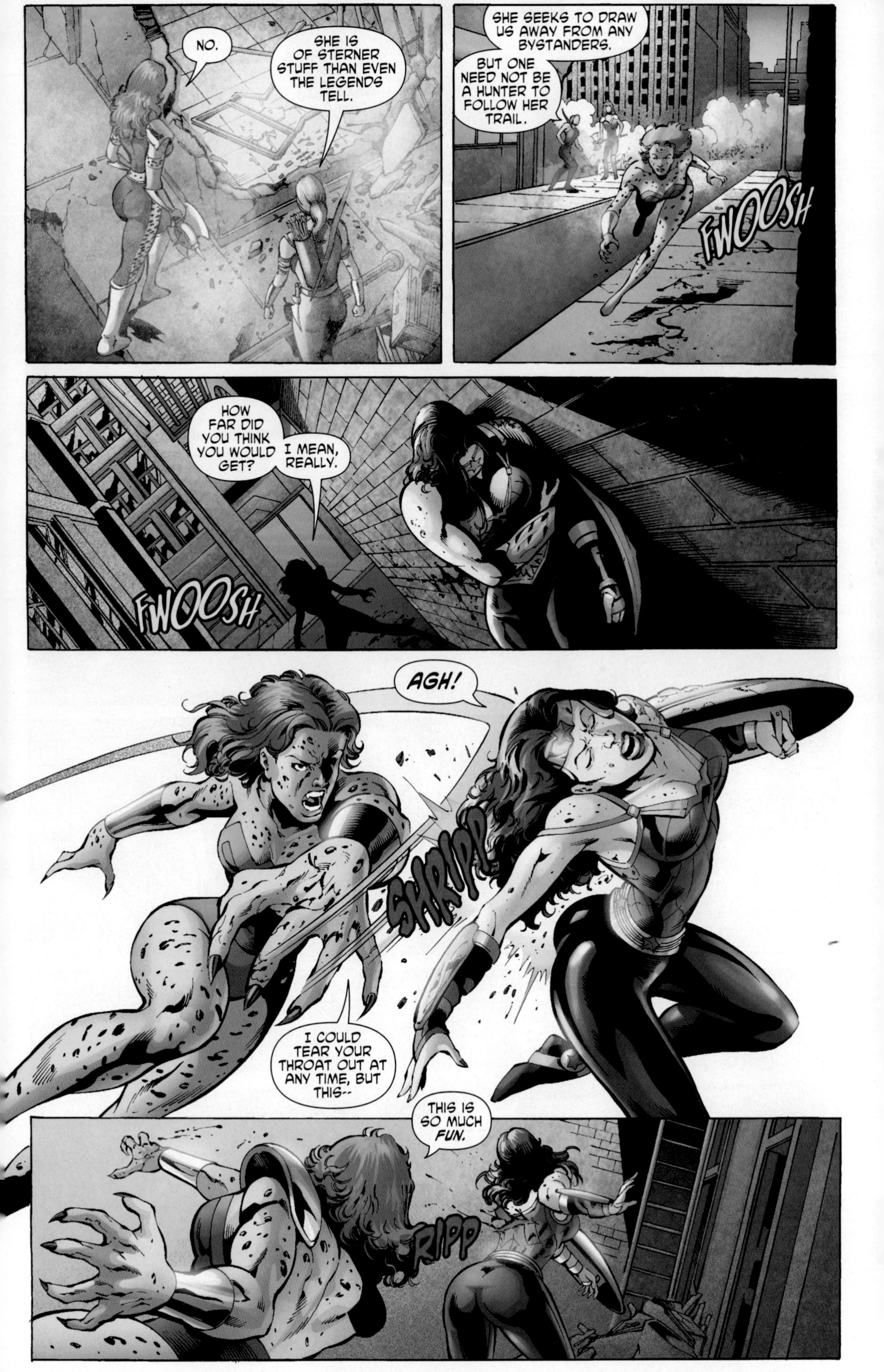
NO.
SHE IS OF STERNER STUFF THAN EVEN THE LEGENDS TELL.
SHE SEEKS TO DRAW US AWAY FROM ANY BYSTANDERS.
BUT ONE NEED NOT BE A HUNTER TO FOLLOW HER TRAIL.
FWOOSH
HOW FAR DID YOU THINK YOU WOULD GET?
I MEAN, REALLY.
FWOOSH
AGH!
SHRIPP
I COULD TEAR YOUR THROAT OUT AT ANY TIME, BUT THIS--
THIS IS SO MUCH FUN.
RIPP

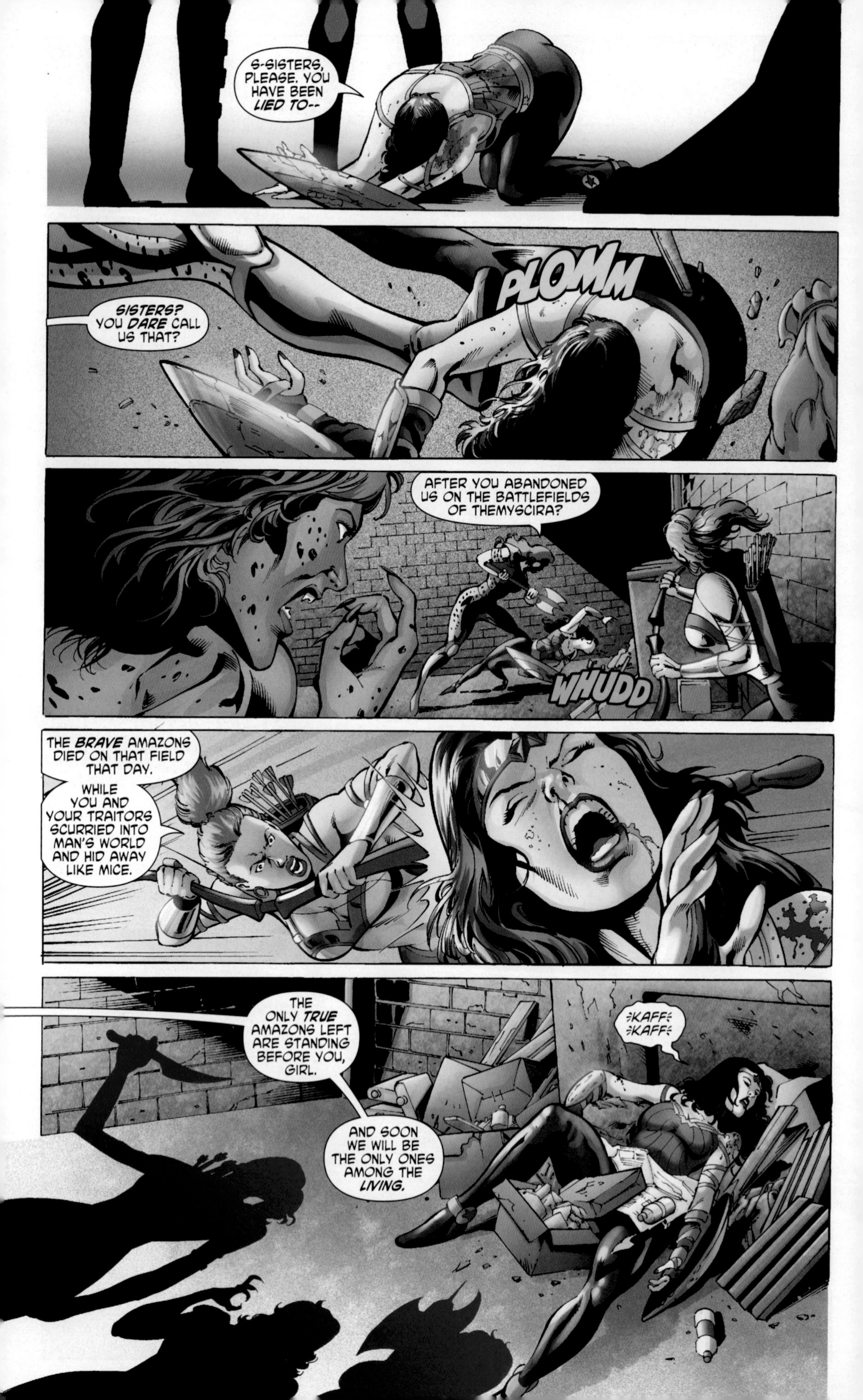
S-SISTERS, PLEASE. YOU HAVE BEEN *LIED TO--*
PLOMM
SISTERS? YOU *DARE* CALL US THAT?
AFTER YOU ABANDONED US ON THE BATTLEFIELDS OF THEMYSCIRA?
WHUDD
THE *BRAVE* AMAZONS DIED ON THAT FIELD THAT DAY.
WHILE YOU AND YOUR TRAITORS SCURRIED INTO MAN'S WORLD AND HID AWAY LIKE MICE.
THE ONLY *TRUE* AMAZONS LEFT ARE STANDING BEFORE YOU, GIRL.
KAFF *KAFF*
AND SOON WE WILL BE THE ONLY ONES AMONG THE *LIVING.*

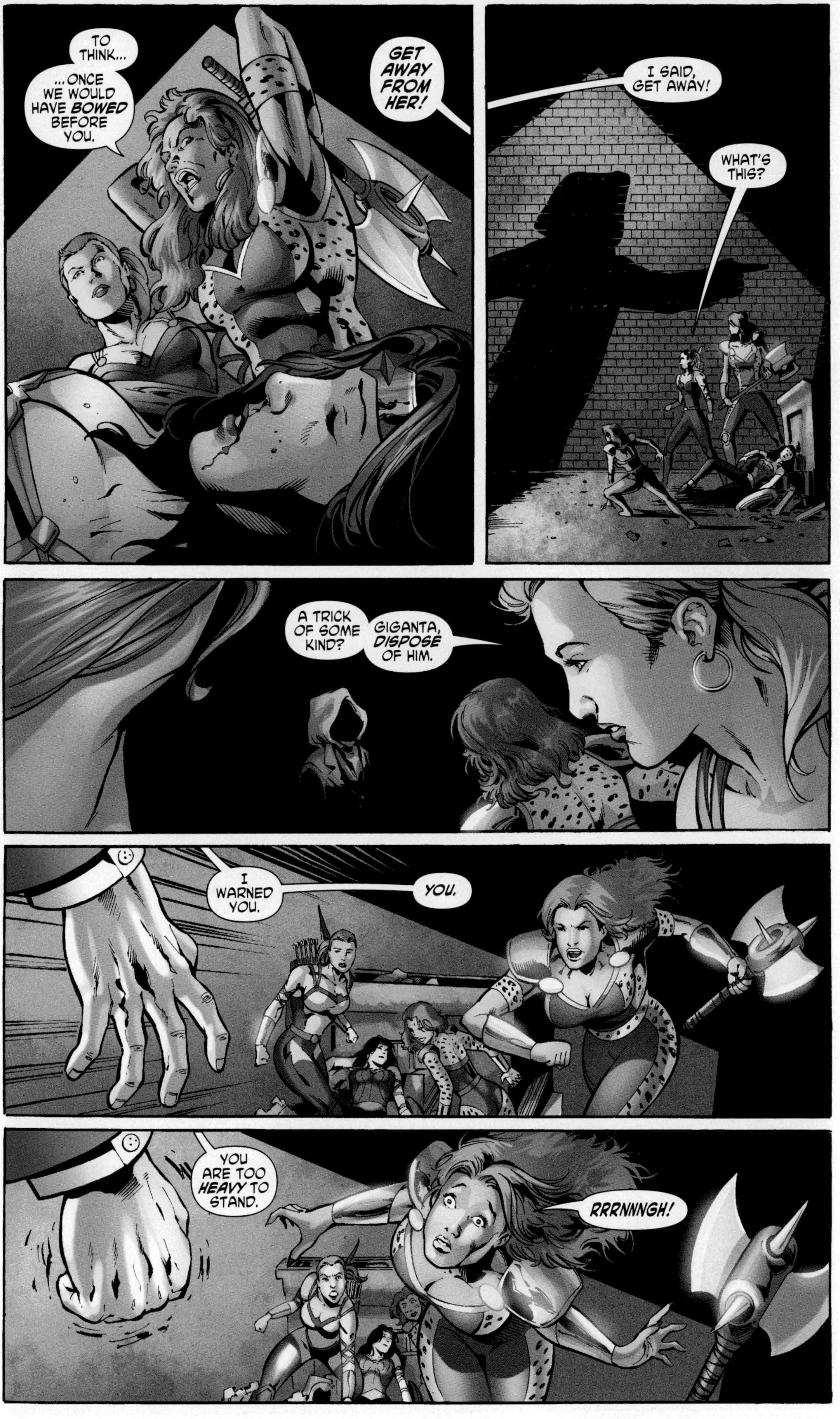
TO THINK...
...ONCE WE WOULD HAVE BOWED BEFORE YOU.
GET AWAY FROM HER!
I SAID, GET AWAY!
WHAT'S THIS?
A TRICK OF SOME KIND?
GIGANTA, DISPOSE OF HIM.
I WARNED YOU.
YOU.
YOU ARE TOO HEAVY TO STAND.
RRRNNNGH!

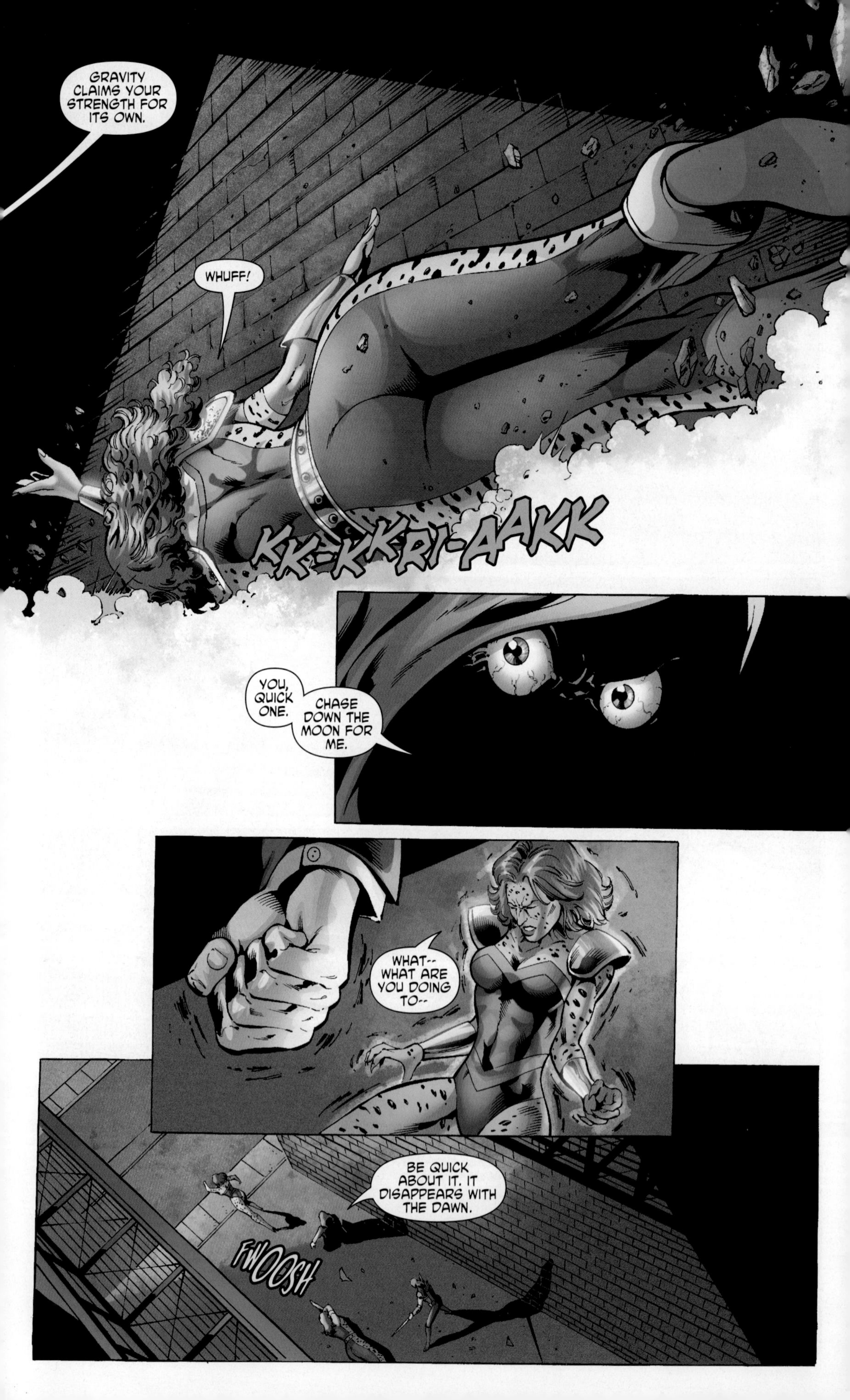
GRAVITY CLAIMS YOUR STRENGTH FOR ITS OWN.
WHUFF!
KK-KKKRI-AAKK
YOU, QUICK ONE.
CHASE DOWN THE MOON FOR ME.
WHAT-- WHAT ARE YOU DOING TO--
BE QUICK ABOUT IT. IT DISAPPEARS WITH THE DAWN.
FWOOSH

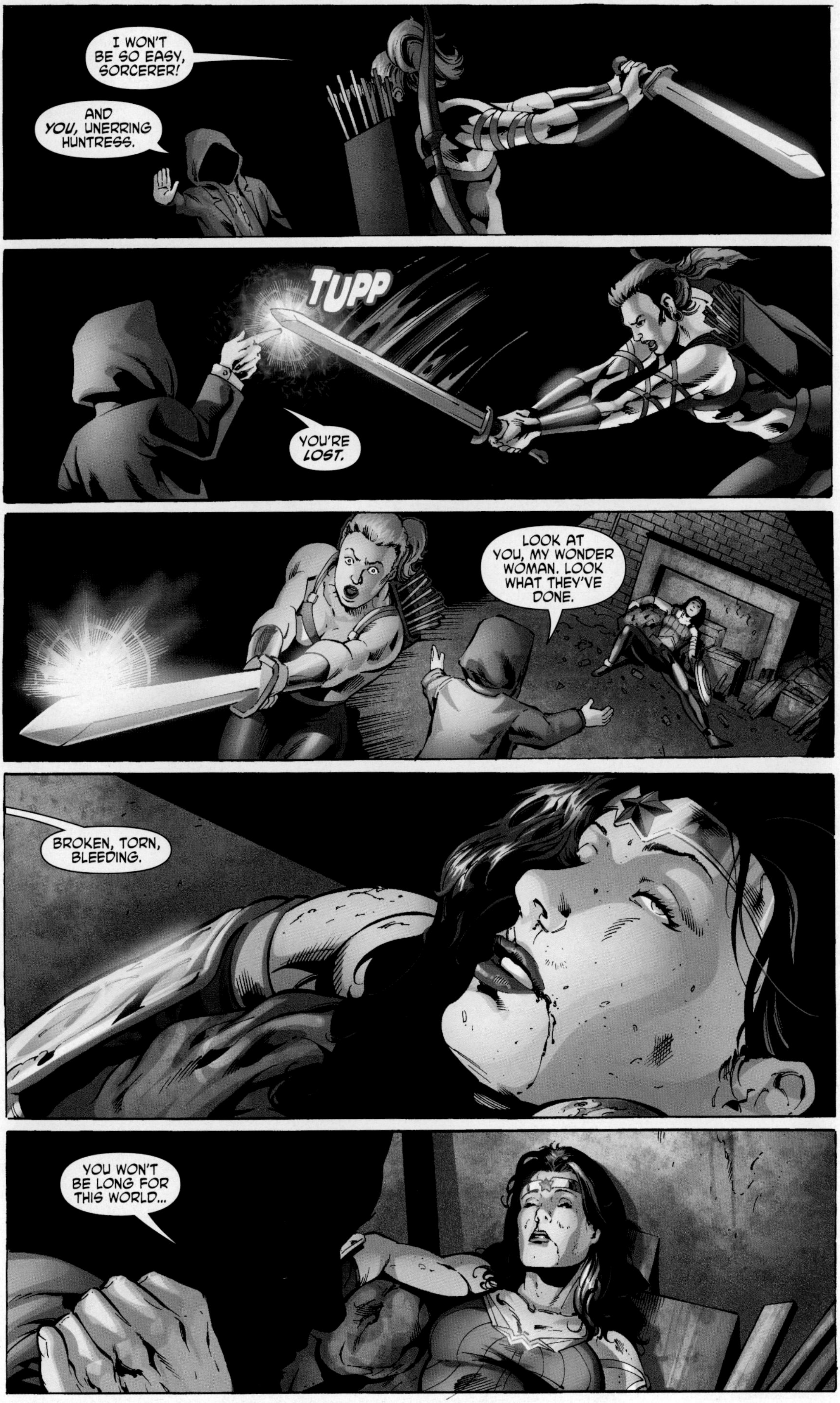
I WON'T BE SO EASY, SORCERER!
AND *YOU*, UNERRING HUNTRESS.
TUPP
YOU'RE *LOST.*
LOOK AT YOU, MY WONDER WOMAN. LOOK WHAT THEY'VE DONE.
BROKEN, TORN, BLEEDING.
YOU WON'T BE LONG FOR THIS WORLD...

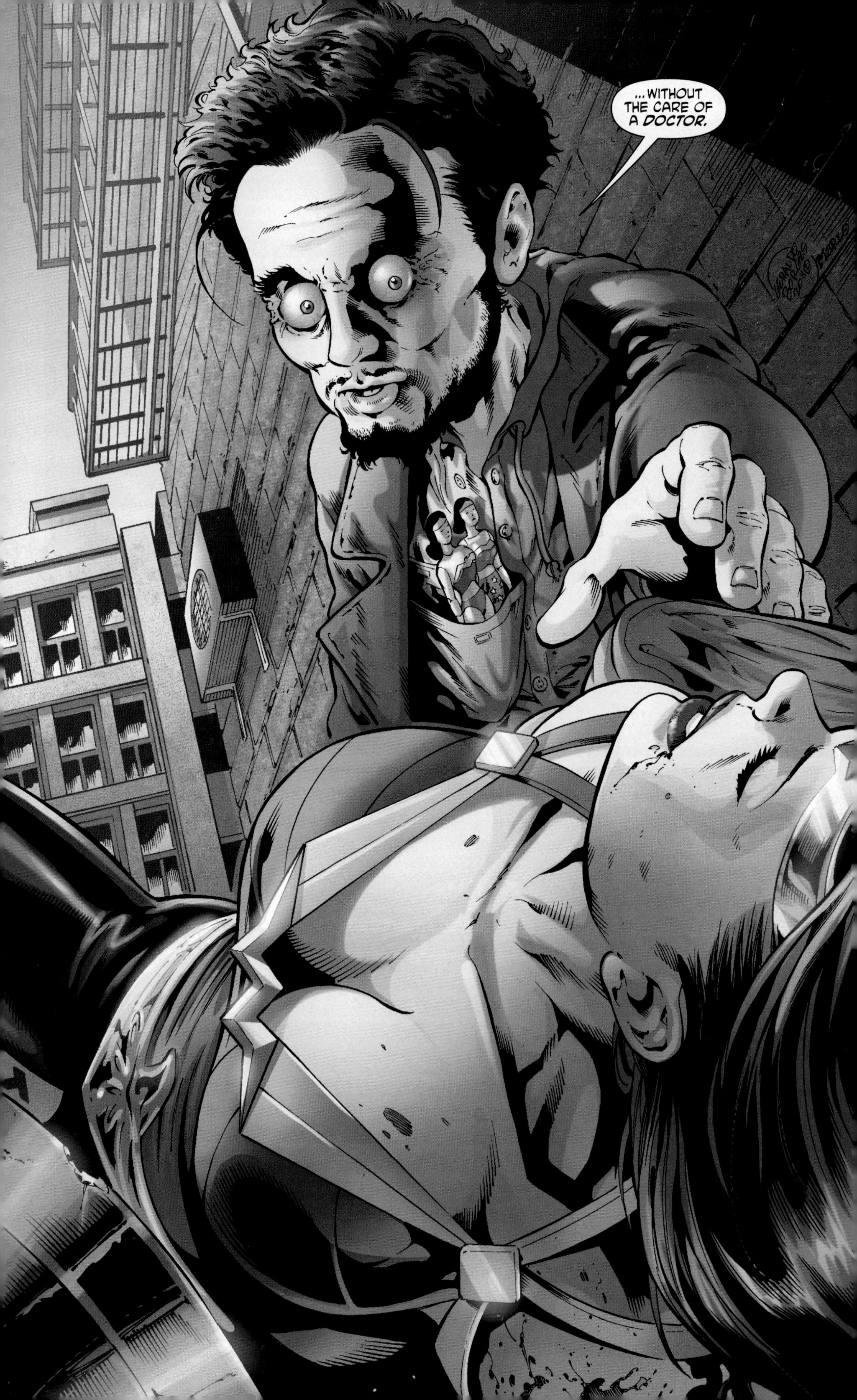
...WITHOUT THE CARE OF A DOCTOR.

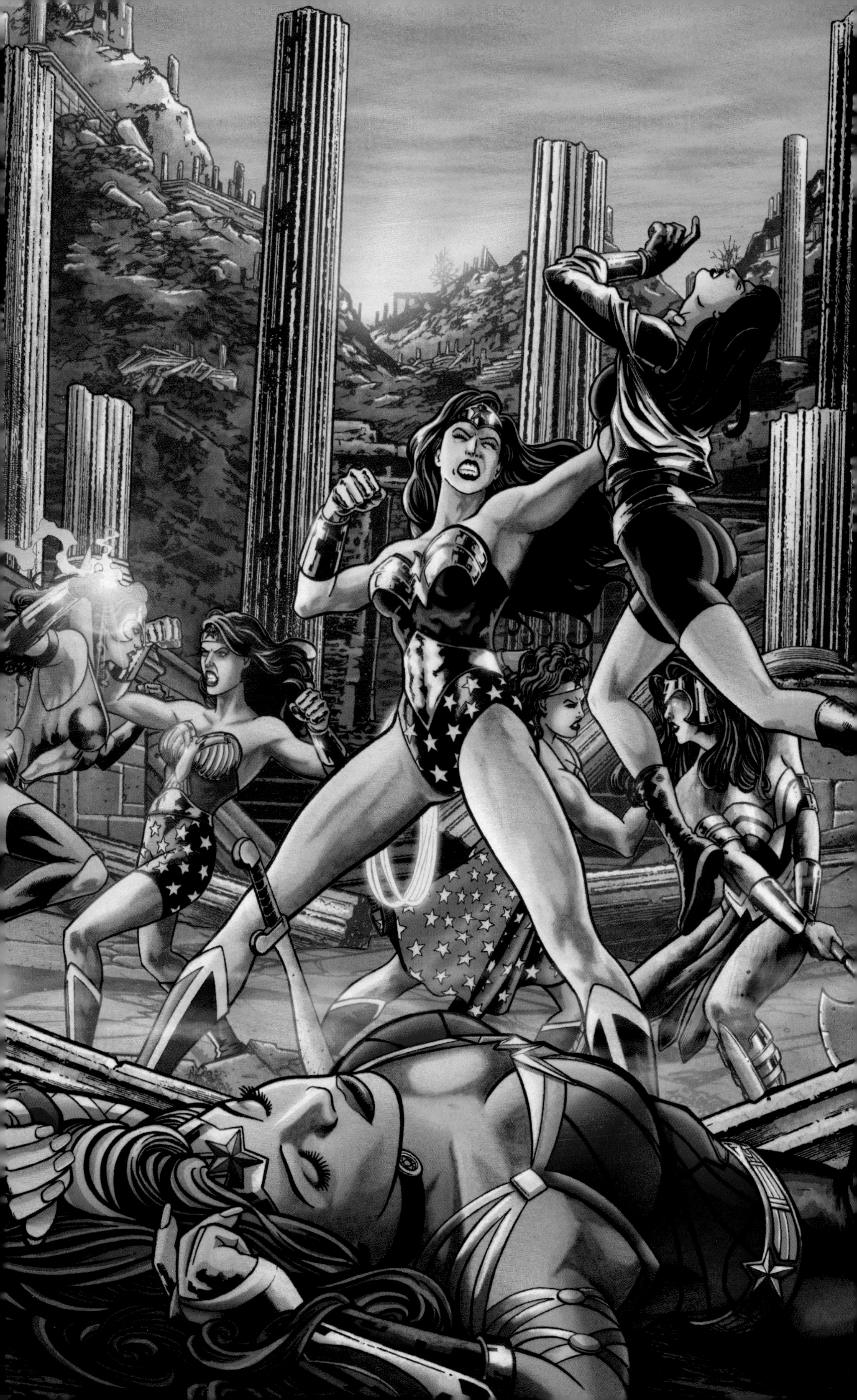

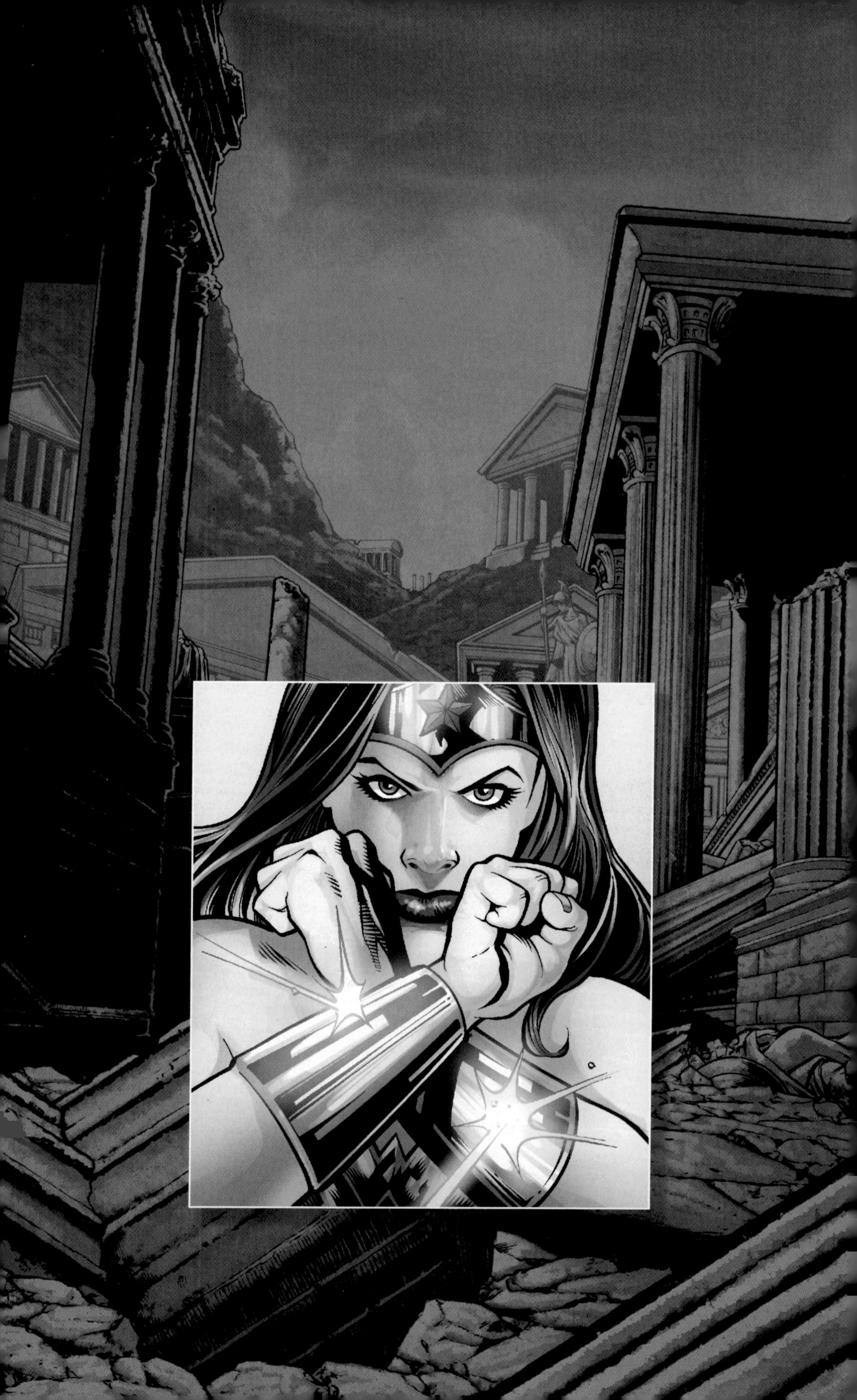

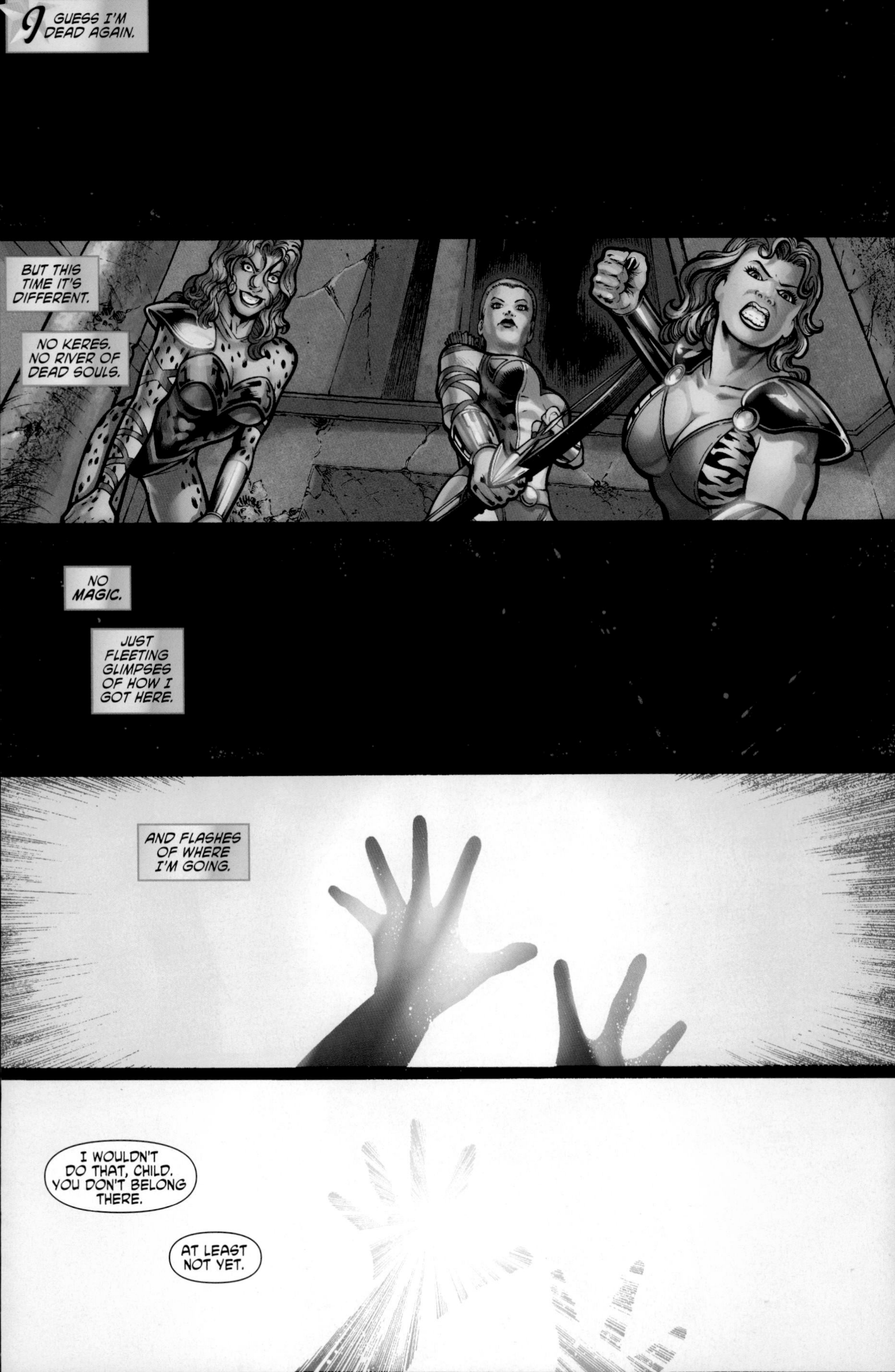
I GUESS I'M DEAD AGAIN.
BUT THIS TIME IT'S DIFFERENT.
NO KERES. NO RIVER OF DEAD SOULS.
NO MAGIC.
JUST FLEETING GLIMPSES OF HOW I GOT HERE.
AND FLASHES OF WHERE I'M GOING.
I WOULDN'T DO THAT, CHILD. YOU DON'T BELONG THERE.
AT LEAST NOT YET.

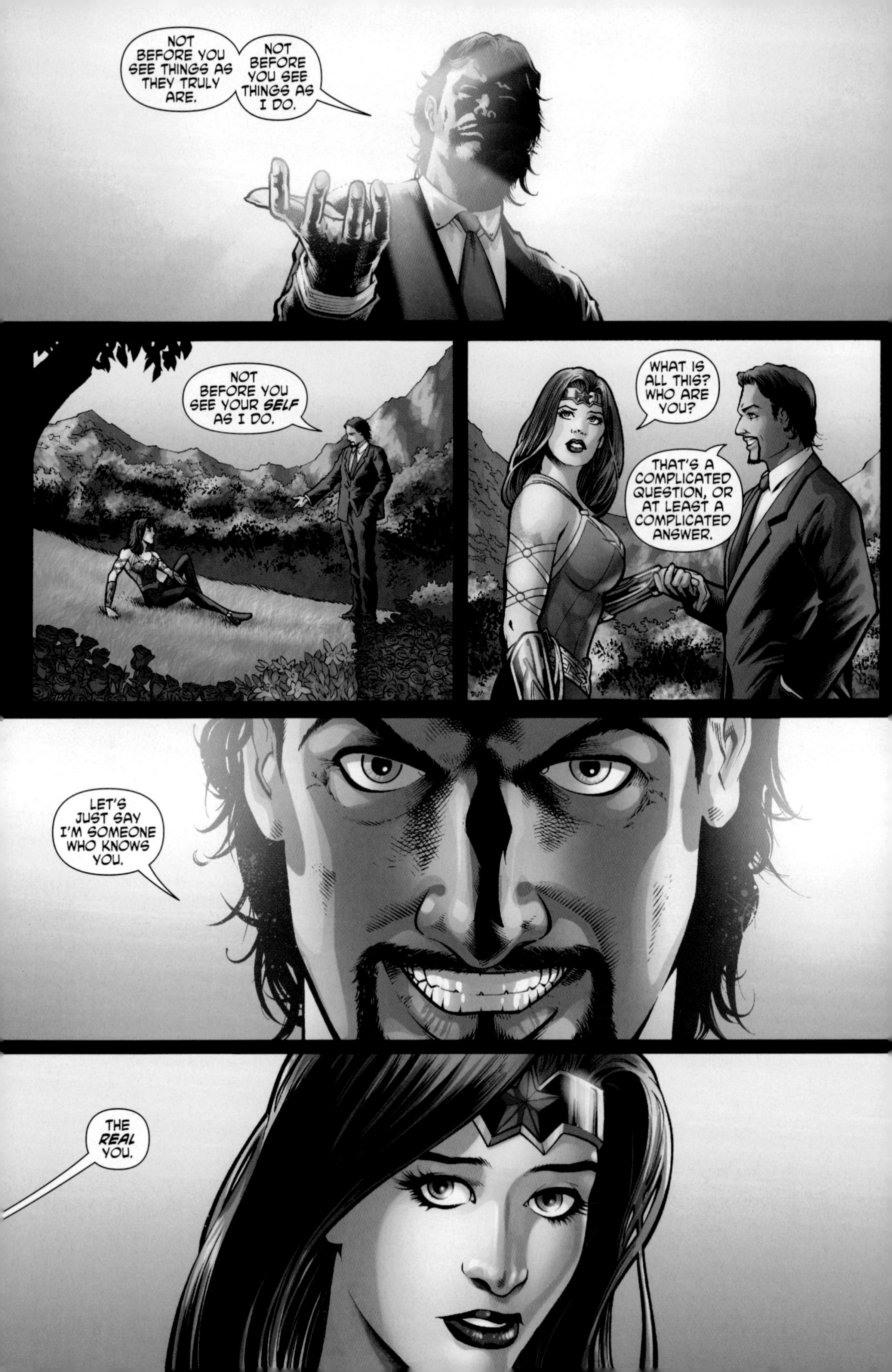
NOT BEFORE YOU SEE THINGS AS THEY TRULY ARE.
NOT BEFORE YOU SEE THINGS AS I DO.
NOT BEFORE YOU SEE YOUR *SELF* AS I DO.
WHAT IS ALL THIS? WHO ARE YOU?
THAT'S A COMPLICATED QUESTION, OR AT LEAST A COMPLICATED ANSWER.
LET'S JUST SAY I'M SOMEONE WHO KNOWS YOU.
THE *REAL* YOU.

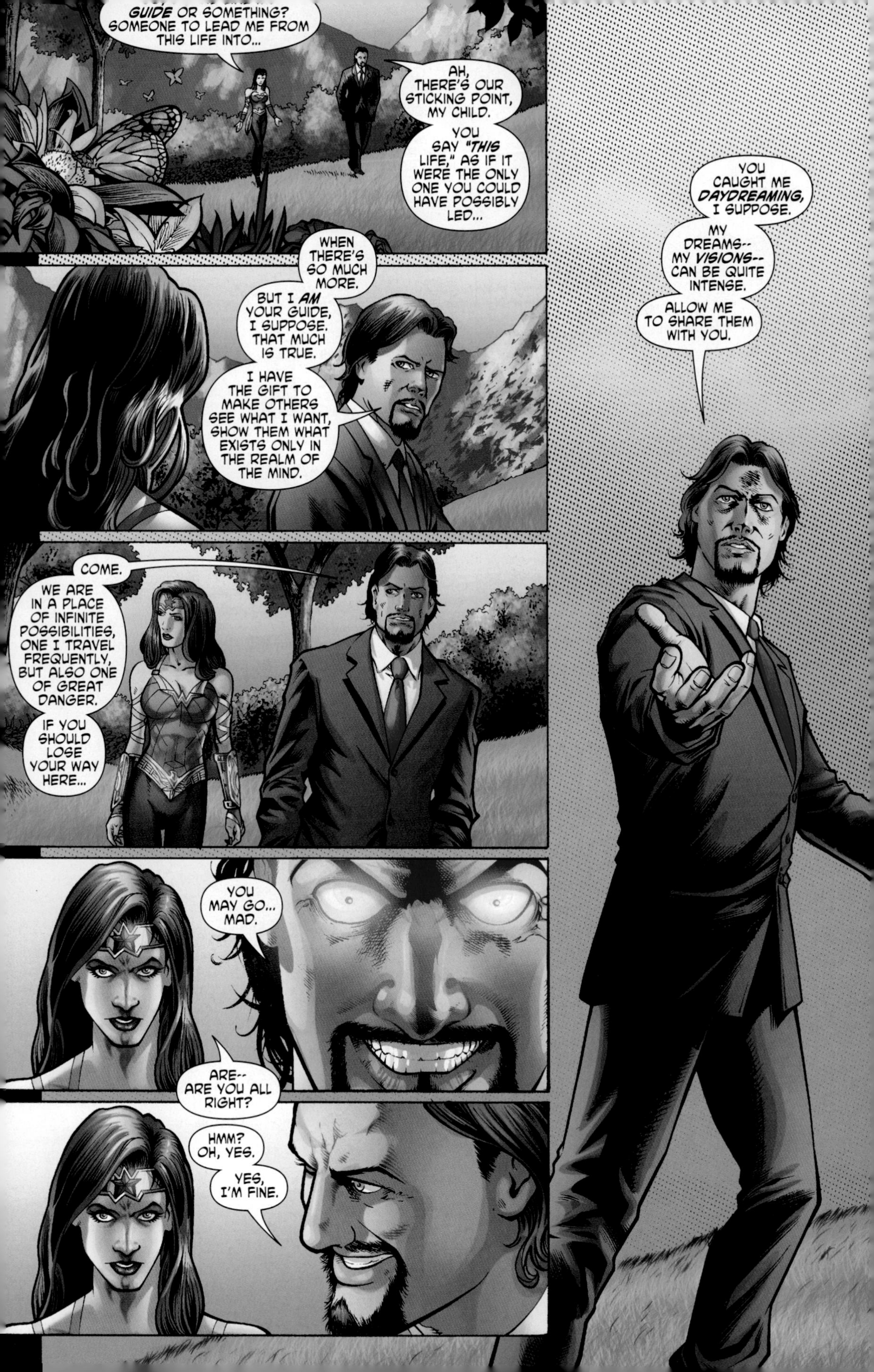
GUIDE OR SOMETHING? SOMEONE TO LEAD ME FROM THIS LIFE INTO...
AH, THERE'S OUR STICKING POINT, MY CHILD.
YOU SAY "THIS LIFE," AS IF IT WERE THE ONLY ONE YOU COULD HAVE POSSIBLY LED...
WHEN THERE'S SO MUCH MORE.
BUT I AM YOUR GUIDE, I SUPPOSE. THAT MUCH IS TRUE.
I HAVE THE GIFT TO MAKE OTHERS SEE WHAT I WANT, SHOW THEM WHAT EXISTS ONLY IN THE REALM OF THE MIND.
COME.
WE ARE IN A PLACE OF INFINITE POSSIBILITIES, ONE I TRAVEL FREQUENTLY, BUT ALSO ONE OF GREAT DANGER.
IF YOU SHOULD LOSE YOUR WAY HERE...
YOU MAY GO... MAD.
ARE-- ARE YOU ALL RIGHT?
HMM? OH, YES.
YES, I'M FINE.
YOU CAUGHT ME DAYDREAMING, I SUPPOSE.
MY DREAMS-- MY VISIONS-- CAN BE QUITE INTENSE.
ALLOW ME TO SHARE THEM WITH YOU.

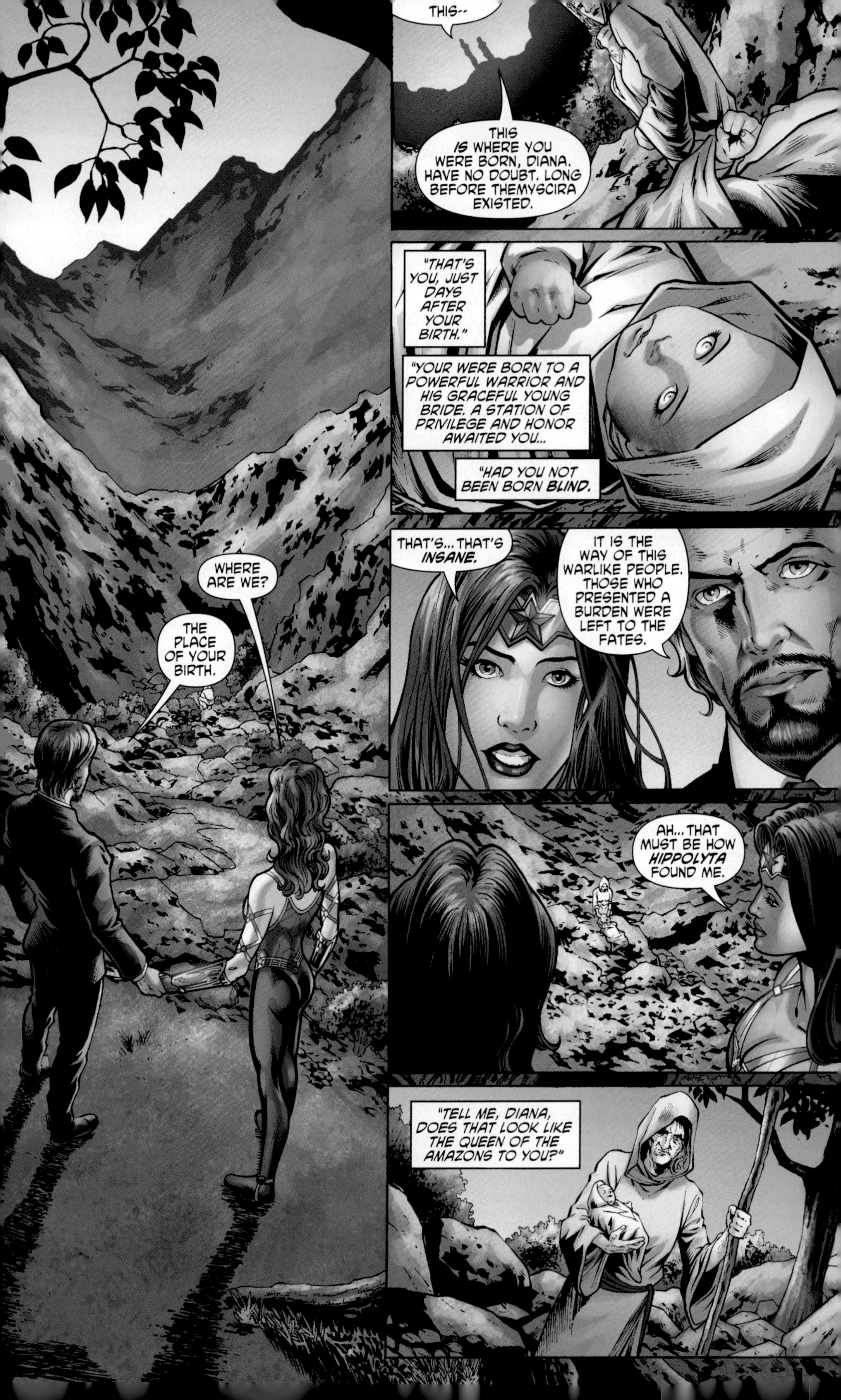
WHERE ARE WE?
THE PLACE OF YOUR BIRTH.
THIS--
THIS *IS* WHERE YOU WERE BORN, DIANA. HAVE NO DOUBT. LONG BEFORE THEMYSCIRA EXISTED.
"THAT'S YOU, JUST DAYS AFTER YOUR BIRTH."
"YOUR WERE BORN TO A POWERFUL WARRIOR AND HIS GRACEFUL YOUNG BRIDE. A STATION OF PRIVILEGE AND HONOR AWAITED YOU...
"HAD YOU NOT BEEN BORN **BLIND.**
THAT'S... THAT'S ***INSANE.***
IT IS THE WAY OF THIS WARLIKE PEOPLE. THOSE WHO PRESENTED A BURDEN WERE LEFT TO THE FATES.
AH... THAT MUST BE HOW ***HIPPOLYTA*** FOUND ME.
"TELL ME, DIANA, DOES THAT LOOK LIKE THE QUEEN OF THE AMAZONS TO YOU?"

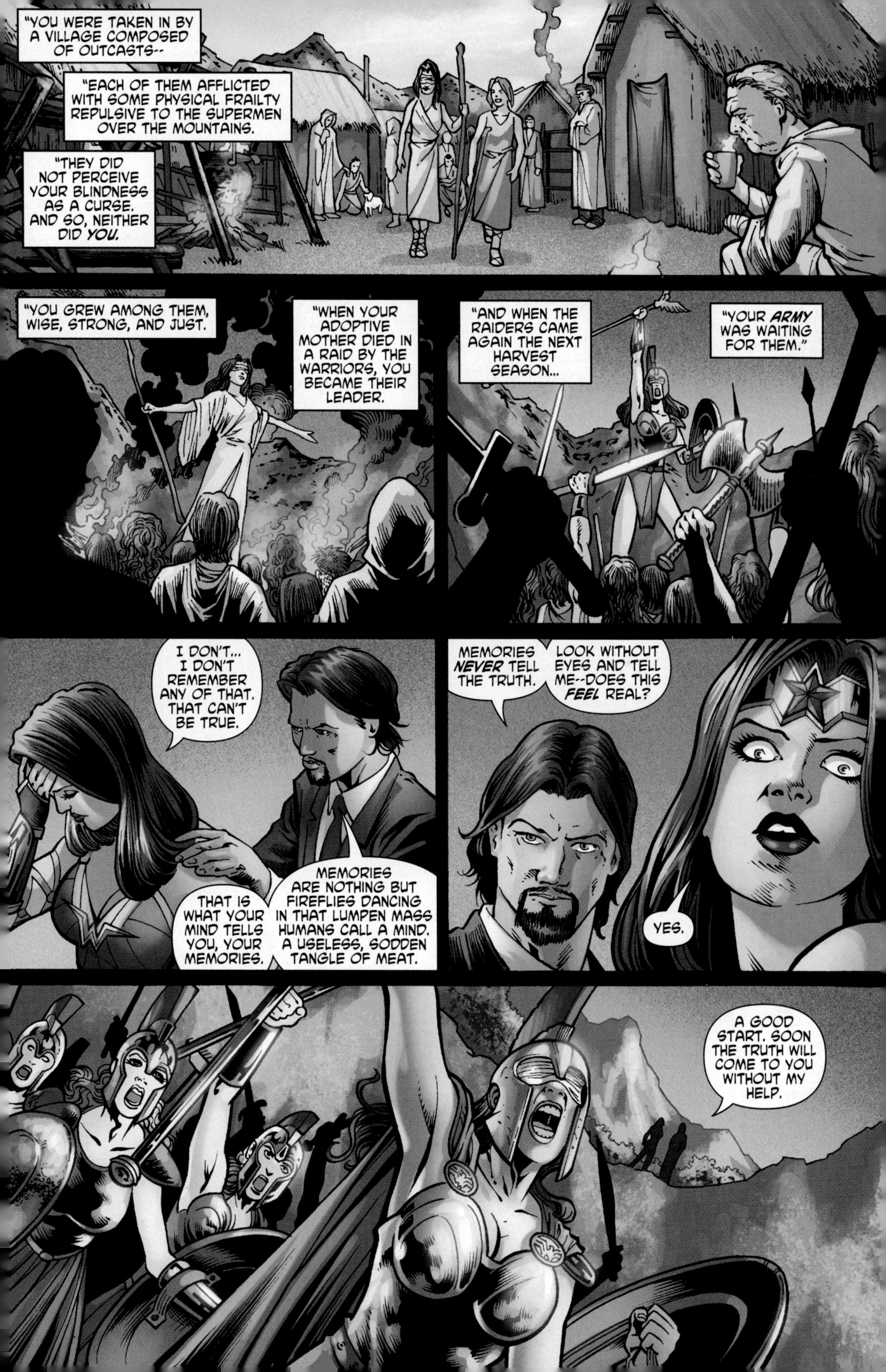
"YOU WERE TAKEN IN BY A VILLAGE COMPOSED OF OUTCASTS--
"EACH OF THEM AFFLICTED WITH SOME PHYSICAL FRAILTY REPULSIVE TO THE SUPERMEN OVER THE MOUNTAINS.
"THEY DID NOT PERCEIVE YOUR BLINDNESS AS A CURSE. AND SO, NEITHER DID *YOU.*
"YOU GREW AMONG THEM, WISE, STRONG, AND JUST.
"WHEN YOUR ADOPTIVE MOTHER DIED IN A RAID BY THE WARRIORS, YOU BECAME THEIR LEADER.
"AND WHEN THE RAIDERS CAME AGAIN THE NEXT HARVEST SEASON...
"YOUR *ARMY* WAS WAITING FOR THEM."
I DON'T... I DON'T REMEMBER ANY OF THAT. THAT CAN'T BE TRUE.
THAT IS WHAT YOUR MIND TELLS YOU, YOUR MEMORIES.
MEMORIES ARE NOTHING BUT FIREFLIES DANCING IN THAT LUMPEN MASS HUMANS CALL A MIND. A USELESS, SODDEN TANGLE OF MEAT.
MEMORIES *NEVER* TELL THE TRUTH.
LOOK WITHOUT EYES AND TELL ME--DOES THIS *FEEL* REAL?
YES.
A GOOD START. SOON THE TRUTH WILL COME TO YOU WITHOUT MY HELP.

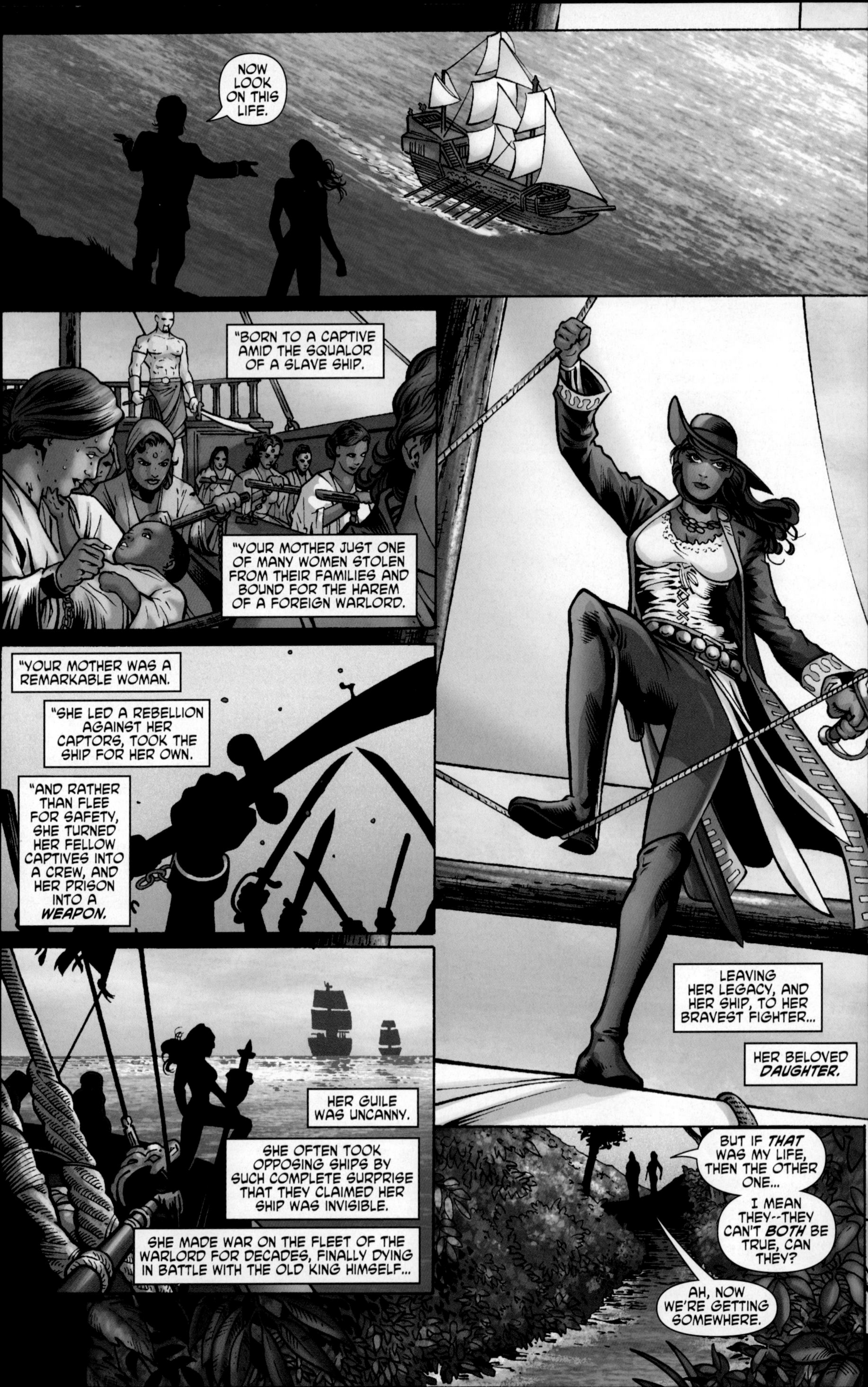
NOW LOOK ON THIS LIFE.
"BORN TO A CAPTIVE AMID THE SQUALOR OF A SLAVE SHIP.
"YOUR MOTHER JUST ONE OF MANY WOMEN STOLEN FROM THEIR FAMILIES AND BOUND FOR THE HAREM OF A FOREIGN WARLORD.
"YOUR MOTHER WAS A REMARKABLE WOMAN.
"SHE LED A REBELLION AGAINST HER CAPTORS, TOOK THE SHIP FOR HER OWN.
"AND RATHER THAN FLEE FOR SAFETY, SHE TURNED HER FELLOW CAPTIVES INTO A CREW, AND HER PRISON INTO A *WEAPON.*
HER GUILE WAS UNCANNY.
SHE OFTEN TOOK OPPOSING SHIPS BY SUCH COMPLETE SURPRISE THAT THEY CLAIMED HER SHIP WAS INVISIBLE.
SHE MADE WAR ON THE FLEET OF THE WARLORD FOR DECADES, FINALLY DYING IN BATTLE WITH THE OLD KING HIMSELF...
LEAVING HER LEGACY, AND HER SHIP, TO HER BRAVEST FIGHTER...
HER BELOVED *DAUGHTER.*
BUT IF *THAT* WAS MY LIFE, THEN THE OTHER ONE...
I MEAN THEY--THEY CAN'T *BOTH* BE TRUE, CAN THEY?
AH, NOW WE'RE GETTING SOMEWHERE.

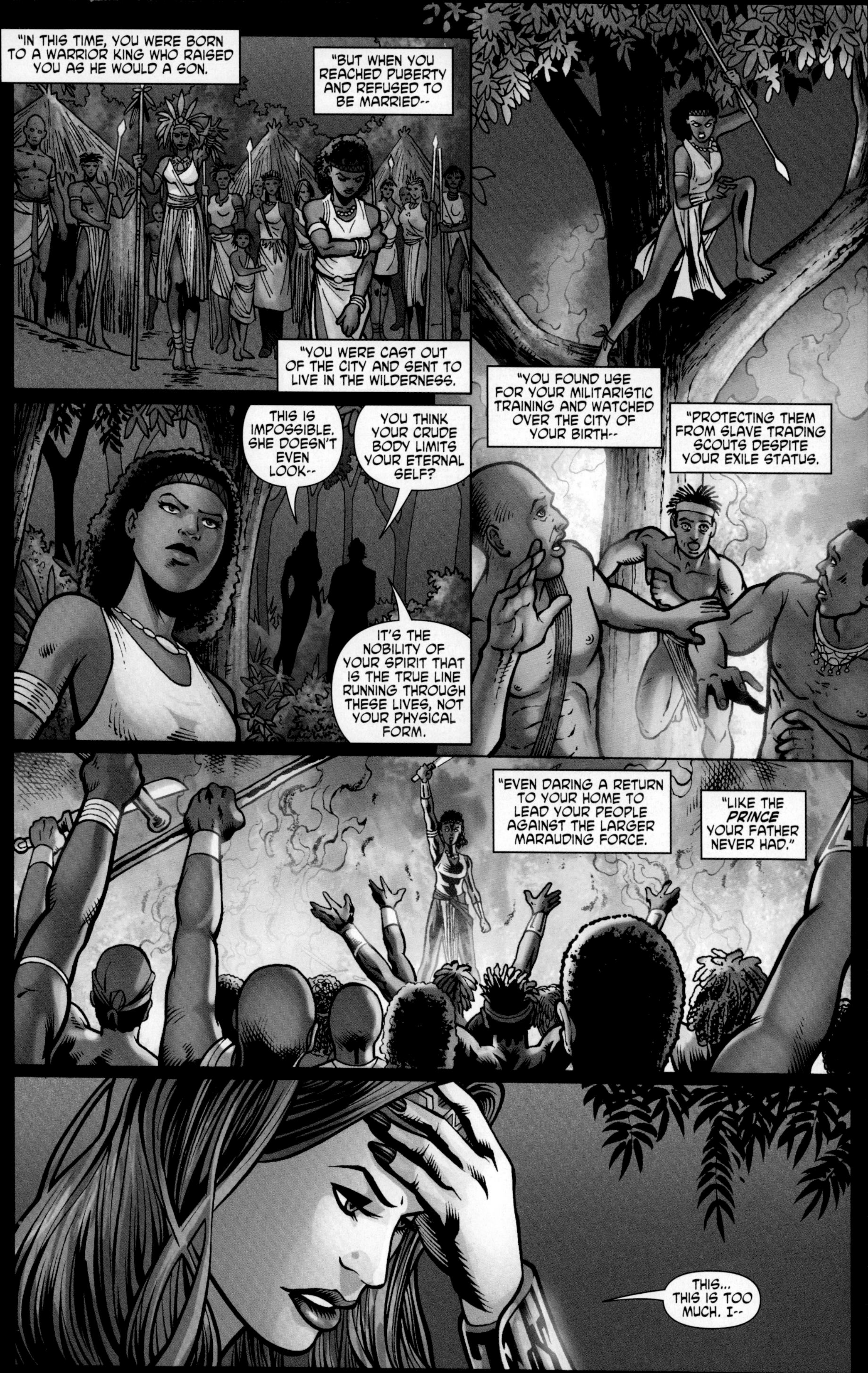

"IN THIS TIME, YOU WERE BORN TO A WARRIOR KING WHO RAISED YOU AS HE WOULD A SON.
"BUT WHEN YOU REACHED PUBERTY AND REFUSED TO BE MARRIED--
"YOU WERE CAST OUT OF THE CITY AND SENT TO LIVE IN THE WILDERNESS.
THIS IS IMPOSSIBLE. SHE DOESN'T EVEN LOOK--
YOU THINK YOUR CRUDE BODY LIMITS YOUR ETERNAL SELF?
IT'S THE NOBILITY OF YOUR SPIRIT THAT IS THE TRUE LINE RUNNING THROUGH THESE LIVES, NOT YOUR PHYSICAL FORM.
"YOU FOUND USE FOR YOUR MILITARISTIC TRAINING AND WATCHED OVER THE CITY OF YOUR BIRTH--
"PROTECTING THEM FROM SLAVE TRADING SCOUTS DESPITE YOUR EXILE STATUS.
"EVEN DARING A RETURN TO YOUR HOME TO LEAD YOUR PEOPLE AGAINST THE LARGER MARAUDING FORCE.
"LIKE THE *PRINCE* YOUR FATHER NEVER HAD."
THIS... THIS IS TOO MUCH. I--

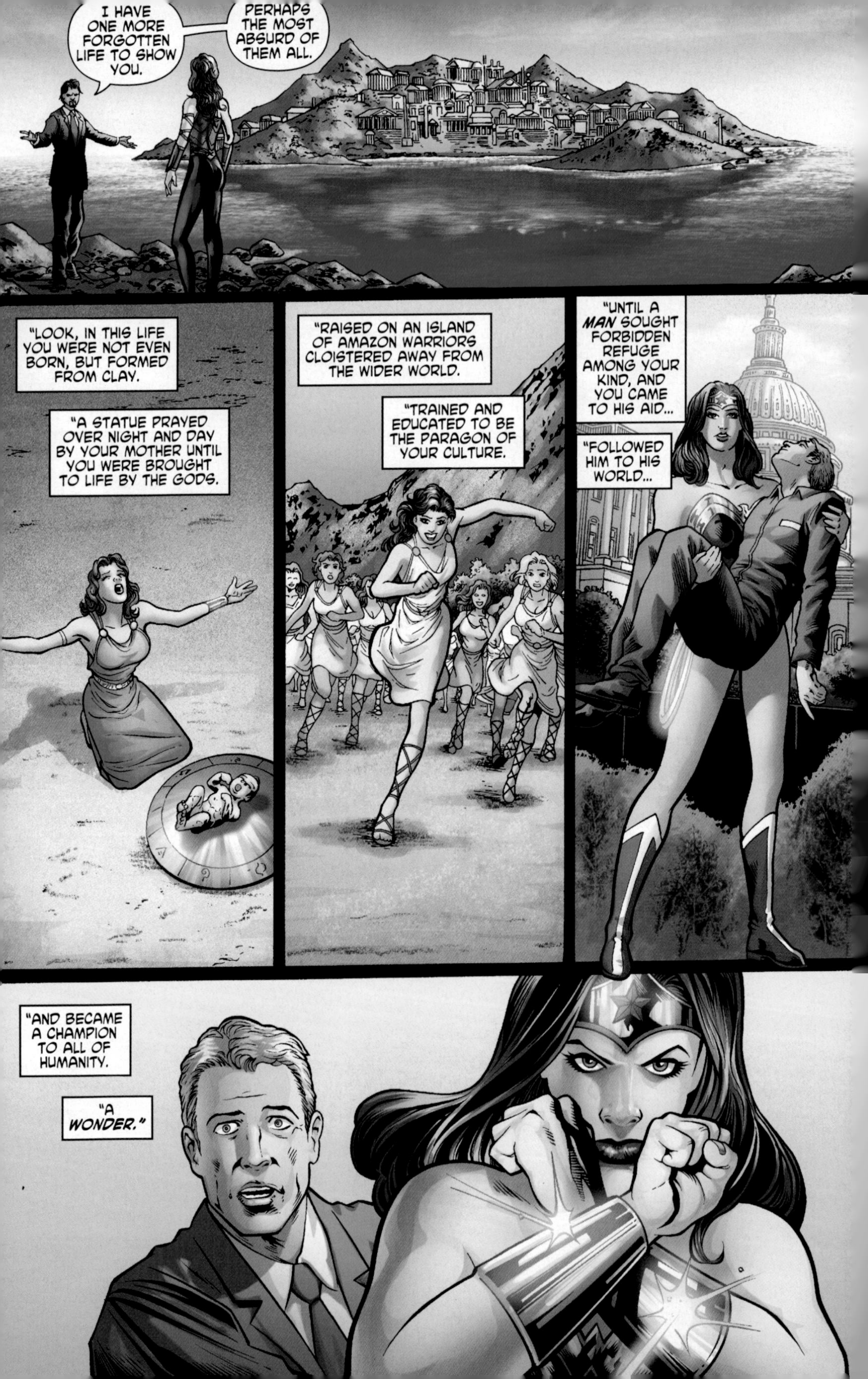
I HAVE ONE MORE FORGOTTEN LIFE TO SHOW YOU.
PERHAPS THE MOST ABSURD OF THEM ALL.
"LOOK, IN THIS LIFE YOU WERE NOT EVEN BORN, BUT FORMED FROM CLAY.
"A STATUE PRAYED OVER NIGHT AND DAY BY YOUR MOTHER UNTIL YOU WERE BROUGHT TO LIFE BY THE GODS.
"RAISED ON AN ISLAND OF AMAZON WARRIORS CLOISTERED AWAY FROM THE WIDER WORLD.
"TRAINED AND EDUCATED TO BE THE PARAGON OF YOUR CULTURE.
"UNTIL A *MAN* SOUGHT FORBIDDEN REFUGE AMONG YOUR KIND, AND YOU CAME TO HIS AID...
"FOLLOWED HIM TO HIS WORLD...
"AND BECAME A CHAMPION TO ALL OF HUMANITY.
"A *WONDER.*"

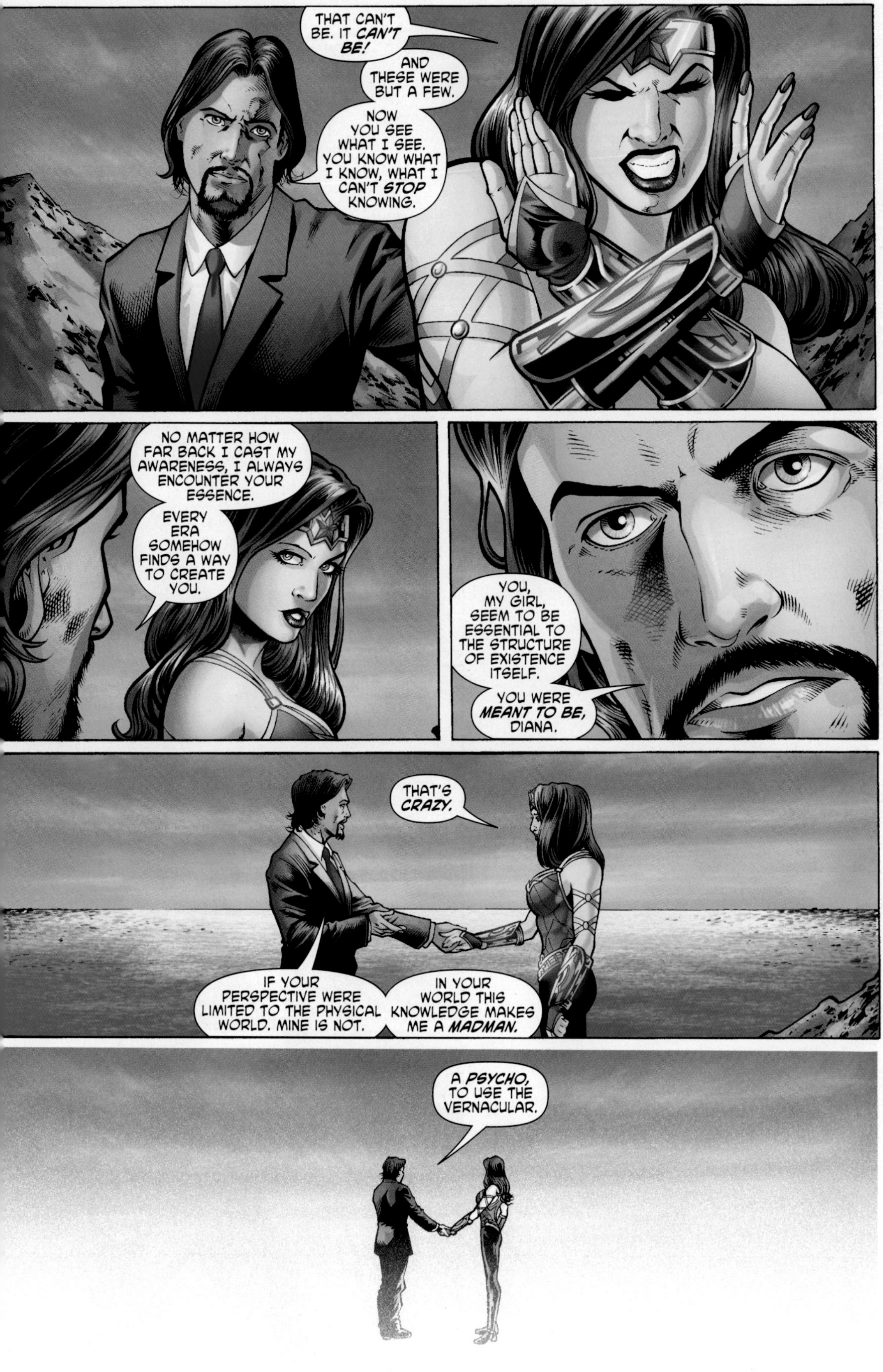
THAT CAN'T BE. IT CAN'T BE!
AND THESE WERE BUT A FEW.
NOW YOU SEE WHAT I SEE. YOU KNOW WHAT I KNOW, WHAT I CAN'T STOP KNOWING.
NO MATTER HOW FAR BACK I CAST MY AWARENESS, I ALWAYS ENCOUNTER YOUR ESSENCE.
EVERY ERA SOMEHOW FINDS A WAY TO CREATE YOU.
YOU, MY GIRL, SEEM TO BE ESSENTIAL TO THE STRUCTURE OF EXISTENCE ITSELF.
YOU WERE MEANT TO BE, DIANA.
THAT'S CRAZY.
IF YOUR PERSPECTIVE WERE LIMITED TO THE PHYSICAL WORLD. MINE IS NOT.
IN YOUR WORLD THIS KNOWLEDGE MAKES ME A MADMAN.
A PSYCHO, TO USE THE VERNACULAR.

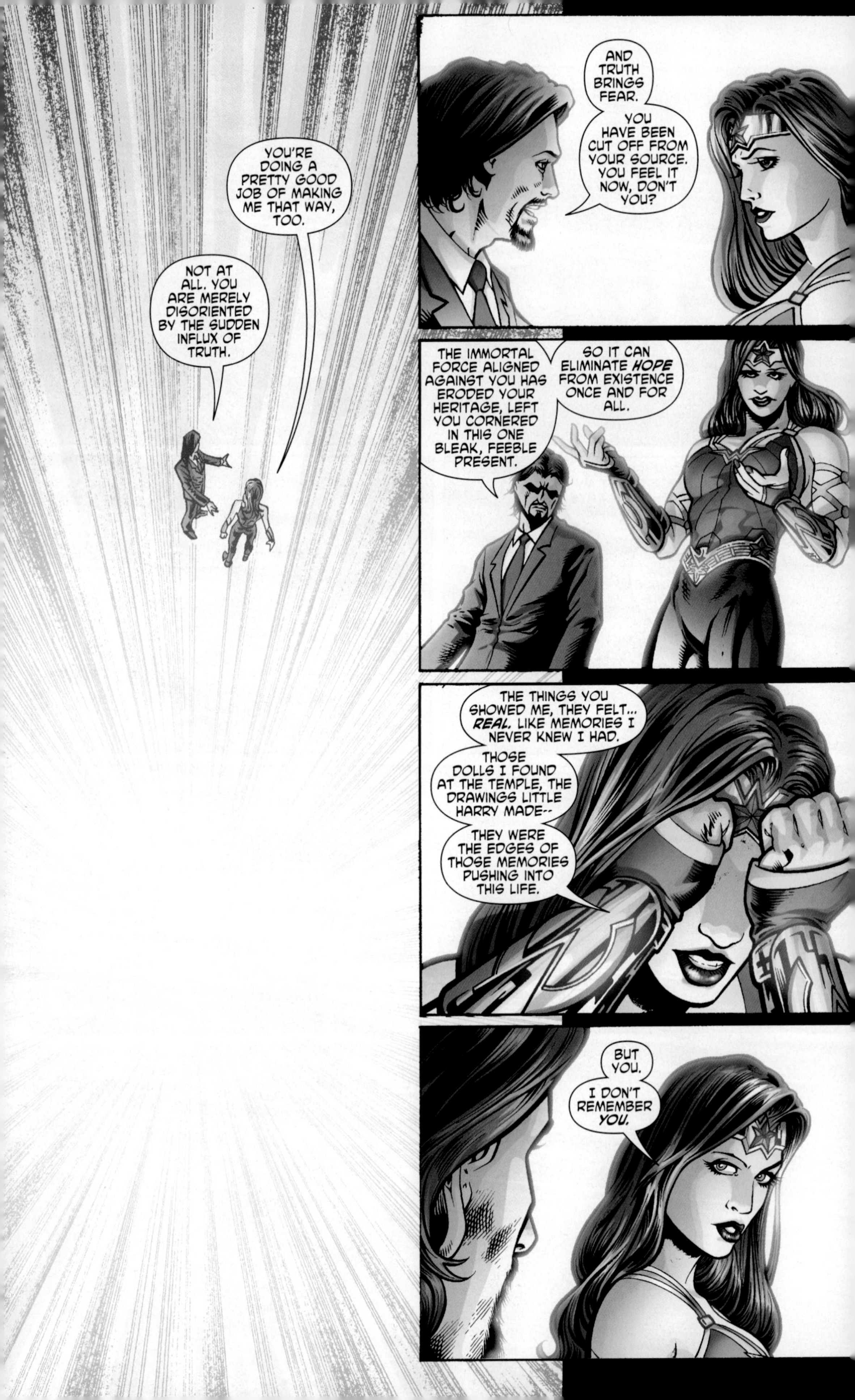
YOU'RE DOING A PRETTY GOOD JOB OF MAKING ME THAT WAY, TOO.
NOT AT ALL. YOU ARE MERELY DISORIENTED BY THE SUDDEN INFLUX OF TRUTH.
AND TRUTH BRINGS FEAR.
YOU HAVE BEEN CUT OFF FROM YOUR SOURCE. YOU FEEL IT NOW, DON'T YOU?
THE IMMORTAL FORCE ALIGNED AGAINST YOU HAS ERODED YOUR HERITAGE, LEFT YOU CORNERED IN THIS ONE BLEAK, FEEBLE PRESENT.
SO IT CAN ELIMINATE HOPE FROM EXISTENCE ONCE AND FOR ALL.
THE THINGS YOU SHOWED ME, THEY FELT... REAL. LIKE MEMORIES I NEVER KNEW I HAD.
THOSE DOLLS I FOUND AT THE TEMPLE, THE DRAWINGS LITTLE HARRY MADE--
THEY WERE THE EDGES OF THOSE MEMORIES PUSHING INTO THIS LIFE.
BUT YOU.
I DON'T REMEMBER YOU.

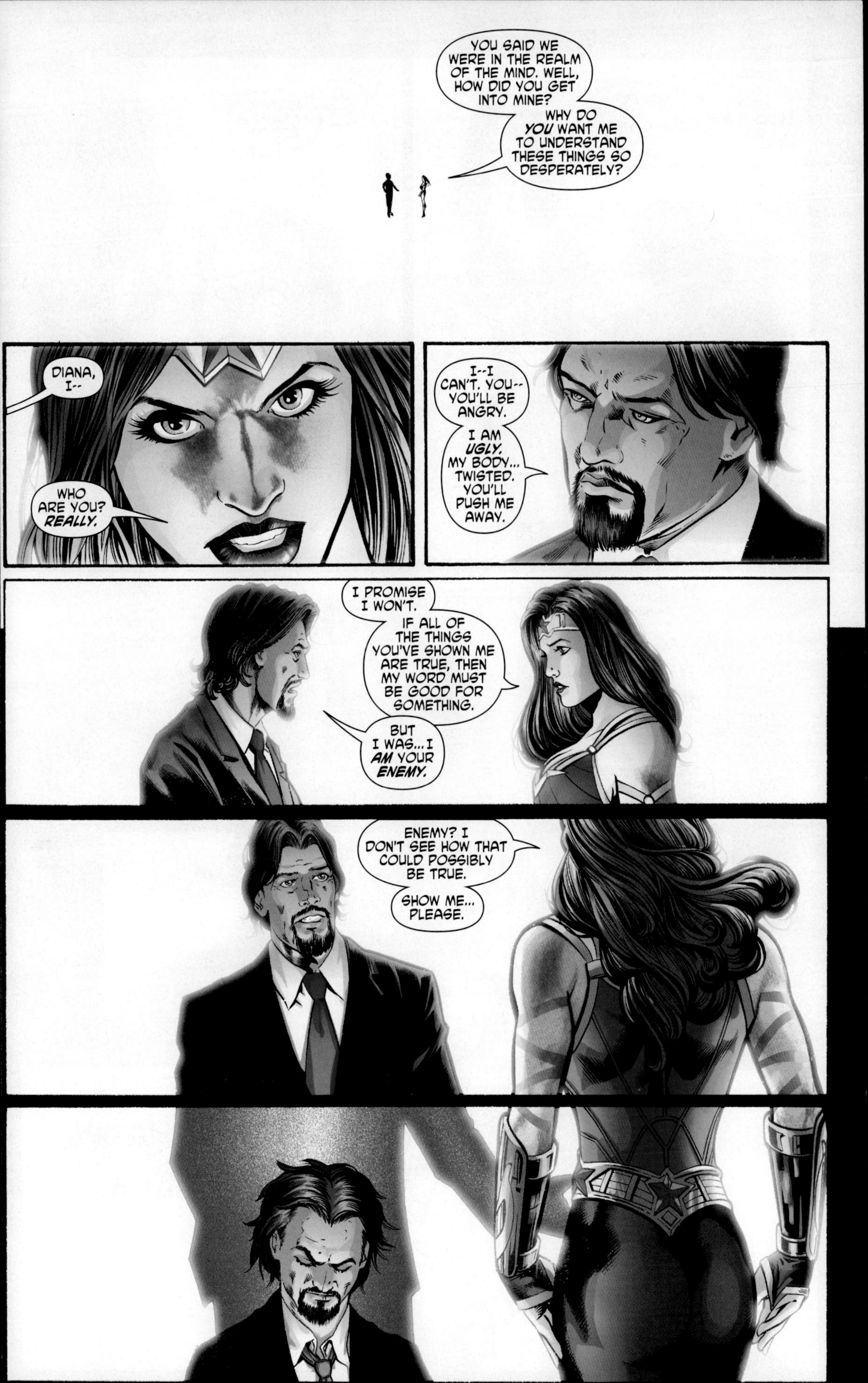
YOU SAID WE WERE IN THE REALM OF THE MIND. WELL, HOW DID YOU GET INTO MINE?
WHY DO *YOU* WANT ME TO UNDERSTAND THESE THINGS SO DESPERATELY?
DIANA, I--
WHO ARE YOU? *REALLY.*
I--I CAN'T. YOU--YOU'LL BE ANGRY.
I AM *UGLY.* MY BODY... TWISTED. YOU'LL PUSH ME AWAY.
I PROMISE I WON'T.
IF ALL OF THE THINGS YOU'VE SHOWN ME ARE TRUE, THEN MY WORD MUST BE GOOD FOR SOMETHING.
BUT I WAS... I *AM* YOUR *ENEMY.*
ENEMY? I DON'T SEE HOW THAT COULD POSSIBLY BE TRUE.
SHOW ME... PLEASE.

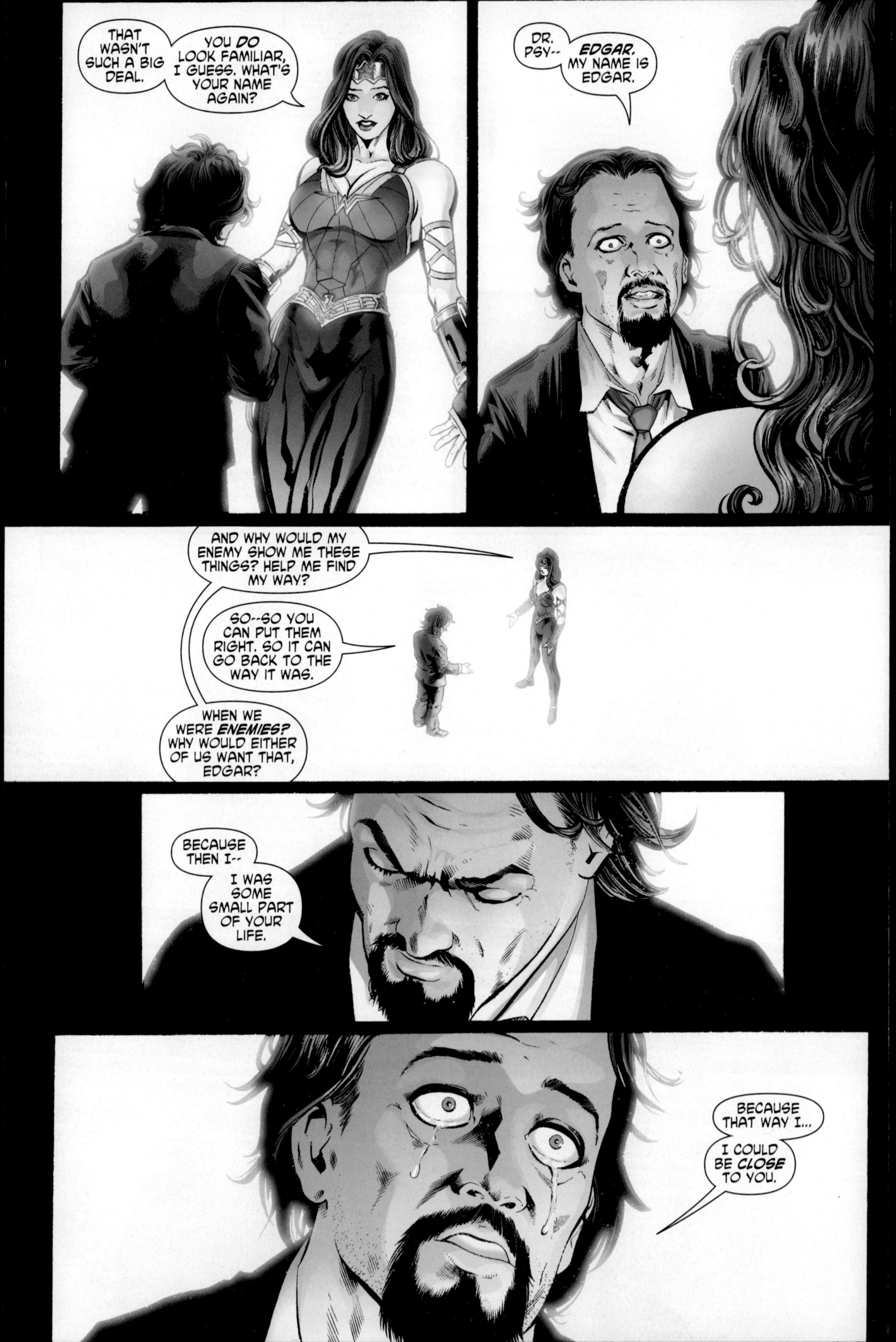
THAT WASN'T SUCH A BIG DEAL.
YOU DO LOOK FAMILIAR, I GUESS. WHAT'S YOUR NAME AGAIN?
DR. PSY--
EDGAR. MY NAME IS EDGAR.
AND WHY WOULD MY ENEMY SHOW ME THESE THINGS? HELP ME FIND MY WAY?
SO--SO YOU CAN PUT THEM RIGHT. SO IT CAN GO BACK TO THE WAY IT WAS.
WHEN WE WERE ENEMIES? WHY WOULD EITHER OF US WANT THAT, EDGAR?
BECAUSE THEN I--
I WAS SOME SMALL PART OF YOUR LIFE.
BECAUSE THAT WAY I...
I COULD BE CLOSE TO YOU.

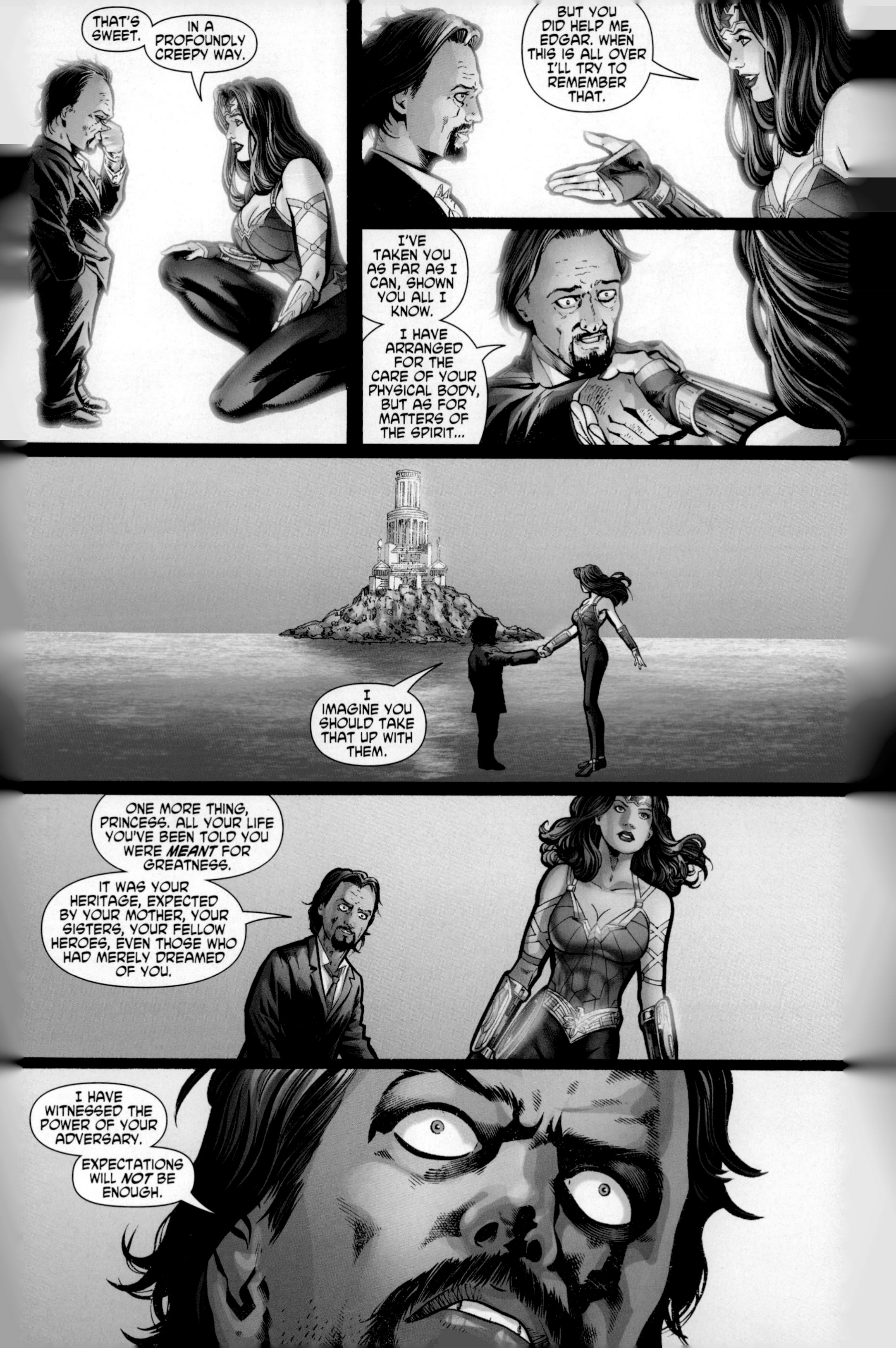
THAT'S SWEET.
IN A PROFOUNDLY CREEPY WAY.
BUT YOU DID HELP ME, EDGAR. WHEN THIS IS ALL OVER I'LL TRY TO REMEMBER THAT.
I'VE TAKEN YOU AS FAR AS I CAN, SHOWN YOU ALL I KNOW.
I HAVE ARRANGED FOR THE CARE OF YOUR PHYSICAL BODY, BUT AS FOR MATTERS OF THE SPIRIT...
I IMAGINE YOU SHOULD TAKE THAT UP WITH THEM.
ONE MORE THING, PRINCESS. ALL YOUR LIFE YOU'VE BEEN TOLD YOU WERE *MEANT* FOR GREATNESS.
IT WAS YOUR HERITAGE, EXPECTED BY YOUR MOTHER, YOUR SISTERS, YOUR FELLOW HEROES, EVEN THOSE WHO HAD MERELY DREAMED OF YOU.
I HAVE WITNESSED THE POWER OF YOUR ADVERSARY.
EXPECTATIONS WILL *NOT* BE ENOUGH.

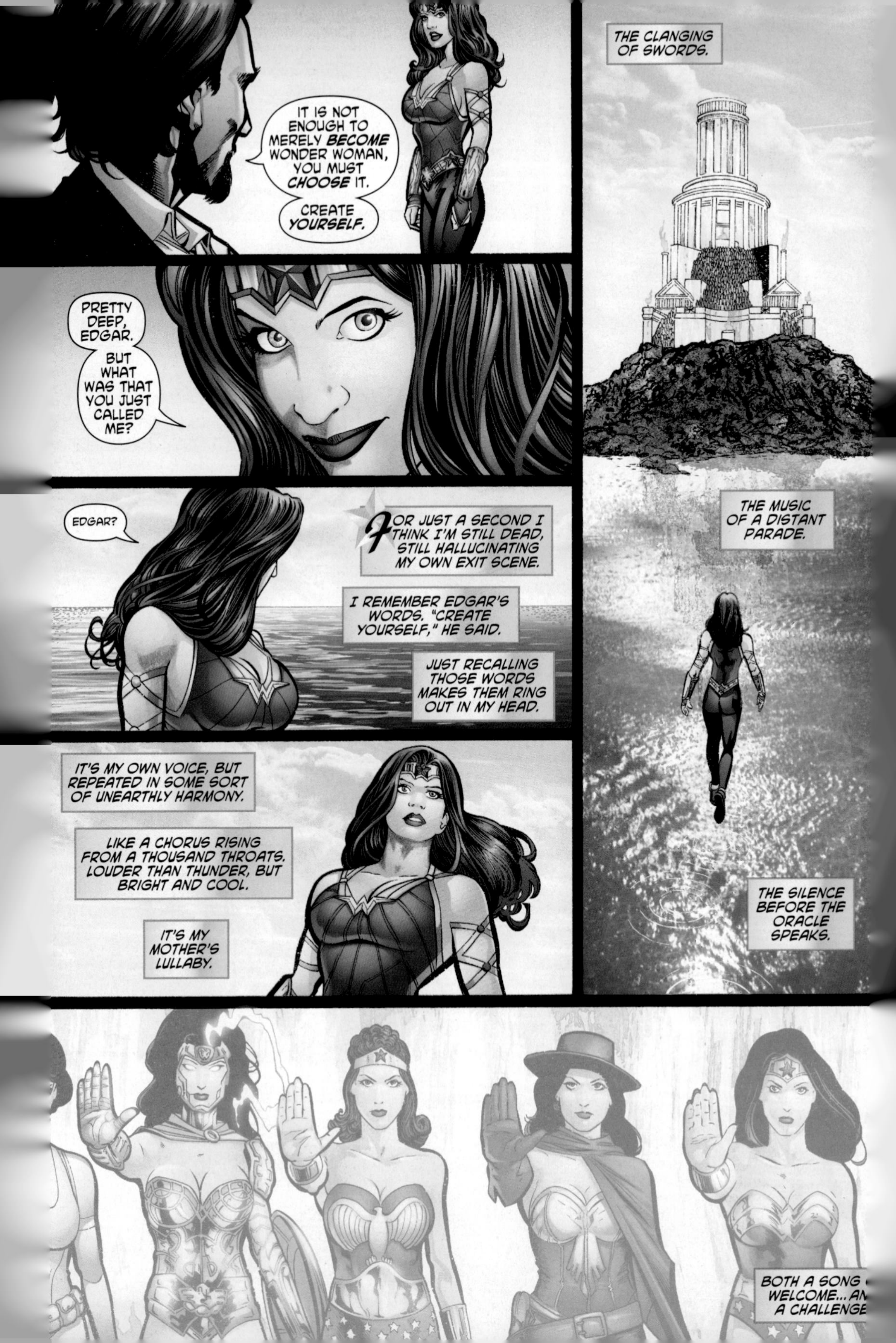
IT IS NOT ENOUGH TO MERELY BECOME WONDER WOMAN, YOU MUST CHOOSE IT.
CREATE YOURSELF.
PRETTY DEEP, EDGAR.
BUT WHAT WAS THAT YOU JUST CALLED ME?
EDGAR?
FOR JUST A SECOND I THINK I'M STILL DEAD, STILL HALLUCINATING MY OWN EXIT SCENE.
I REMEMBER EDGAR'S WORDS. "CREATE YOURSELF," HE SAID.
JUST RECALLING THOSE WORDS MAKES THEM RING OUT IN MY HEAD.
IT'S MY OWN VOICE, BUT REPEATED IN SOME SORT OF UNEARTHLY HARMONY.
LIKE A CHORUS RISING FROM A THOUSAND THROATS. LOUDER THAN THUNDER, BUT BRIGHT AND COOL.
IT'S MY MOTHER'S LULLABY.
THE CLANGING OF SWORDS.
THE MUSIC OF A DISTANT PARADE.
THE SILENCE BEFORE THE ORACLE SPEAKS.
BOTH A SONG
WELCOME... AN
A CHALLENGE

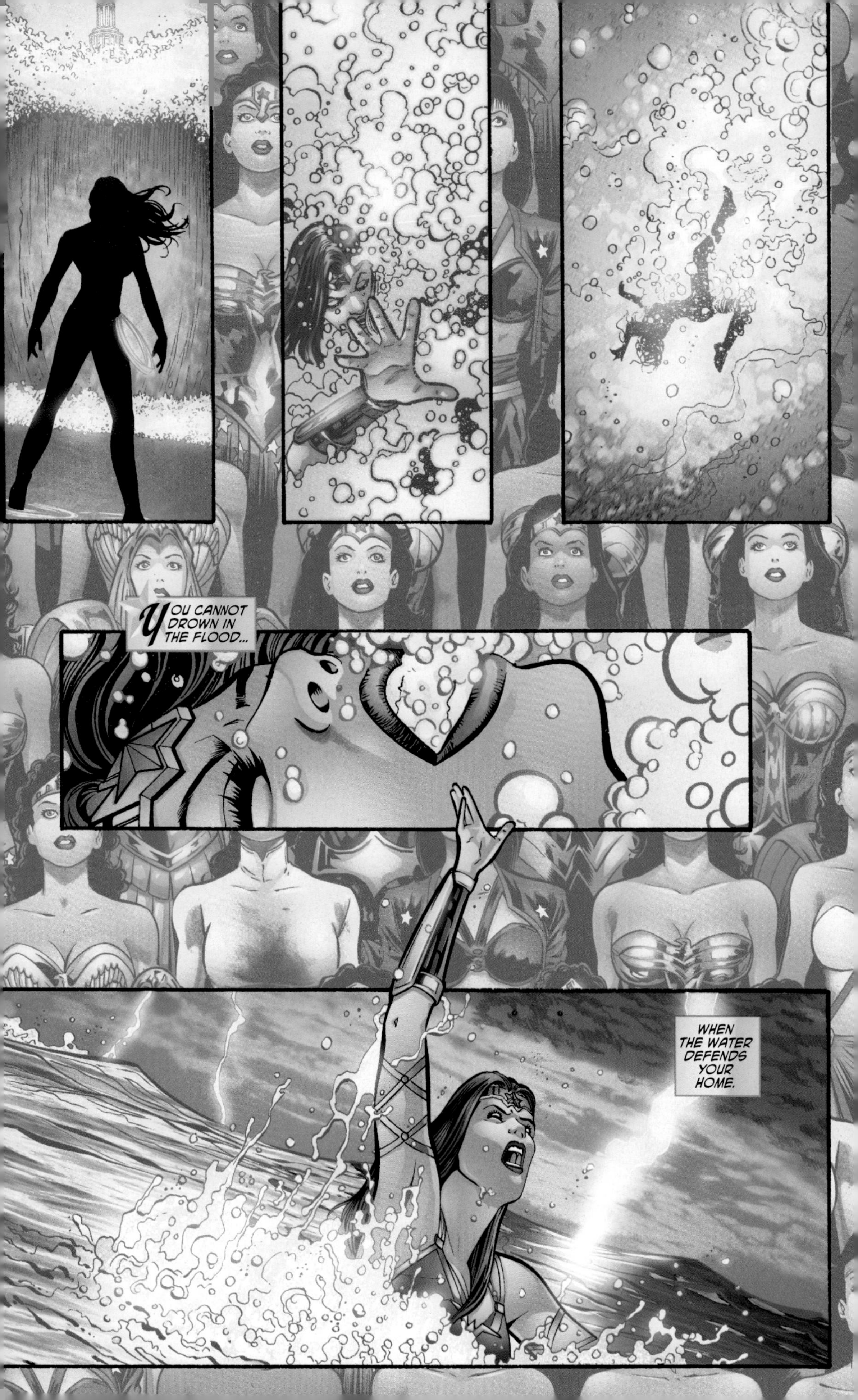
YOU CANNOT DROWN IN THE FLOOD...
WHEN THE WATER DEFENDS YOUR HOME.

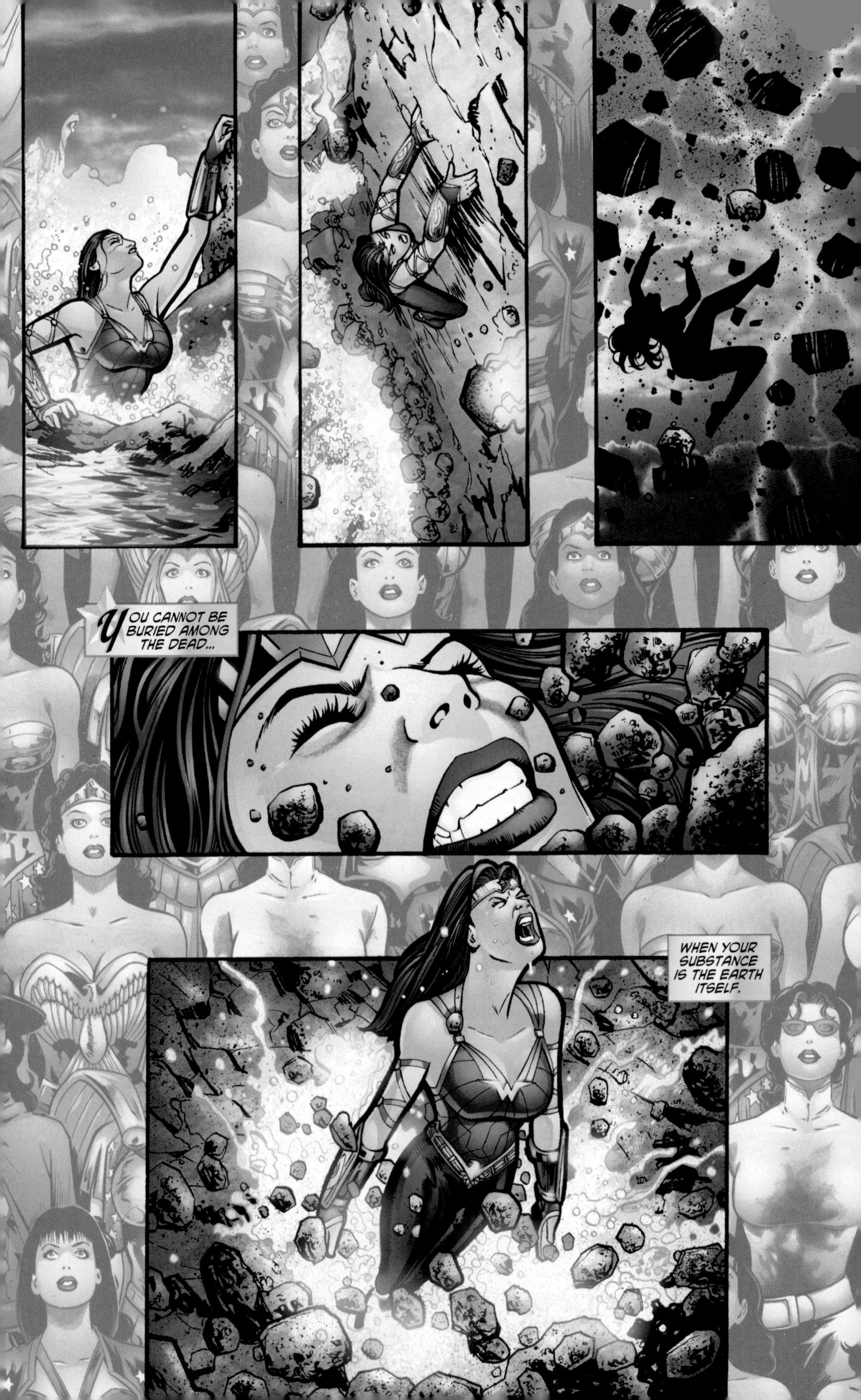
YOU CANNOT BE BURIED AMONG THE DEAD...
WHEN YOUR SUBSTANCE IS THE EARTH ITSELF.

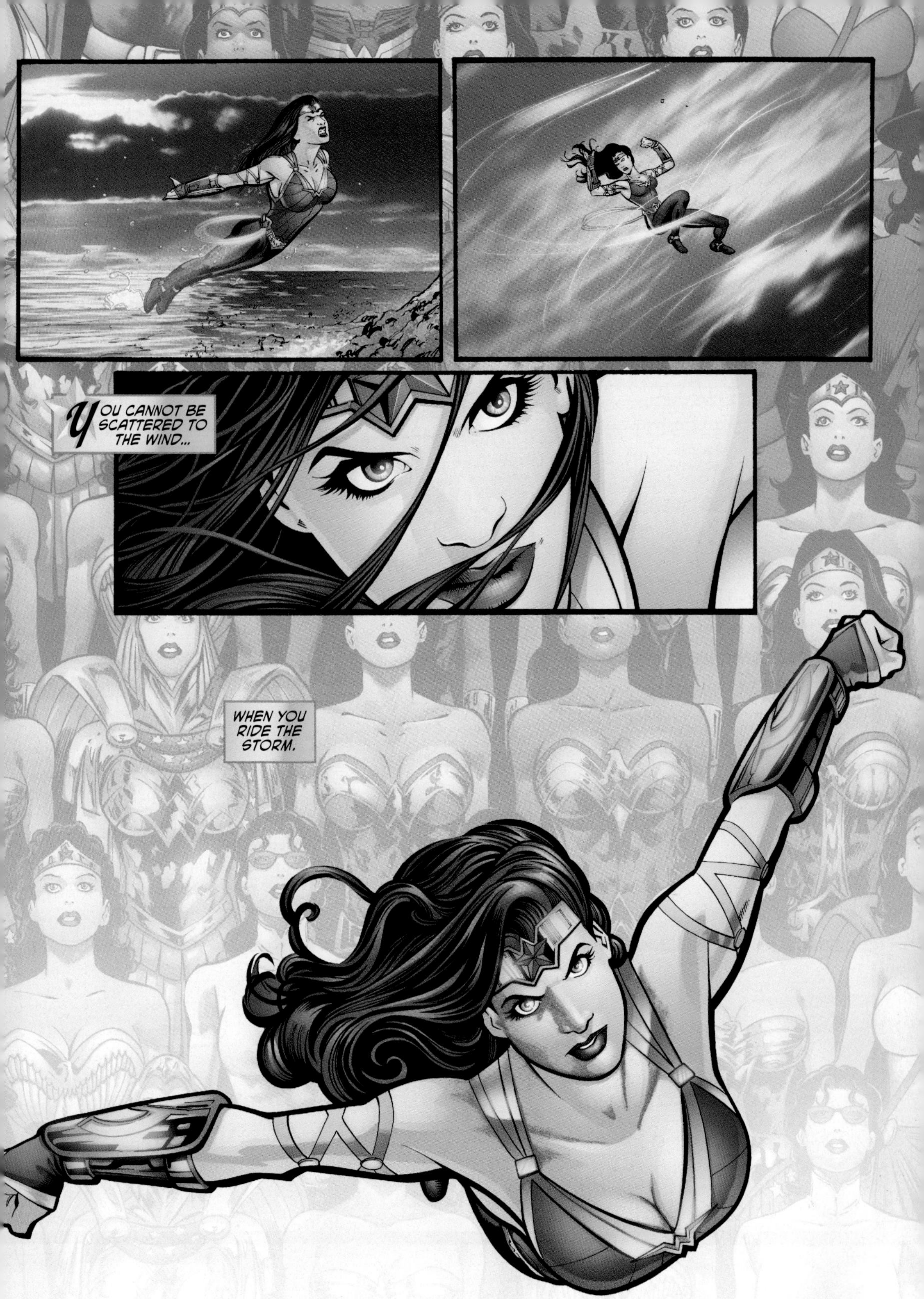
YOU CANNOT BE SCATTERED TO THE WIND...
WHEN YOU RIDE THE STORM.

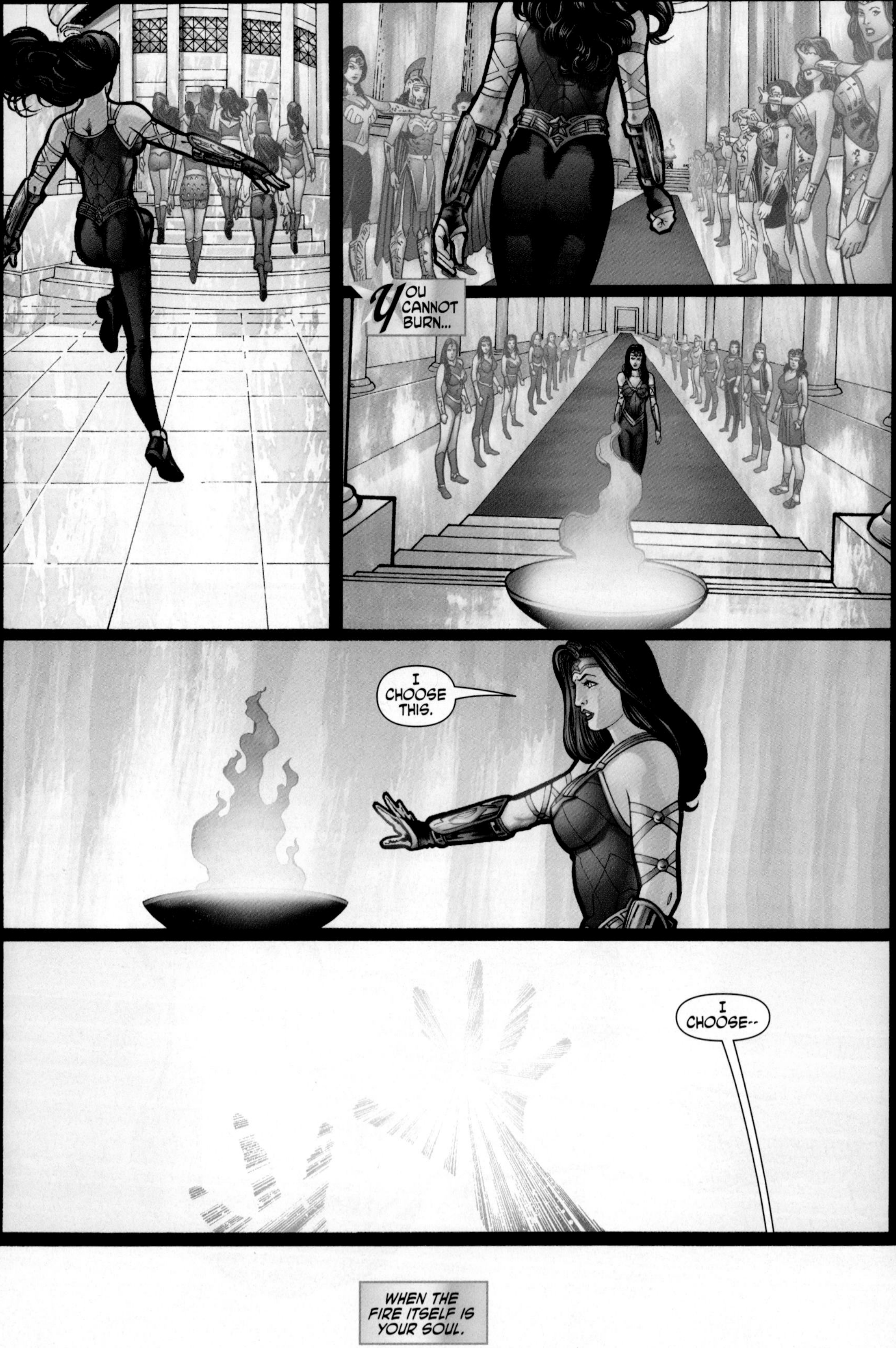
YOU CANNOT BURN...
I CHOOSE THIS.
I CHOOSE--
WHEN THE FIRE ITSELF IS YOUR SOUL.

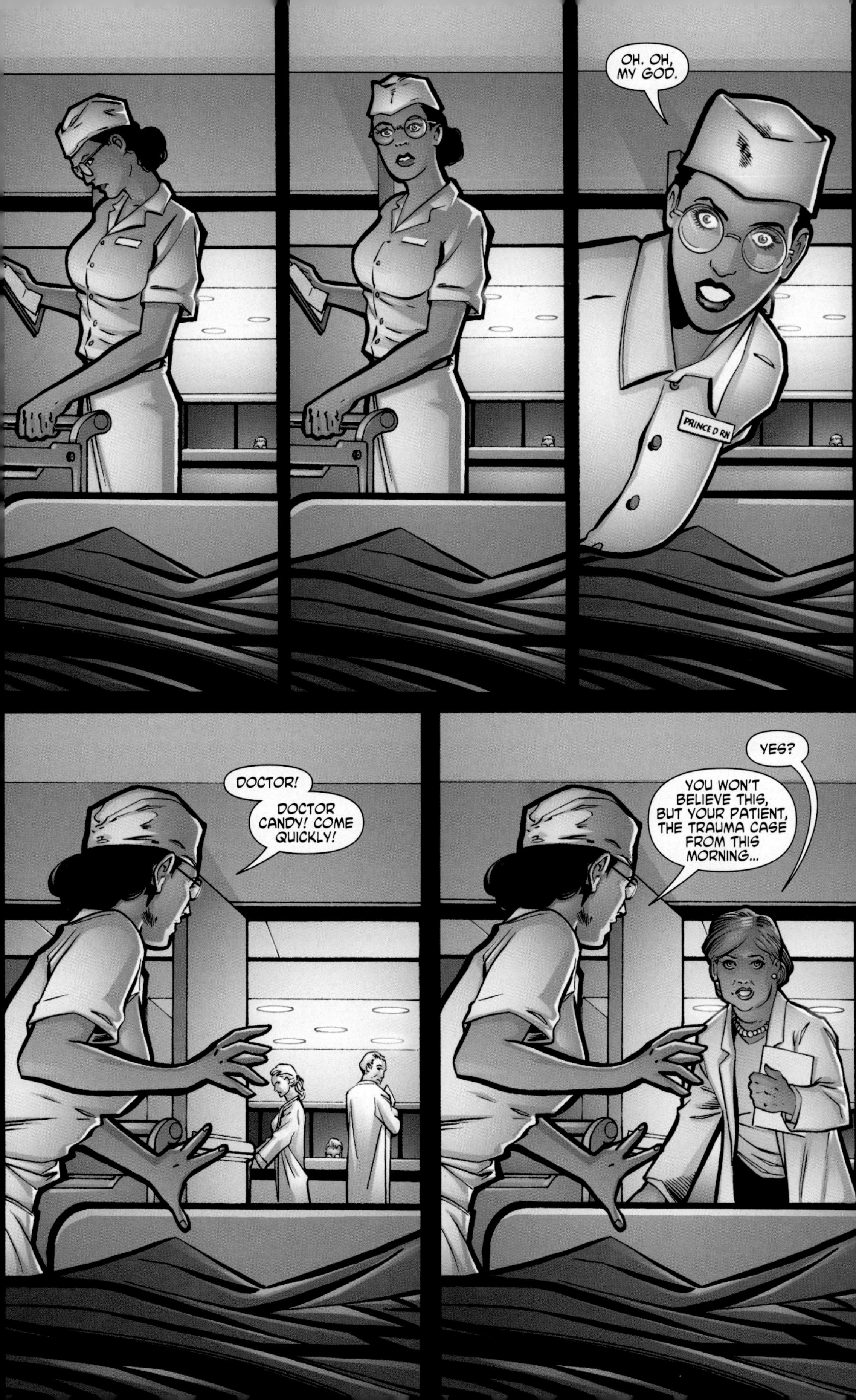
OH. OH, MY GOD.
PRINCE D RN
DOCTOR!
DOCTOR CANDY! COME QUICKLY!
YES?
YOU WON'T BELIEVE THIS, BUT YOUR PATIENT, THE TRAUMA CASE FROM THIS MORNING...

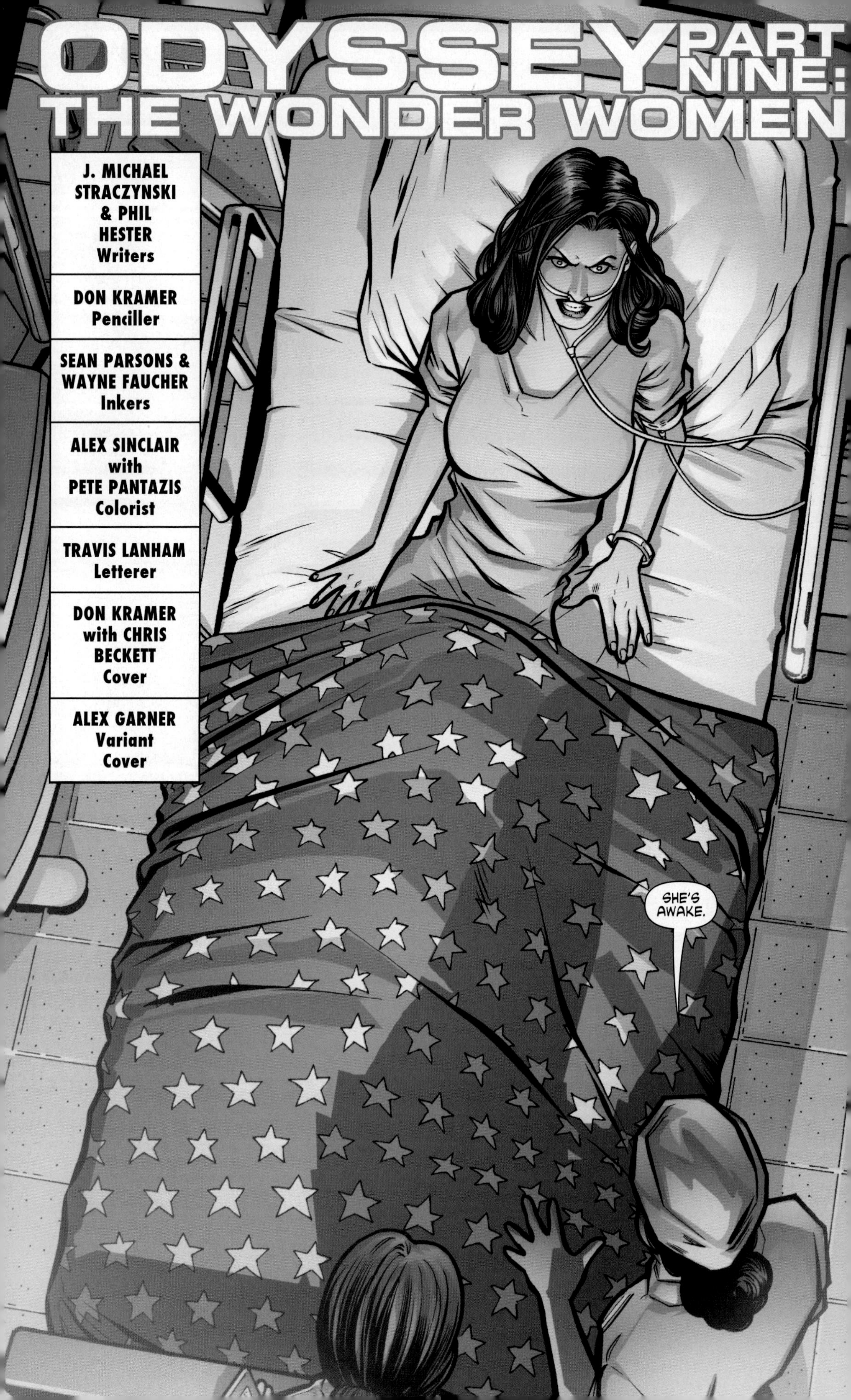
ODYSSEY PART NINE: THE WONDER WOMEN
J. MICHAEL STRACZYNSKI & PHIL HESTER Writers
DON KRAMER Penciller
SEAN PARSONS & WAYNE FAUCHER Inkers
ALEX SINCLAIR with PETE PANTAZIS Colorist
TRAVIS LANHAM Letterer
DON KRAMER with CHRIS BECKETT Cover
ALEX GARNER Variant Cover
SHE'S AWAKE.

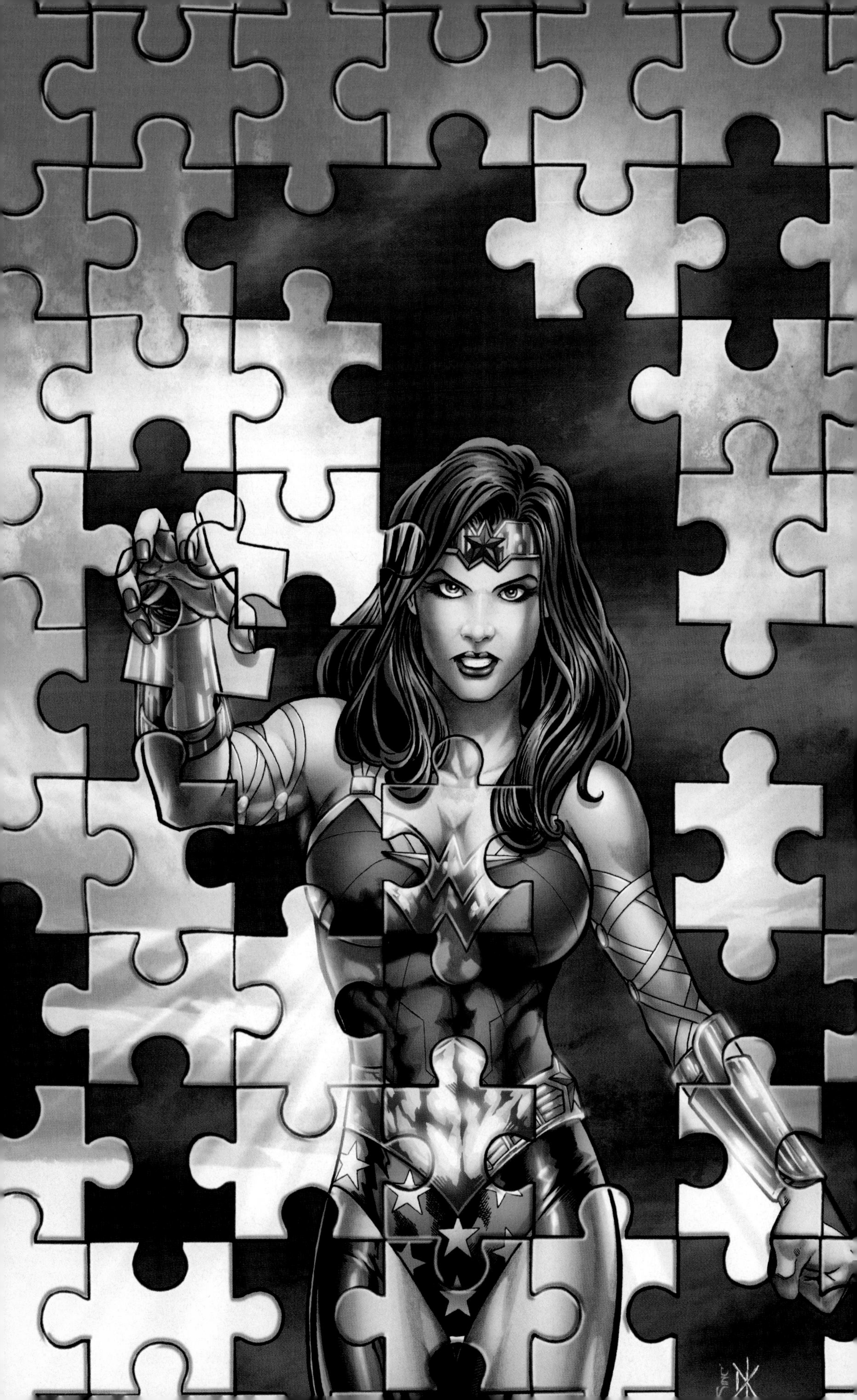

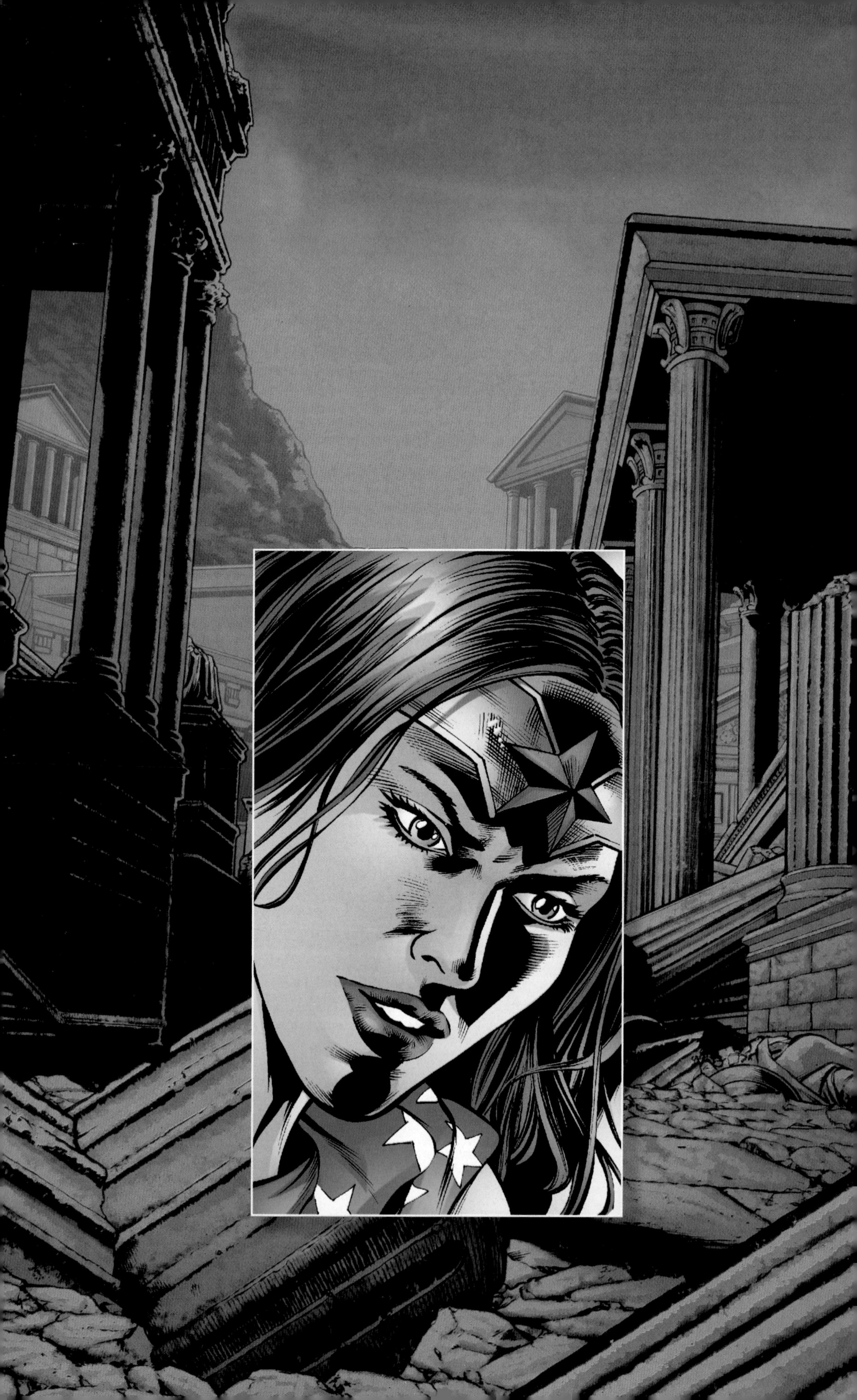

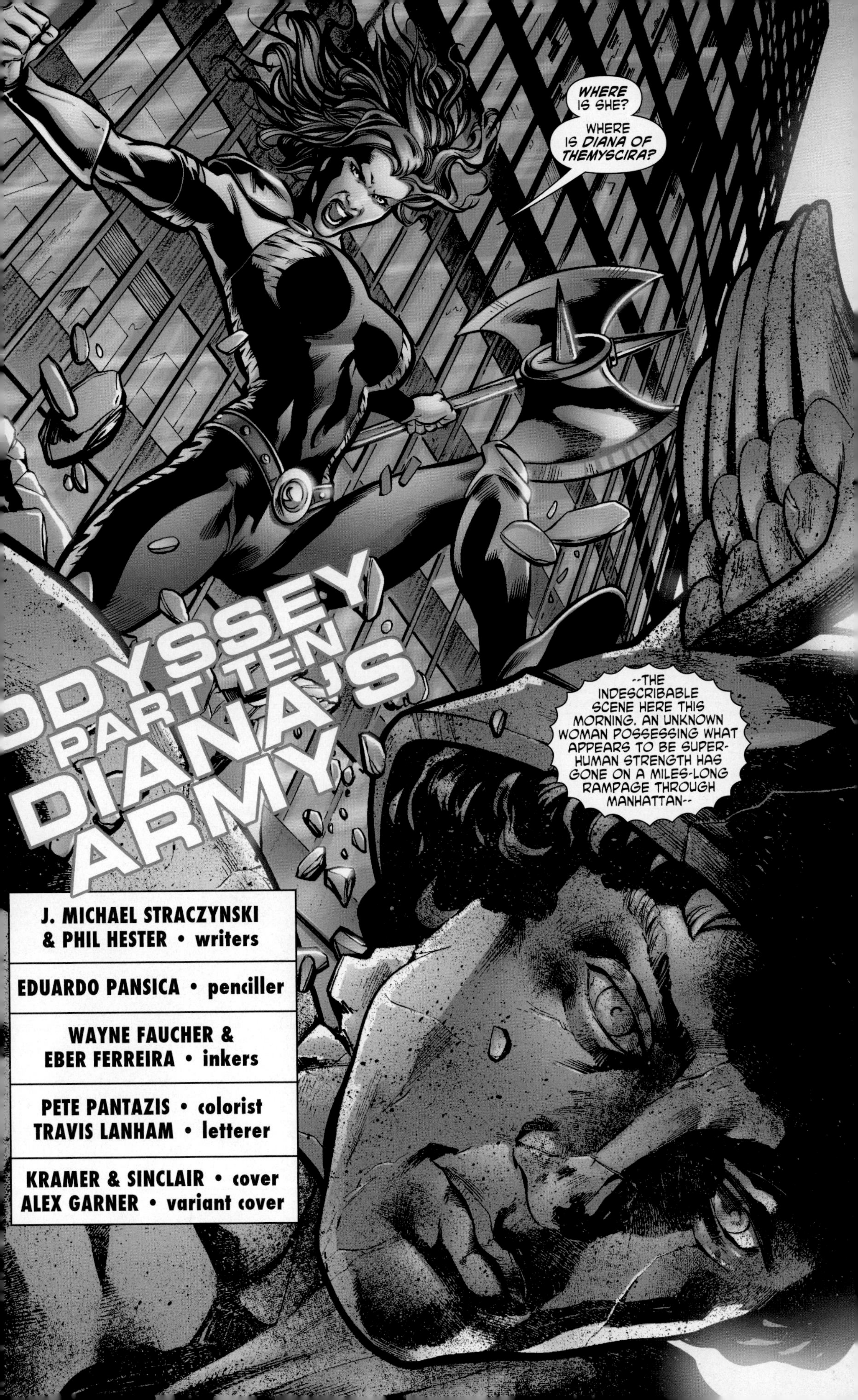
WHERE IS SHE?
WHERE IS DIANA OF THEMYSCIRA?
ODYSSEY PART TEN DIANA'S ARMY
--THE INDESCRIBABLE SCENE HERE THIS MORNING. AN UNKNOWN WOMAN POSSESSING WHAT APPEARS TO BE SUPER-HUMAN STRENGTH HAS GONE ON A MILES-LONG RAMPAGE THROUGH MANHATTAN--
J. MICHAEL STRACZYNSKI & PHIL HESTER • writers
EDUARDO PANSICA • penciller
WAYNE FAUCHER & EBER FERREIRA • inkers
PETE PANTAZIS • colorist
TRAVIS LANHAM • letterer
KRAMER & SINCLAIR • cover
ALEX GARNER • variant cover

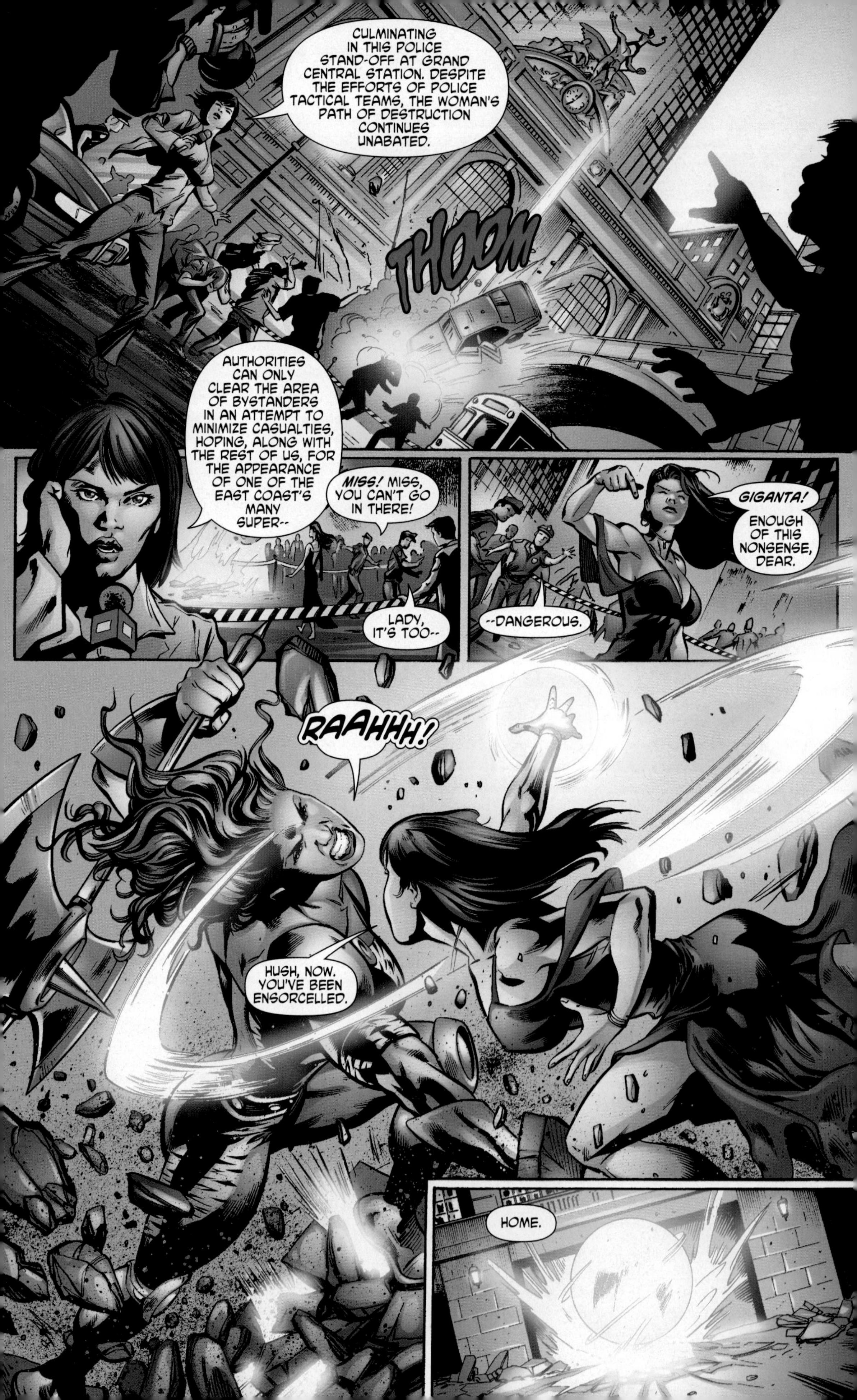
CULMINATING IN THIS POLICE STAND-OFF AT GRAND CENTRAL STATION. DESPITE THE EFFORTS OF POLICE TACTICAL TEAMS, THE WOMAN'S PATH OF DESTRUCTION CONTINUES UNABATED.
THOOM
AUTHORITIES CAN ONLY CLEAR THE AREA OF BYSTANDERS IN AN ATTEMPT TO MINIMIZE CASUALTIES, HOPING, ALONG WITH THE REST OF US, FOR THE APPEARANCE OF ONE OF THE EAST COAST'S MANY SUPER--
MISS! MISS, YOU CAN'T GO IN THERE!
LADY, IT'S TOO--
--DANGEROUS.
GIGANTA!
ENOUGH OF THIS NONSENSE, DEAR.
RAAHHH!
HUSH, NOW. YOU'VE BEEN ENSORCELLED.
HOME.

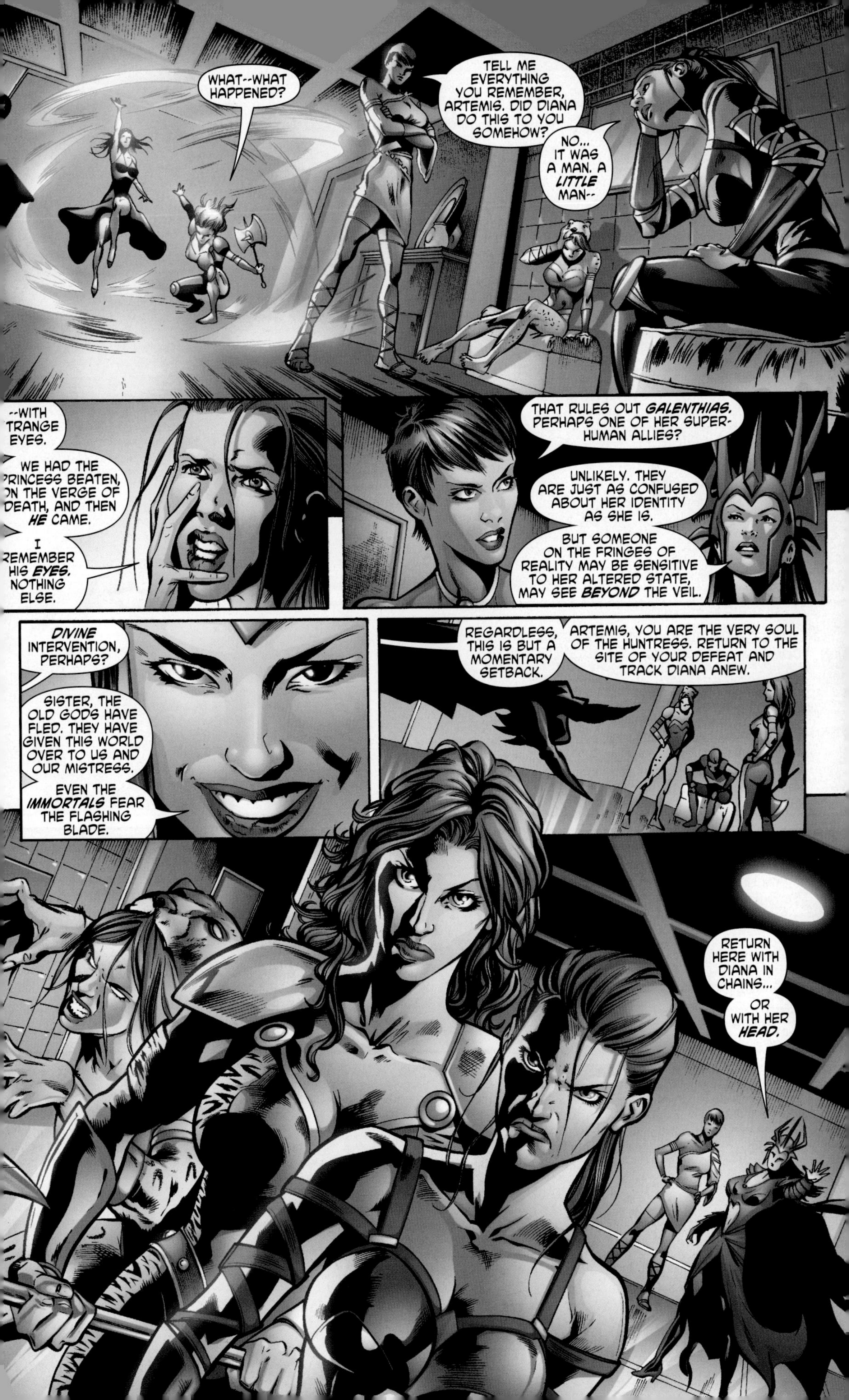
WHAT--WHAT HAPPENED?
TELL ME EVERYTHING YOU REMEMBER, ARTEMIS. DID DIANA DO THIS TO YOU SOMEHOW?
NO... IT WAS A MAN. A *LITTLE* MAN--
--WITH TRANGE EYES.
WE HAD THE PRINCESS BEATEN, ON THE VERGE OF DEATH, AND THEN *HE* CAME.
I REMEMBER HIS *EYES.* NOTHING ELSE.
THAT RULES OUT *GALENTHIAS.* PERHAPS ONE OF HER SUPER-HUMAN ALLIES?
UNLIKELY. THEY ARE JUST AS CONFUSED ABOUT HER IDENTITY AS SHE IS.
BUT SOMEONE ON THE FRINGES OF REALITY MAY BE SENSITIVE TO HER ALTERED STATE, MAY SEE *BEYOND* THE VEIL.
DIVINE INTERVENTION, PERHAPS?
SISTER, THE OLD GODS HAVE FLED. THEY HAVE GIVEN THIS WORLD OVER TO US AND OUR MISTRESS.
EVEN THE *IMMORTALS* FEAR THE FLASHING BLADE.
REGARDLESS, THIS IS BUT A MOMENTARY SETBACK.
ARTEMIS, YOU ARE THE VERY SOUL OF THE HUNTRESS. RETURN TO THE SITE OF YOUR DEFEAT AND TRACK DIANA ANEW.
RETURN HERE WITH DIANA IN CHAINS...
OR WITH HER *HEAD.*

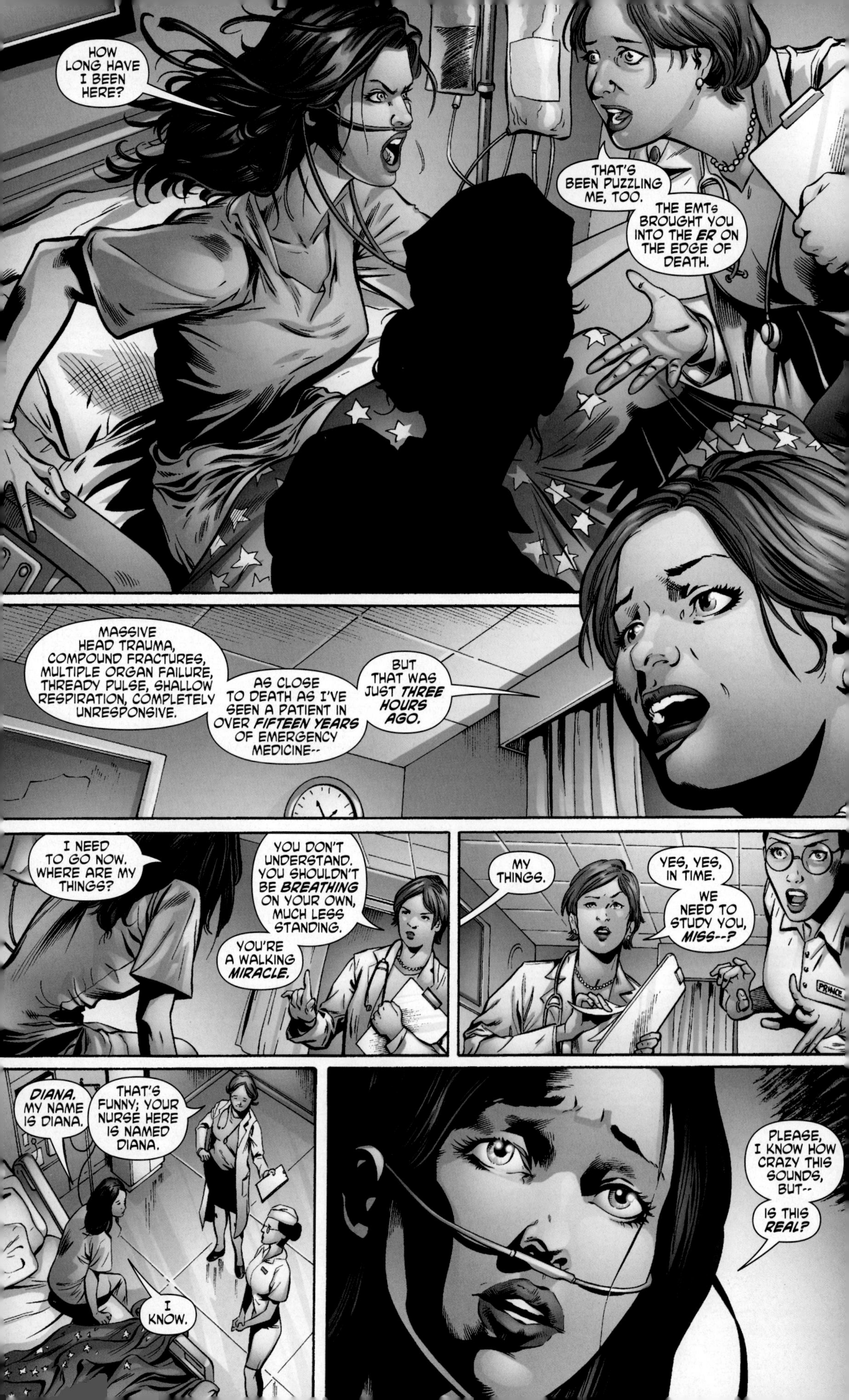
HOW LONG HAVE I BEEN HERE?
THAT'S BEEN PUZZLING ME, TOO.
THE EMTs BROUGHT YOU INTO THE *ER* ON THE EDGE OF DEATH.
MASSIVE HEAD TRAUMA, COMPOUND FRACTURES, MULTIPLE ORGAN FAILURE, THREADY PULSE, SHALLOW RESPIRATION, COMPLETELY UNRESPONSIVE.
AS CLOSE TO DEATH AS I'VE SEEN A PATIENT IN OVER *FIFTEEN YEARS* OF EMERGENCY MEDICINE--
BUT THAT WAS JUST *THREE HOURS AGO.*
I NEED TO GO NOW. WHERE ARE MY THINGS?
YOU DON'T UNDERSTAND. YOU SHOULDN'T BE *BREATHING* ON YOUR OWN, MUCH LESS STANDING.
YOU'RE A WALKING *MIRACLE.*
MY THINGS.
YES, YES, IN TIME.
WE NEED TO STUDY YOU, *MISS--?*
PRINCE
DIANA. MY NAME IS DIANA.
THAT'S FUNNY; YOUR NURSE HERE IS NAMED DIANA.
I KNOW.
PLEASE, I KNOW HOW CRAZY THIS SOUNDS, BUT--
IS THIS *REAL?*

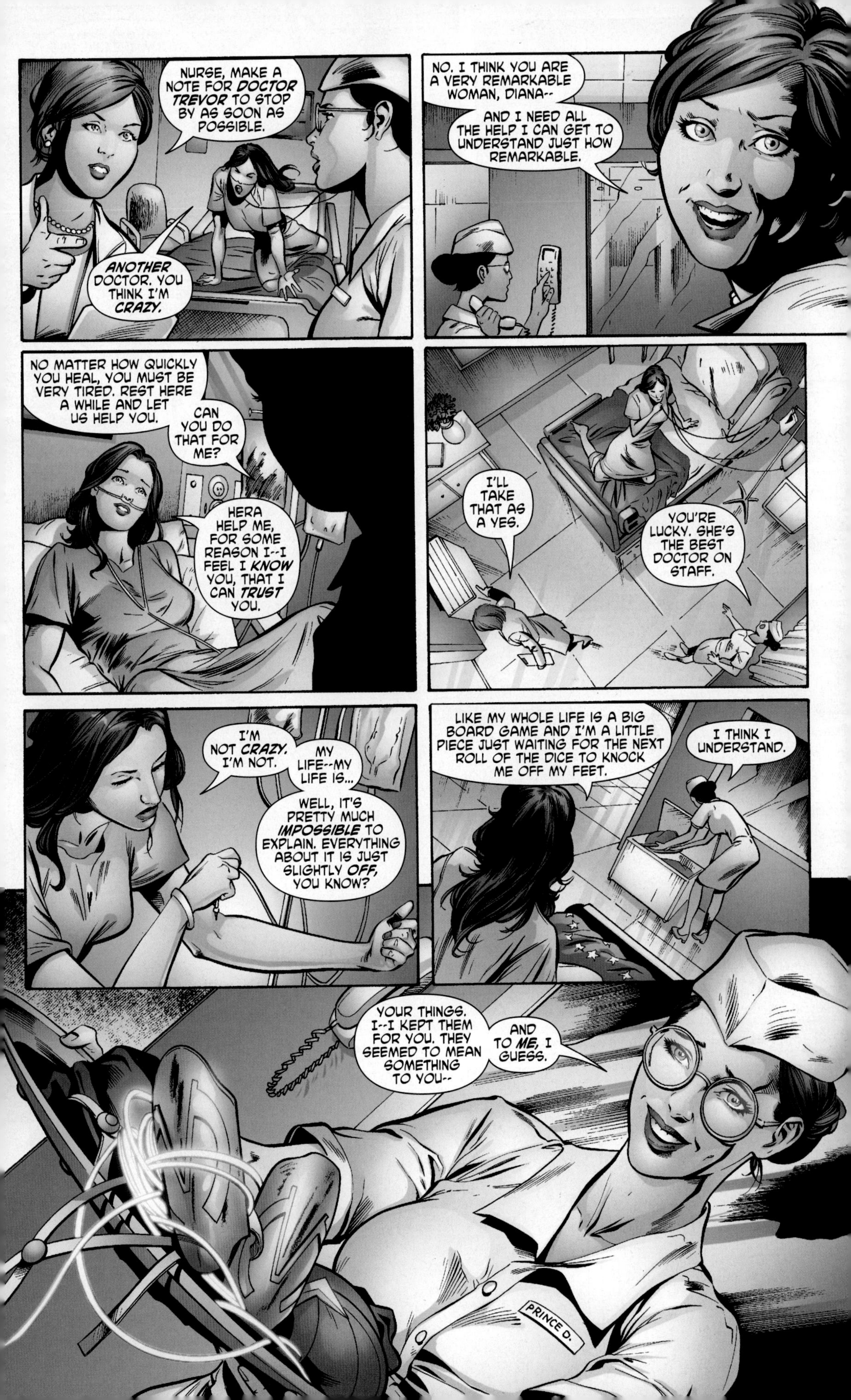

NURSE, MAKE A NOTE FOR DOCTOR TREVOR TO STOP BY AS SOON AS POSSIBLE.
ANOTHER DOCTOR. YOU THINK I'M CRAZY.
NO. I THINK YOU ARE A VERY REMARKABLE WOMAN, DIANA--
AND I NEED ALL THE HELP I CAN GET TO UNDERSTAND JUST HOW REMARKABLE.
NO MATTER HOW QUICKLY YOU HEAL, YOU MUST BE VERY TIRED. REST HERE A WHILE AND LET US HELP YOU.
CAN YOU DO THAT FOR ME?
HERA HELP ME, FOR SOME REASON I--I FEEL I KNOW YOU, THAT I CAN TRUST YOU.
I'LL TAKE THAT AS A YES.
YOU'RE LUCKY. SHE'S THE BEST DOCTOR ON STAFF.
I'M NOT CRAZY. I'M NOT.
MY LIFE--MY LIFE IS...
WELL, IT'S PRETTY MUCH IMPOSSIBLE TO EXPLAIN. EVERYTHING ABOUT IT IS JUST SLIGHTLY OFF, YOU KNOW?
LIKE MY WHOLE LIFE IS A BIG BOARD GAME AND I'M A LITTLE PIECE JUST WAITING FOR THE NEXT ROLL OF THE DICE TO KNOCK ME OFF MY FEET.
I THINK I UNDERSTAND.
YOUR THINGS. I--I KEPT THEM FOR YOU. THEY SEEMED TO MEAN SOMETHING TO YOU--
AND TO ME, I GUESS.
PRINCE D.

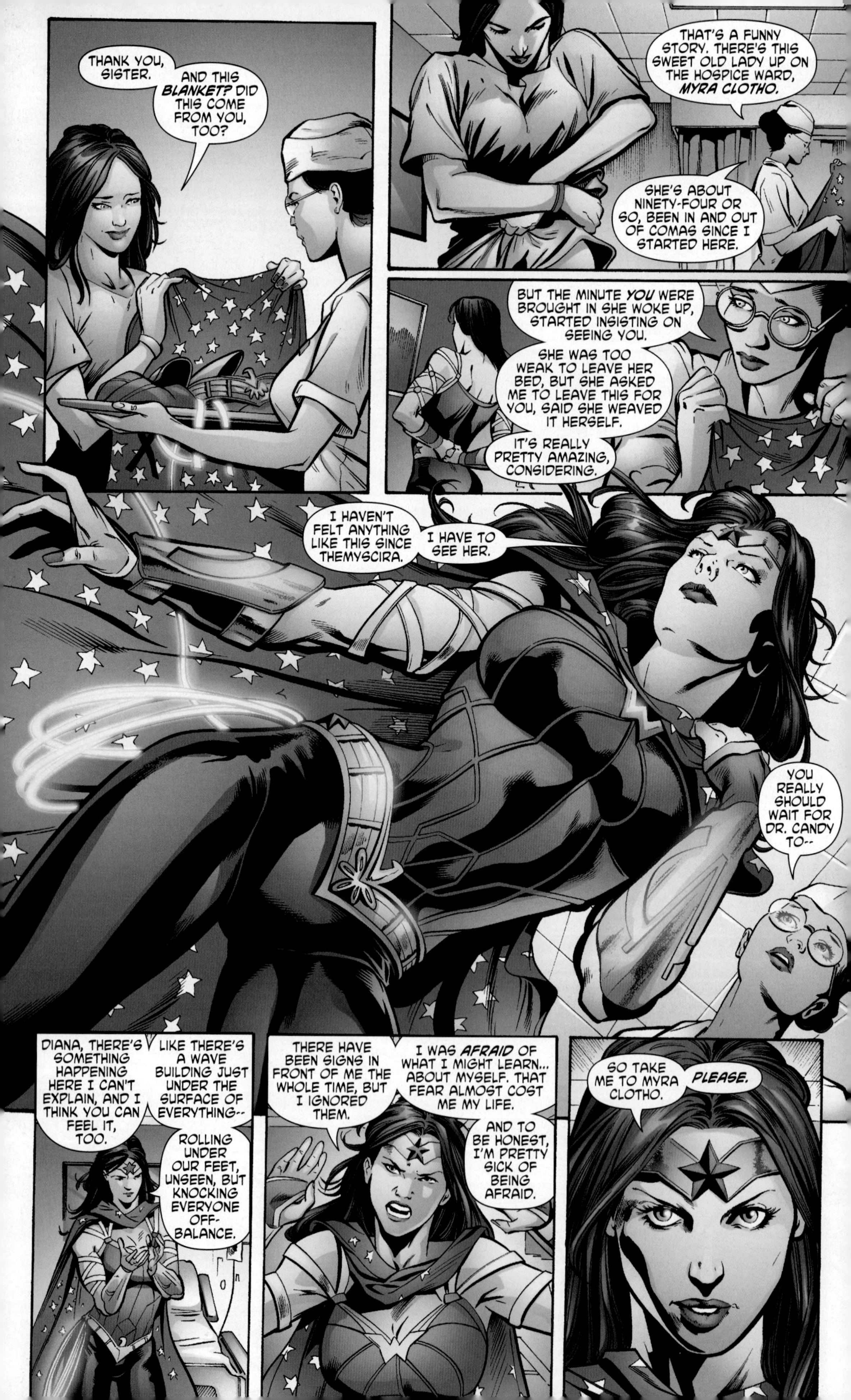
THANK YOU, SISTER.
AND THIS BLANKET? DID THIS COME FROM YOU, TOO?
THAT'S A FUNNY STORY. THERE'S THIS SWEET OLD LADY UP ON THE HOSPICE WARD, MYRA CLOTHO.
SHE'S ABOUT NINETY-FOUR OR SO, BEEN IN AND OUT OF COMAS SINCE I STARTED HERE.
BUT THE MINUTE YOU WERE BROUGHT IN SHE WOKE UP, STARTED INSISTING ON SEEING YOU.
SHE WAS TOO WEAK TO LEAVE HER BED, BUT SHE ASKED ME TO LEAVE THIS FOR YOU, SAID SHE WEAVED IT HERSELF.
IT'S REALLY PRETTY AMAZING, CONSIDERING.
I HAVEN'T FELT ANYTHING LIKE THIS SINCE THEMYSCIRA.
I HAVE TO SEE HER.
YOU REALLY SHOULD WAIT FOR DR. CANDY TO--
DIANA, THERE'S SOMETHING HAPPENING HERE I CAN'T EXPLAIN, AND I THINK YOU CAN FEEL IT, TOO.
LIKE THERE'S A WAVE BUILDING JUST UNDER THE SURFACE OF EVERYTHING--
ROLLING UNDER OUR FEET, UNSEEN, BUT KNOCKING EVERYONE OFF-BALANCE.
THERE HAVE BEEN SIGNS IN FRONT OF ME THE WHOLE TIME, BUT I IGNORED THEM.
I WAS AFRAID OF WHAT I MIGHT LEARN... ABOUT MYSELF. THAT FEAR ALMOST COST ME MY LIFE.
AND TO BE HONEST, I'M PRETTY SICK OF BEING AFRAID.
SO TAKE ME TO MYRA CLOTHO.
PLEASE.

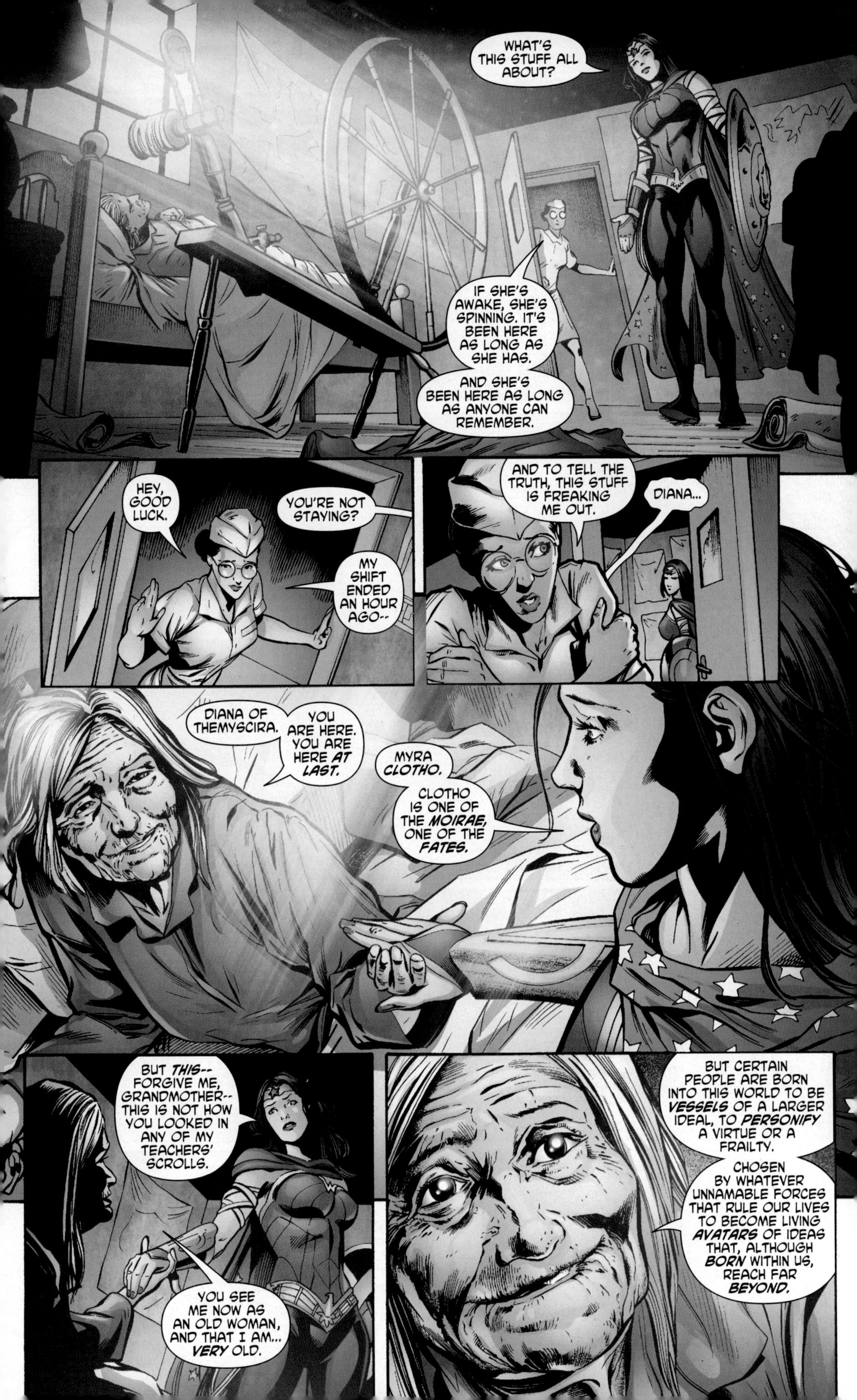
WHAT'S THIS STUFF ALL ABOUT?
IF SHE'S AWAKE, SHE'S SPINNING. IT'S BEEN HERE AS LONG AS SHE HAS.
AND SHE'S BEEN HERE AS LONG AS ANYONE CAN REMEMBER.
HEY, GOOD LUCK.
YOU'RE NOT STAYING?
MY SHIFT ENDED AN HOUR AGO--
AND TO TELL THE TRUTH, THIS STUFF IS FREAKING ME OUT.
DIANA...
DIANA OF THEMYSCIRA.
YOU ARE HERE. YOU ARE HERE *AT LAST.*
MYRA *CLOTHO.*
CLOTHO IS ONE OF THE *MOIRAE,* ONE OF THE *FATES.*
BUT *THIS*-- FORGIVE ME, GRANDMOTHER-- THIS IS NOT HOW YOU LOOKED IN ANY OF MY TEACHERS' SCROLLS.
YOU SEE ME NOW AS AN OLD WOMAN, AND THAT I AM... *VERY* OLD.
BUT CERTAIN PEOPLE ARE BORN INTO THIS WORLD TO BE *VESSELS* OF A LARGER IDEAL, TO *PERSONIFY* A VIRTUE OR A FRAILTY.
CHOSEN BY WHATEVER UNNAMABLE FORCES THAT RULE OUR LIVES TO BECOME LIVING *AVATARS* OF IDEAS THAT, ALTHOUGH *BORN* WITHIN US, REACH FAR *BEYOND.*

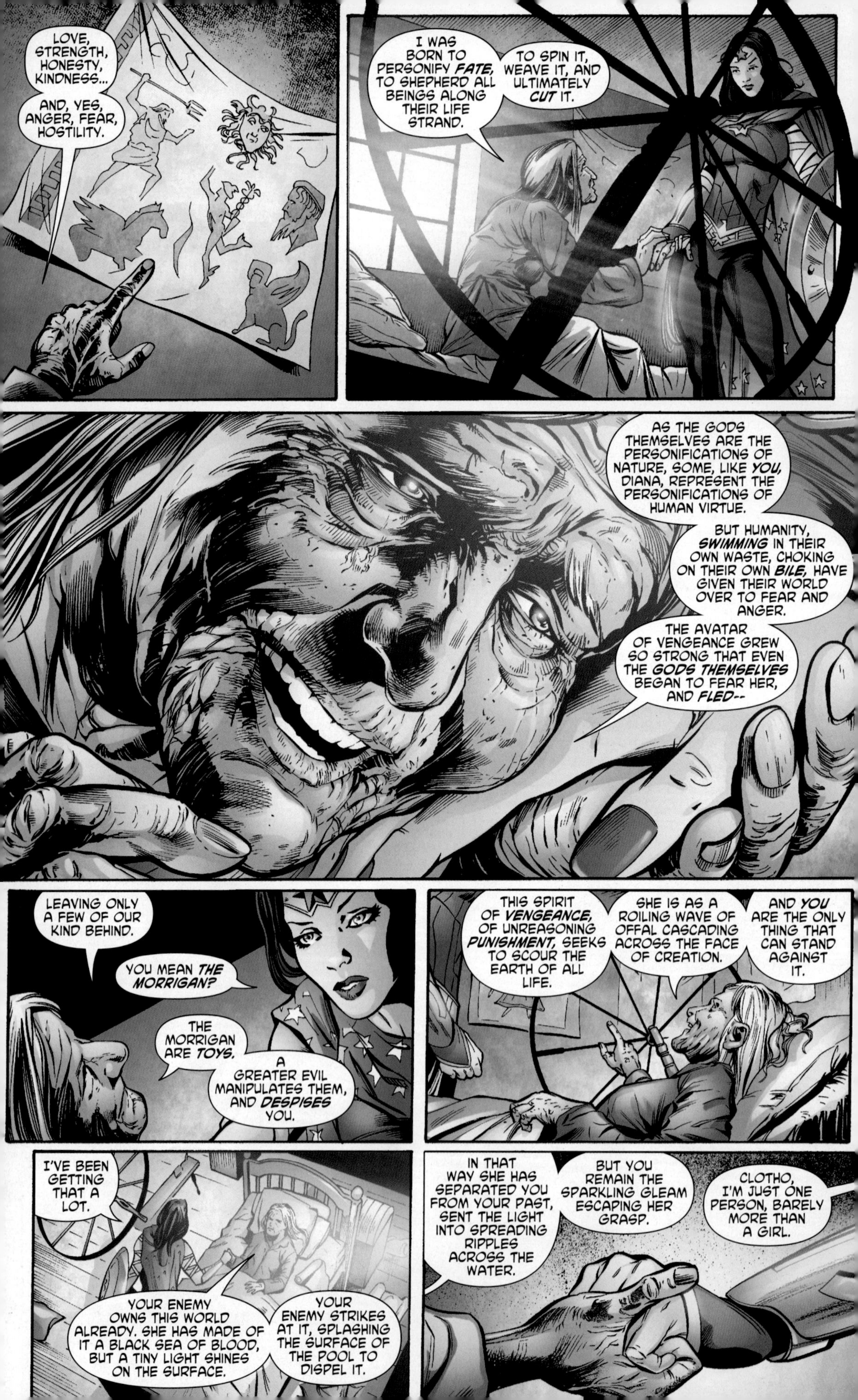
LOVE, STRENGTH, HONESTY, KINDNESS...
AND, YES, ANGER, FEAR, HOSTILITY.
I WAS BORN TO PERSONIFY FATE, TO SHEPHERD ALL BEINGS ALONG THEIR LIFE STRAND.
TO SPIN IT, WEAVE IT, AND ULTIMATELY CUT IT.
AS THE GODS THEMSELVES ARE THE PERSONIFICATIONS OF NATURE, SOME, LIKE YOU, DIANA, REPRESENT THE PERSONIFICATIONS OF HUMAN VIRTUE.
BUT HUMANITY, SWIMMING IN THEIR OWN WASTE, CHOKING ON THEIR OWN BILE, HAVE GIVEN THEIR WORLD OVER TO FEAR AND ANGER.
THE AVATAR OF VENGEANCE GREW SO STRONG THAT EVEN THE GODS THEMSELVES BEGAN TO FEAR HER, AND FLED--
LEAVING ONLY A FEW OF OUR KIND BEHIND.
YOU MEAN THE MORRIGAN?
THE MORRIGAN ARE TOYS.
A GREATER EVIL MANIPULATES THEM, AND DESPISES YOU.
THIS SPIRIT OF VENGEANCE, OF UNREASONING PUNISHMENT, SEEKS TO SCOUR THE EARTH OF ALL LIFE.
SHE IS AS A ROILING WAVE OF OFFAL CASCADING ACROSS THE FACE OF CREATION.
AND YOU ARE THE ONLY THING THAT CAN STAND AGAINST IT.
I'VE BEEN GETTING THAT A LOT.
YOUR ENEMY OWNS THIS WORLD ALREADY. SHE HAS MADE OF IT A BLACK SEA OF BLOOD, BUT A TINY LIGHT SHINES ON THE SURFACE.
YOUR ENEMY STRIKES AT IT, SPLASHING THE SURFACE OF THE POOL TO DISPEL IT.
IN THAT WAY SHE HAS SEPARATED YOU FROM YOUR PAST, SENT THE LIGHT INTO SPREADING RIPPLES ACROSS THE WATER.
BUT YOU REMAIN THE SPARKLING GLEAM ESCAPING HER GRASP.
CLOTHO, I'M JUST ONE PERSON, BARELY MORE THAN A GIRL.

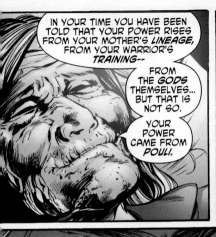

IN YOUR TIME YOU HAVE BEEN TOLD THAT YOUR POWER RISES FROM YOUR MOTHER'S *LINEAGE*, FROM YOUR WARRIOR'S *TRAINING*--

FROM THE *GODS* THEMSELVES... BUT THAT IS NOT SO.

YOUR POWER CAME FROM *POULI*.

UH...I'M SORRY.

WHAT?

POULI. THAT IS WHAT YOU CALLED THE *BIRD*, ISN'T IT?

OH, MY.

I--I BARELY REMEMBER.

YOU SECRETLY FOLLOWED YOUR OLDER SISTERS ON A HUNTING PARTY.

"ARTEMIS WOUNDED A SMALL GAME BIRD, BUT LARGER PREY DISTRACTED HER FROM FINISHING IT OFF."

I REMEMBER NOW.

I KEPT HIM HIDDEN IN A BASKET, FED HIM BUGS, CLEANED HIS WOUND.

"SOME OF MY SISTERS TEASED ME...

"AT FIRST."

I THOUGHT HE WOULD GET BETTER AND FLY AWAY.

BUT HE NEVER DID.

NEVERTHELESS, HE DIED A RECIPIENT OF YOUR *LOVE*.

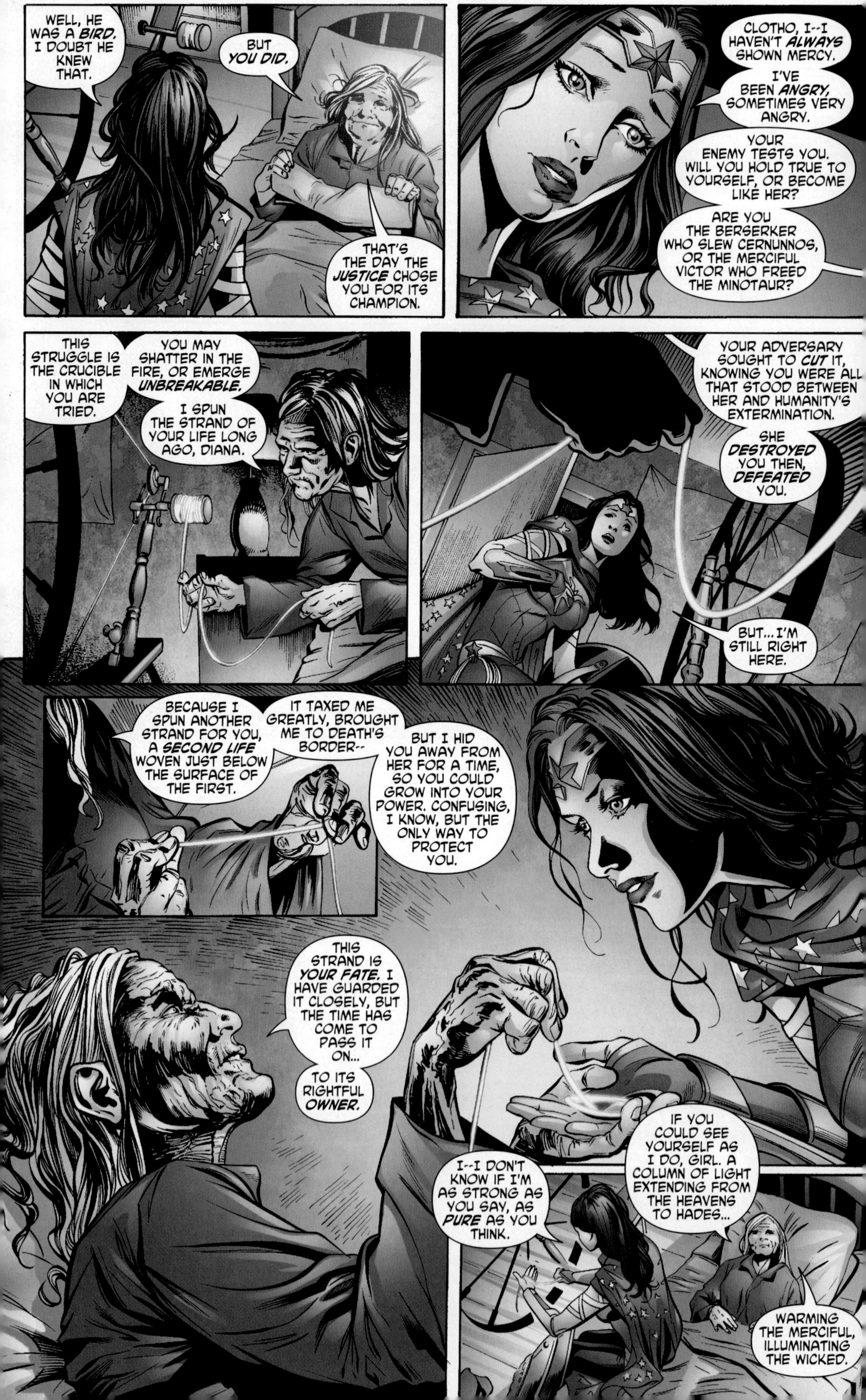
WELL, HE WAS A BIRD. I DOUBT HE KNEW THAT.
BUT YOU DID.
THAT'S THE DAY THE JUSTICE CHOSE YOU FOR ITS CHAMPION.
CLOTHO, I--I HAVEN'T ALWAYS SHOWN MERCY.
I'VE BEEN ANGRY, SOMETIMES VERY ANGRY.
YOUR ENEMY TESTS YOU. WILL YOU HOLD TRUE TO YOURSELF, OR BECOME LIKE HER?
ARE YOU THE BERSERKER WHO SLEW CERNUNNOS, OR THE MERCIFUL VICTOR WHO FREED THE MINOTAUR?
THIS STRUGGLE IS THE CRUCIBLE IN WHICH YOU ARE TRIED.
YOU MAY SHATTER IN THE FIRE, OR EMERGE UNBREAKABLE.
I SPUN THE STRAND OF YOUR LIFE LONG AGO, DIANA.
YOUR ADVERSARY SOUGHT TO CUT IT, KNOWING YOU WERE ALL THAT STOOD BETWEEN HER AND HUMANITY'S EXTERMINATION.
SHE DESTROYED YOU THEN, DEFEATED YOU.
BUT... I'M STILL RIGHT HERE.
BECAUSE I SPUN ANOTHER STRAND FOR YOU, A SECOND LIFE WOVEN JUST BELOW THE SURFACE OF THE FIRST.
IT TAXED ME GREATLY, BROUGHT ME TO DEATH'S BORDER--
BUT I HID YOU AWAY FROM HER FOR A TIME, SO YOU COULD GROW INTO YOUR POWER. CONFUSING, I KNOW, BUT THE ONLY WAY TO PROTECT YOU.
THIS STRAND IS YOUR FATE. I HAVE GUARDED IT CLOSELY, BUT THE TIME HAS COME TO PASS IT ON...
TO ITS RIGHTFUL OWNER.
I--I DON'T KNOW IF I'M AS STRONG AS YOU SAY, AS PURE AS YOU THINK.
IF YOU COULD SEE YOURSELF AS I DO, GIRL. A COLUMN OF LIGHT EXTENDING FROM THE HEAVENS TO HADES...
WARMING THE MERCIFUL, ILLUMINATING THE WICKED.

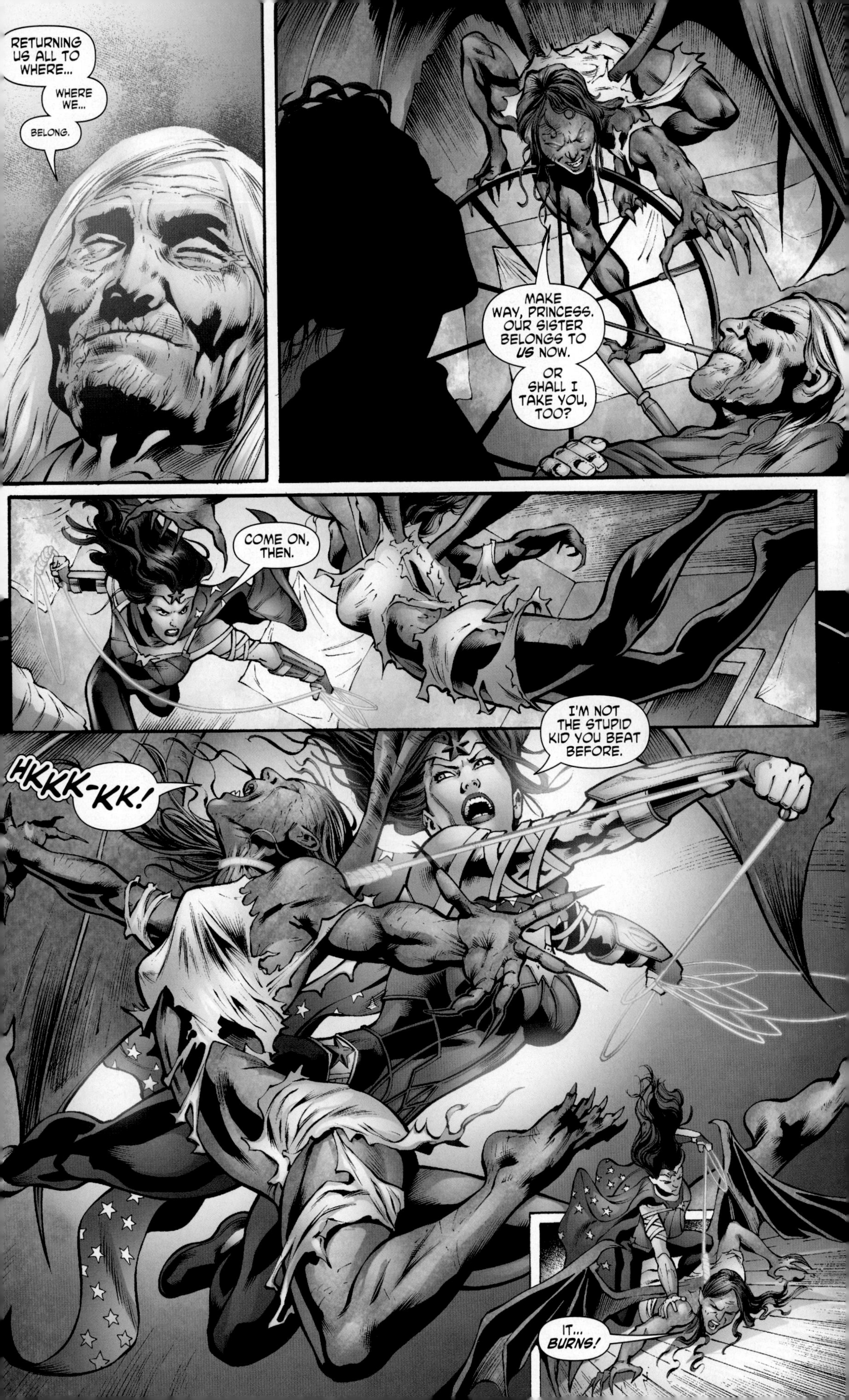
RETURNING US ALL TO WHERE...
WHERE WE...
BELONG.
MAKE WAY, PRINCESS. OUR SISTER BELONGS TO *US* NOW.
OR SHALL I TAKE YOU, TOO?
COME ON, THEN.
I'M NOT THE STUPID KID YOU BEAT BEFORE.
HKKK-KK!
IT... *BURNS!*

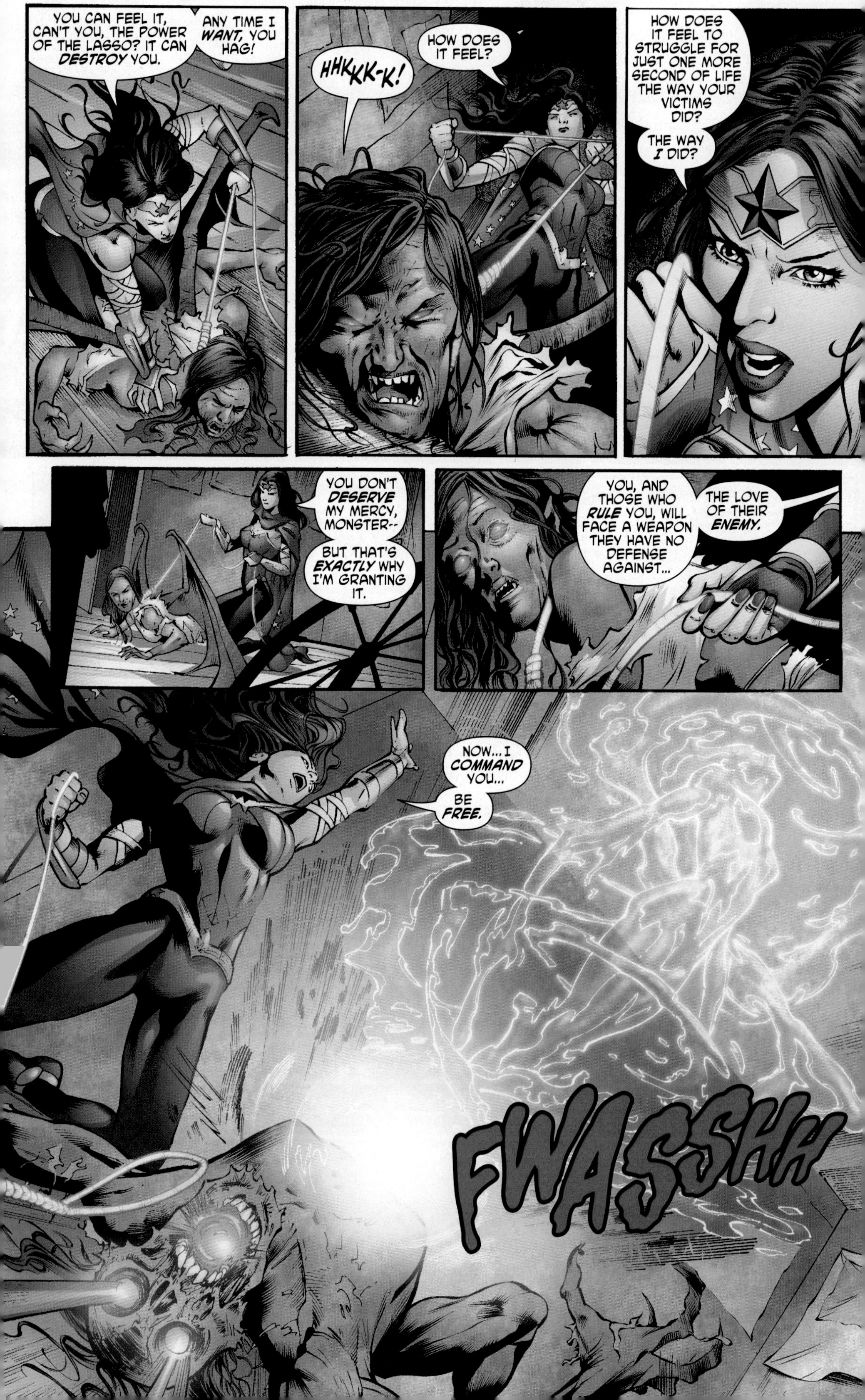
YOU CAN FEEL IT, CAN'T YOU, THE POWER OF THE LASSO? IT CAN DESTROY YOU.
ANY TIME I WANT, YOU HAG!
HHKKK-K!
HOW DOES IT FEEL?
HOW DOES IT FEEL TO STRUGGLE FOR JUST ONE MORE SECOND OF LIFE THE WAY YOUR VICTIMS DID?
THE WAY I DID?
YOU DON'T DESERVE MY MERCY, MONSTER--
BUT THAT'S EXACTLY WHY I'M GRANTING IT.
YOU, AND THOSE WHO RULE YOU, WILL FACE A WEAPON THEY HAVE NO DEFENSE AGAINST...
THE LOVE OF THEIR ENEMY.
NOW... I COMMAND YOU...
BE FREE.
FWASSHH

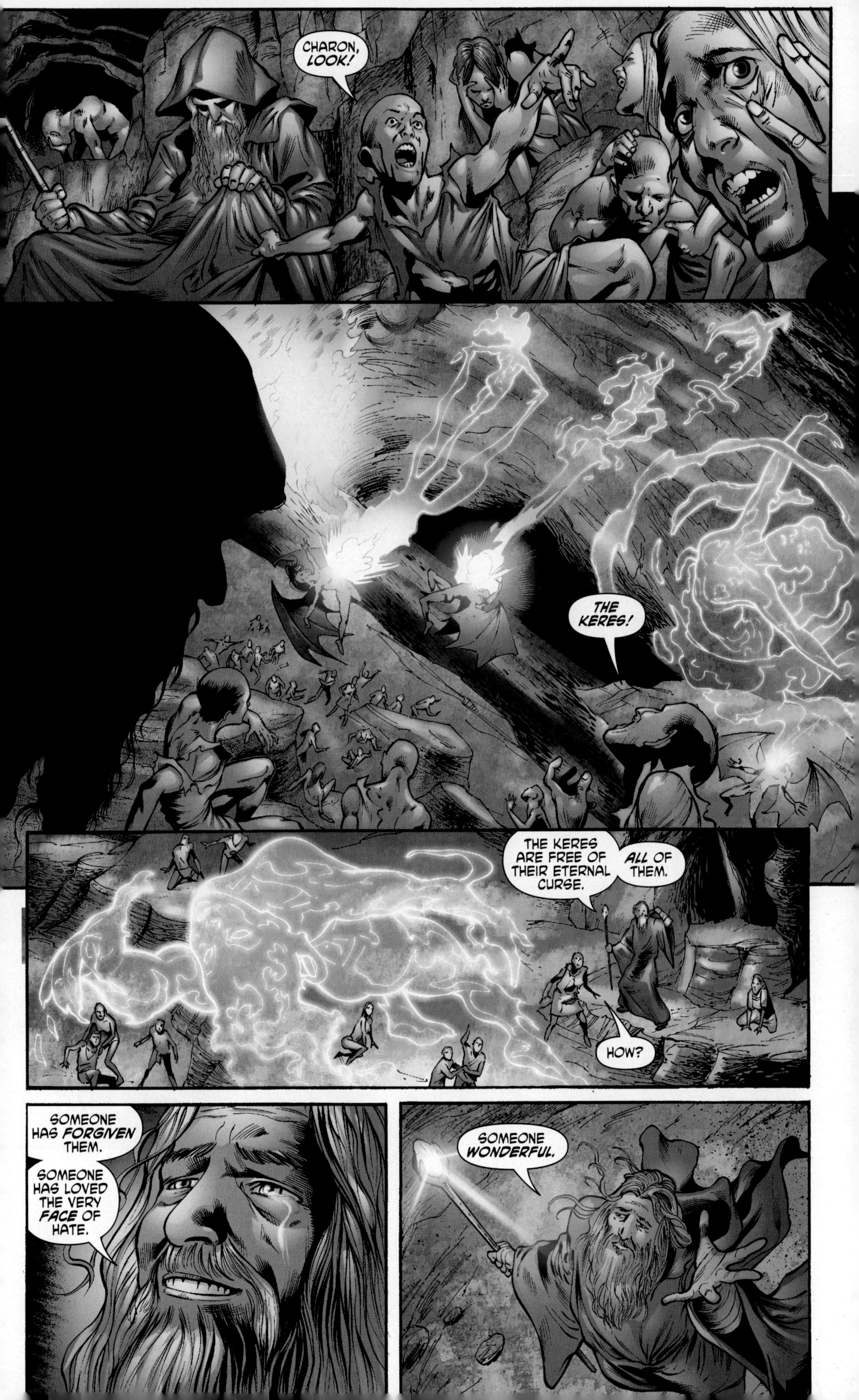
CHARON, LOOK!
THE KERES!
THE KERES ARE FREE OF THEIR ETERNAL CURSE.
ALL OF THEM.
HOW?
SOMEONE HAS FORGIVEN THEM.
SOMEONE HAS LOVED THE VERY FACE OF HATE.
SOMEONE WONDERFUL.

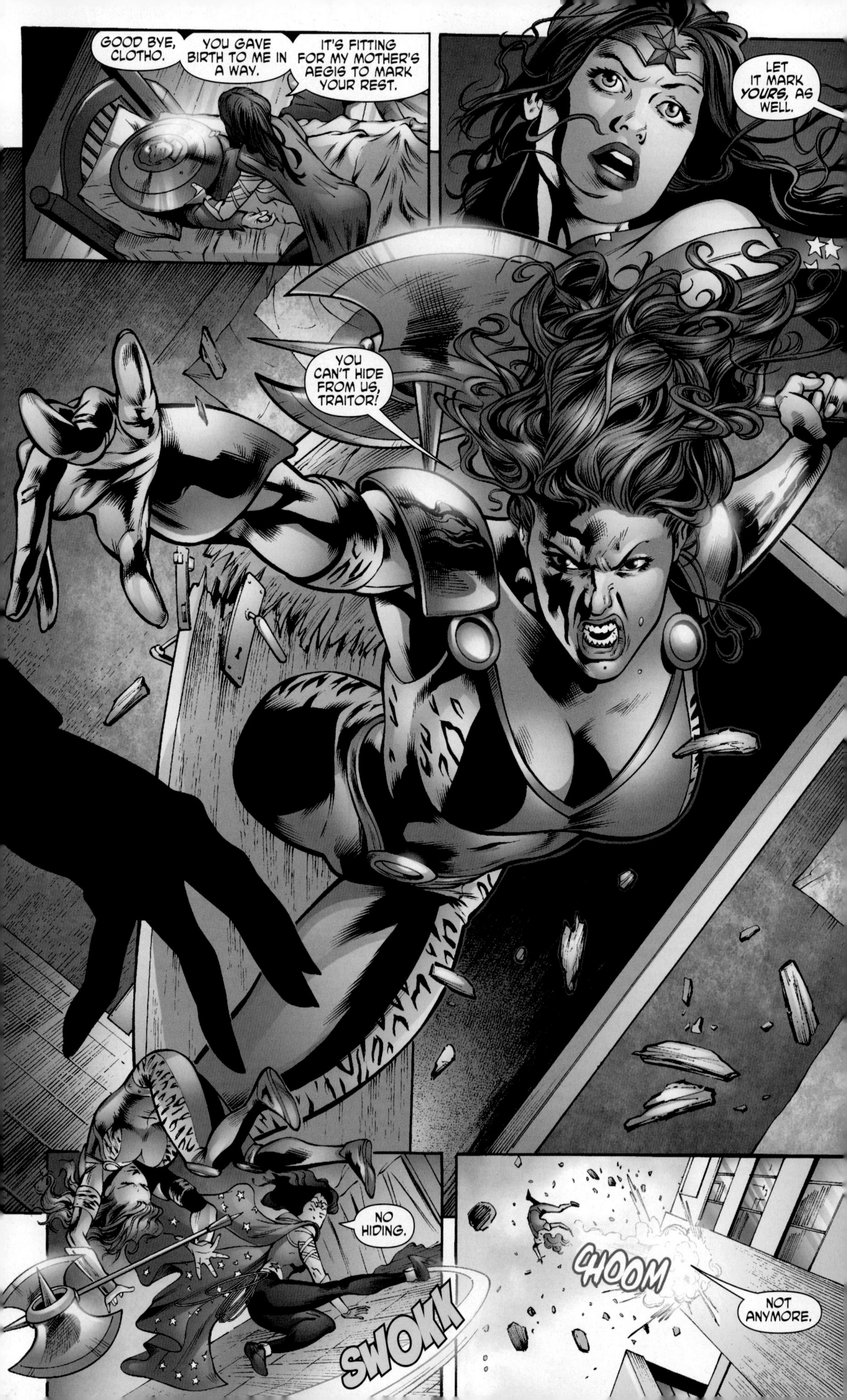
GOOD BYE, CLOTHO.
YOU GAVE BIRTH TO ME IN A WAY.
IT'S FITTING FOR MY MOTHER'S AEGIS TO MARK YOUR REST.
LET IT MARK YOURS, AS WELL.
YOU CAN'T HIDE FROM US, TRAITOR!
NO HIDING.
SWOKK
CHOOM
NOT ANYMORE.

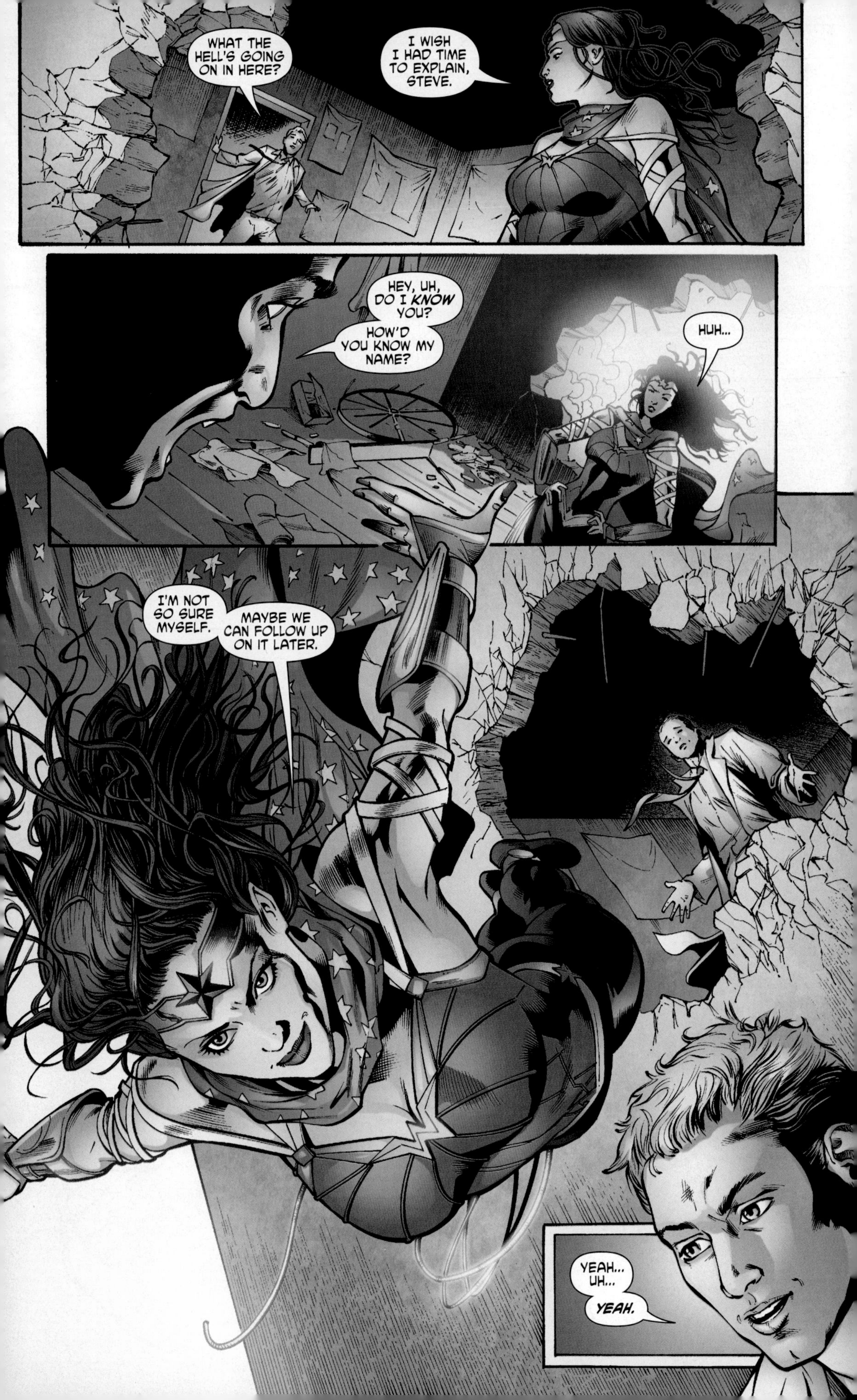
WHAT THE HELL'S GOING ON IN HERE?
I WISH I HAD TIME TO EXPLAIN, STEVE.
HEY, UH, DO I *KNOW* YOU?
HOW'D YOU KNOW MY NAME?
HUH...
I'M NOT SO SURE MYSELF.
MAYBE WE CAN FOLLOW UP ON IT LATER.
YEAH... UH...
YEAH.

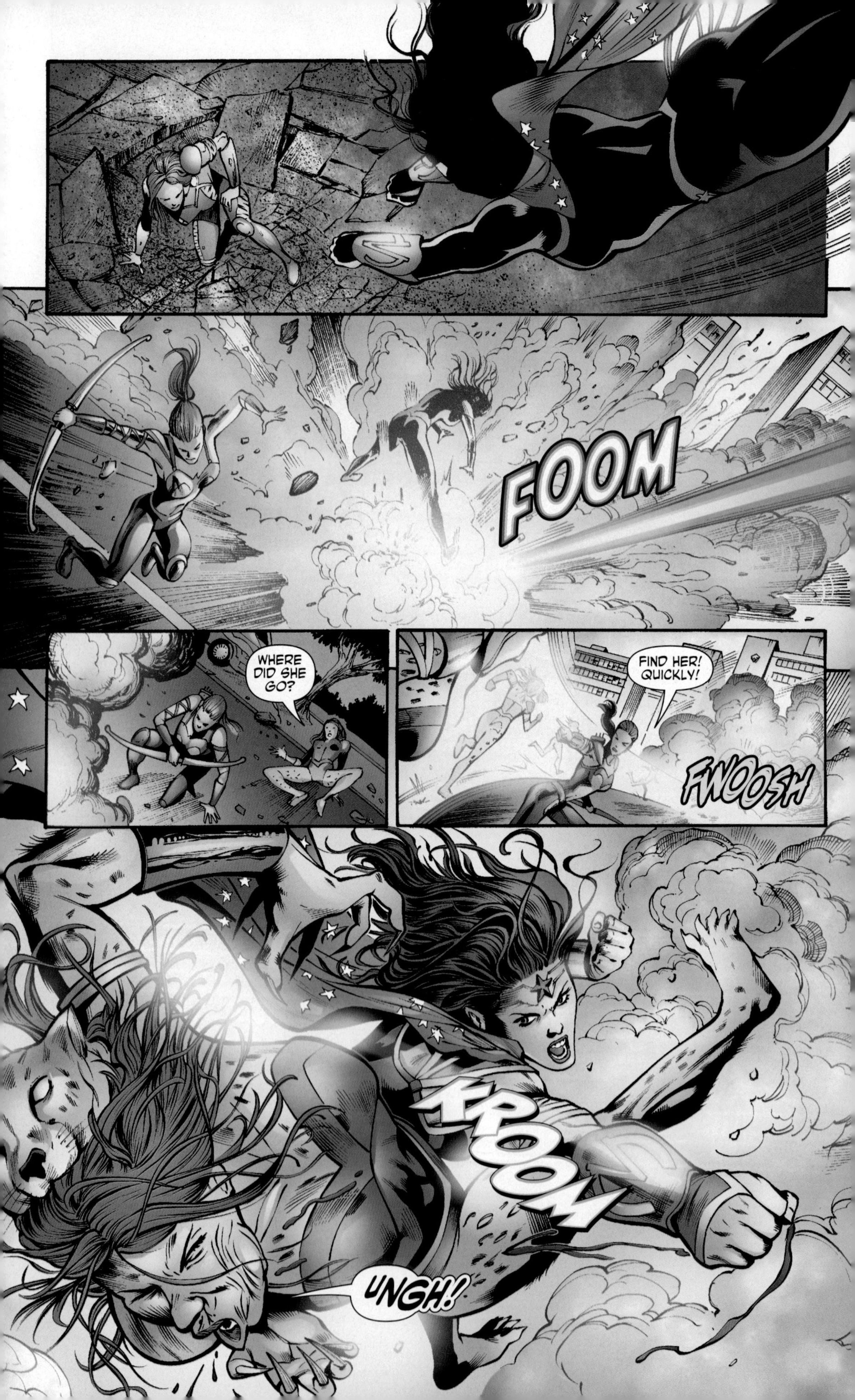
FOOM
WHERE DID SHE GO?
FIND HER! QUICKLY!
FWOOSH
KROOM
UNGH!

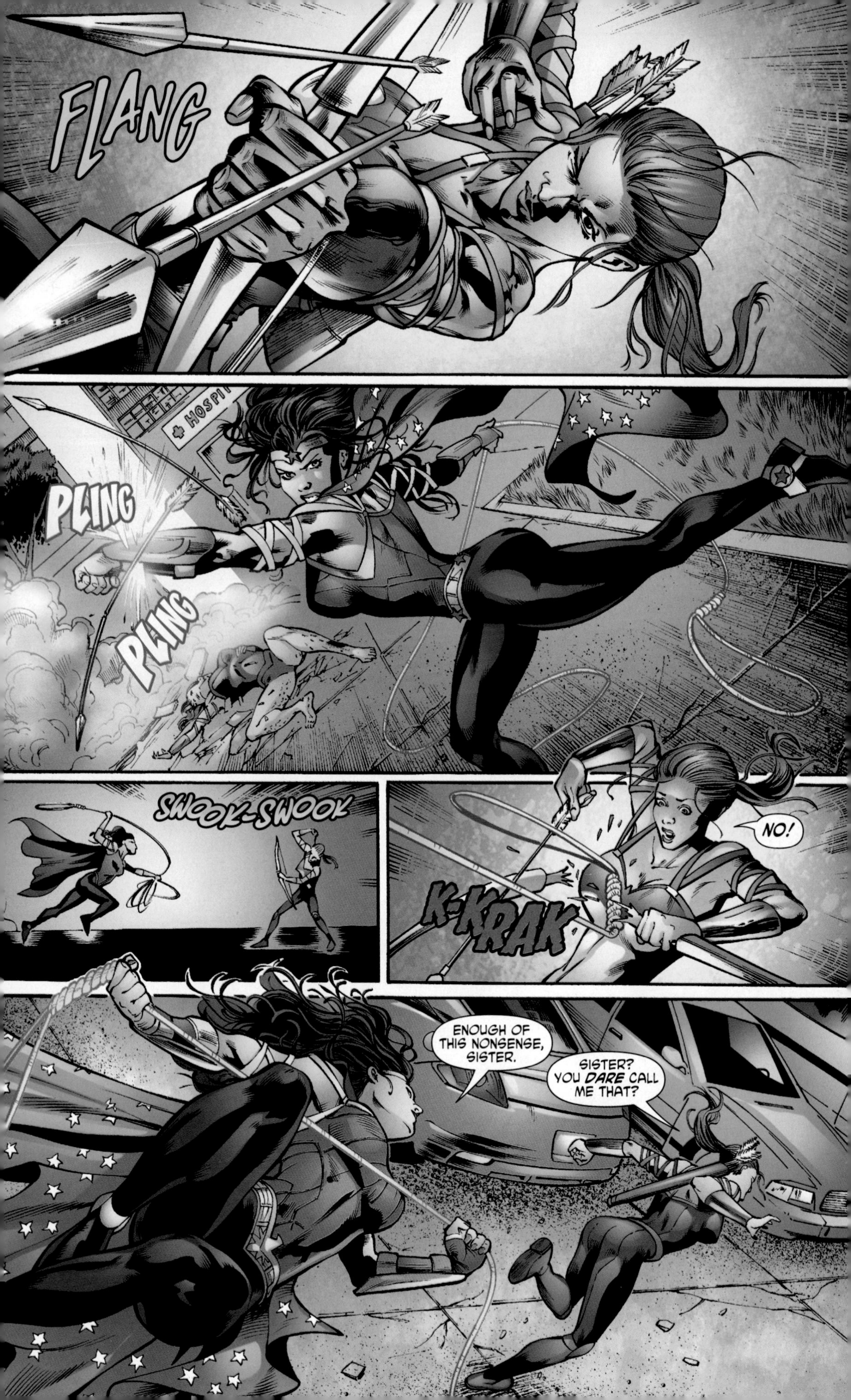
FLANG
HOSPI
PLING
PLING
SWOOK-SWOOK
NO!
K-KRAK
ENOUGH OF THIS NONSENSE, SISTER.
SISTER? YOU DARE CALL ME THAT?

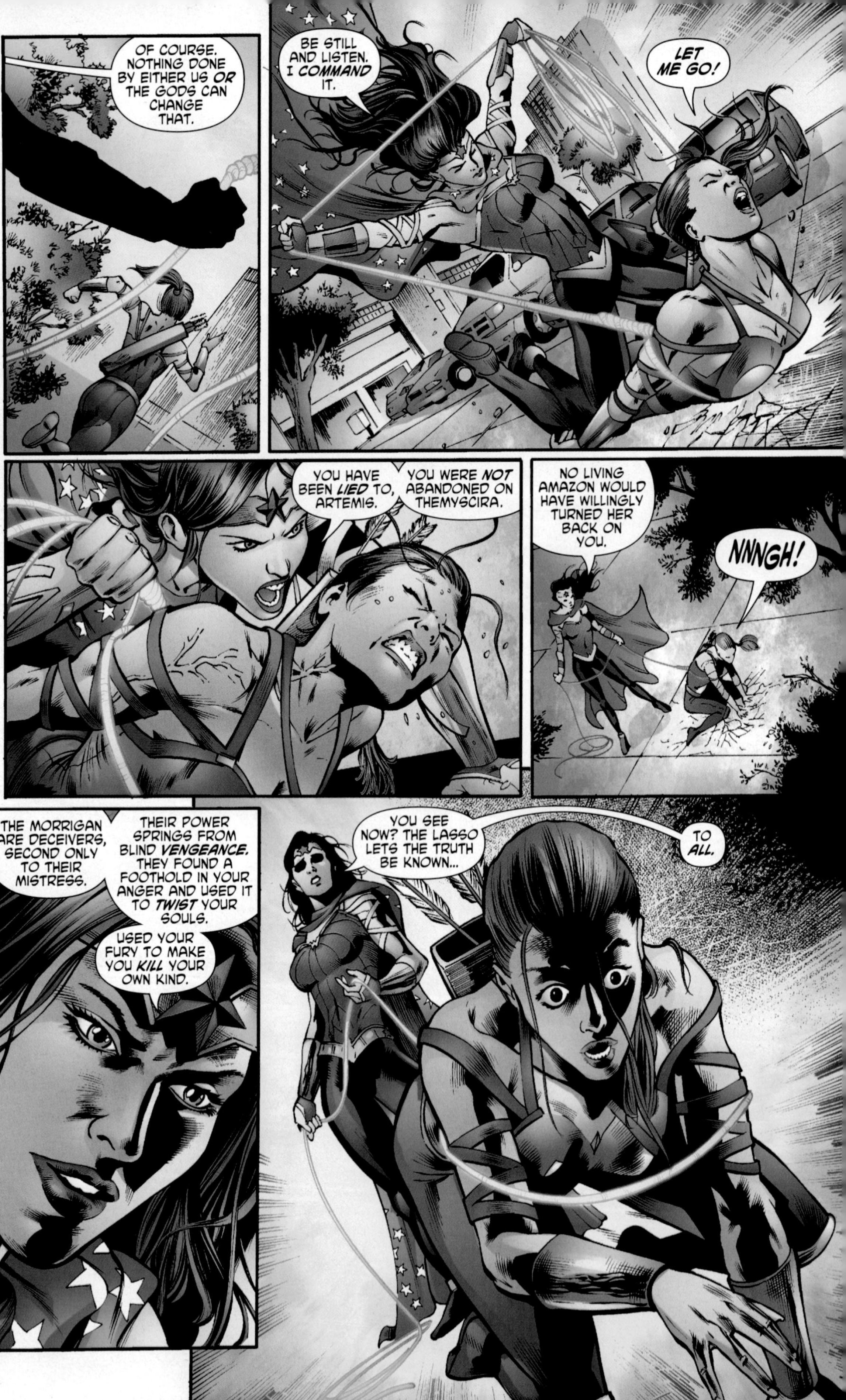
OF COURSE. NOTHING DONE BY EITHER US *OR* THE GODS CAN CHANGE THAT.
BE STILL AND LISTEN. I *COMMAND* IT.
LET ME GO!
YOU HAVE BEEN *LIED* TO, ARTEMIS.
YOU WERE *NOT* ABANDONED ON THEMYSCIRA.
NO LIVING AMAZON WOULD HAVE WILLINGLY TURNED HER BACK ON YOU.
NNNGH!
THE MORRIGAN ARE DECEIVERS, SECOND ONLY TO THEIR MISTRESS.
THEIR POWER SPRINGS FROM BLIND *VENGEANCE.* THEY FOUND A FOOTHOLD IN YOUR ANGER AND USED IT TO *TWIST* YOUR SOULS.
USED YOUR FURY TO MAKE YOU *KILL* YOUR OWN KIND.
YOU SEE NOW? THE LASSO LETS THE TRUTH BE KNOWN...
TO *ALL.*

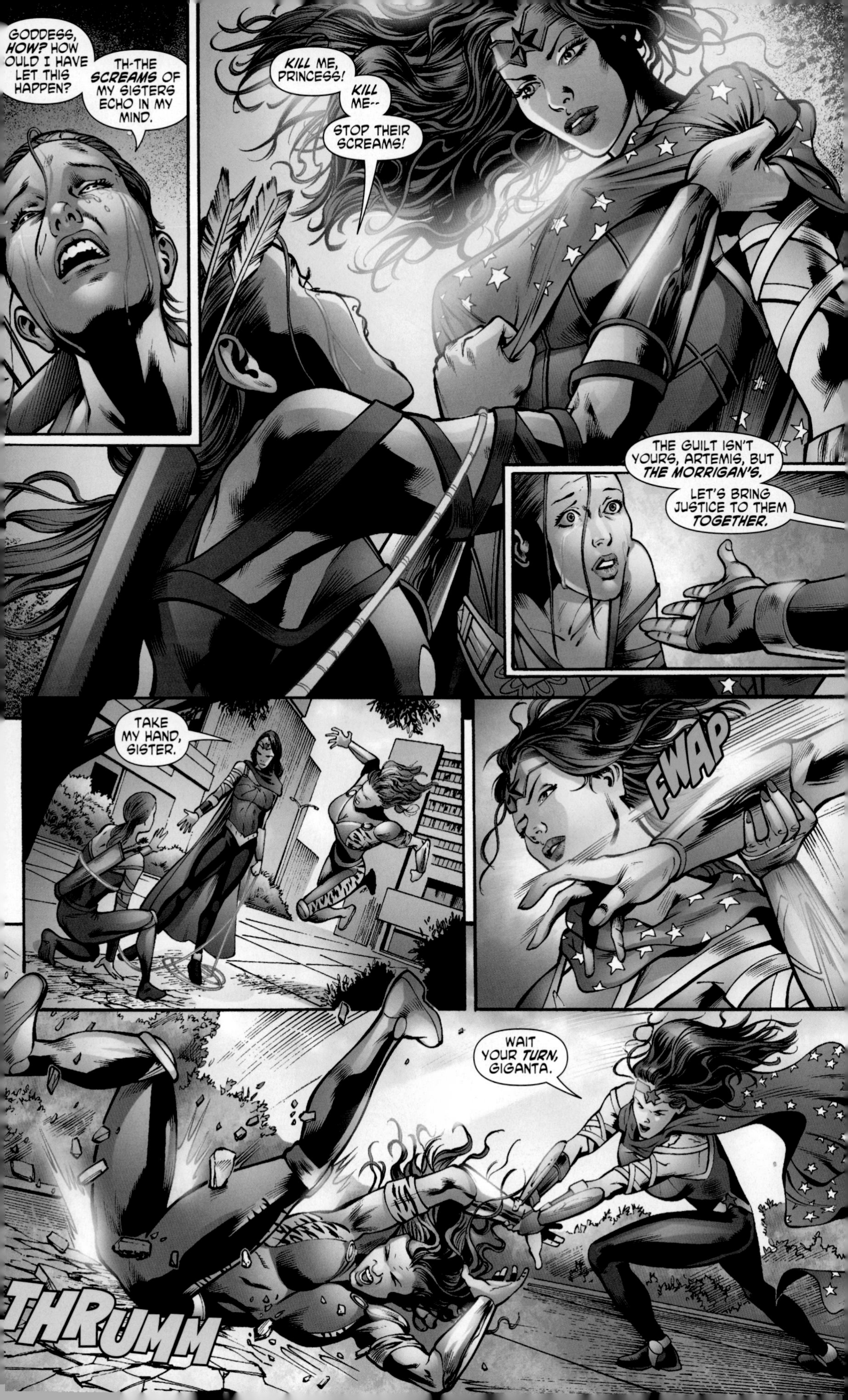
GODDESS, HOW? HOW OULD I HAVE LET THIS HAPPEN?
TH-THE SCREAMS OF MY SISTERS ECHO IN MY MIND.
KILL ME, PRINCESS!
KILL ME--
STOP THEIR SCREAMS!
THE GUILT ISN'T YOURS, ARTEMIS, BUT THE MORRIGAN'S.
LET'S BRING JUSTICE TO THEM TOGETHER.
TAKE MY HAND, SISTER.
FWAP
WAIT YOUR TURN, GIGANTA.
THRUMM

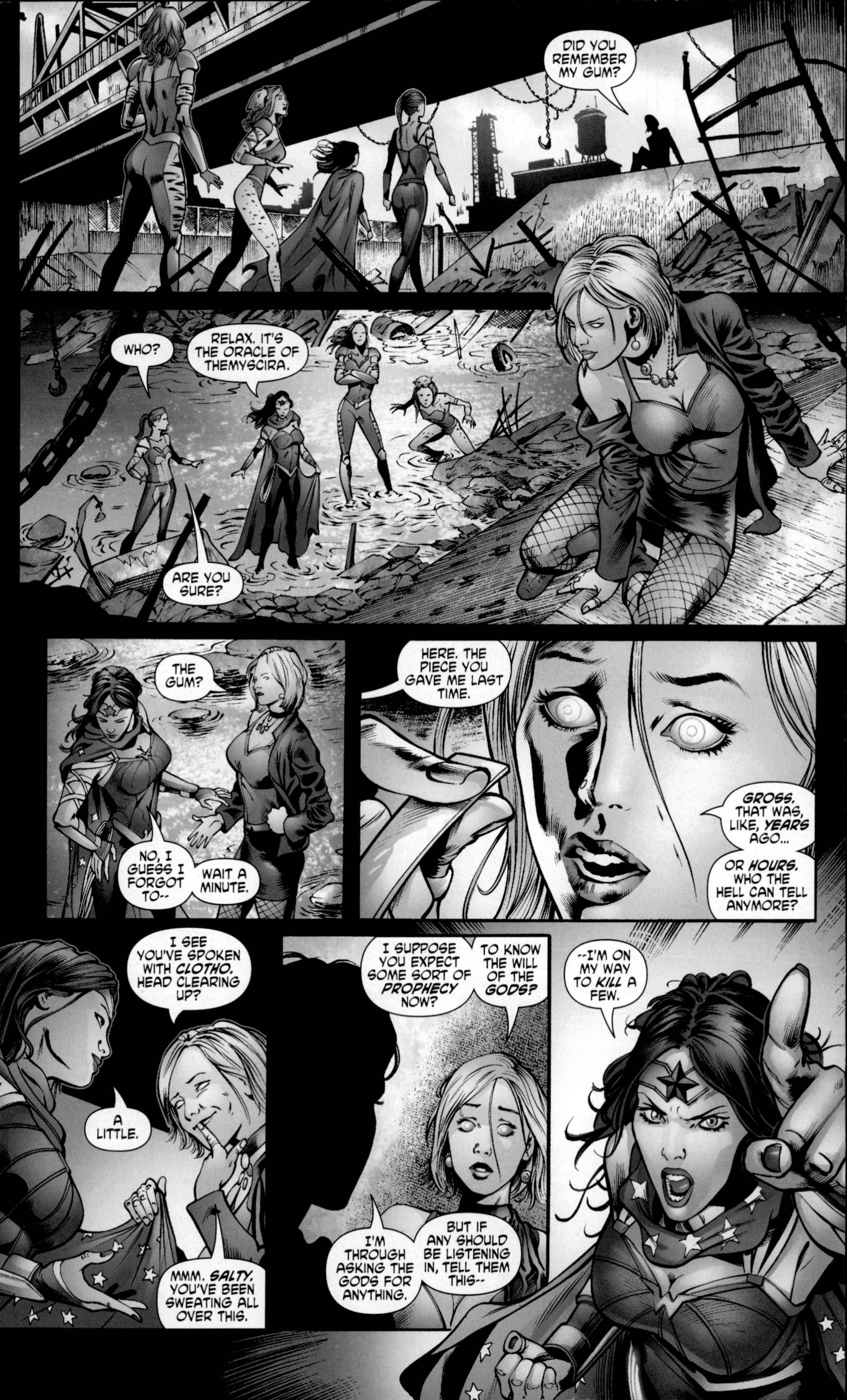
DID YOU REMEMBER MY GUM?
WHO?
RELAX. IT'S THE ORACLE OF THEMYSCIRA.
ARE YOU SURE?
THE GUM?
NO, I GUESS I FORGOT TO--
WAIT A MINUTE.
HERE. THE PIECE YOU GAVE ME LAST TIME.
GROSS. THAT WAS, LIKE, YEARS AGO...
OR HOURS. WHO THE HELL CAN TELL ANYMORE?
I SEE YOU'VE SPOKEN WITH CLOTHO. HEAD CLEARING UP?
A LITTLE.
MMM. SALTY. YOU'VE BEEN SWEATING ALL OVER THIS.
I SUPPOSE YOU EXPECT SOME SORT OF PROPHECY NOW?
TO KNOW THE WILL OF THE GODS?
I'M THROUGH ASKING THE GODS FOR ANYTHING.
BUT IF ANY SHOULD BE LISTENING IN, TELL THEM THIS--
--I'M ON MY WAY TO KILL A FEW.

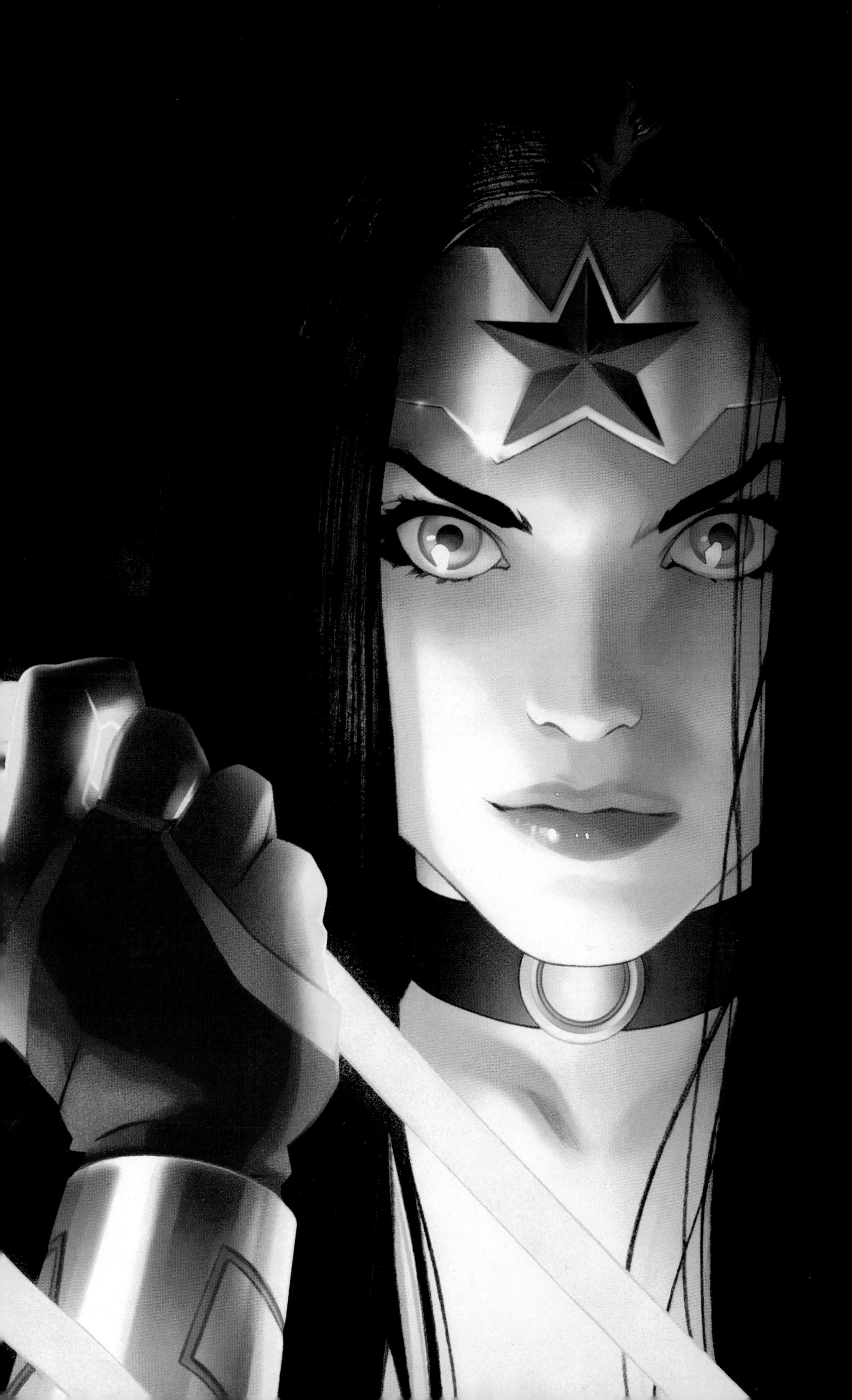

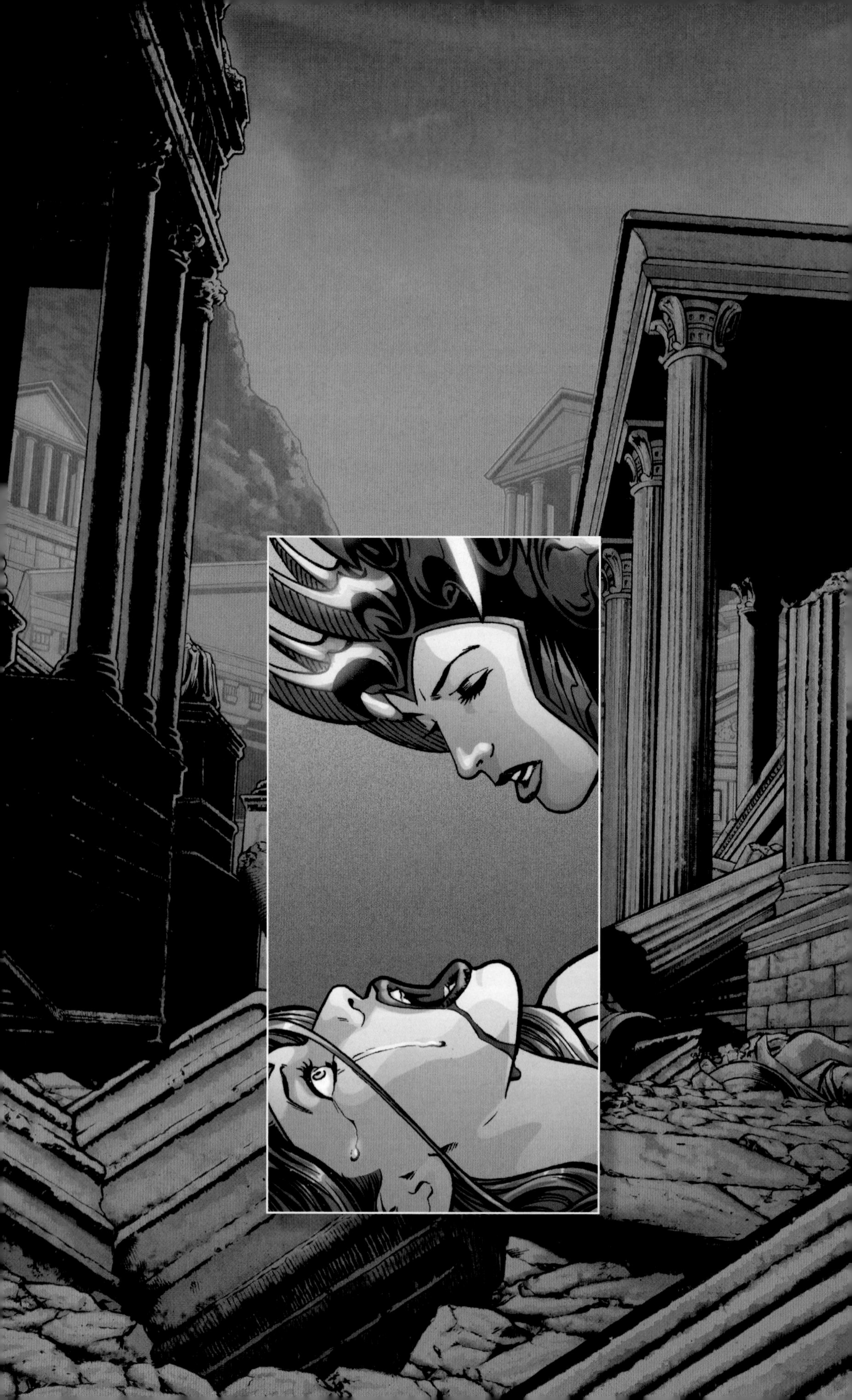

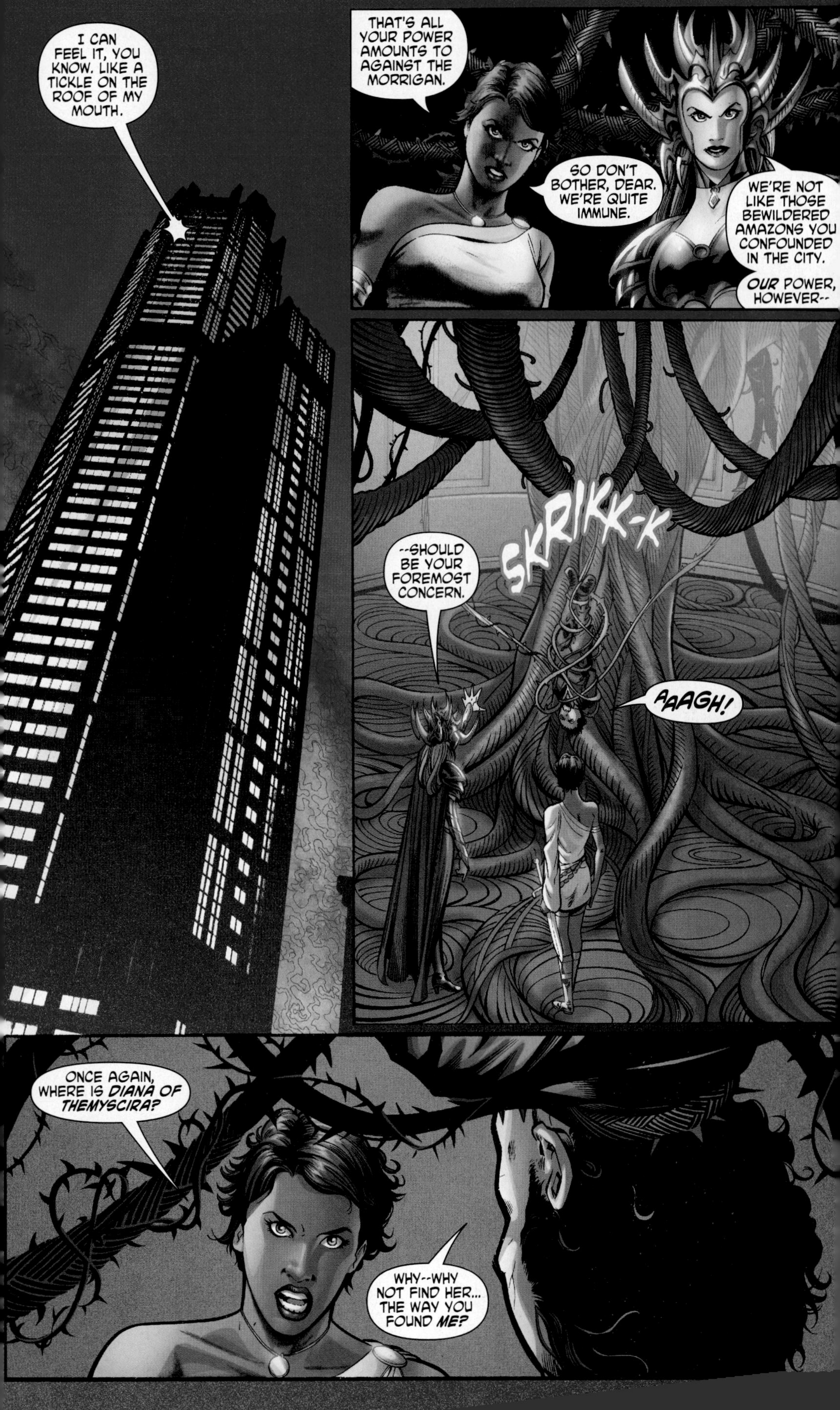
I CAN FEEL IT, YOU KNOW. LIKE A TICKLE ON THE ROOF OF MY MOUTH.
THAT'S ALL YOUR POWER AMOUNTS TO AGAINST THE MORRIGAN.
SO DON'T BOTHER, DEAR. WE'RE QUITE IMMUNE.
WE'RE NOT LIKE THOSE BEWILDERED AMAZONS YOU CONFOUNDED IN THE CITY.
OUR POWER, HOWEVER--
SKRIKK-K
--SHOULD BE YOUR FOREMOST CONCERN.
AAAGH!
ONCE AGAIN, WHERE IS DIANA OF THEMYSCIRA?
WHY--WHY NOT FIND HER... THE WAY YOU FOUND ME?

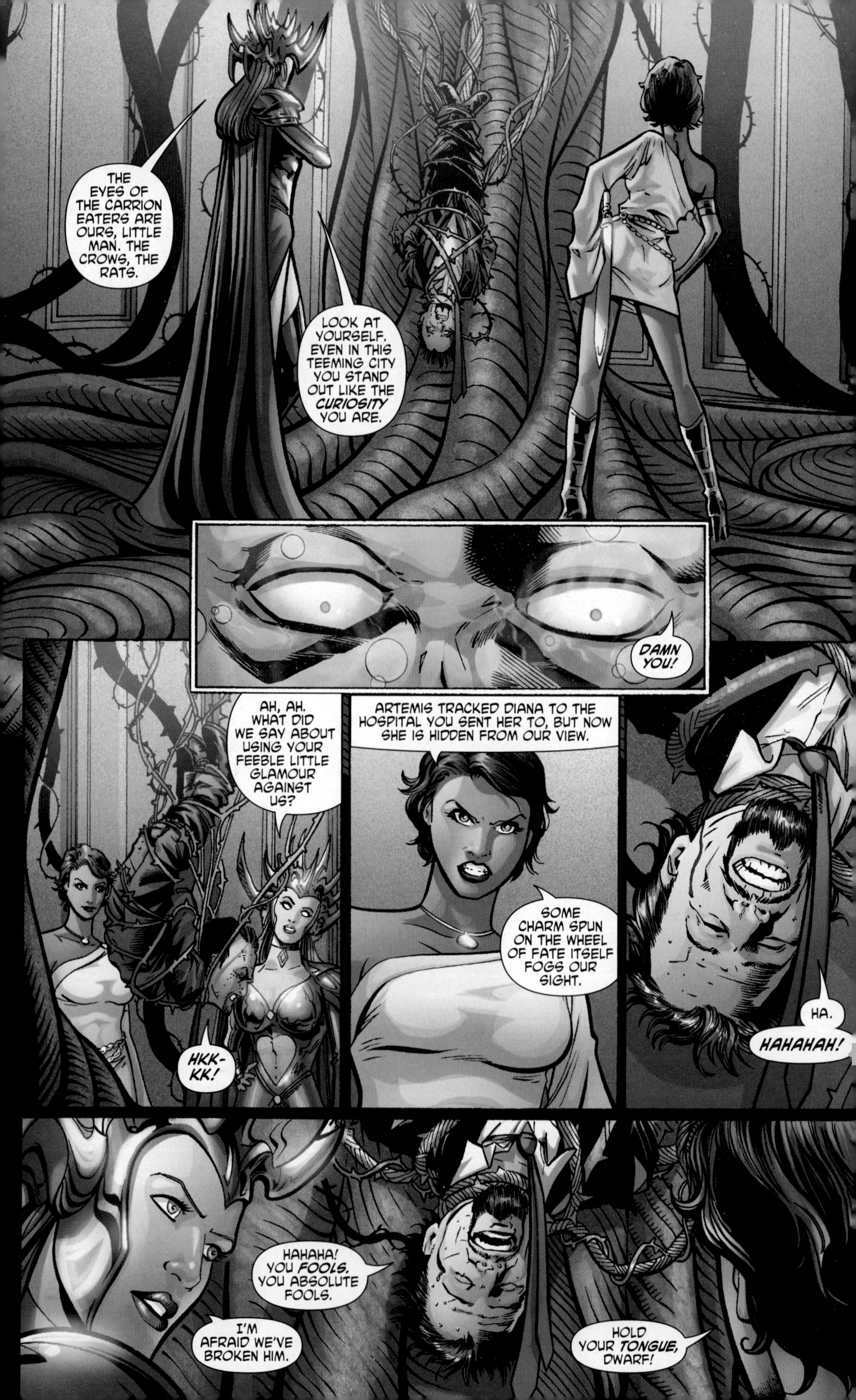
THE EYES OF THE CARRION EATERS ARE OURS, LITTLE MAN. THE CROWS, THE RATS.
LOOK AT YOURSELF. EVEN IN THIS TEEMING CITY YOU STAND OUT LIKE THE *CURIOSITY* YOU ARE.
DAMN YOU!
AH, AH. WHAT DID WE SAY ABOUT USING YOUR FEEBLE LITTLE GLAMOUR AGAINST US?
HKK-KK!
ARTEMIS TRACKED DIANA TO THE HOSPITAL YOU SENT HER TO, BUT NOW SHE IS HIDDEN FROM OUR VIEW.
SOME CHARM SPUN ON THE WHEEL OF FATE ITSELF FOGS OUR SIGHT.
HA.
HAHAHAH!
HAHAHA! YOU *FOOLS.* YOU ABSOLUTE FOOLS.
I'M AFRAID WE'VE BROKEN HIM.
HOLD YOUR *TONGUE,* DWARF!

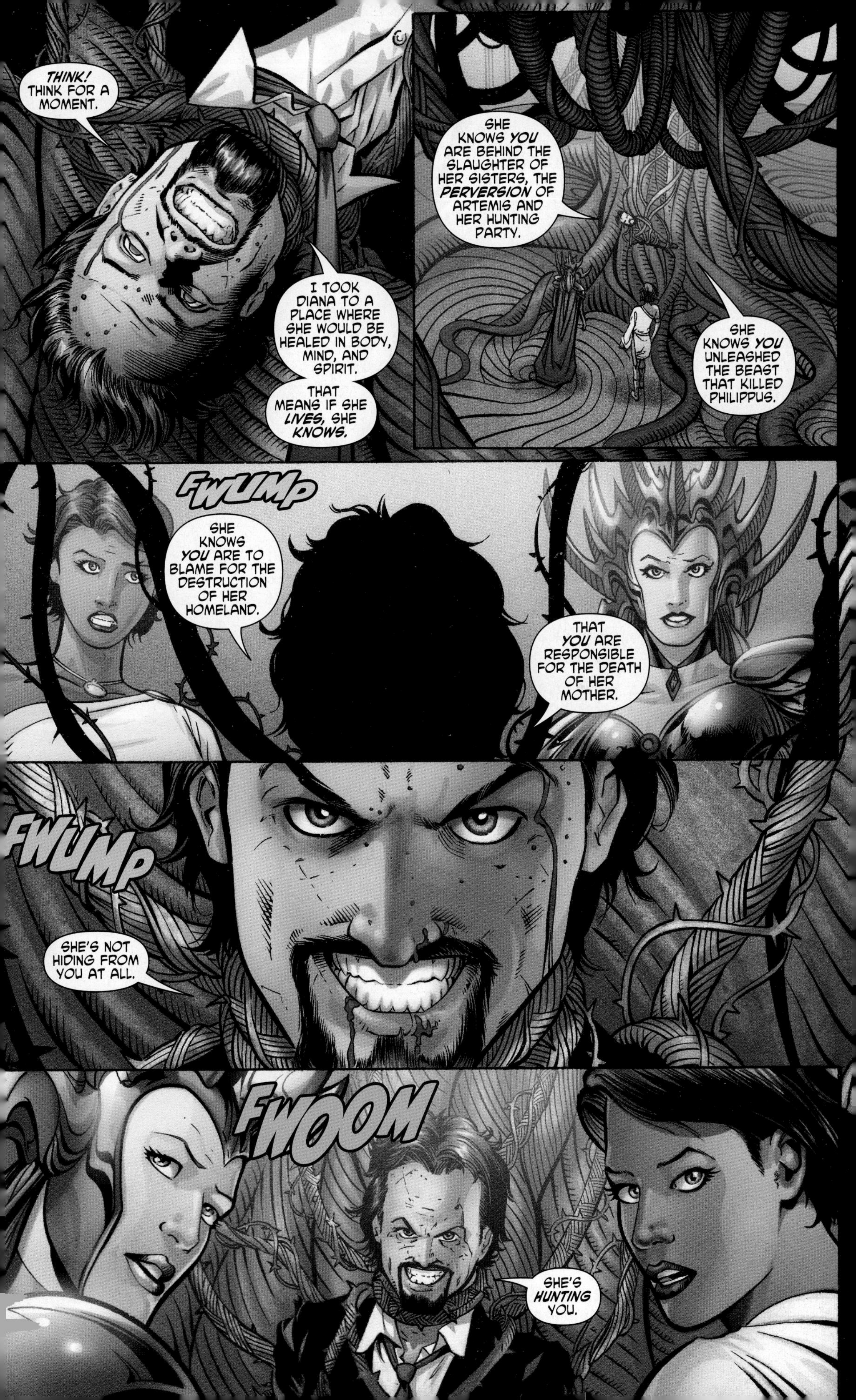
THINK! THINK FOR A MOMENT.
I TOOK DIANA TO A PLACE WHERE SHE WOULD BE HEALED IN BODY, MIND, AND SPIRIT.
THAT MEANS IF SHE LIVES, SHE KNOWS.
SHE KNOWS YOU ARE BEHIND THE SLAUGHTER OF HER SISTERS, THE PERVERSION OF ARTEMIS AND HER HUNTING PARTY.
SHE KNOWS YOU UNLEASHED THE BEAST THAT KILLED PHILIPPUS.
FWUMP
SHE KNOWS YOU ARE TO BLAME FOR THE DESTRUCTION OF HER HOMELAND.
THAT YOU ARE RESPONSIBLE FOR THE DEATH OF HER MOTHER.
FWUMP
SHE'S NOT HIDING FROM YOU AT ALL.
FWOOM
SHE'S HUNTING YOU.

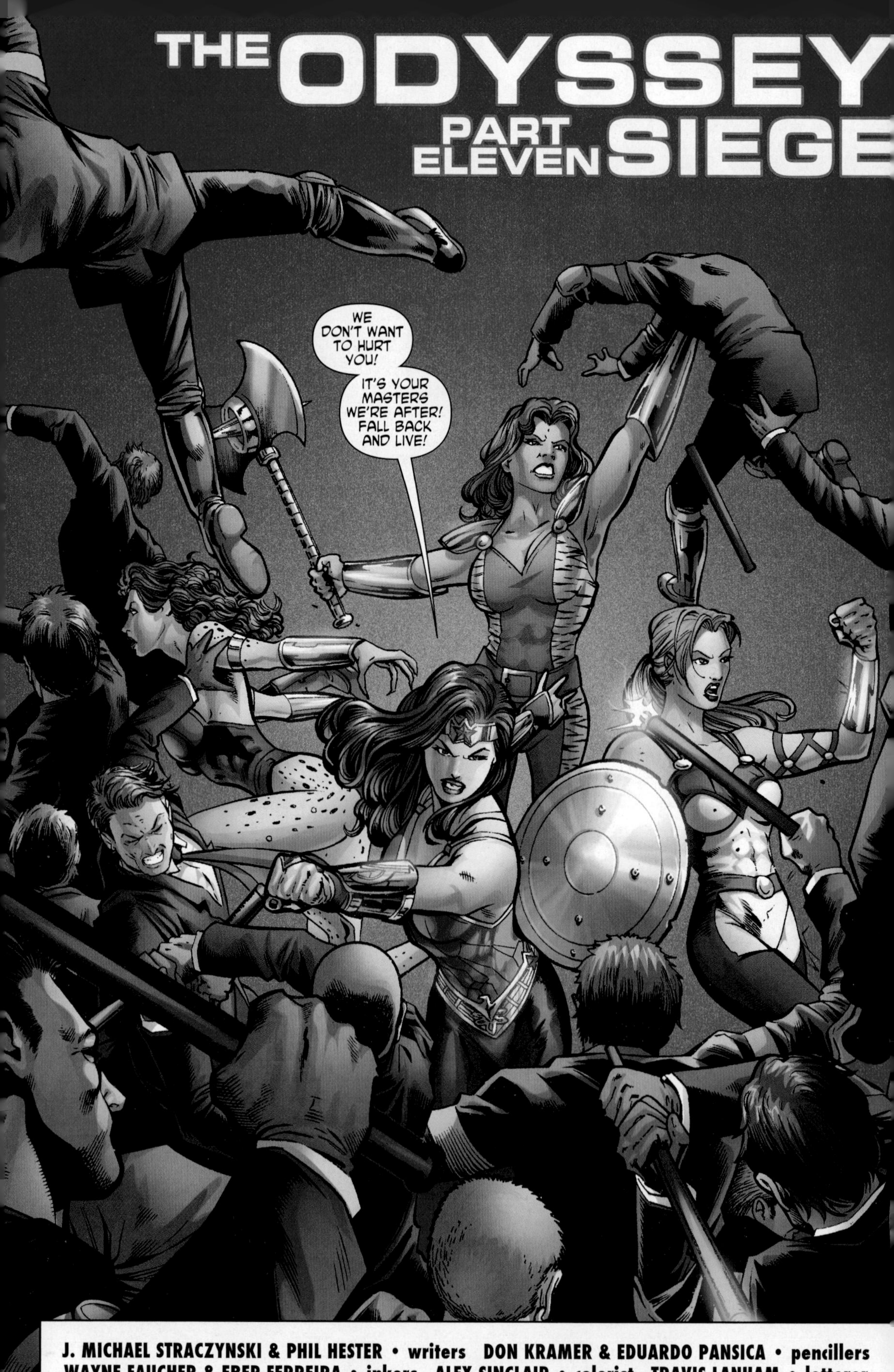
THE ODYSSEY
PART ELEVEN SIEGE
WE DON'T WANT TO HURT YOU!
IT'S YOUR MASTERS WE'RE AFTER! FALL BACK AND LIVE!

J. MICHAEL STRACZYNSKI & PHIL HESTER • writers DON KRAMER & EDUARDO PANSICA • pencillers
WAYNE FAUCHER & EBER FERREIRA • inkers ALEX SINCLAIR • colorist TRAVIS LANHAM • letterer
JOSH MIDDLETON • cover ALEX GARNER • variant cover CHRIS CONROY • associate editor
WONDER WOMAN created by WILLIAM MOULTON MARSTON

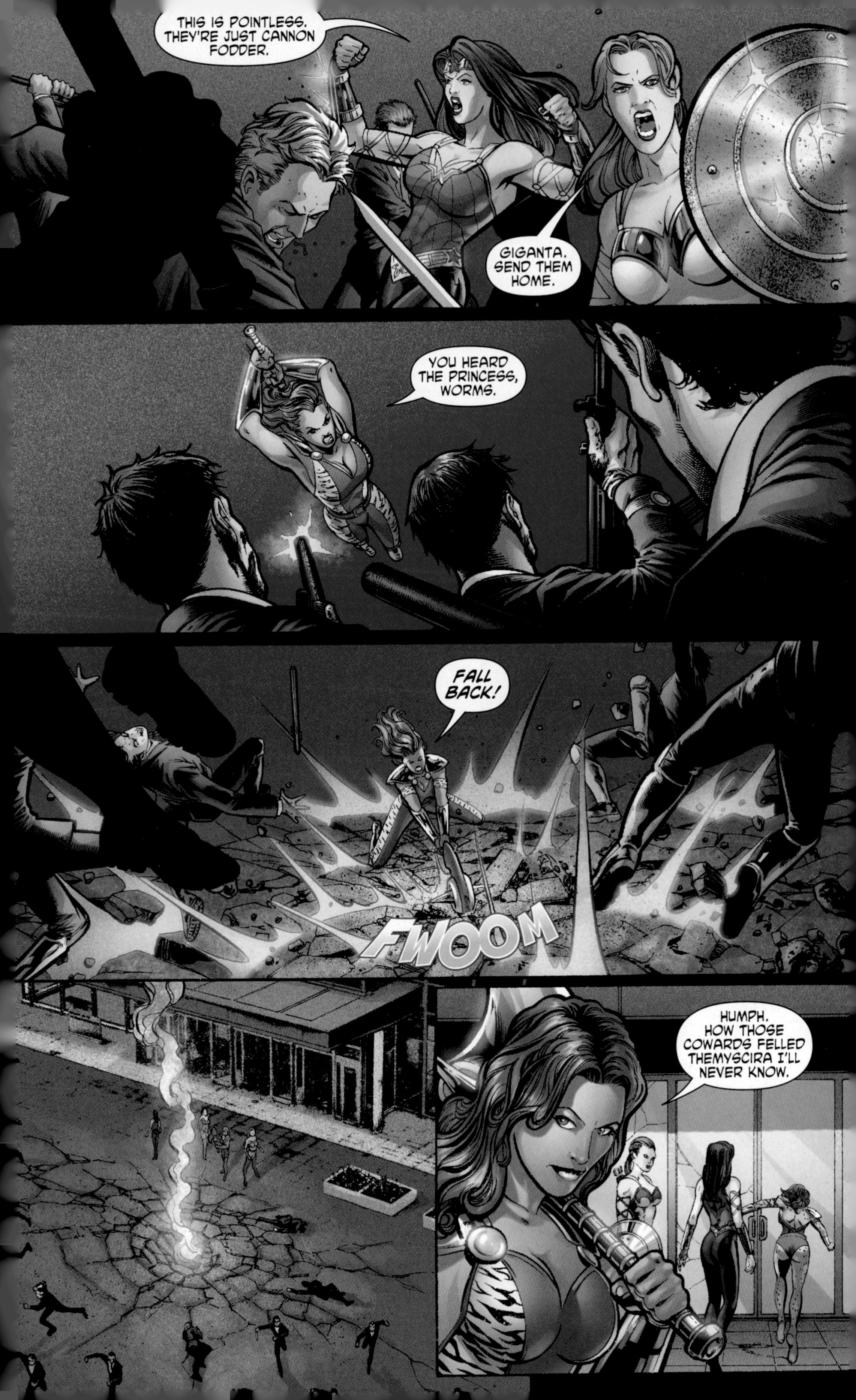
THIS IS POINTLESS. THEY'RE JUST CANNON FODDER.
GIGANTA. SEND THEM HOME.
YOU HEARD THE PRINCESS, WORMS.
FALL BACK!
FWOOM
HUMPH. HOW THOSE COWARDS FELLED THEMYSCIRA I'LL NEVER KNOW.

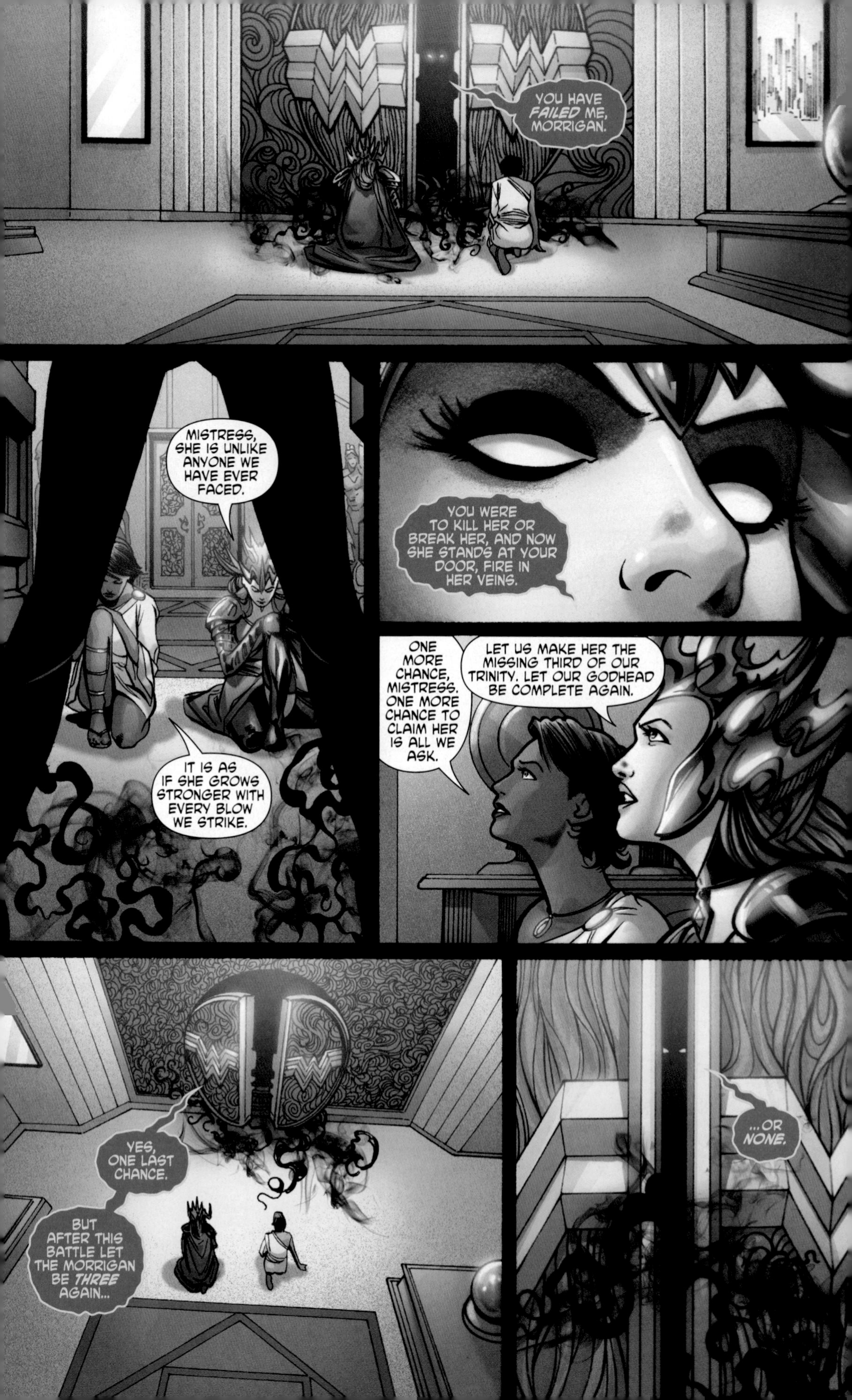
YOU HAVE FAILED ME, MORRIGAN.
MISTRESS, SHE IS UNLIKE ANYONE WE HAVE EVER FACED.
IT IS AS IF SHE GROWS STRONGER WITH EVERY BLOW WE STRIKE.
YOU WERE TO KILL HER OR BREAK HER, AND NOW SHE STANDS AT YOUR DOOR, FIRE IN HER VEINS.
ONE MORE CHANCE, MISTRESS. ONE MORE CHANCE TO CLAIM HER IS ALL WE ASK.
LET US MAKE HER THE MISSING THIRD OF OUR TRINITY. LET OUR GODHEAD BE COMPLETE AGAIN.
YES, ONE LAST CHANCE.
BUT AFTER THIS BATTLE LET THE MORRIGAN BE THREE AGAIN...
...OR NONE.

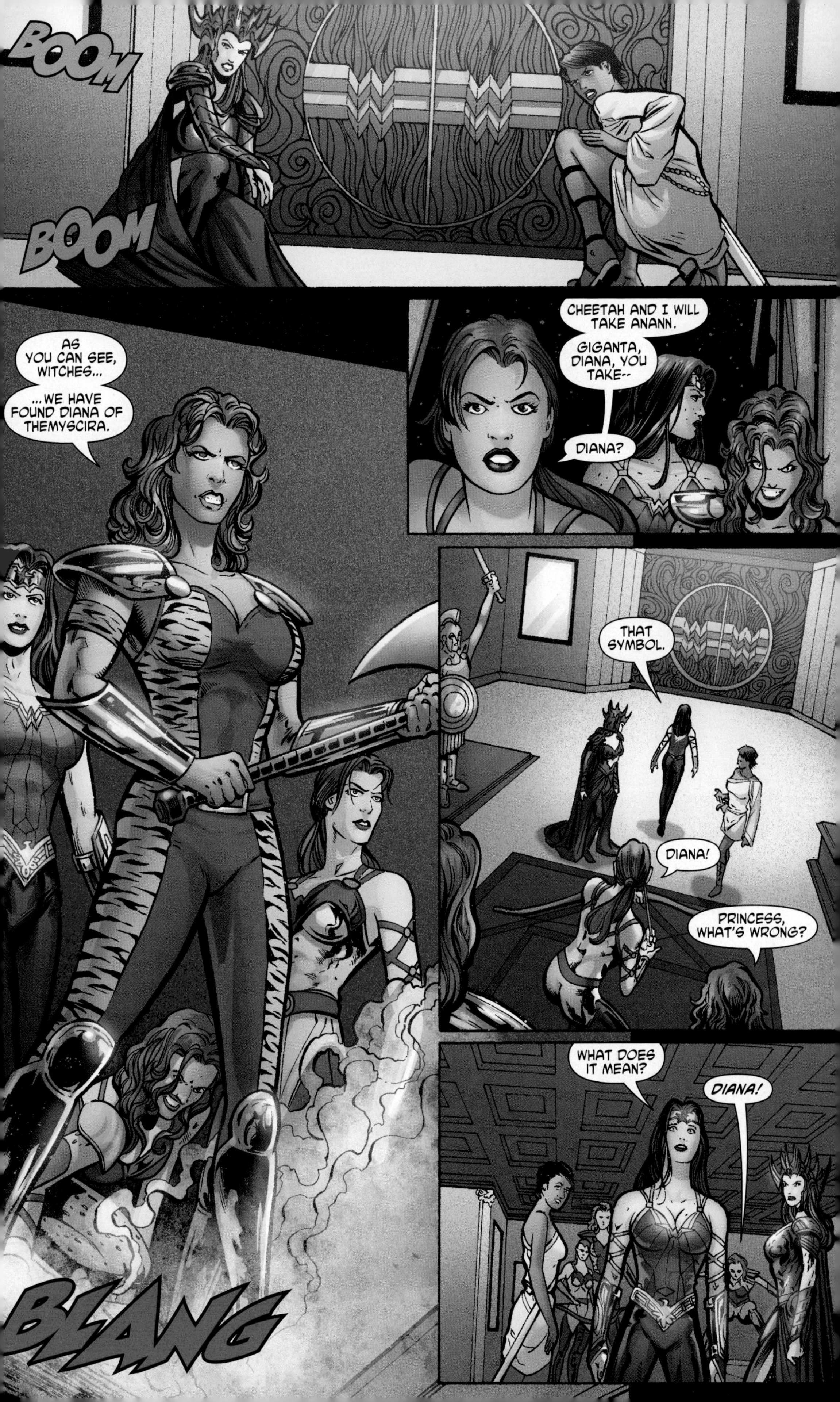
BOOM
BOOM
AS YOU CAN SEE, WITCHES...
...WE HAVE FOUND DIANA OF THEMYSCIRA.
BLANG
CHEETAH AND I WILL TAKE ANANN.
GIGANTA, DIANA, YOU TAKE--
DIANA?
THAT SYMBOL.
DIANA!
PRINCESS, WHAT'S WRONG?
WHAT DOES IT MEAN?
DIANA!

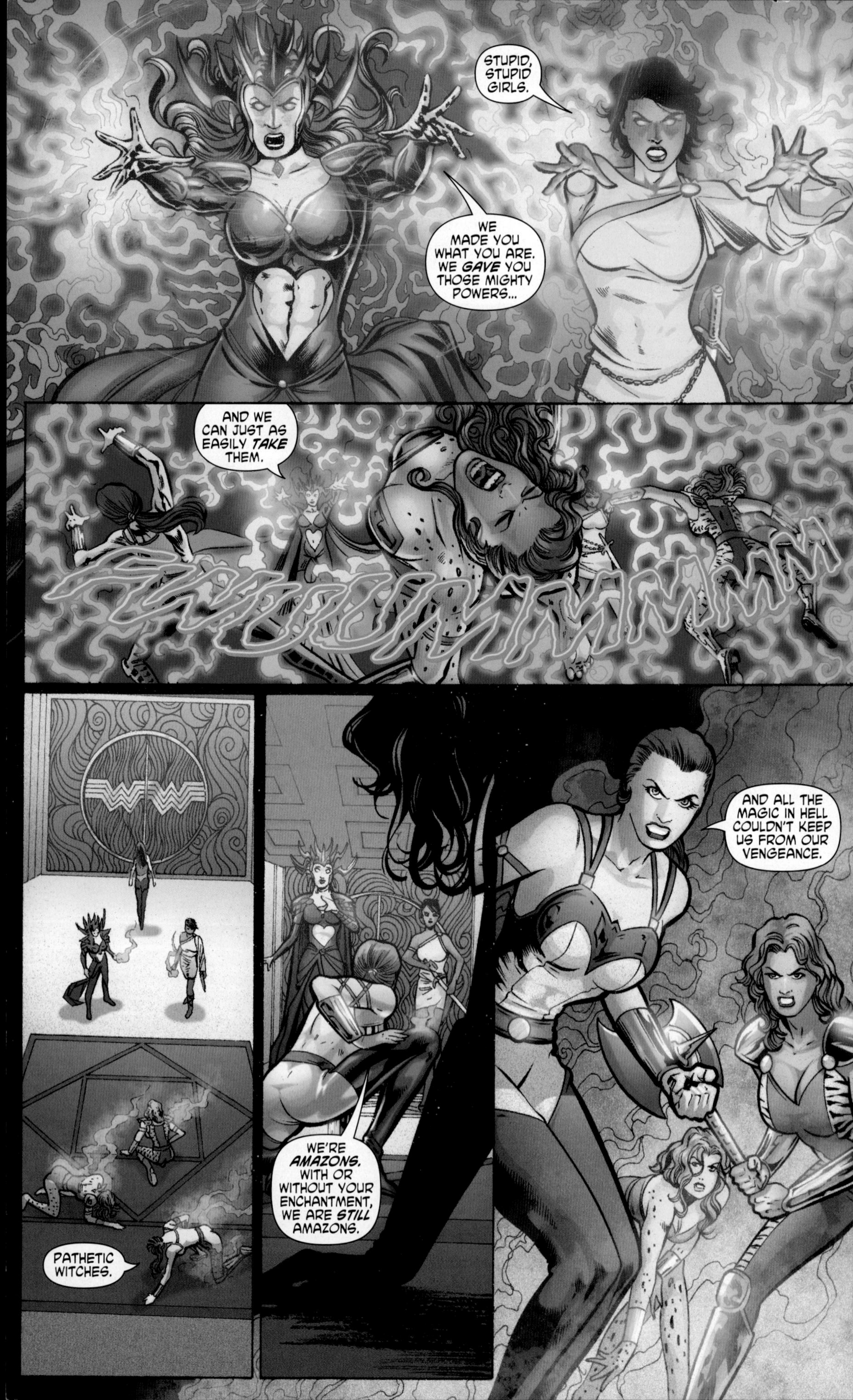
STUPID, STUPID GIRLS.
WE MADE YOU WHAT YOU ARE. WE *GAVE* YOU THOSE MIGHTY POWERS...
AND WE CAN JUST AS EASILY *TAKE* THEM.
FZSHOOMMMMMM
PATHETIC WITCHES.
WE'RE *AMAZONS.* WITH OR WITHOUT YOUR ENCHANTMENT, WE ARE *STILL* AMAZONS.
AND ALL THE MAGIC IN HELL COULDN'T KEEP US FROM OUR VENGEANCE.

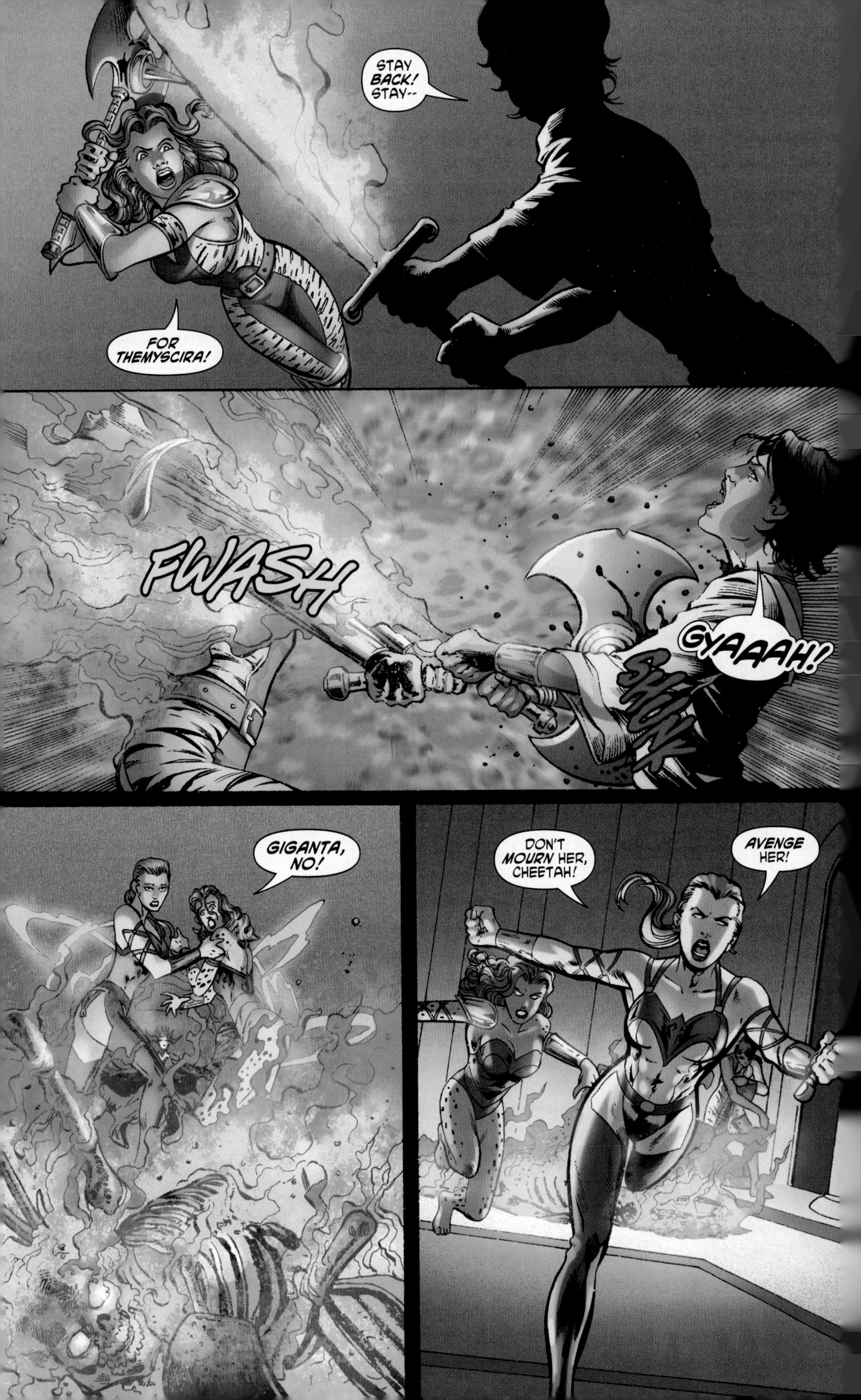
STAY BACK! STAY--
FOR THEMYSCIRA!
FWASH
GYAAAH!
SHUNK
GIGANTA, NO!
DON'T MOURN HER, CHEETAH!
AVENGE HER!

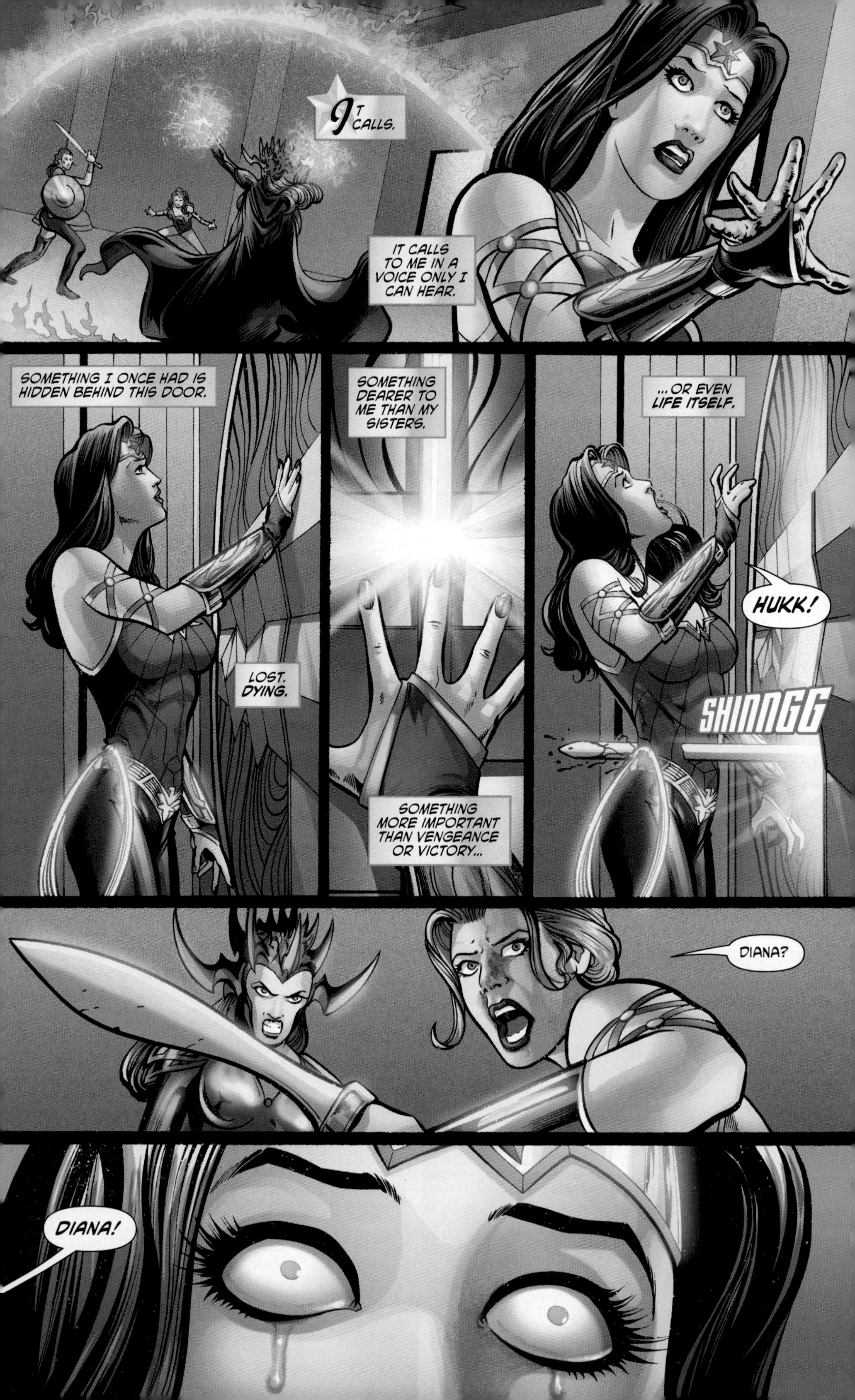
IT CALLS.
IT CALLS TO ME IN A VOICE ONLY I CAN HEAR.
SOMETHING I ONCE HAD IS HIDDEN BEHIND THIS DOOR.
LOST. DYING.
SOMETHING DEARER TO ME THAN MY SISTERS.
SOMETHING MORE IMPORTANT THAN VENGEANCE OR VICTORY...
...OR EVEN LIFE ITSELF.
HUKK!
SHINNGG
DIANA?
DIANA!

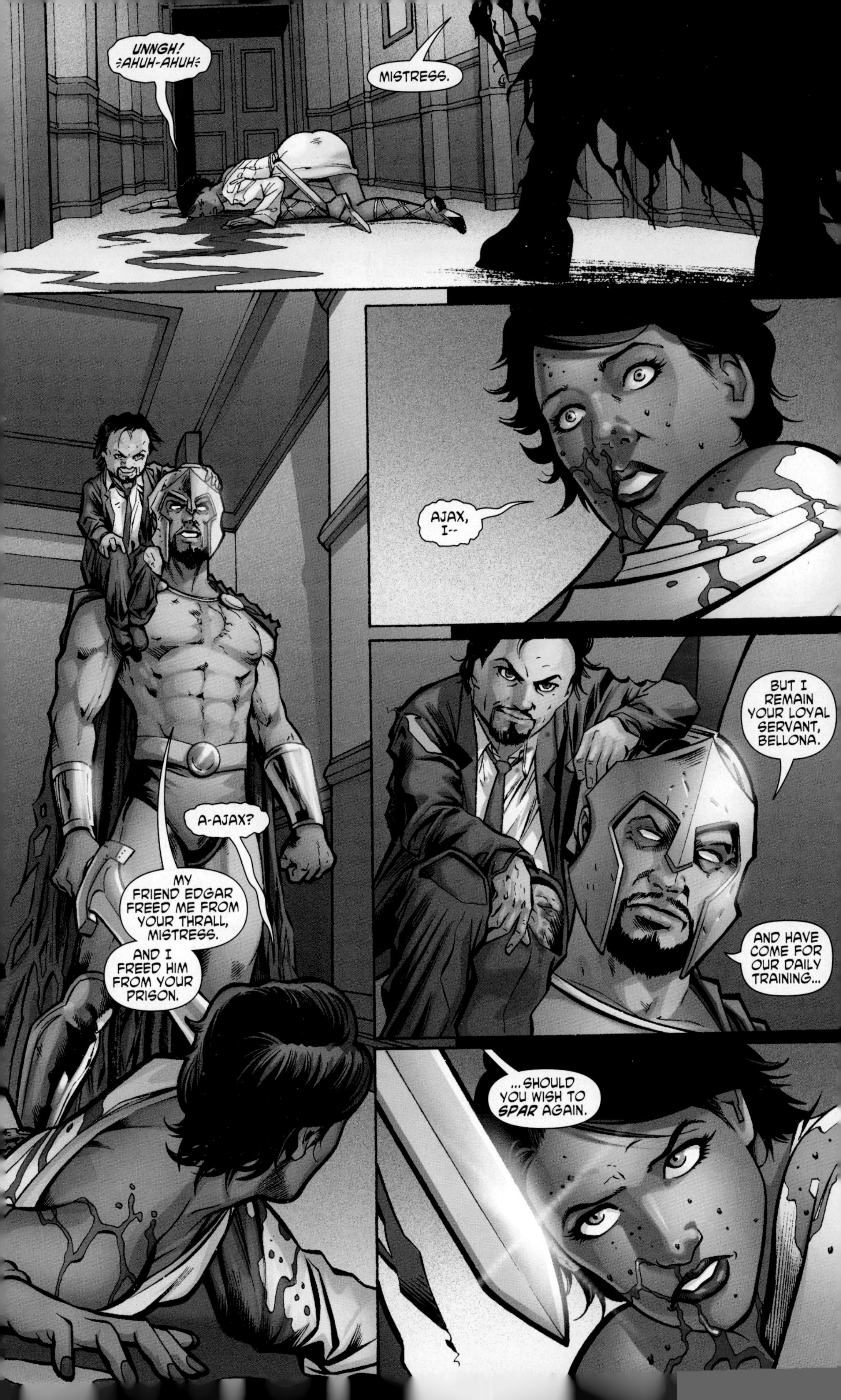
UNNGH! AHUH-AHUH
MISTRESS.
AJAX, I--
A-AJAX?
MY FRIEND EDGAR FREED ME FROM YOUR THRALL, MISTRESS.
AND I FREED HIM FROM YOUR PRISON.
BUT I REMAIN YOUR LOYAL SERVANT, BELLONA.
AND HAVE COME FOR OUR DAILY TRAINING...
...SHOULD YOU WISH TO SPAR AGAIN.

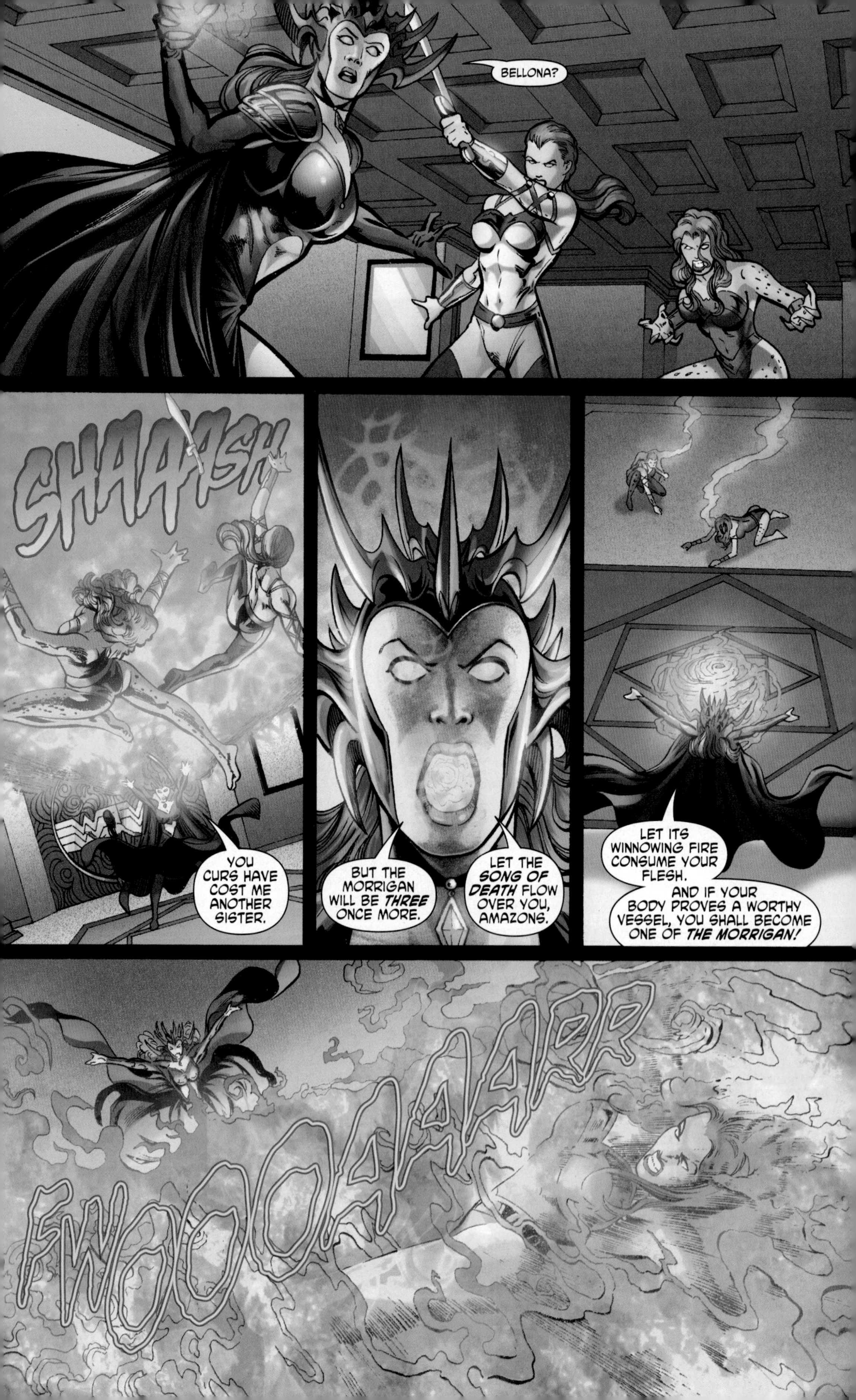
BELLONA?
SHAAASH
YOU CURS HAVE COST ME ANOTHER SISTER.
BUT THE MORRIGAN WILL BE *THREE* ONCE MORE.
LET THE *SONG OF DEATH* FLOW OVER YOU, AMAZONS.
LET ITS WINNOWING FIRE CONSUME YOUR FLESH.
AND IF YOUR BODY PROVES A WORTHY VESSEL, YOU SHALL BECOME ONE OF *THE MORRIGAN!*
FWOOOAAAARR

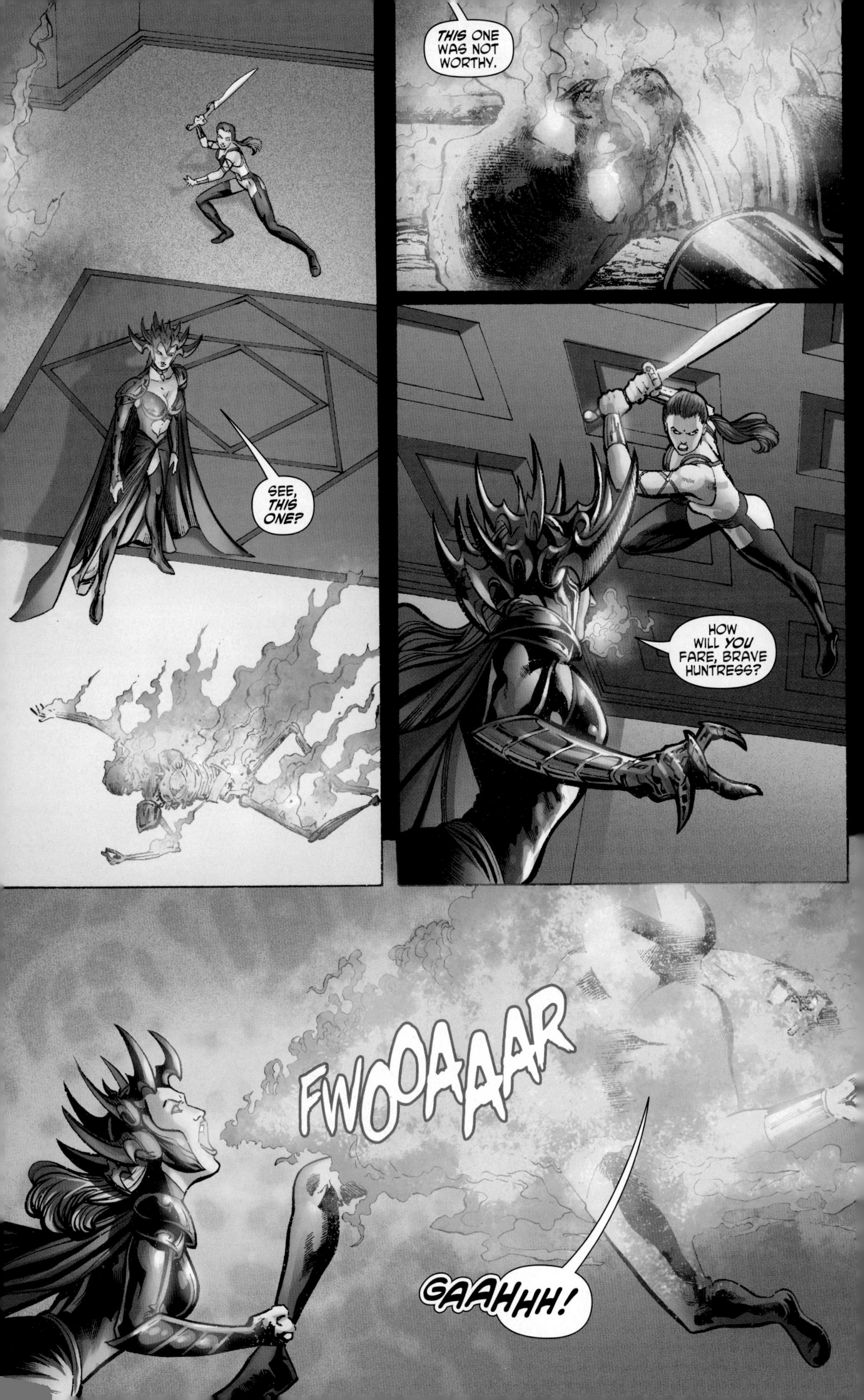
SEE, THIS ONE?
THIS ONE WAS NOT WORTHY.
HOW WILL YOU FARE, BRAVE HUNTRESS?
FWOOAAAR
GAAHHH!

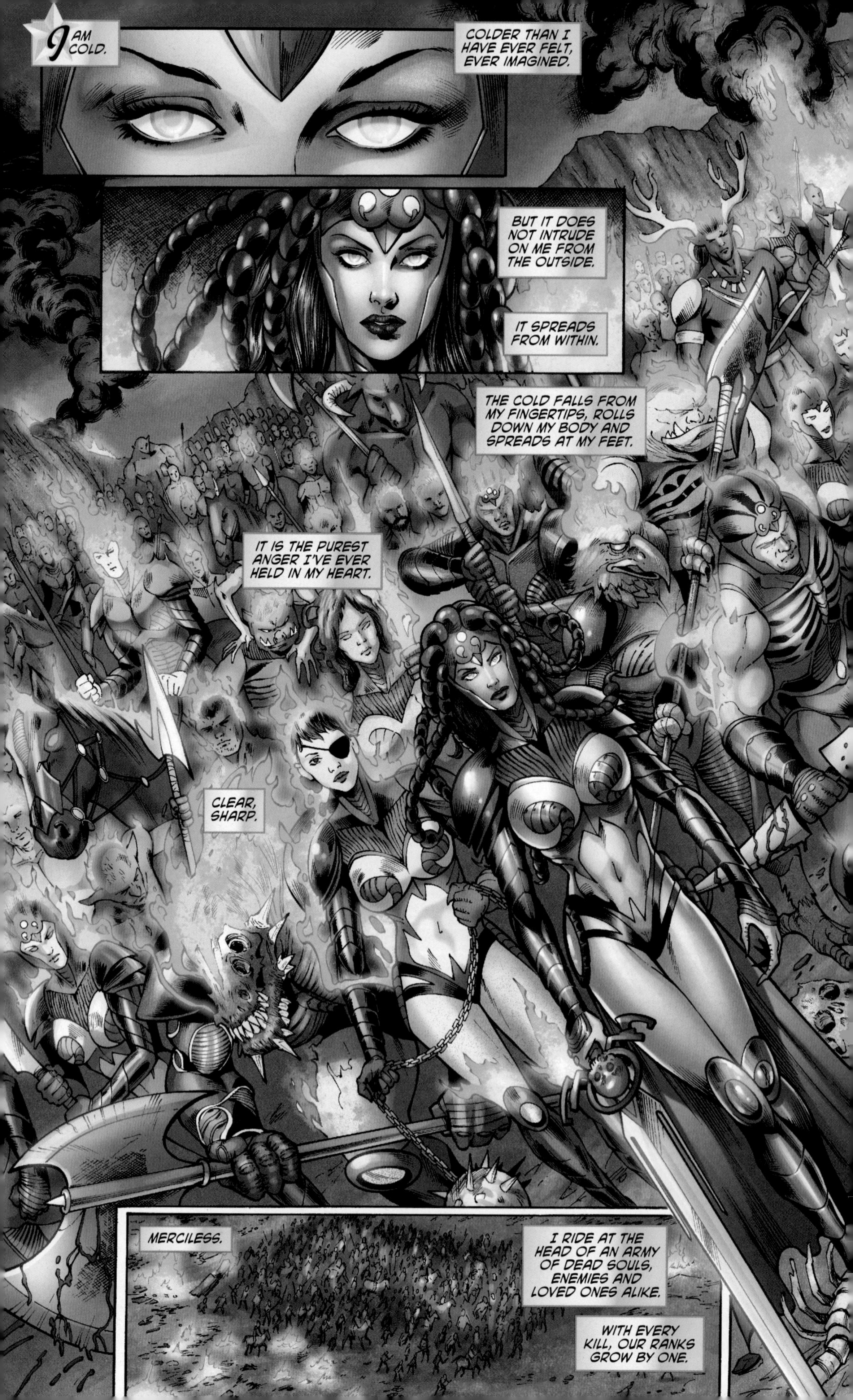
I AM COLD.
COLDER THAN I HAVE EVER FELT, EVER IMAGINED.
BUT IT DOES NOT INTRUDE ON ME FROM THE OUTSIDE.
IT SPREADS FROM WITHIN.
THE COLD FALLS FROM MY FINGERTIPS, ROLLS DOWN MY BODY AND SPREADS AT MY FEET.
IT IS THE PUREST ANGER I'VE EVER HELD IN MY HEART.
CLEAR, SHARP.
MERCILESS.
I RIDE AT THE HEAD OF AN ARMY OF DEAD SOULS, ENEMIES AND LOVED ONES ALIKE.
WITH EVERY KILL, OUR RANKS GROW BY ONE.

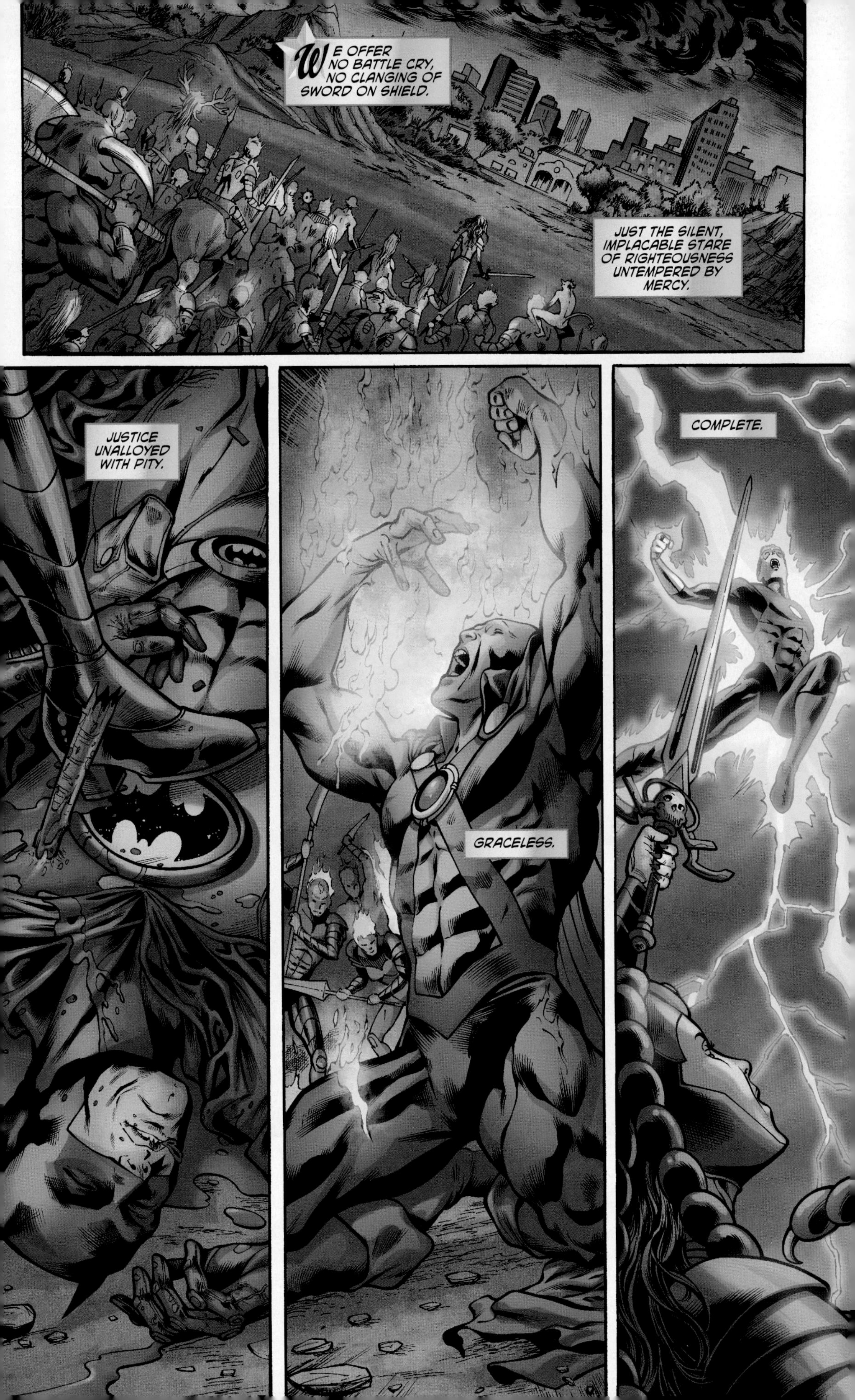
WE OFFER NO BATTLE CRY, NO CLANGING OF SWORD ON SHIELD.
JUST THE SILENT, IMPLACABLE STARE OF RIGHTEOUSNESS UNTEMPERED BY MERCY.
JUSTICE UNALLOYED WITH PITY.
GRACELESS.
COMPLETE.

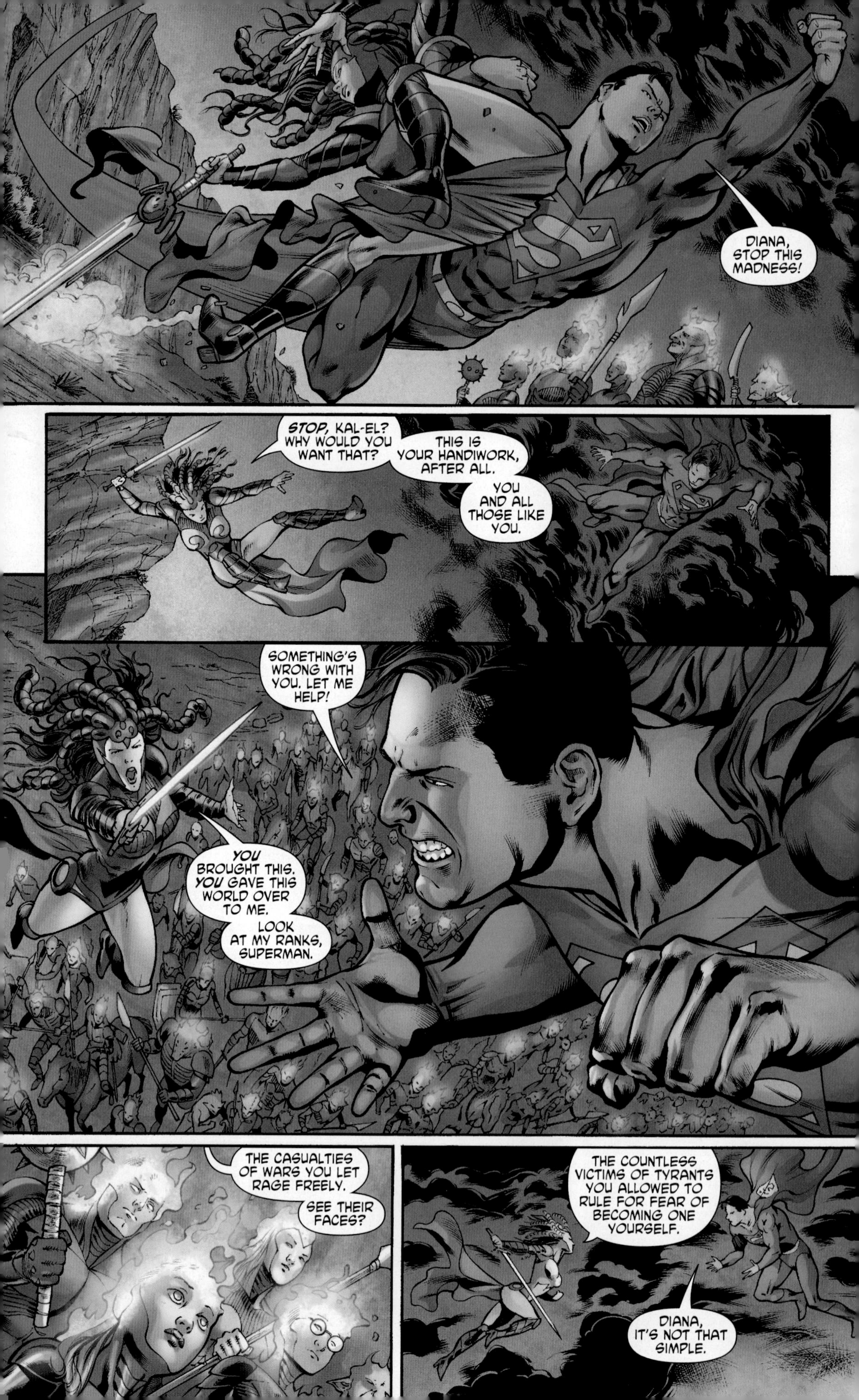
DIANA, STOP THIS MADNESS!
STOP, KAL-EL? WHY WOULD YOU WANT THAT?
THIS IS YOUR HANDIWORK, AFTER ALL.
YOU AND ALL THOSE LIKE YOU.
SOMETHING'S WRONG WITH YOU. LET ME HELP!
YOU BROUGHT THIS. YOU GAVE THIS WORLD OVER TO ME.
LOOK AT MY RANKS, SUPERMAN.
THE CASUALTIES OF WARS YOU LET RAGE FREELY.
SEE THEIR FACES?
THE COUNTLESS VICTIMS OF TYRANTS YOU ALLOWED TO RULE FOR FEAR OF BECOMING ONE YOURSELF.
DIANA, IT'S NOT THAT SIMPLE.

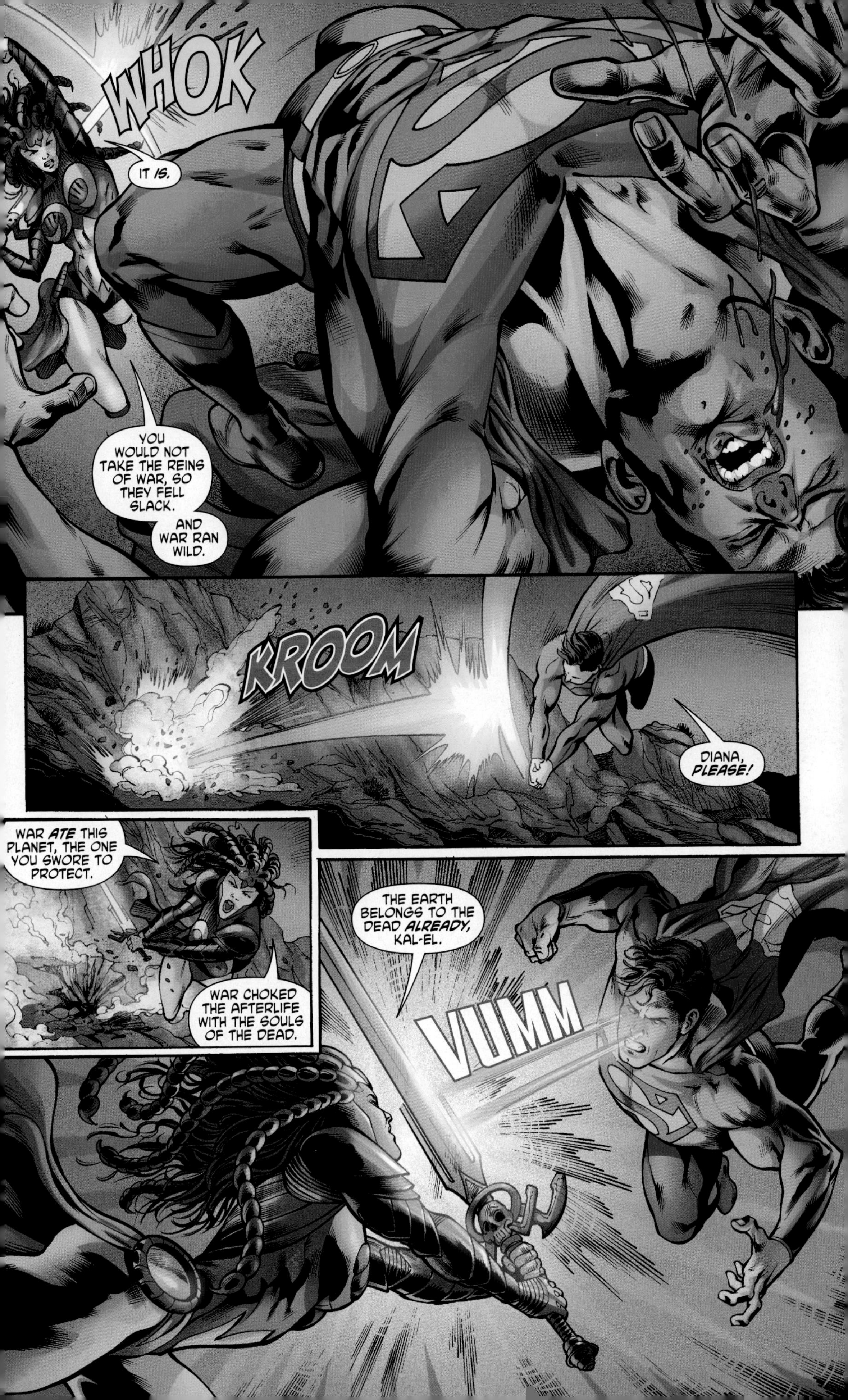
WHOK
IT IS.
YOU WOULD NOT TAKE THE REINS OF WAR, SO THEY FELL SLACK.
AND WAR RAN WILD.
KROOM
DIANA, PLEASE!
WAR ATE THIS PLANET, THE ONE YOU SWORE TO PROTECT.
WAR CHOKED THE AFTERLIFE WITH THE SOULS OF THE DEAD.
THE EARTH BELONGS TO THE DEAD ALREADY, KAL-EL.
VUMM

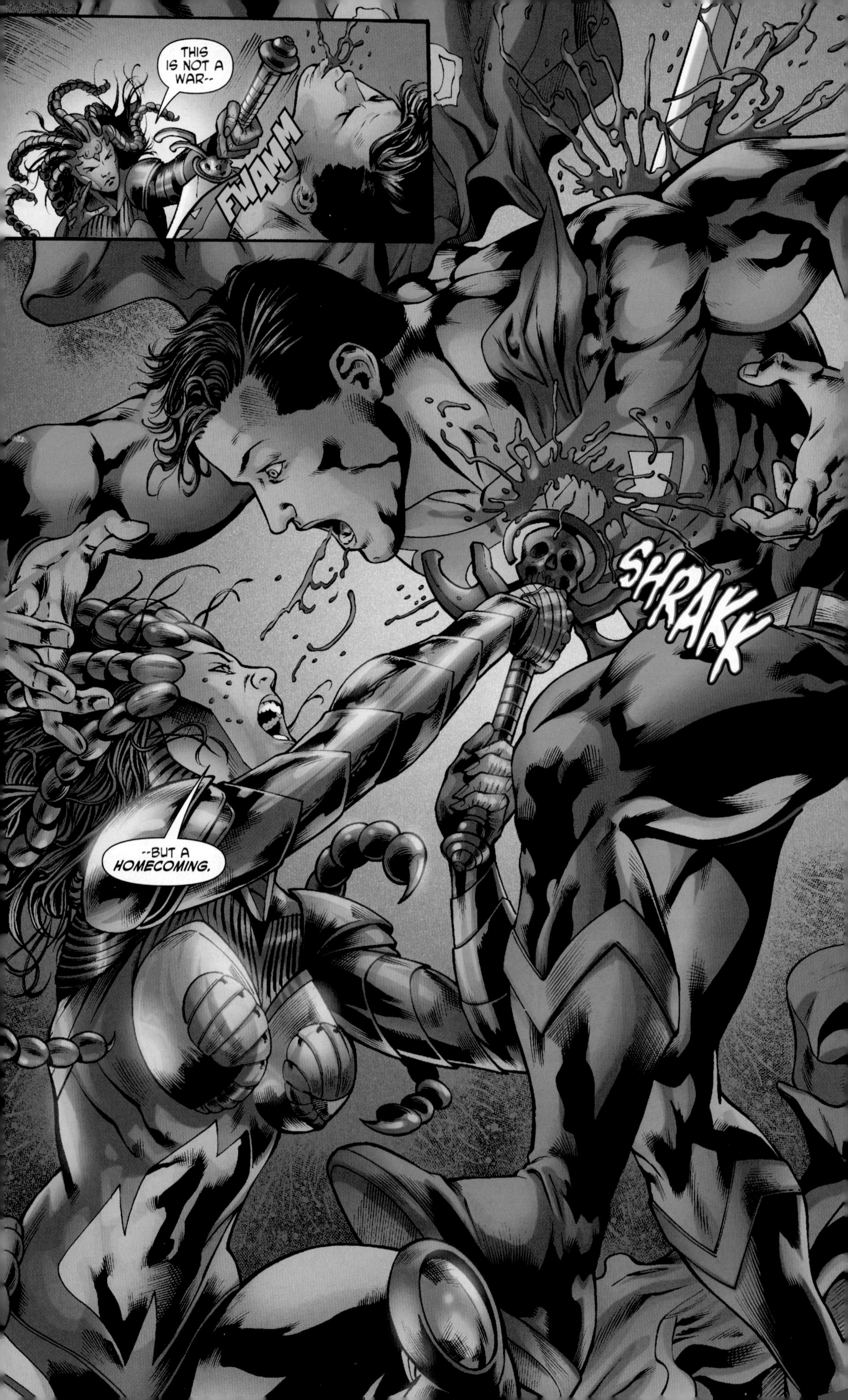
THIS IS NOT A WAR--
FWAMM
SHRAKK
--BUT A HOMECOMING.

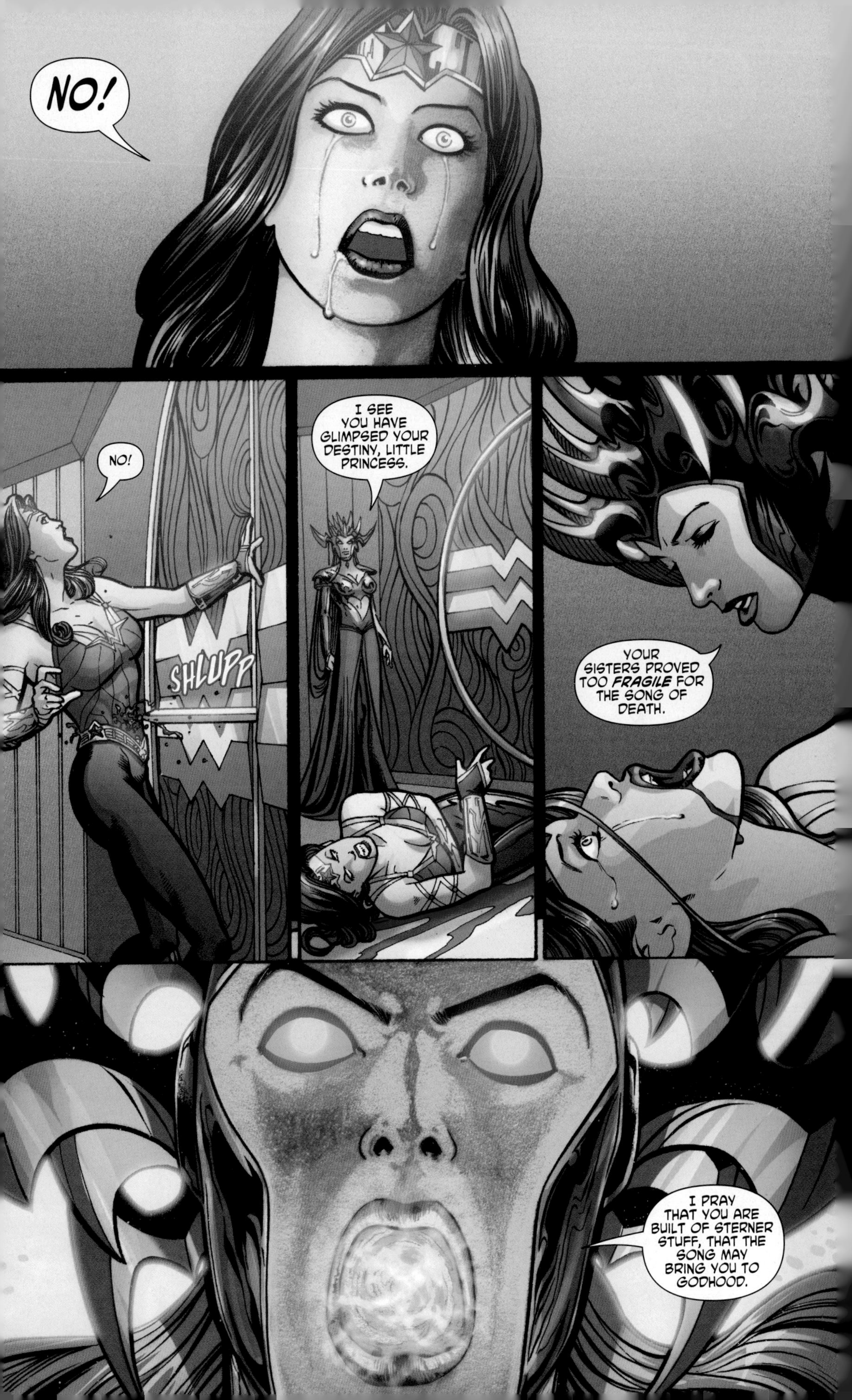
NO!
NO!
SHLUPP
I SEE YOU HAVE GLIMPSED YOUR DESTINY, LITTLE PRINCESS.
YOUR SISTERS PROVED TOO FRAGILE FOR THE SONG OF DEATH.
I PRAY THAT YOU ARE BUILT OF STERNER STUFF, THAT THE SONG MAY BRING YOU TO GODHOOD.

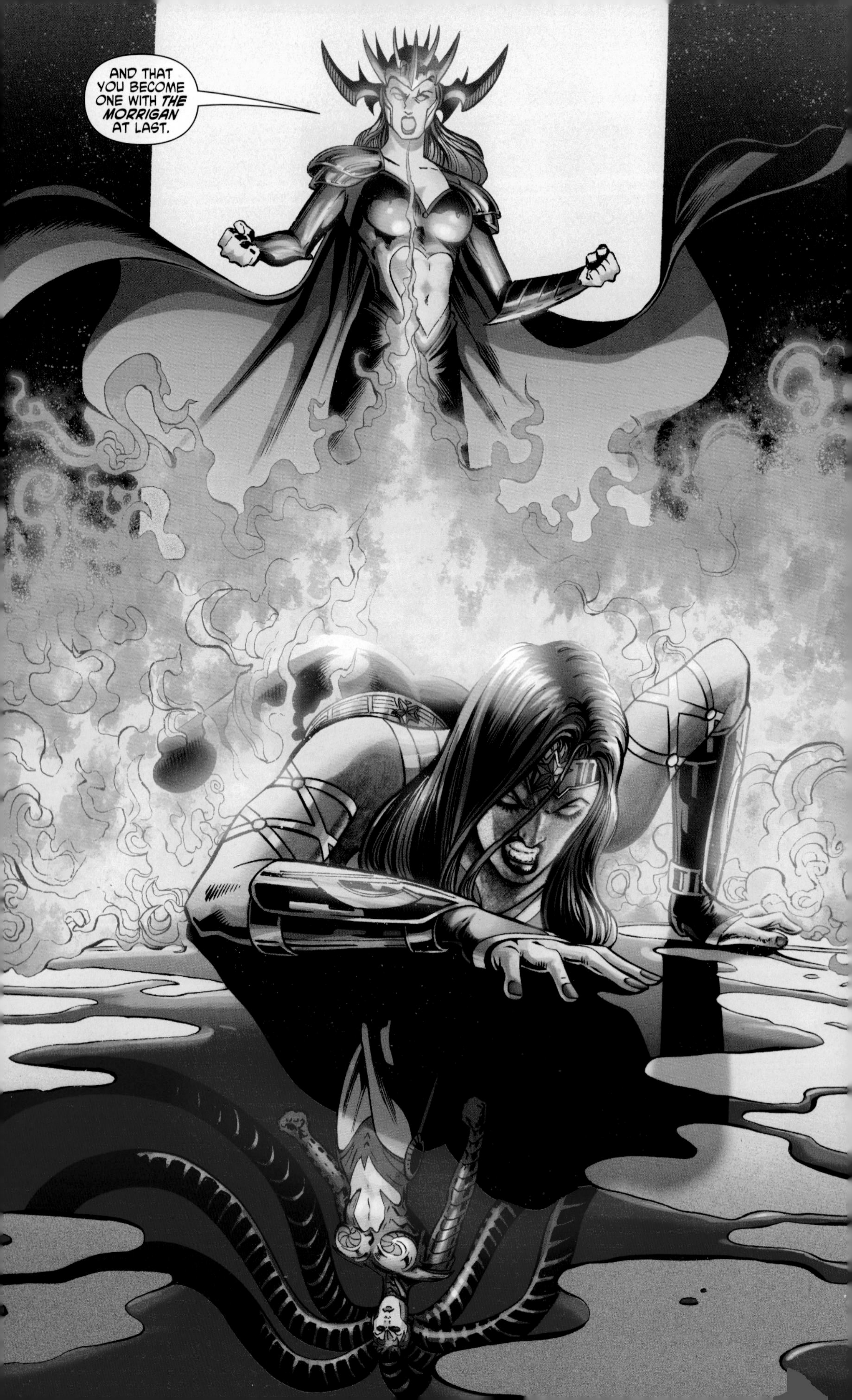
AND THAT YOU BECOME ONE WITH *THE MORRIGAN* AT LAST.

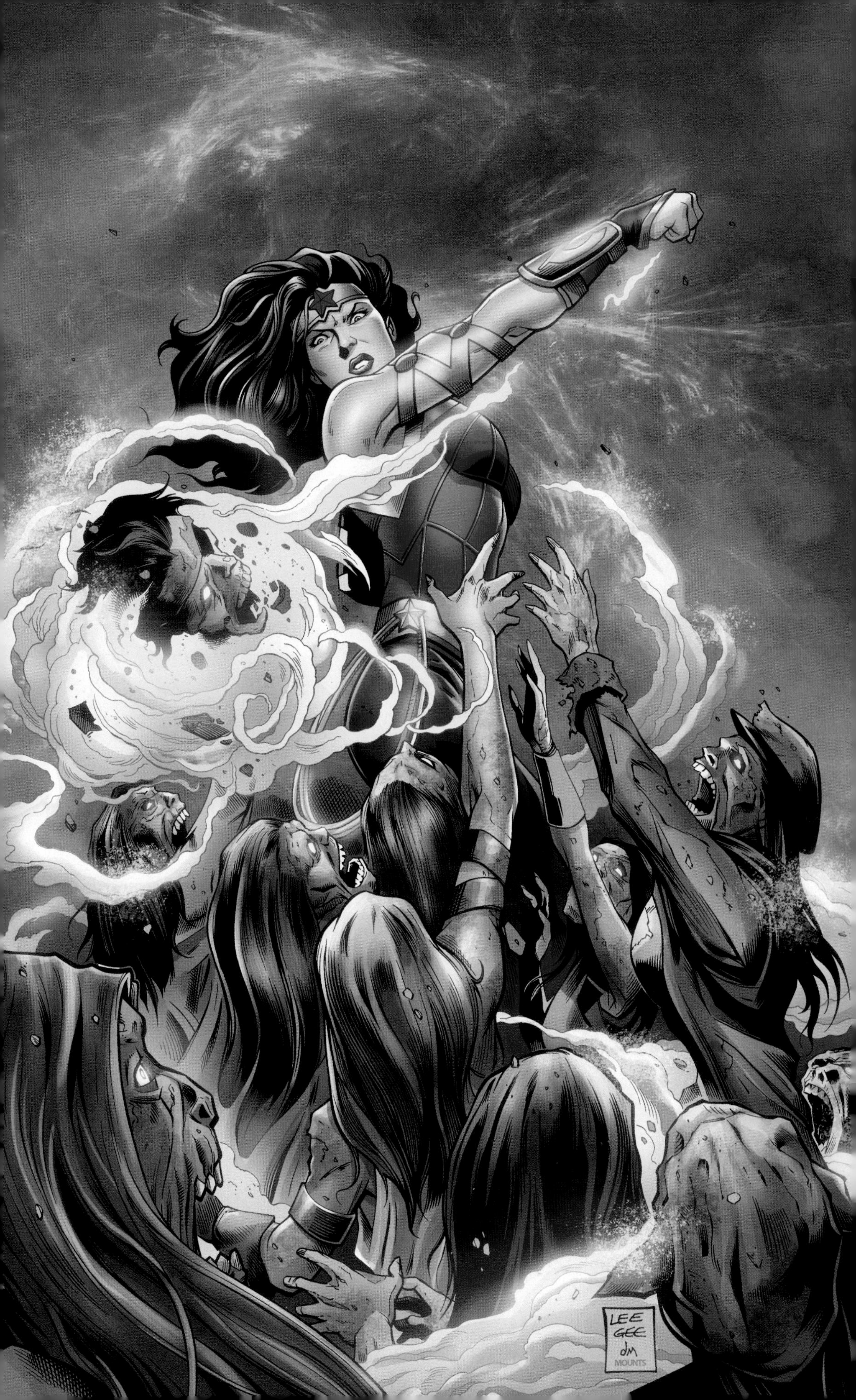
LEE
GEE
MOUNTS

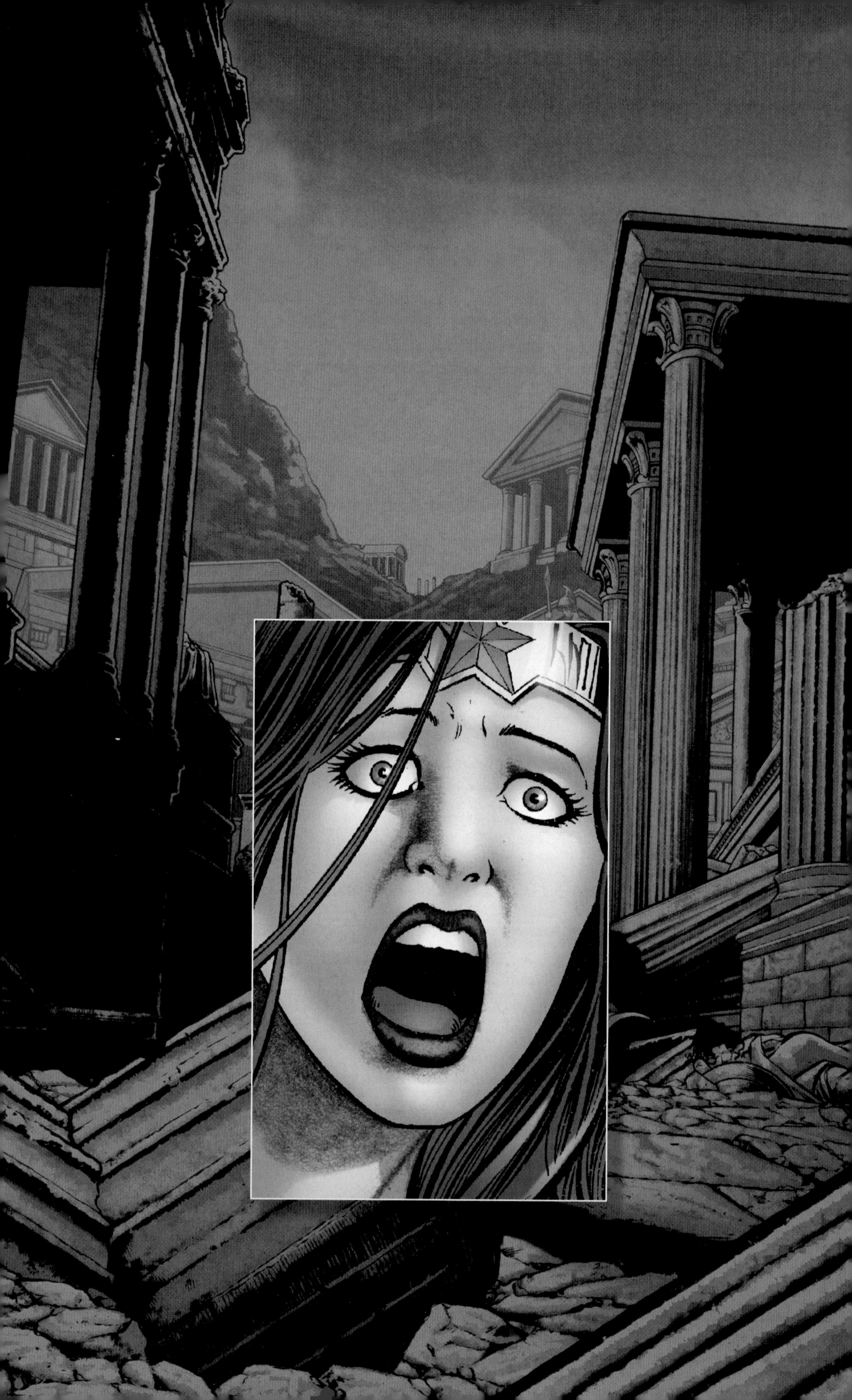

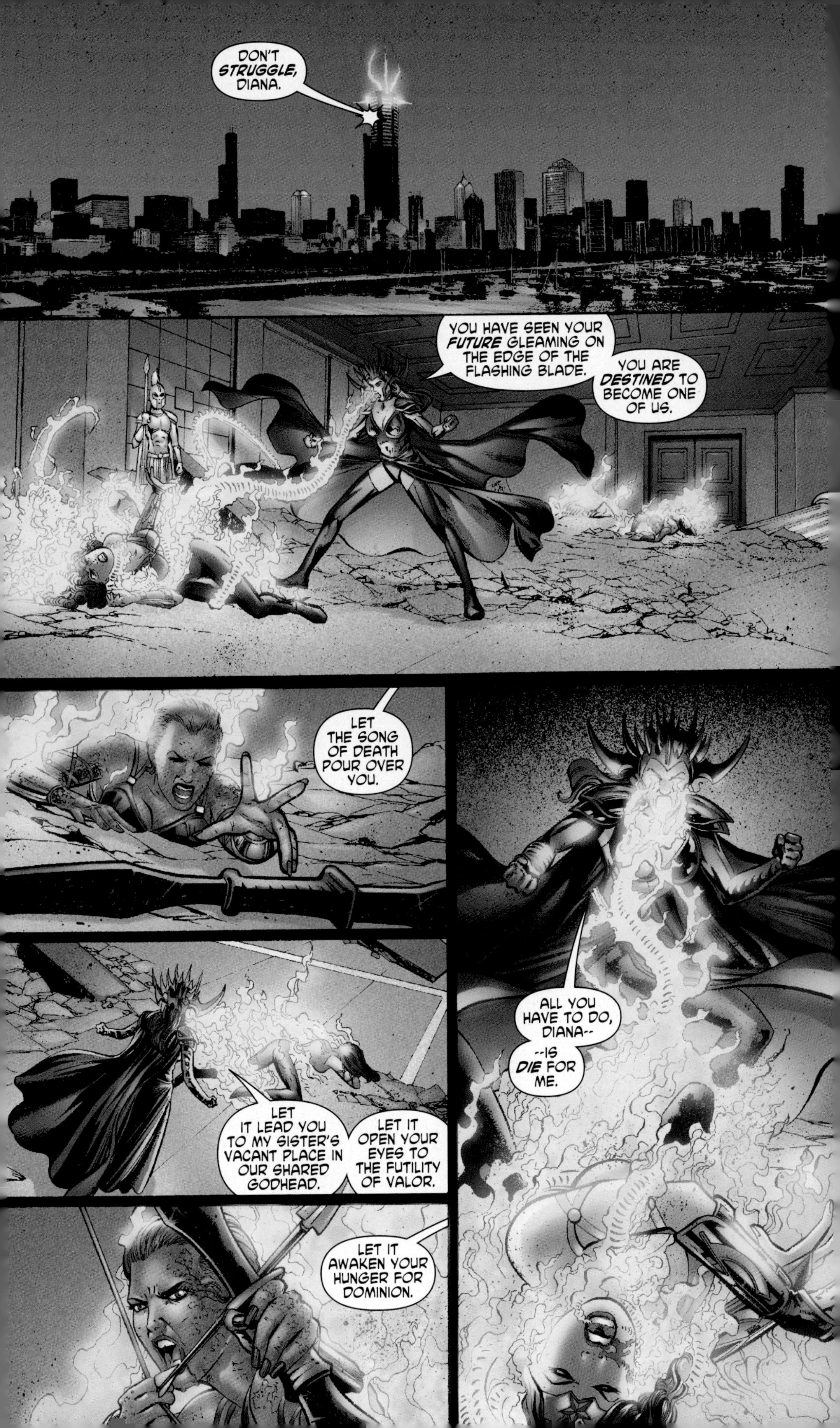
DON'T STRUGGLE, DIANA.
YOU HAVE SEEN YOUR FUTURE GLEAMING ON THE EDGE OF THE FLASHING BLADE.
YOU ARE DESTINED TO BECOME ONE OF US.
LET THE SONG OF DEATH POUR OVER YOU.
LET IT LEAD YOU TO MY SISTER'S VACANT PLACE IN OUR SHARED GODHEAD.
LET IT OPEN YOUR EYES TO THE FUTILITY OF VALOR.
LET IT AWAKEN YOUR HUNGER FOR DOMINION.
ALL YOU HAVE TO DO, DIANA--
--IS DIE FOR ME.

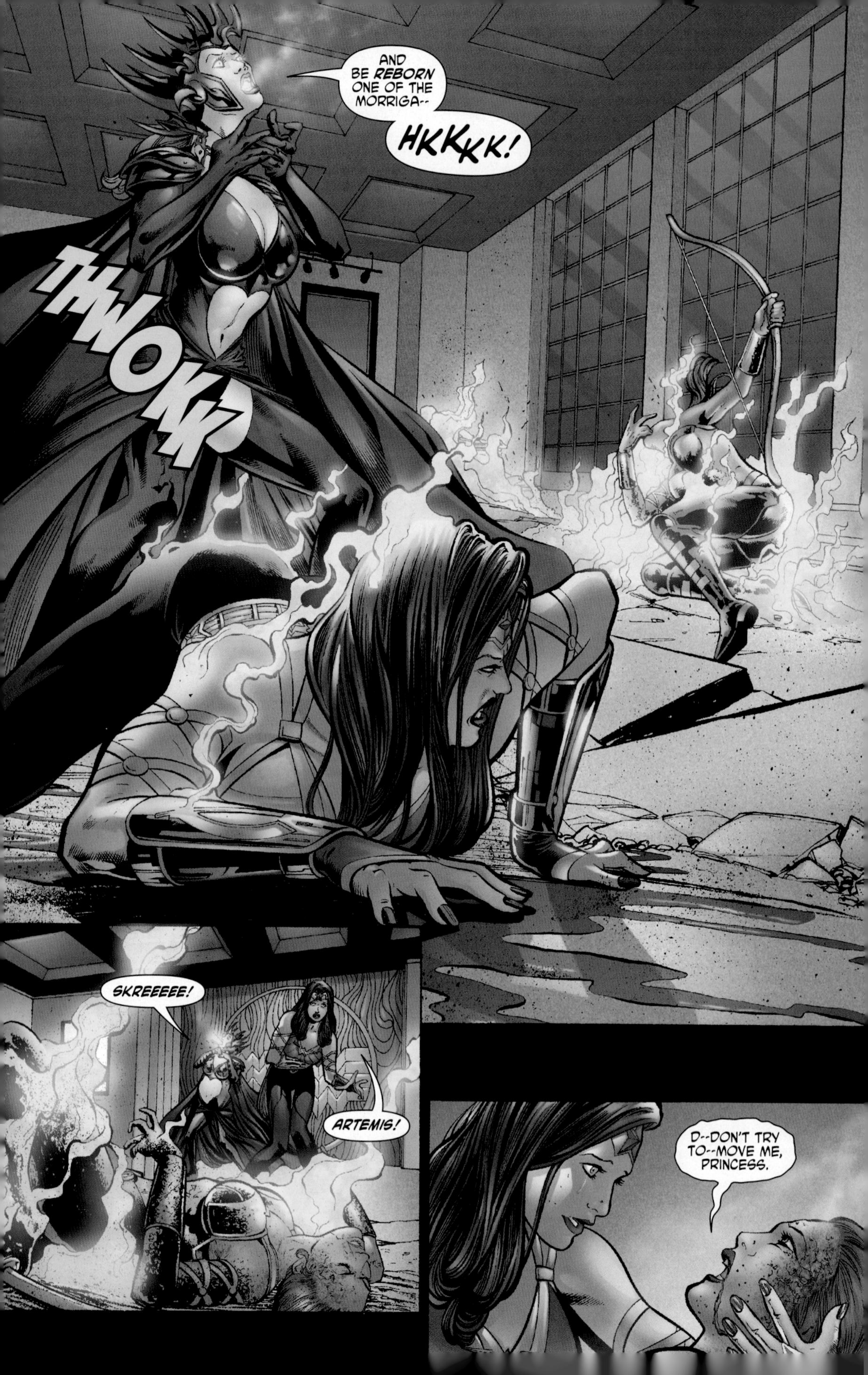

AND BE REBORN ONE OF THE MORRIGA--
HKKKK!
THWOKK
SKREEEEE!
ARTEMIS!
D--DON'T TRY TO--MOVE ME, PRINCESS.

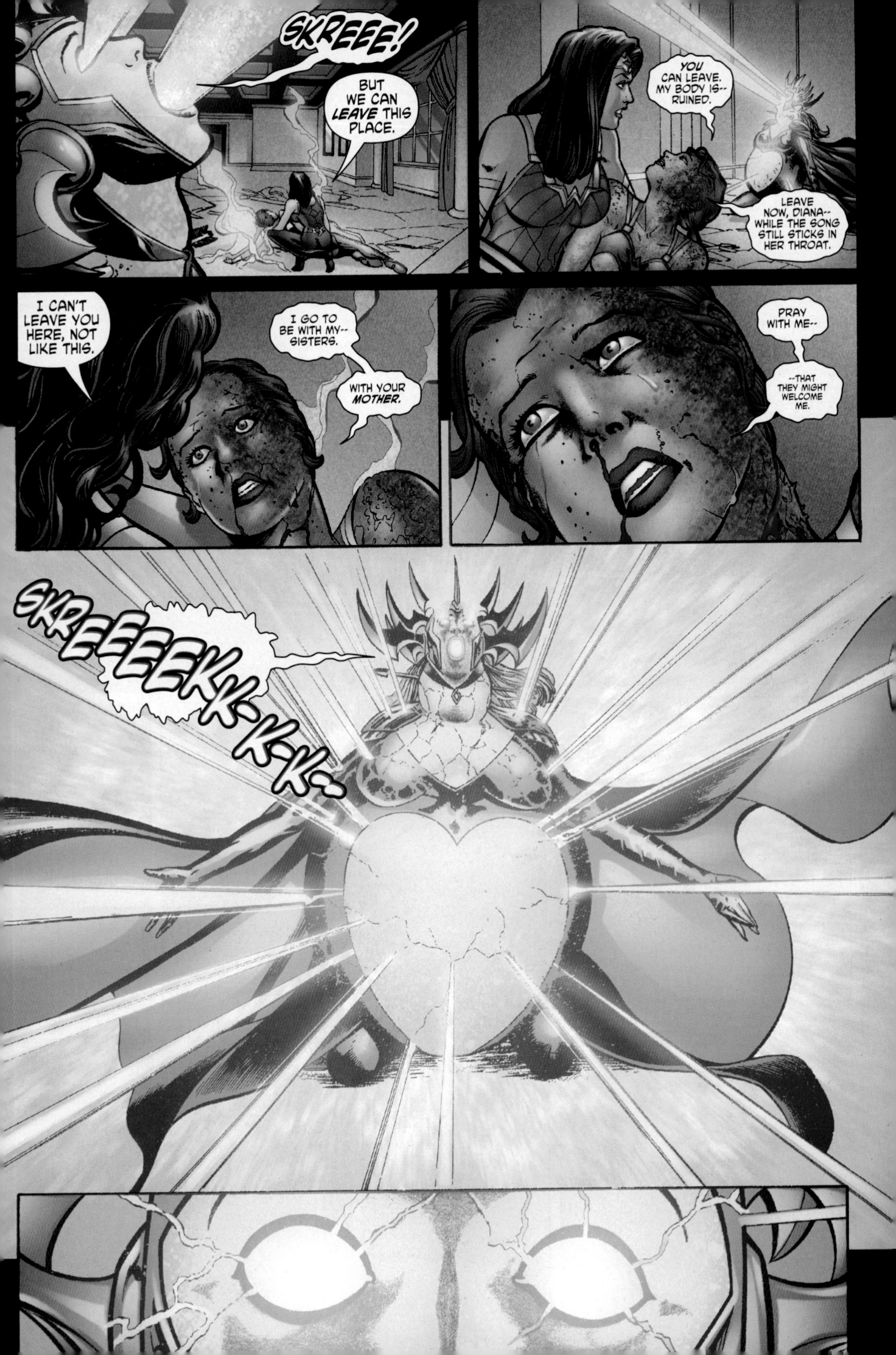
SKREEE!
BUT WE CAN LEAVE THIS PLACE.
YOU CAN LEAVE. MY BODY IS-- RUINED.
LEAVE NOW, DIANA-- WHILE THE SONG STILL STICKS IN HER THROAT.
I CAN'T LEAVE YOU HERE, NOT LIKE THIS.
I GO TO BE WITH MY-- SISTERS.
WITH YOUR MOTHER.
PRAY WITH ME--
--THAT THEY MIGHT WELCOME ME.
SKREEEEKK-K-K--

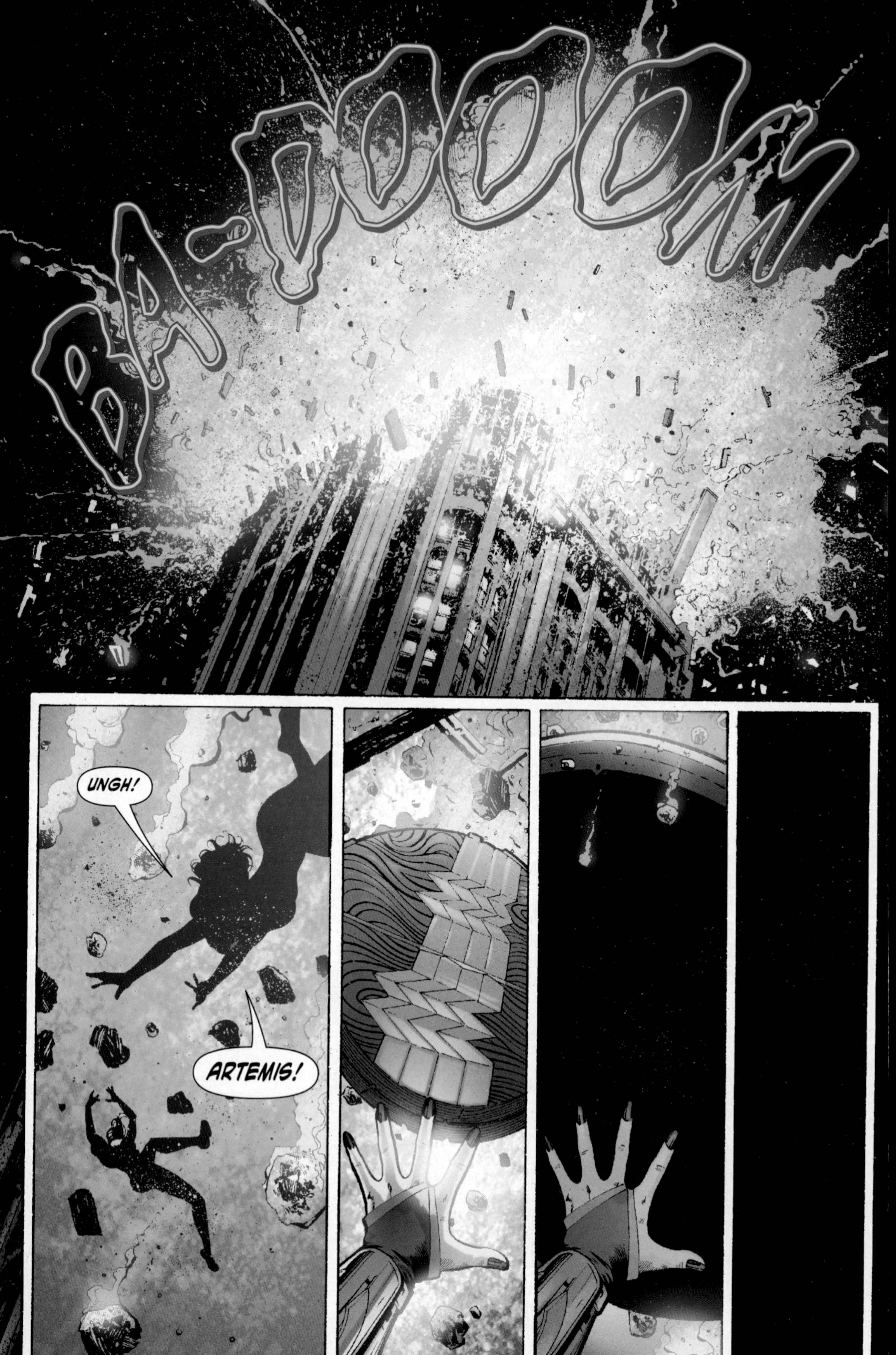
BA-DOOOM
UNGH!
ARTEMIS!

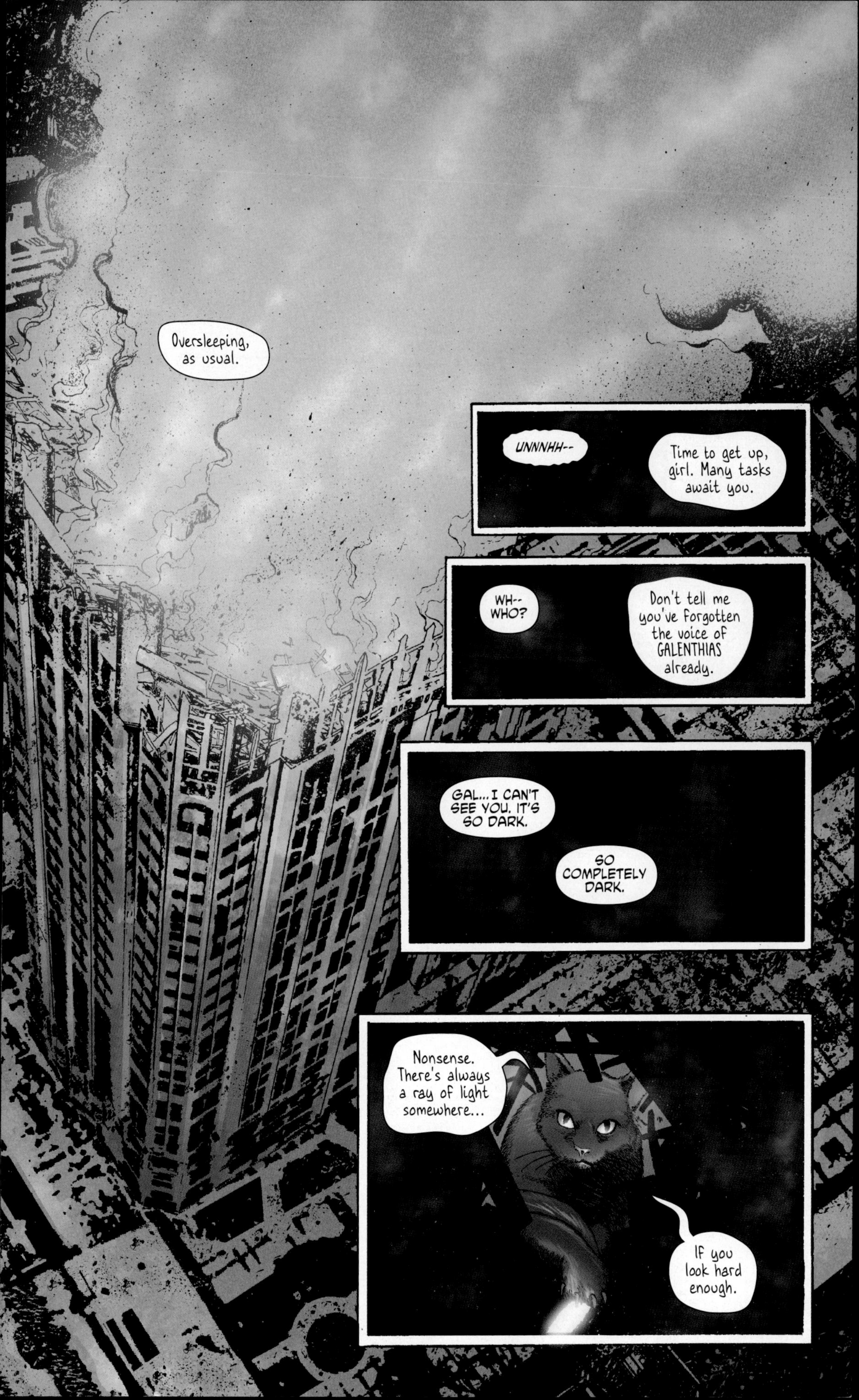
Oversleeping, as usual.
UNNNHH--
Time to get up, girl. Many tasks await you.
WH-- WHO?
Don't tell me you've forgotten the voice of GALENTHIAS already.
GAL... I CAN'T SEE YOU. IT'S SO DARK.
SO COMPLETELY DARK.
Nonsense. There's always a ray of light somewhere...
If you look hard enough.

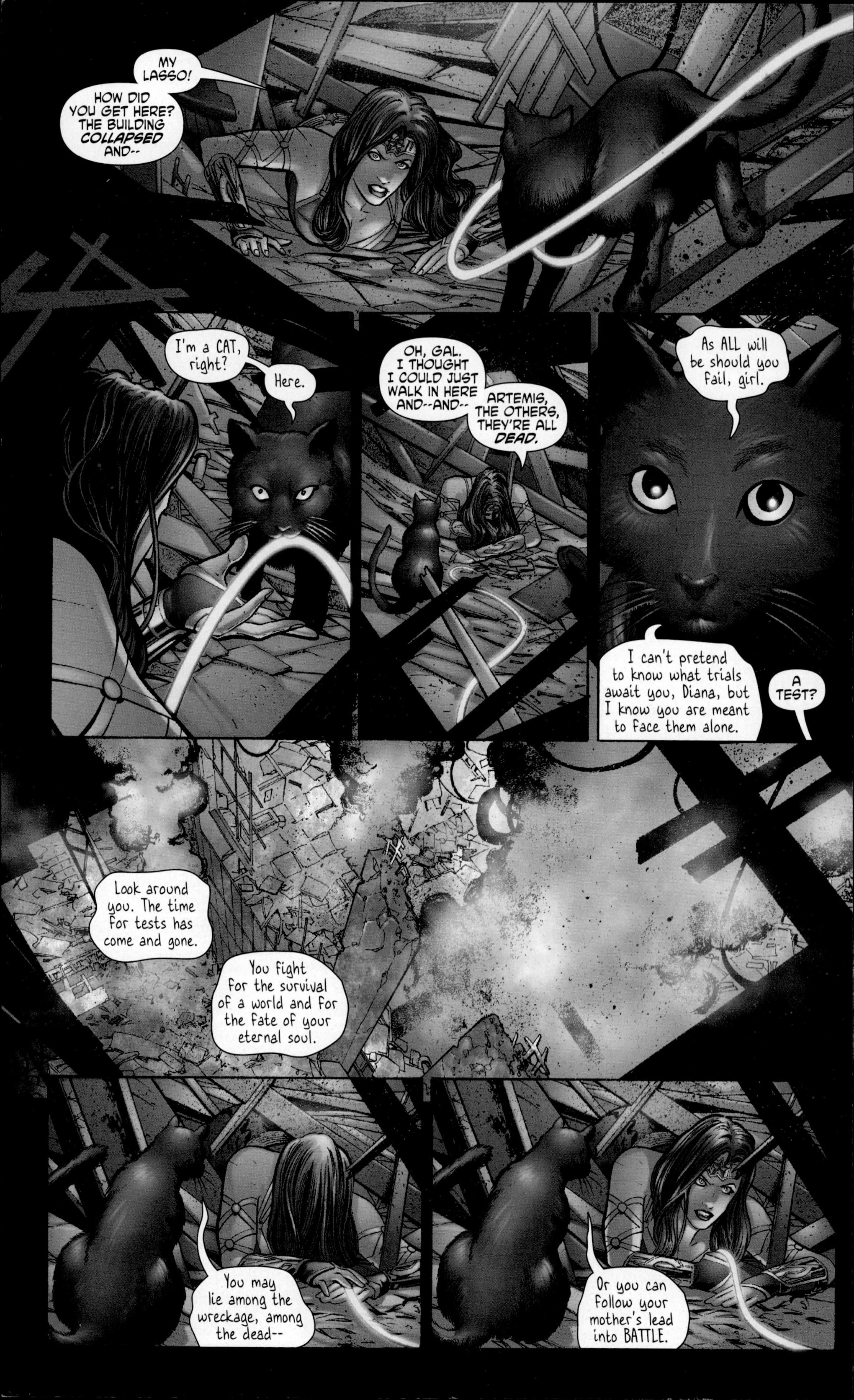
MY LASSO!
HOW DID YOU GET HERE? THE BUILDING *COLLAPSED* AND--
I'm a CAT, right?
Here.
OH, GAL. I THOUGHT I COULD JUST WALK IN HERE AND--AND--
ARTEMIS, THE OTHERS, THEY'RE ALL *DEAD.*
As ALL will be should you fail, girl.
I can't pretend to know what trials await you, Diana, but I know you are meant to face them alone.
A TEST?
Look around you. The time for tests has come and gone.
You fight for the survival of a world and for the fate of your eternal soul.
You may lie among the wreckage, among the dead--
Or you can follow your mother's lead into BATTLE.

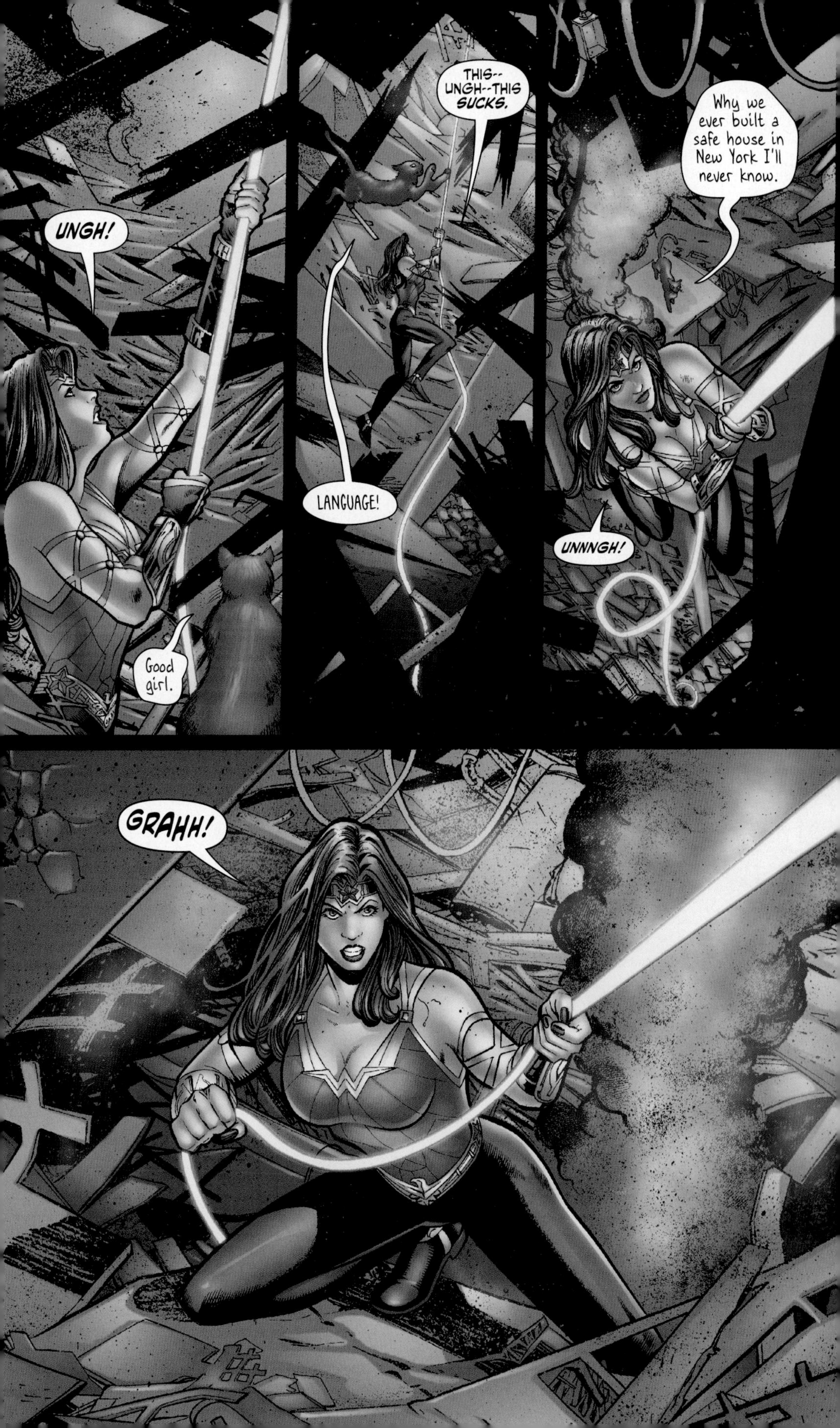
UNGH!
Good girl.
THIS-- UNGH--THIS SUCKS.
LANGUAGE!
Why we ever built a safe house in New York I'll never know.
UNNNGH!
GRAHH!

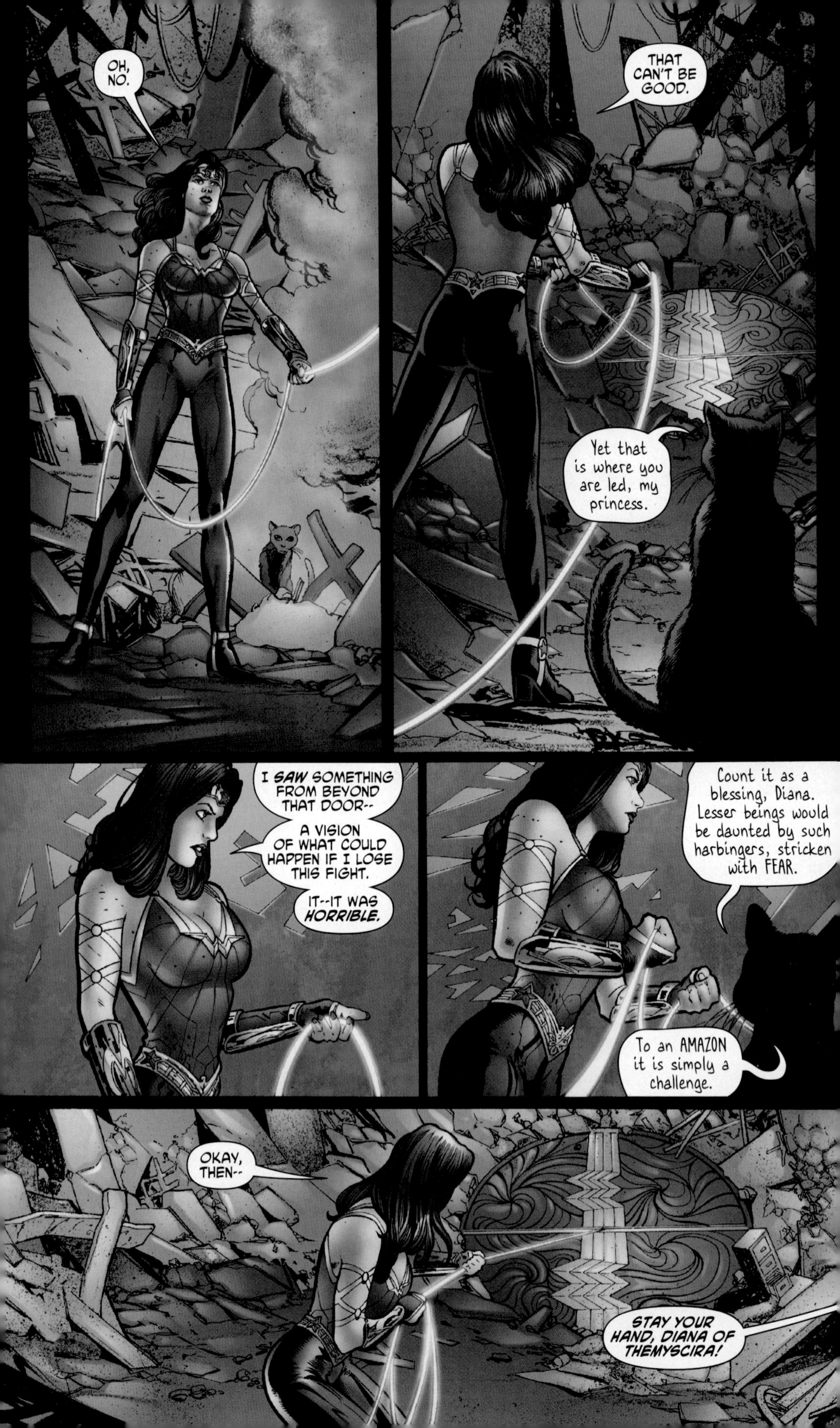
OH, NO.
THAT CAN'T BE GOOD.
Yet that is where you are led, my princess.
I SAW SOMETHING FROM BEYOND THAT DOOR--
A VISION OF WHAT COULD HAPPEN IF I LOSE THIS FIGHT.
IT--IT WAS HORRIBLE.
Count it as a blessing, Diana. Lesser beings would be daunted by such harbingers, stricken with FEAR.
To an AMAZON it is simply a challenge.
OKAY, THEN--
STAY YOUR HAND, DIANA OF THEMYSCIRA!

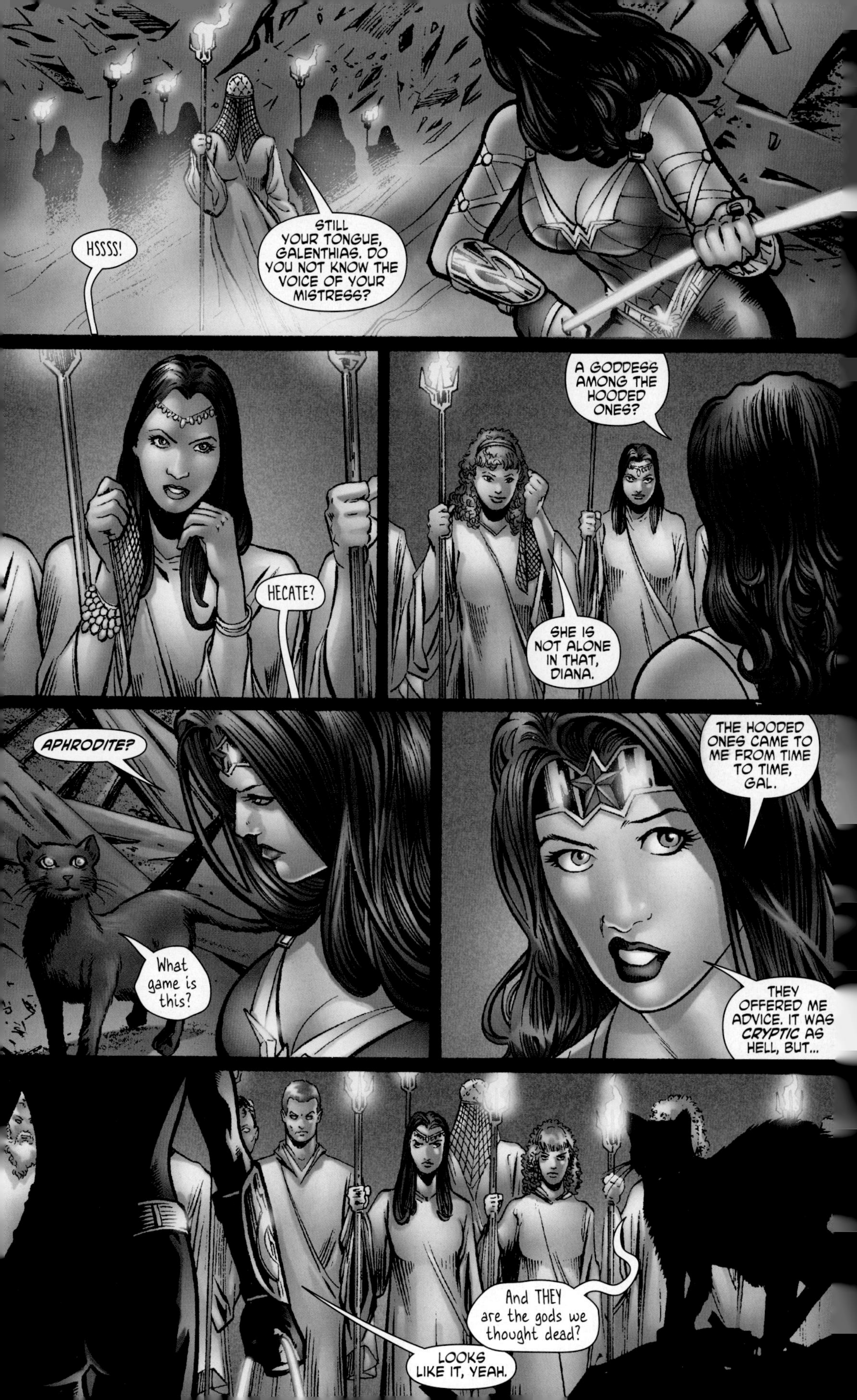
HSSSS!
STILL YOUR TONGUE, GALENTHIAS. DO YOU NOT KNOW THE VOICE OF YOUR MISTRESS?
HECATE?
A GODDESS AMONG THE HOODED ONES?
SHE IS NOT ALONE IN THAT, DIANA.
APHRODITE?
What game is this?
THE HOODED ONES CAME TO ME FROM TIME TO TIME, GAL.
THEY OFFERED ME ADVICE. IT WAS CRYPTIC AS HELL, BUT...
And THEY are the gods we thought dead?
LOOKS LIKE IT, YEAH.

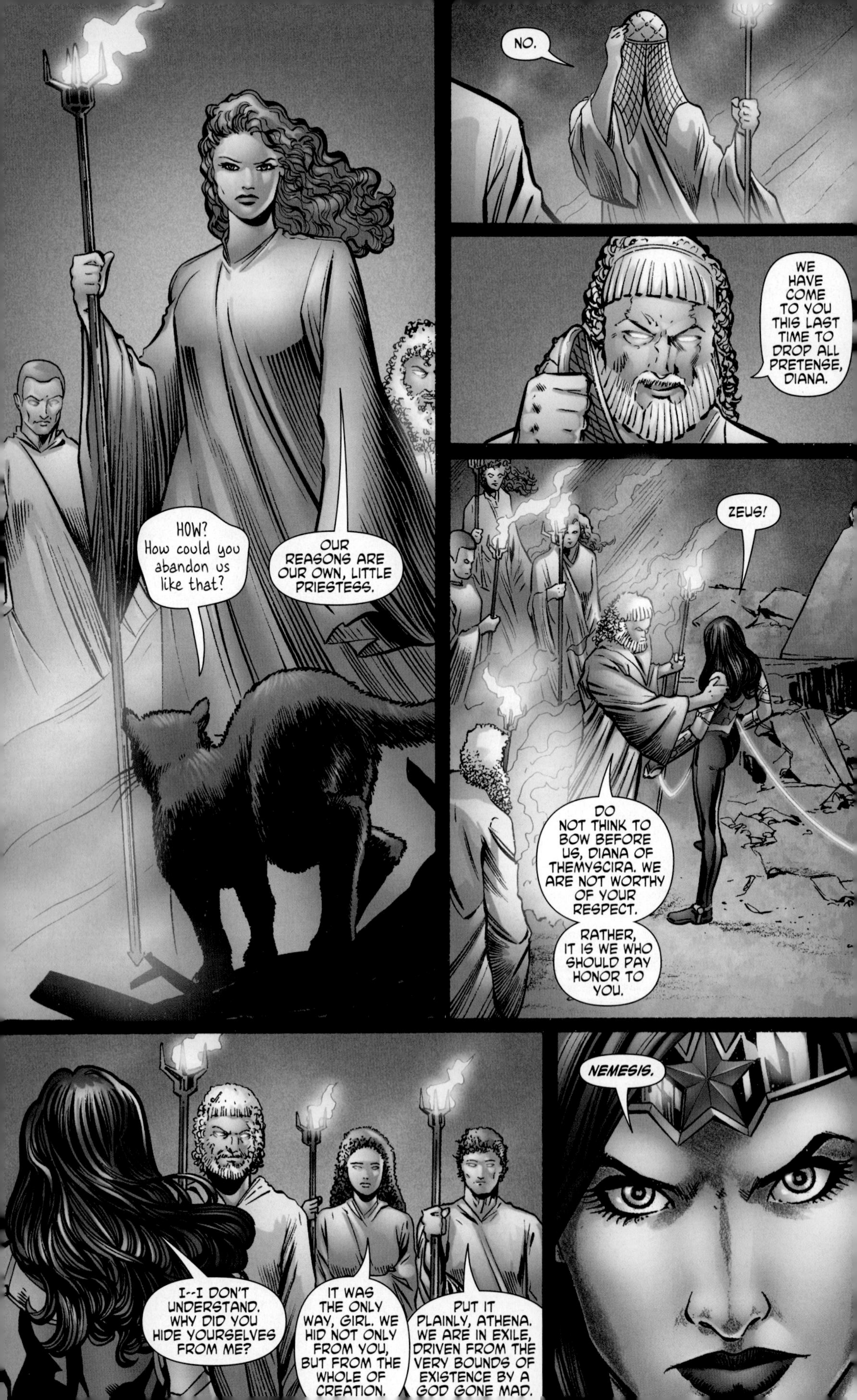
HOW? How could you abandon us like that?
OUR REASONS ARE OUR OWN, LITTLE PRIESTESS.
NO.
WE HAVE COME TO YOU THIS LAST TIME TO DROP ALL PRETENSE, DIANA.
ZEUS!
DO NOT THINK TO BOW BEFORE US, DIANA OF THEMYSCIRA. WE ARE NOT WORTHY OF YOUR RESPECT.
RATHER, IT IS WE WHO SHOULD PAY HONOR TO YOU.
I--I DON'T UNDERSTAND. WHY DID YOU HIDE YOURSELVES FROM ME?
IT WAS THE ONLY WAY, GIRL. WE HID NOT ONLY FROM YOU, BUT FROM THE WHOLE OF CREATION.
PUT IT PLAINLY, ATHENA. WE ARE IN EXILE, DRIVEN FROM THE VERY BOUNDS OF EXISTENCE BY A GOD GONE MAD.
NEMESIS.

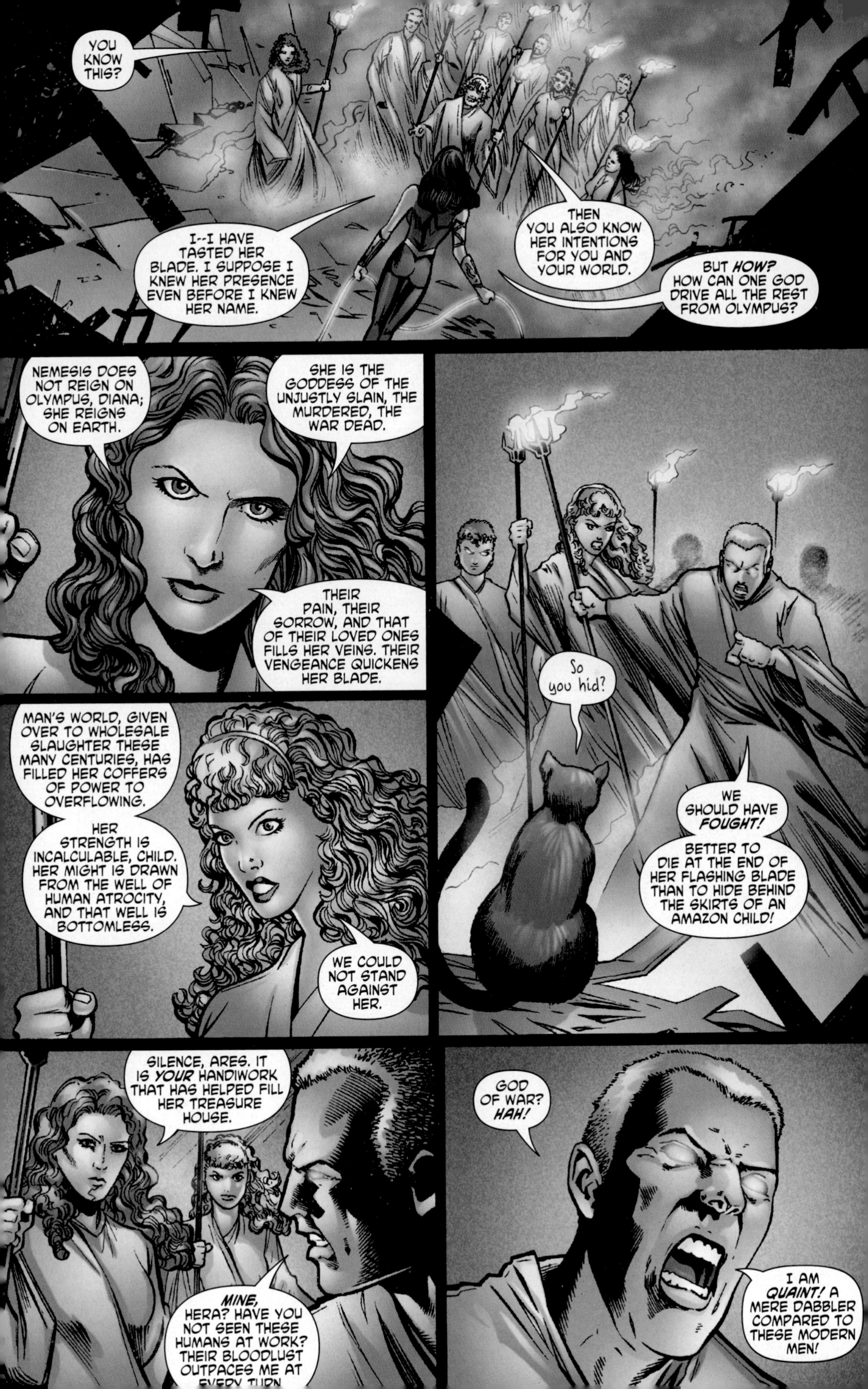
YOU KNOW THIS?
I--I HAVE TASTED HER BLADE. I SUPPOSE I KNEW HER PRESENCE EVEN BEFORE I KNEW HER NAME.
THEN YOU ALSO KNOW HER INTENTIONS FOR YOU AND YOUR WORLD.
BUT HOW? HOW CAN ONE GOD DRIVE ALL THE REST FROM OLYMPUS?
NEMESIS DOES NOT REIGN ON OLYMPUS, DIANA; SHE REIGNS ON EARTH.
SHE IS THE GODDESS OF THE UNJUSTLY SLAIN, THE MURDERED, THE WAR DEAD.
THEIR PAIN, THEIR SORROW, AND THAT OF THEIR LOVED ONES FILLS HER VEINS. THEIR VENGEANCE QUICKENS HER BLADE.
MAN'S WORLD, GIVEN OVER TO WHOLESALE SLAUGHTER THESE MANY CENTURIES, HAS FILLED HER COFFERS OF POWER TO OVERFLOWING.
HER STRENGTH IS INCALCULABLE, CHILD. HER MIGHT IS DRAWN FROM THE WELL OF HUMAN ATROCITY, AND THAT WELL IS BOTTOMLESS.
WE COULD NOT STAND AGAINST HER.
So you hid?
WE SHOULD HAVE FOUGHT!
BETTER TO DIE AT THE END OF HER FLASHING BLADE THAN TO HIDE BEHIND THE SKIRTS OF AN AMAZON CHILD!
SILENCE, ARES. IT IS YOUR HANDIWORK THAT HAS HELPED FILL HER TREASURE HOUSE.
MINE, HERA? HAVE YOU NOT SEEN THESE HUMANS AT WORK? THEIR BLOODLUST OUTPACES ME AT EVERY TURN
GOD OF WAR? HAH!
I AM QUAINT! A MERE DABBLER COMPARED TO THESE MODERN MEN!

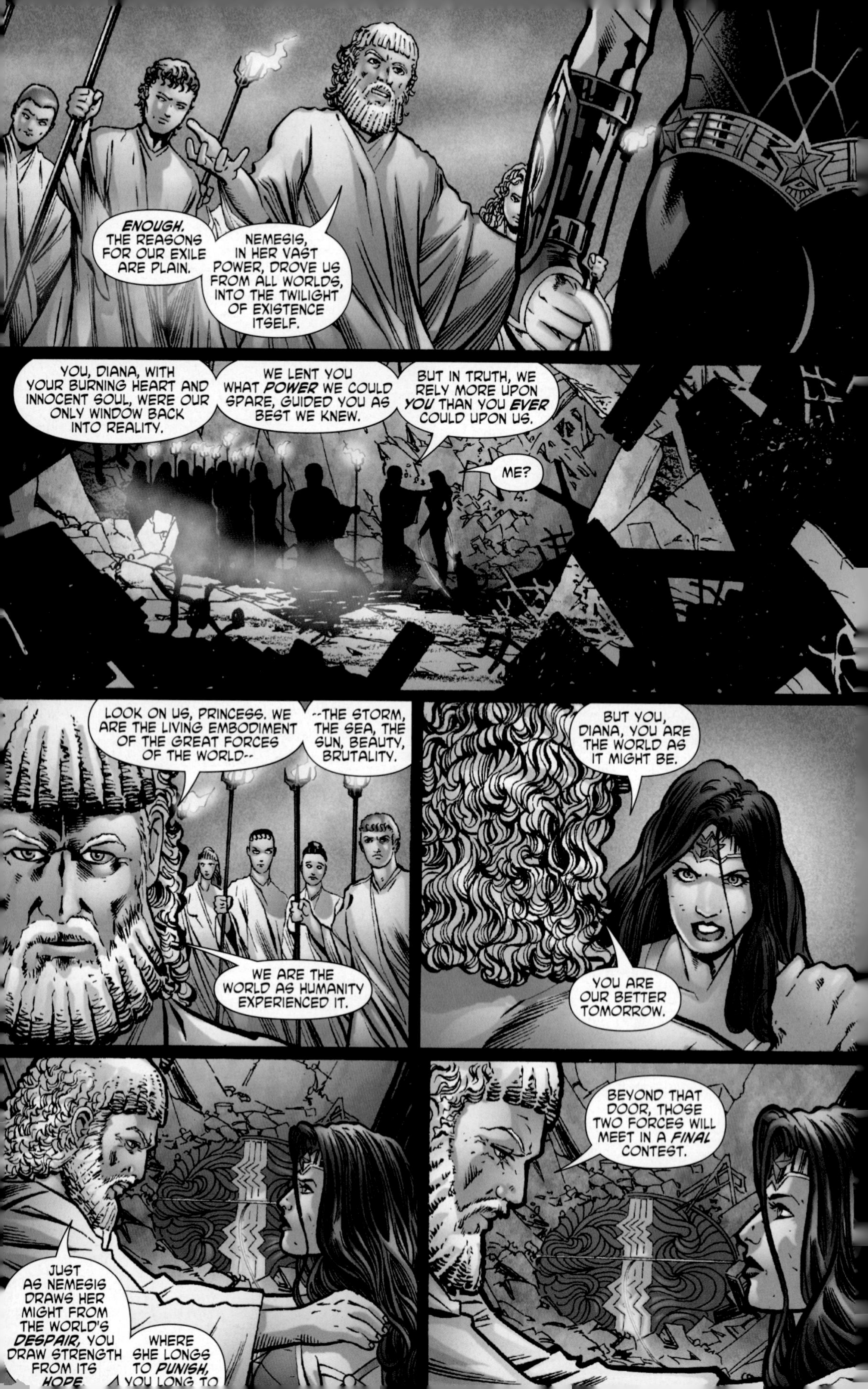
ENOUGH. THE REASONS FOR OUR EXILE ARE PLAIN.
NEMESIS, IN HER VAST POWER, DROVE US FROM ALL WORLDS, INTO THE TWILIGHT OF EXISTENCE ITSELF.
YOU, DIANA, WITH YOUR BURNING HEART AND INNOCENT SOUL, WERE OUR ONLY WINDOW BACK INTO REALITY.
WE LENT YOU WHAT POWER WE COULD SPARE, GUIDED YOU AS BEST WE KNEW.
BUT IN TRUTH, WE RELY MORE UPON YOU THAN YOU EVER COULD UPON US.
ME?
LOOK ON US, PRINCESS. WE ARE THE LIVING EMBODIMENT OF THE GREAT FORCES OF THE WORLD--
--THE STORM, THE SEA, THE SUN, BEAUTY, BRUTALITY.
WE ARE THE WORLD AS HUMANITY EXPERIENCED IT.
BUT YOU, DIANA, YOU ARE THE WORLD AS IT MIGHT BE.
YOU ARE OUR BETTER TOMORROW.
JUST AS NEMESIS DRAWS HER MIGHT FROM THE WORLD'S DESPAIR, YOU DRAW STRENGTH FROM ITS HOPE.
WHERE SHE LONGS TO PUNISH, YOU LONG TO
BEYOND THAT DOOR, THOSE TWO FORCES WILL MEET IN A FINAL CONTEST.

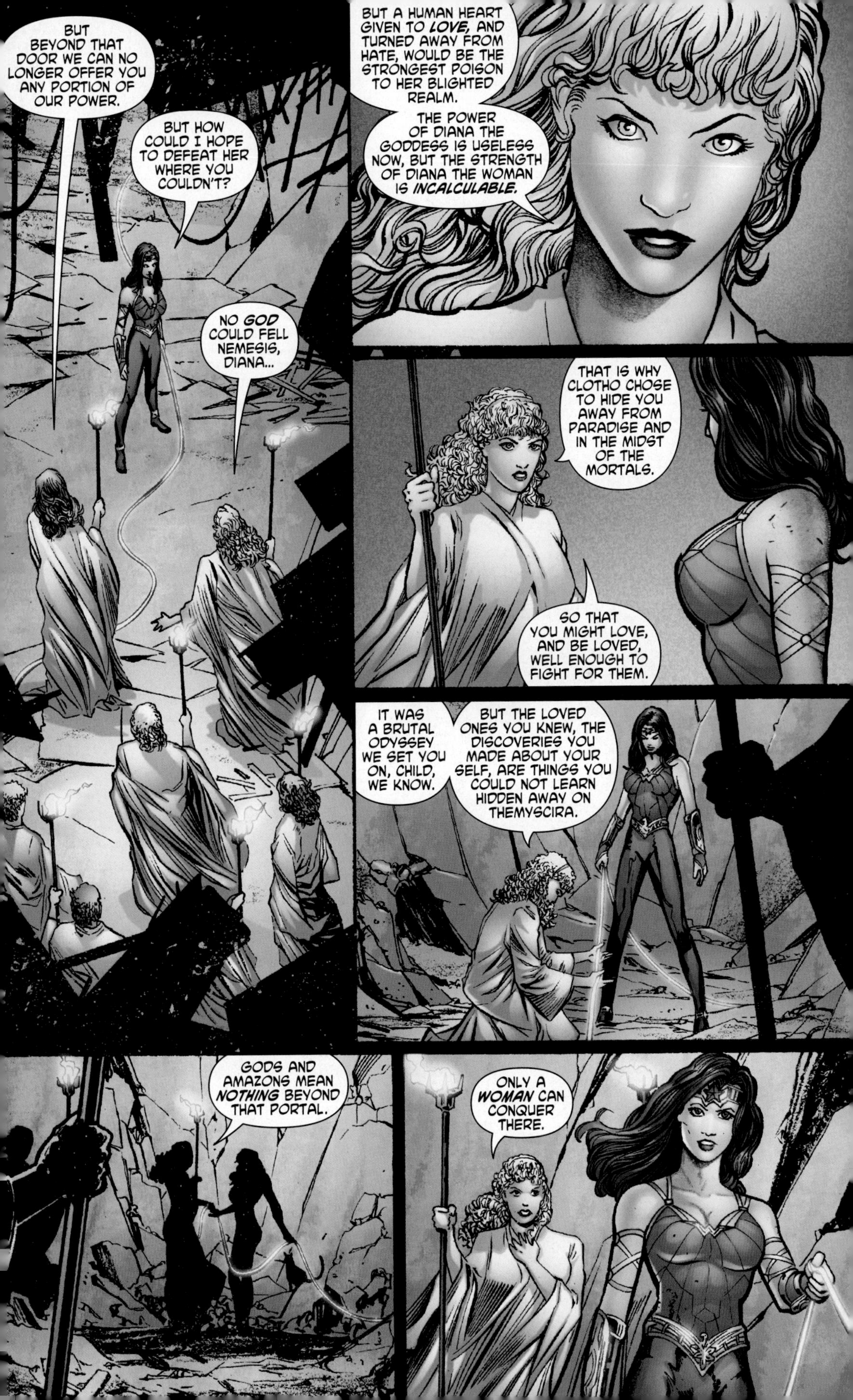
BUT BEYOND THAT DOOR WE CAN NO LONGER OFFER YOU ANY PORTION OF OUR POWER.
BUT HOW COULD I HOPE TO DEFEAT HER WHERE YOU COULDN'T?
NO GOD COULD FELL NEMESIS, DIANA...
BUT A HUMAN HEART GIVEN TO LOVE, AND TURNED AWAY FROM HATE, WOULD BE THE STRONGEST POISON TO HER BLIGHTED REALM.
THE POWER OF DIANA THE GODDESS IS USELESS NOW, BUT THE STRENGTH OF DIANA THE WOMAN IS INCALCULABLE.
THAT IS WHY CLOTHO CHOSE TO HIDE YOU AWAY FROM PARADISE AND IN THE MIDST OF THE MORTALS.
SO THAT YOU MIGHT LOVE, AND BE LOVED, WELL ENOUGH TO FIGHT FOR THEM.
IT WAS A BRUTAL ODYSSEY WE SET YOU ON, CHILD, WE KNOW.
BUT THE LOVED ONES YOU KNEW, THE DISCOVERIES YOU MADE ABOUT YOUR SELF, ARE THINGS YOU COULD NOT LEARN HIDDEN AWAY ON THEMYSCIRA.
GODS AND AMAZONS MEAN NOTHING BEYOND THAT PORTAL.
ONLY A WOMAN CAN CONQUER THERE.

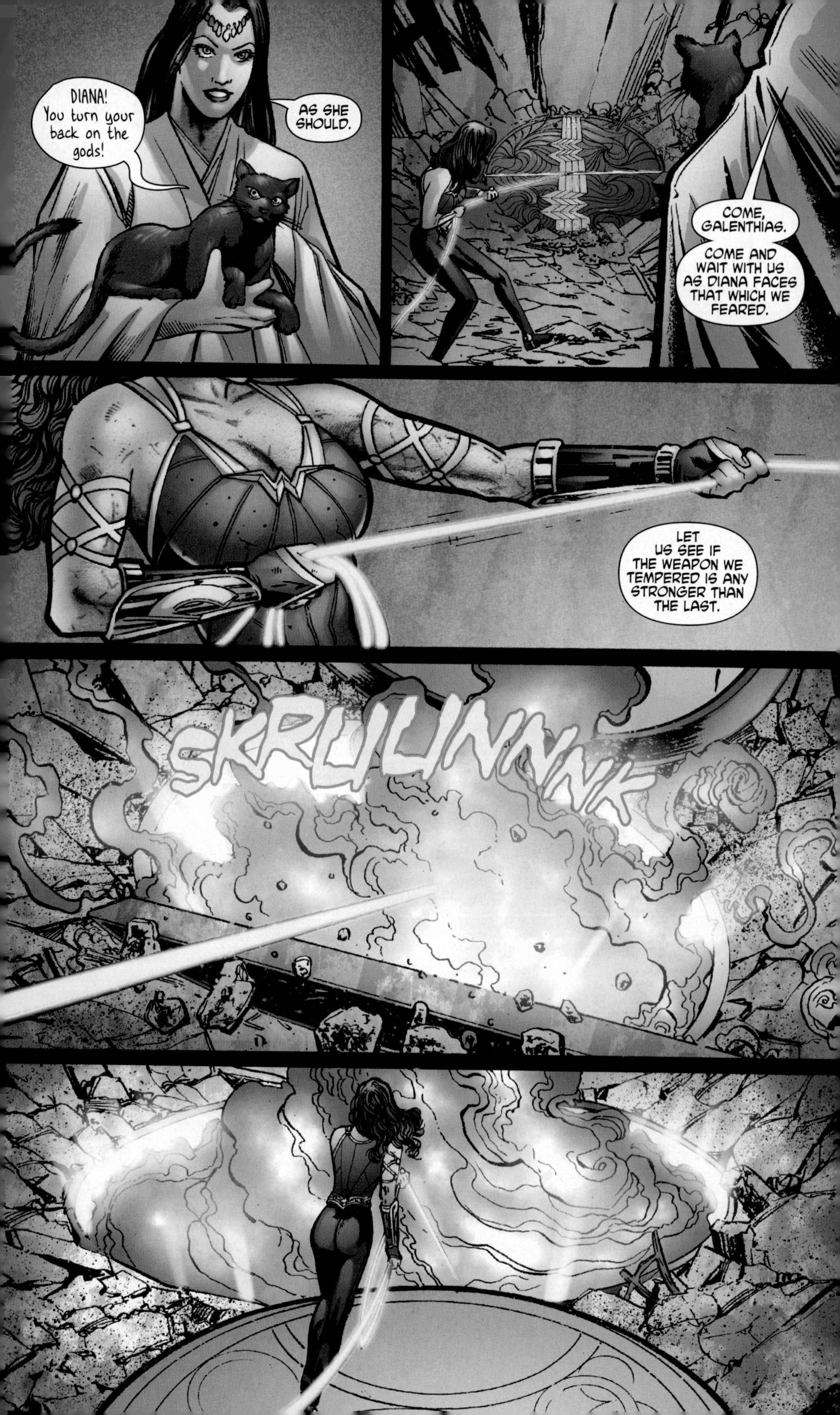
DIANA! You turn your back on the gods!
AS SHE SHOULD.
COME, GALENTHIAS.
COME AND WAIT WITH US AS DIANA FACES THAT WHICH WE FEARED.
LET US SEE IF THE WEAPON WE TEMPERED IS ANY STRONGER THAN THE LAST.
SKRUUNNNK

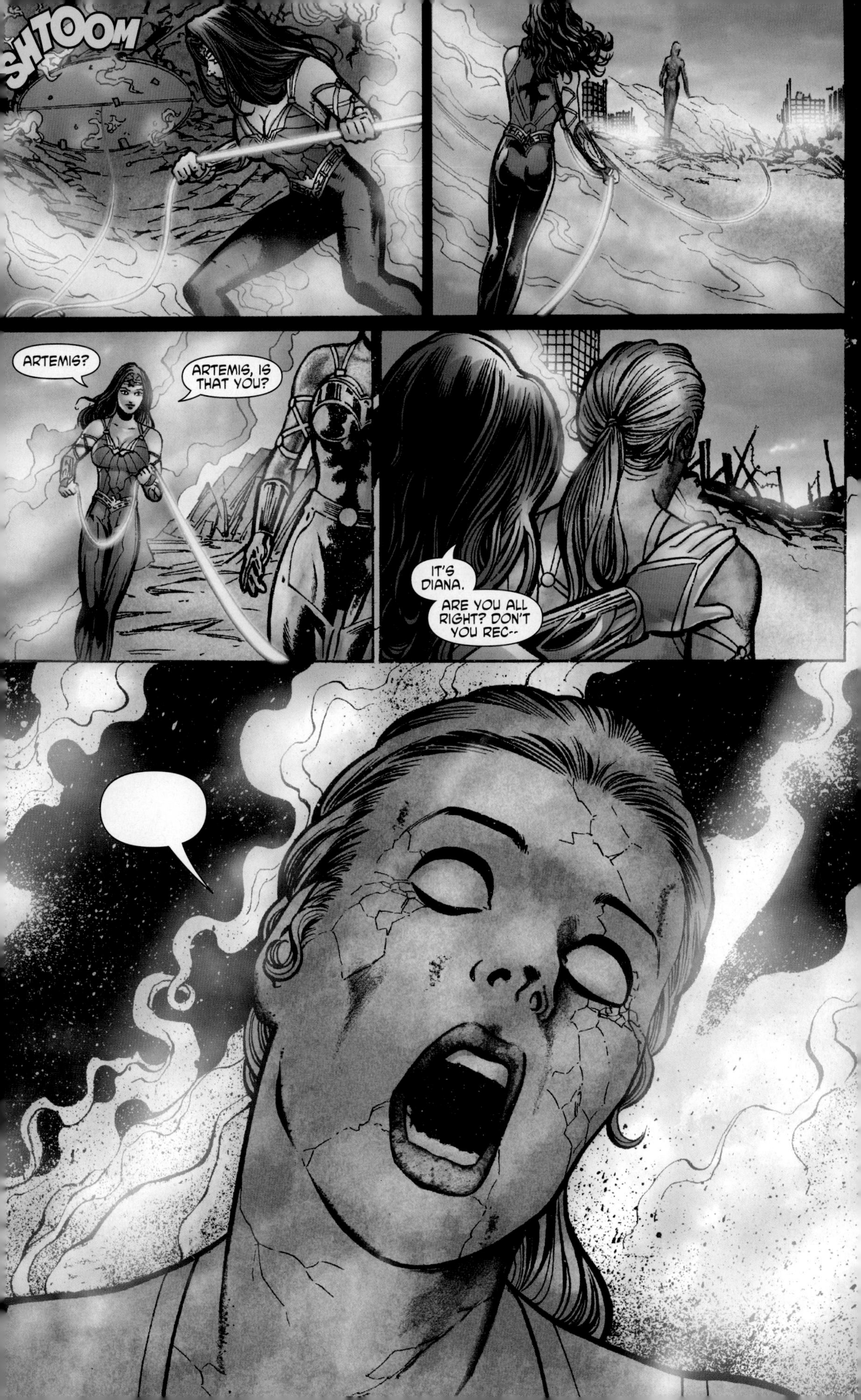
SHTOOM
ARTEMIS?
ARTEMIS, IS THAT YOU?
IT'S DIANA.
ARE YOU ALL RIGHT? DON'T YOU REC--

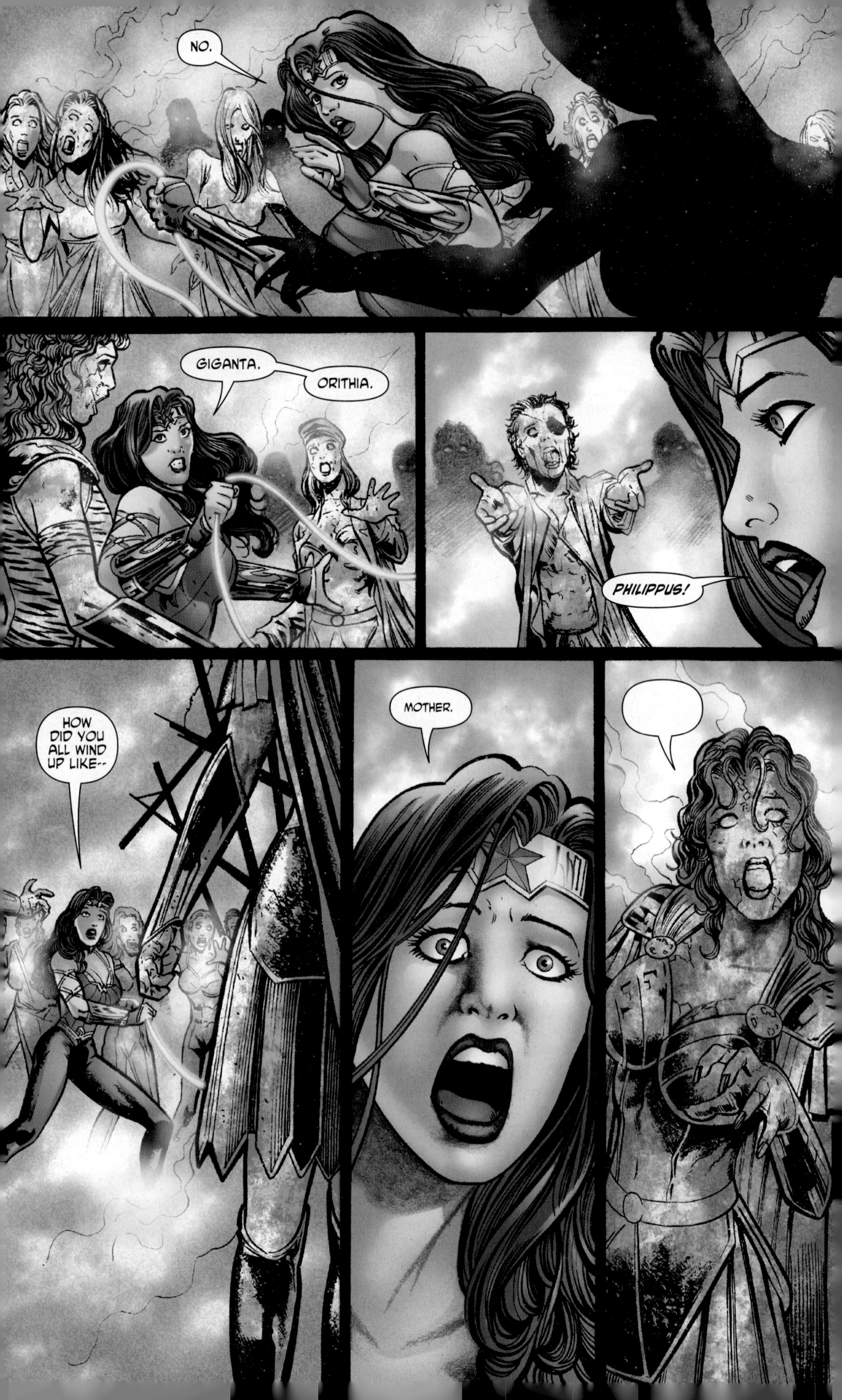

NO.
GIGANTA.
ORITHIA.
PHILIPPUS!
HOW DID YOU ALL WIND UP LIKE--
MOTHER.

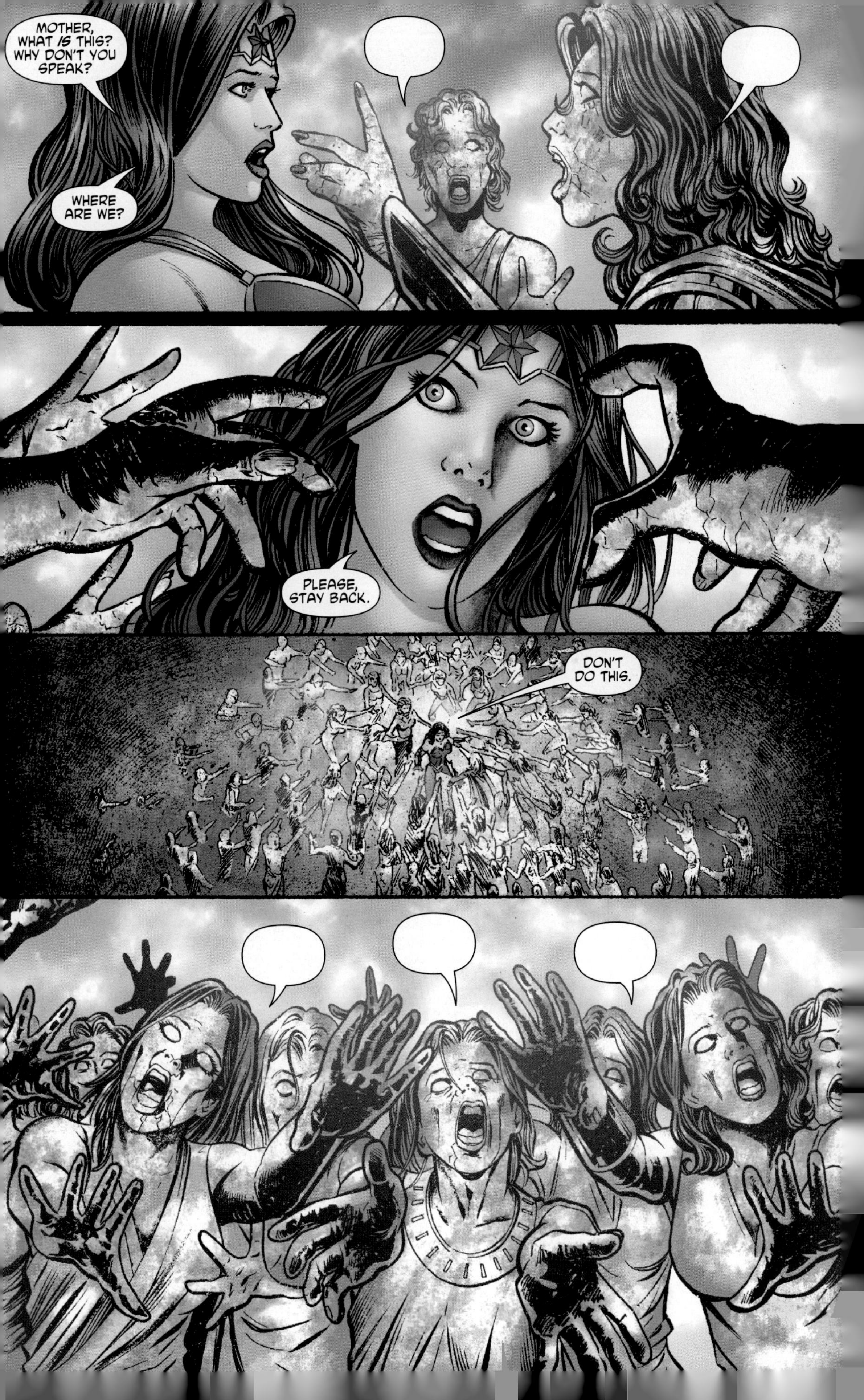

MOTHER, WHAT *IS* THIS? WHY DON'T YOU SPEAK?
WHERE ARE WE?
PLEASE, STAY BACK.
DON'T DO THIS.

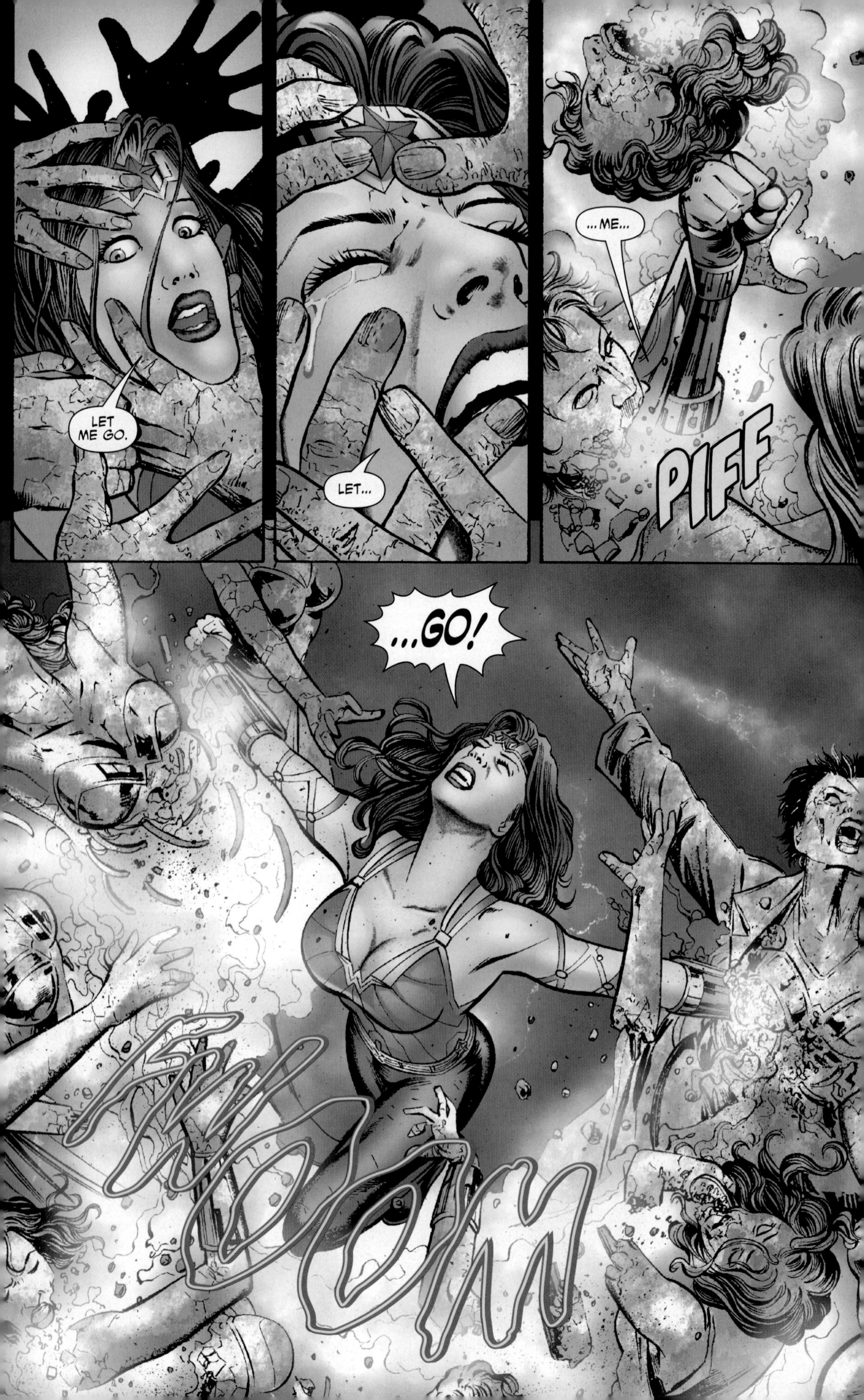

LET ME GO.
LET...
...ME...
PIFF
...GO!

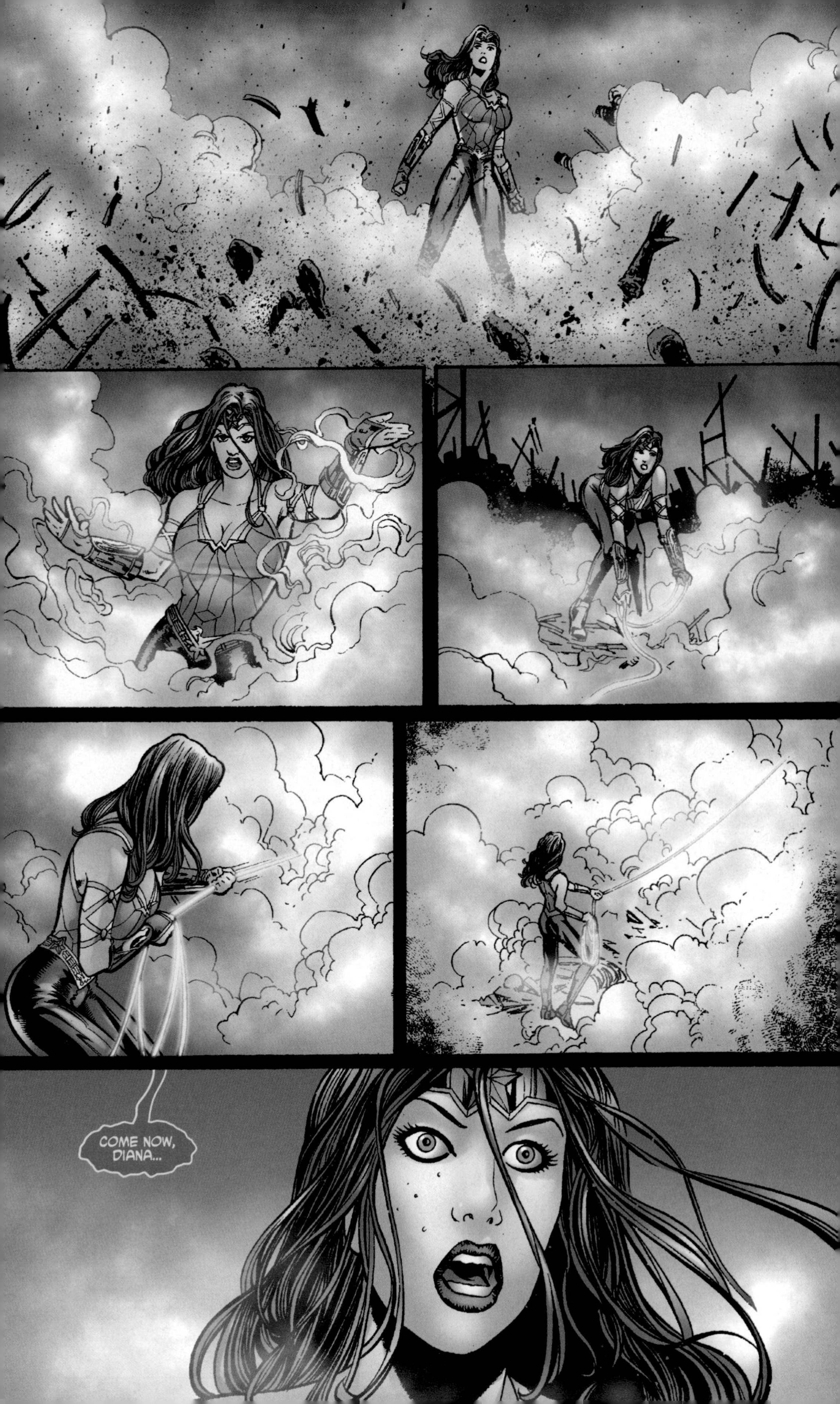
COME NOW, DIANA...

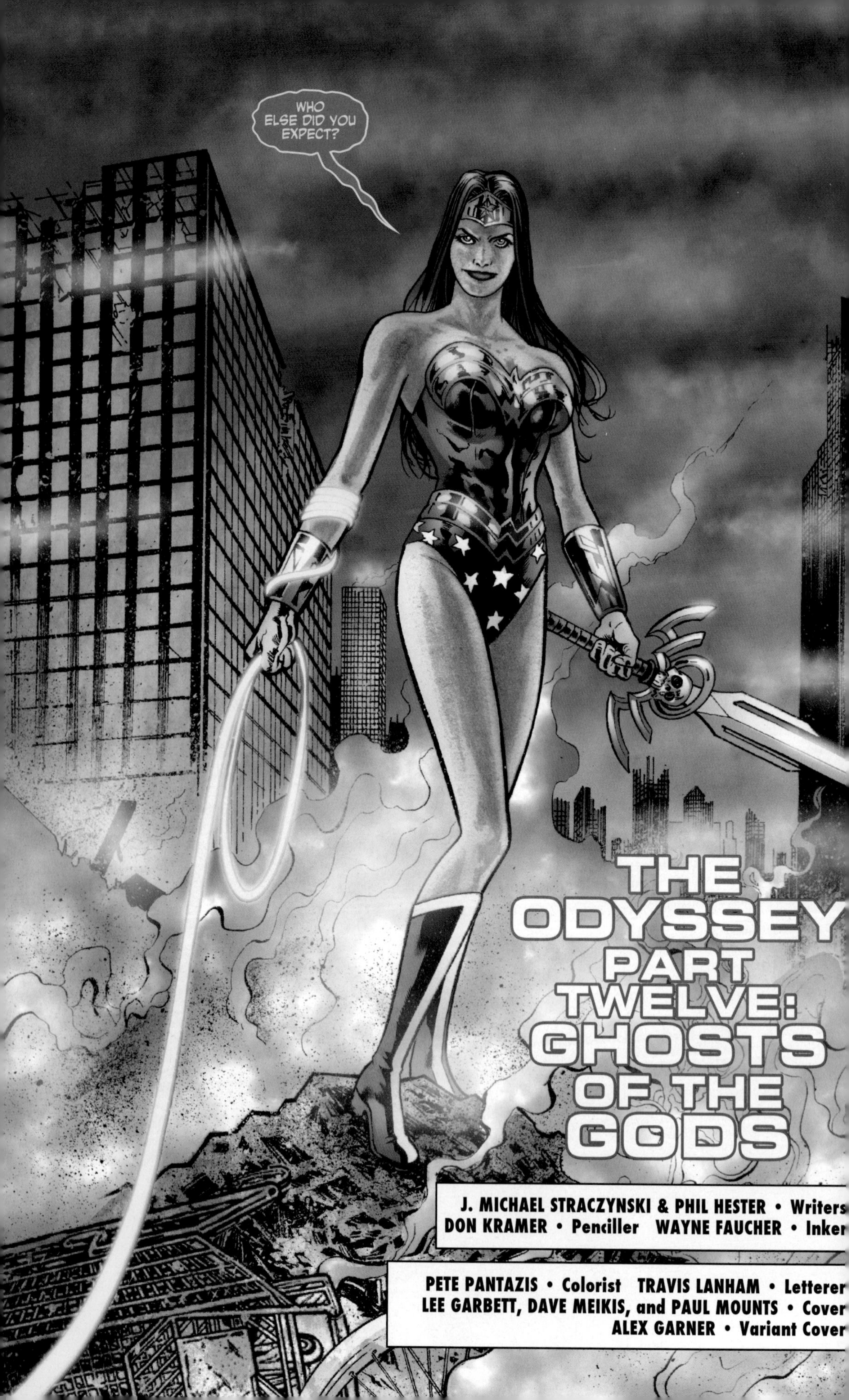
WHO ELSE DID YOU EXPECT?
THE ODYSSEY PART TWELVE: GHOSTS OF THE GODS
J. MICHAEL STRACZYNSKI & PHIL HESTER • Writers
DON KRAMER • Penciller WAYNE FAUCHER • Inker
PETE PANTAZIS • Colorist TRAVIS LANHAM • Letterer
LEE GARBETT, DAVE MEIKIS, and PAUL MOUNTS • Cover
ALEX GARNER • Variant Cover

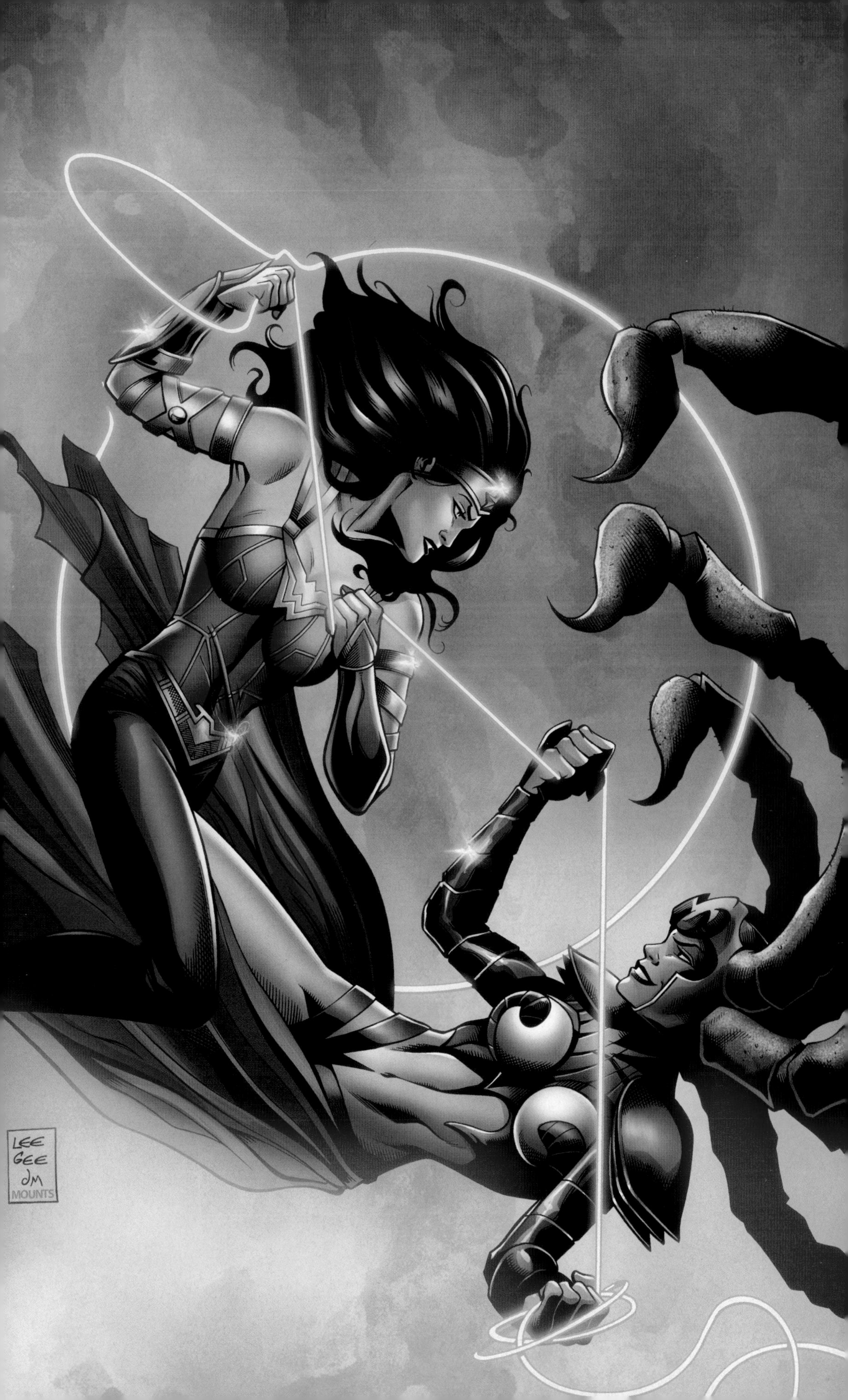
LEE
GEE
JM
MOUNTS

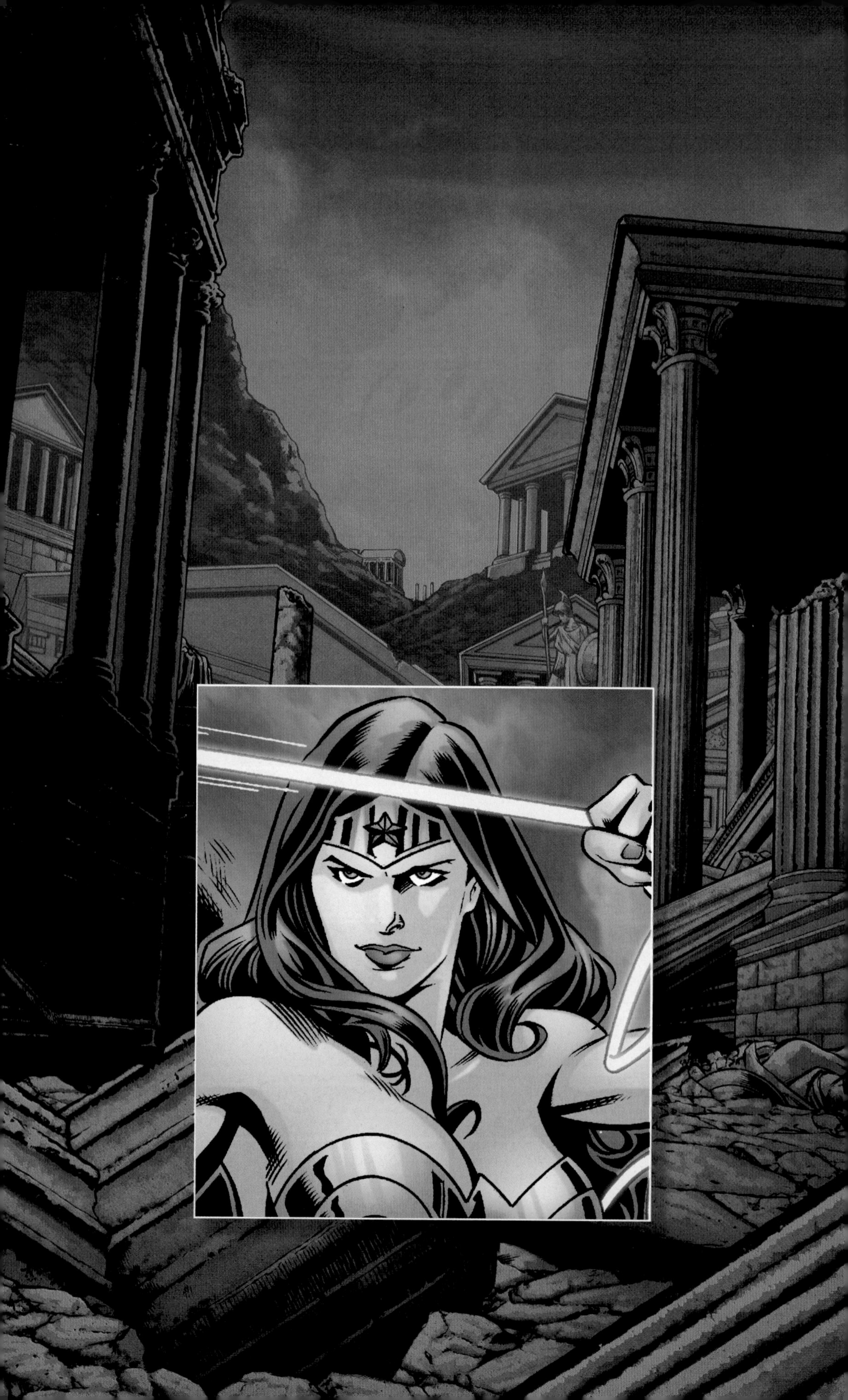

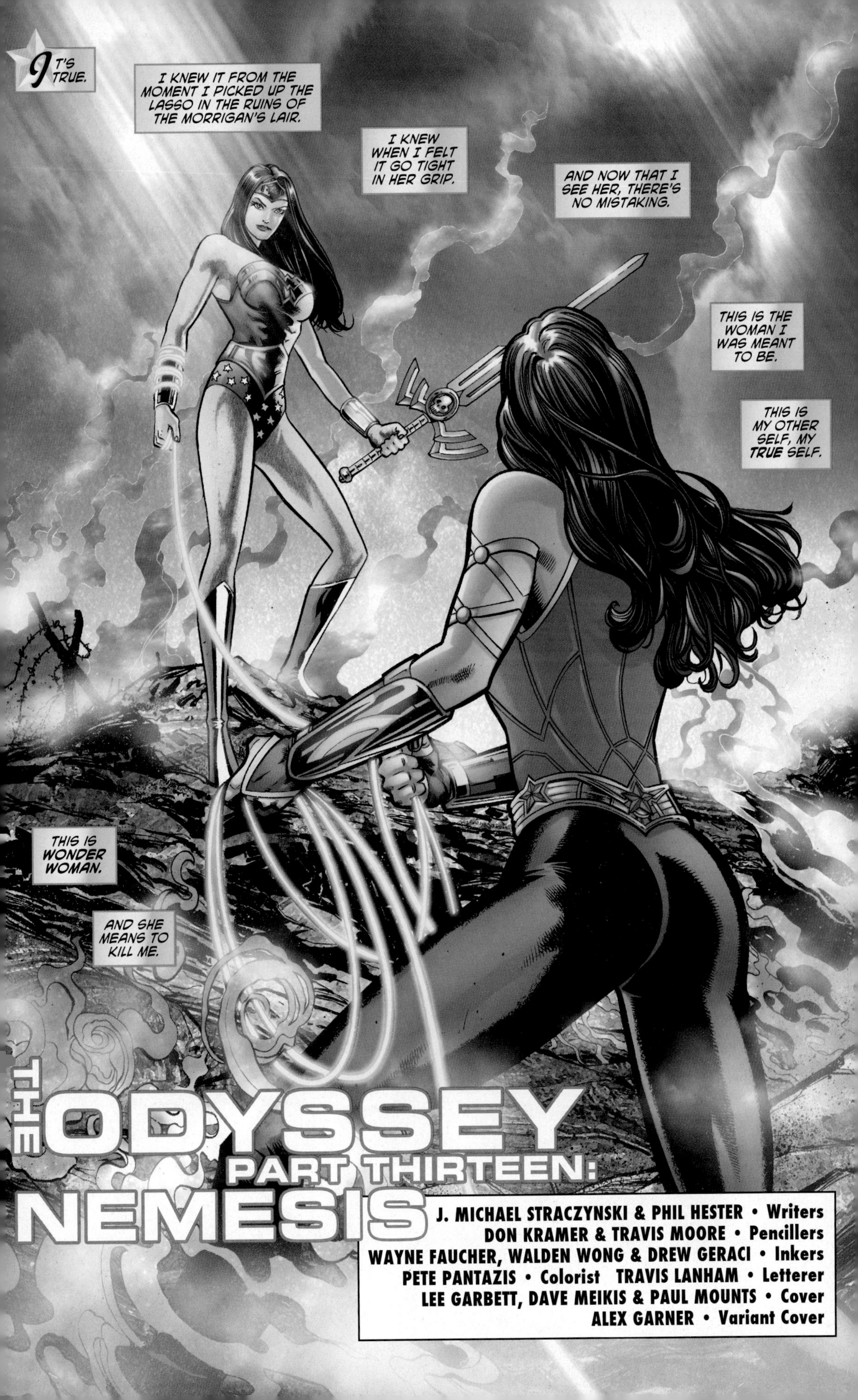
IT'S TRUE.
I KNEW IT FROM THE MOMENT I PICKED UP THE LASSO IN THE RUINS OF THE MORRIGAN'S LAIR.
I KNEW WHEN I FELT IT GO TIGHT IN HER GRIP.
AND NOW THAT I SEE HER, THERE'S NO MISTAKING.
THIS IS THE WOMAN I WAS MEANT TO BE.
THIS IS MY OTHER SELF, MY TRUE SELF.
THIS IS WONDER WOMAN.
AND SHE MEANS TO KILL ME.
THE ODYSSEY
PART THIRTEEN:
NEMESIS
J. MICHAEL STRACZYNSKI & PHIL HESTER • Writers
DON KRAMER & TRAVIS MOORE • Pencillers
WAYNE FAUCHER, WALDEN WONG & DREW GERACI • Inkers
PETE PANTAZIS • Colorist TRAVIS LANHAM • Letterer
LEE GARBETT, DAVE MEIKIS & PAUL MOUNTS • Cover
ALEX GARNER • Variant Cover

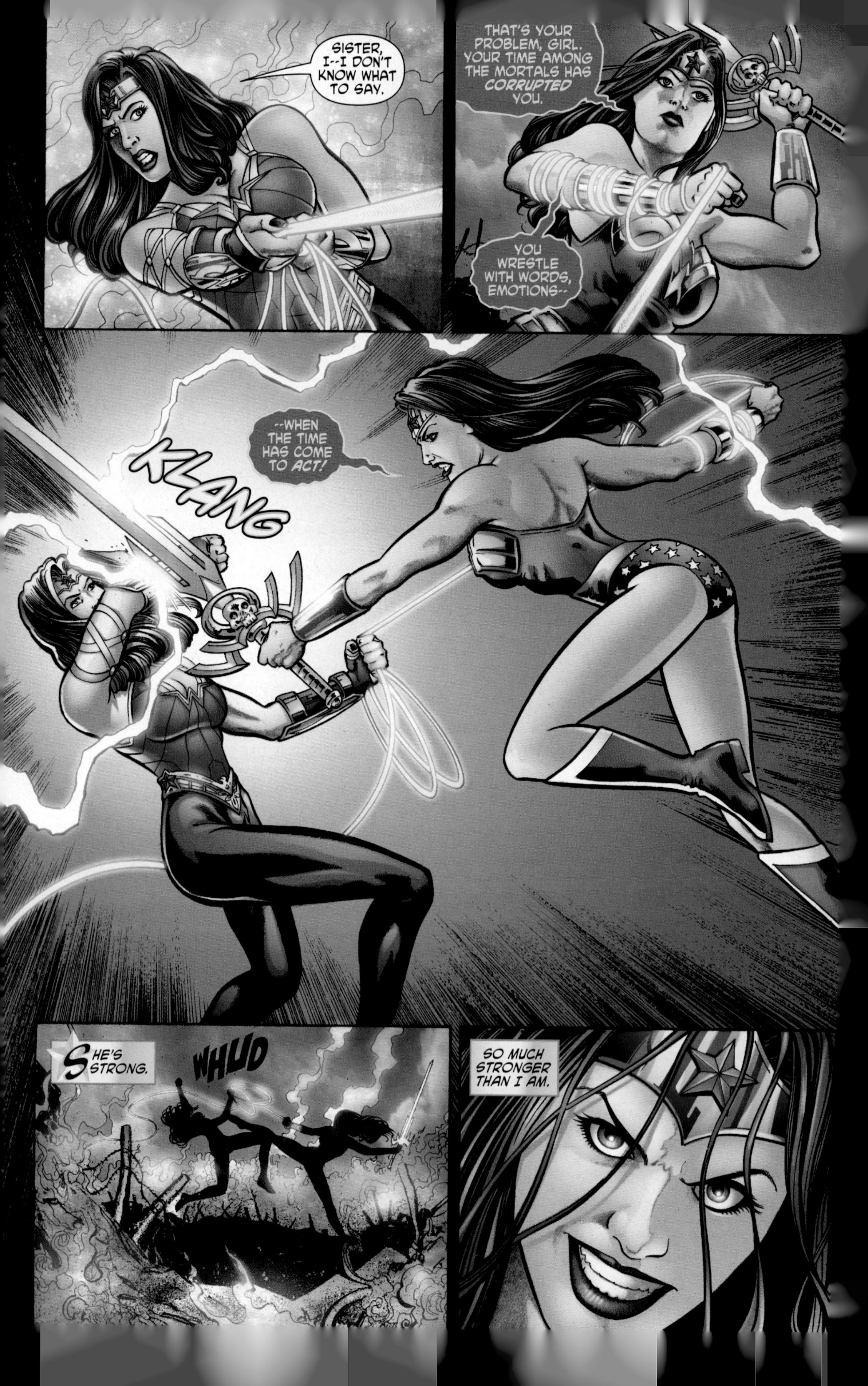
SISTER, I--I DON'T KNOW WHAT TO SAY.
THAT'S YOUR PROBLEM, GIRL. YOUR TIME AMONG THE MORTALS HAS CORRUPTED YOU.
YOU WRESTLE WITH WORDS, EMOTIONS--
--WHEN THE TIME HAS COME TO ACT!
KLANG
SHE'S STRONG.
WHUD
SO MUCH STRONGER THAN I AM.

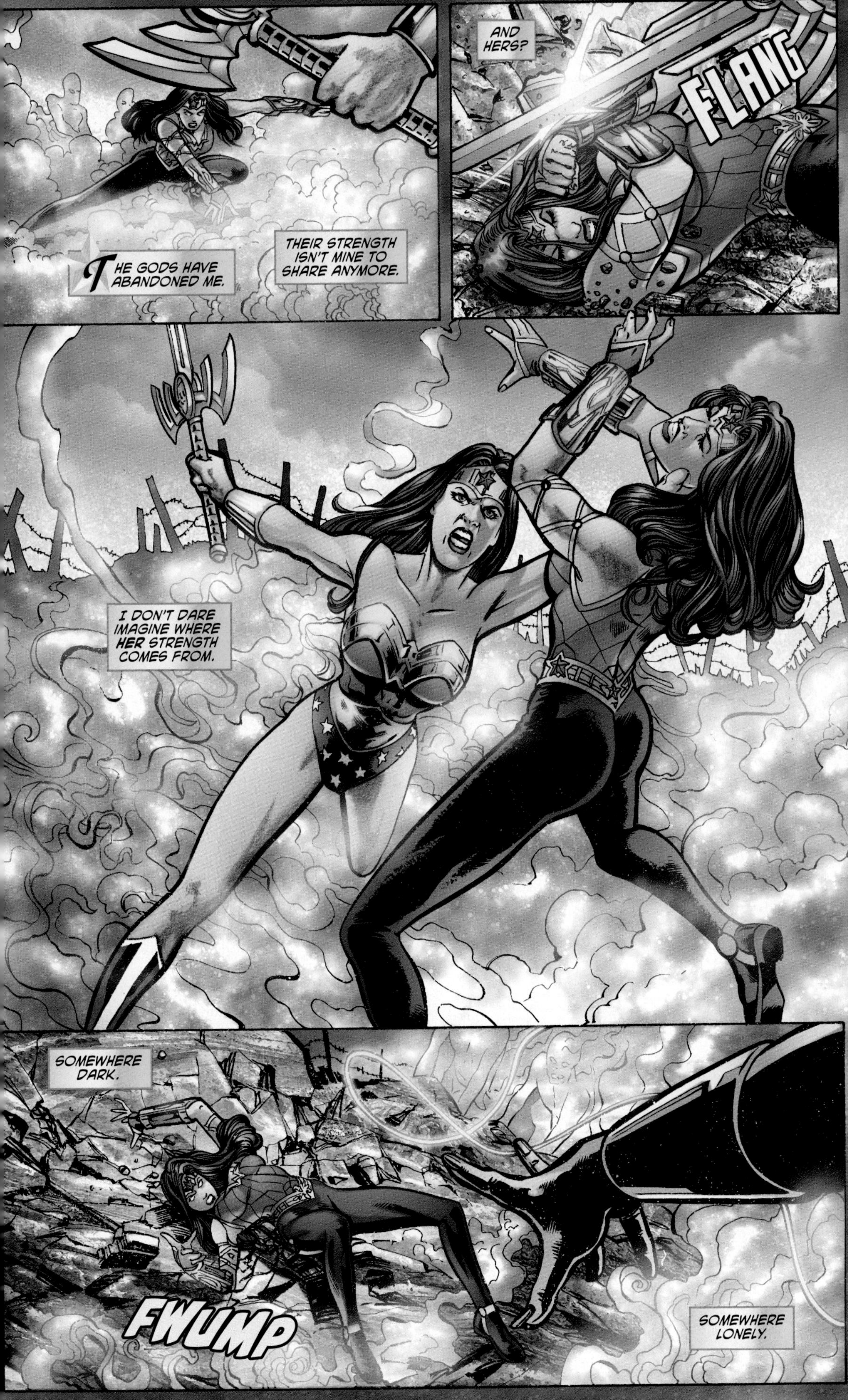
THE GODS HAVE ABANDONED ME.
THEIR STRENGTH ISN'T MINE TO SHARE ANYMORE.
AND HERS?
FLANG
I DON'T DARE IMAGINE WHERE HER STRENGTH COMES FROM.
SOMEWHERE DARK.
FWUMP
SOMEWHERE LONELY.

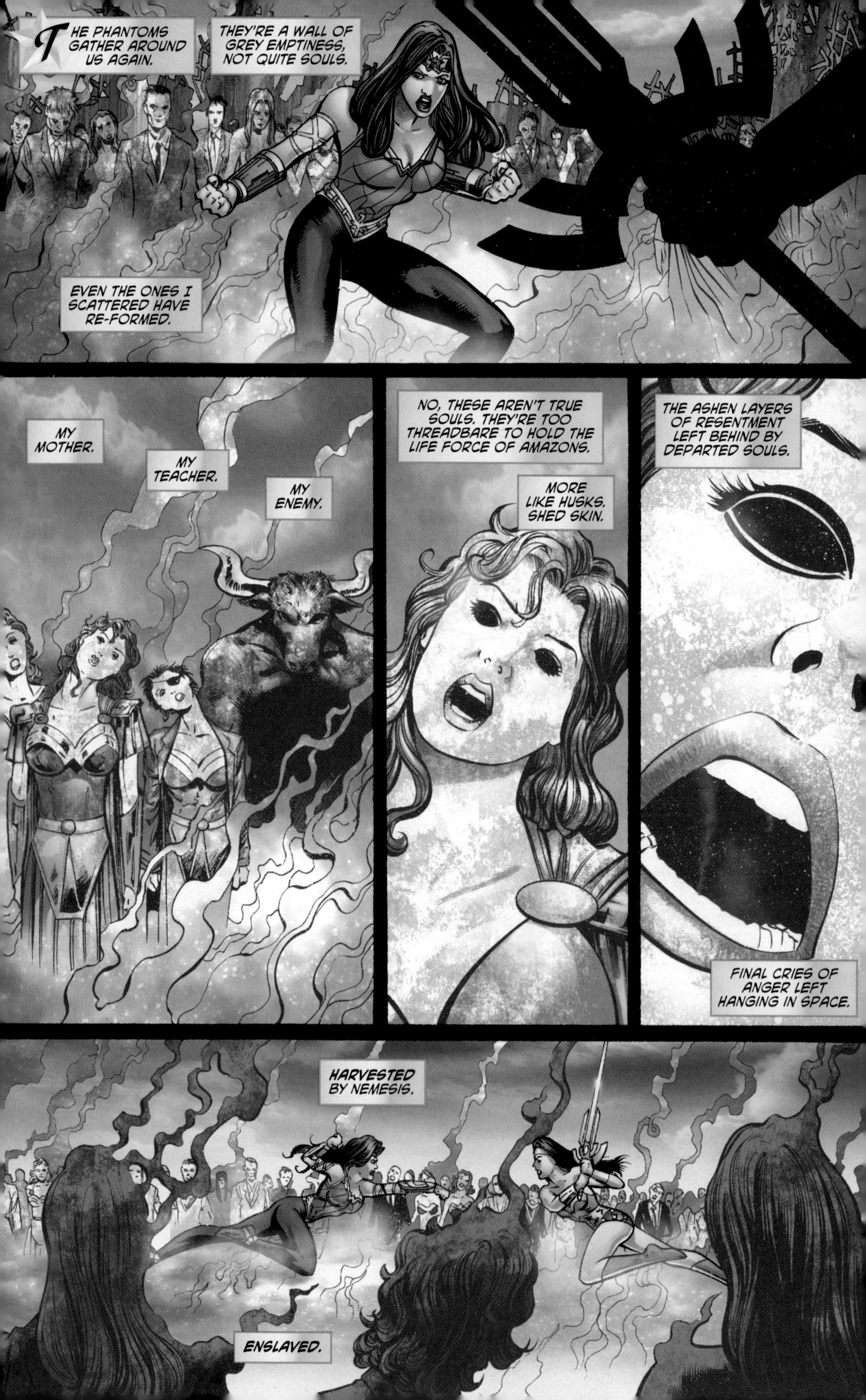
THE PHANTOMS GATHER AROUND US AGAIN.
THEY'RE A WALL OF GREY EMPTINESS, NOT QUITE SOULS.
EVEN THE ONES I SCATTERED HAVE RE-FORMED.
MY MOTHER.
MY TEACHER.
MY ENEMY.
NO, THESE AREN'T TRUE SOULS. THEY'RE TOO THREADBARE TO HOLD THE LIFE FORCE OF AMAZONS.
MORE LIKE HUSKS. SHED SKIN.
THE ASHEN LAYERS OF RESENTMENT LEFT BEHIND BY DEPARTED SOULS.
FINAL CRIES OF ANGER LEFT HANGING IN SPACE.
HARVESTED BY NEMESIS.
ENSLAVED.

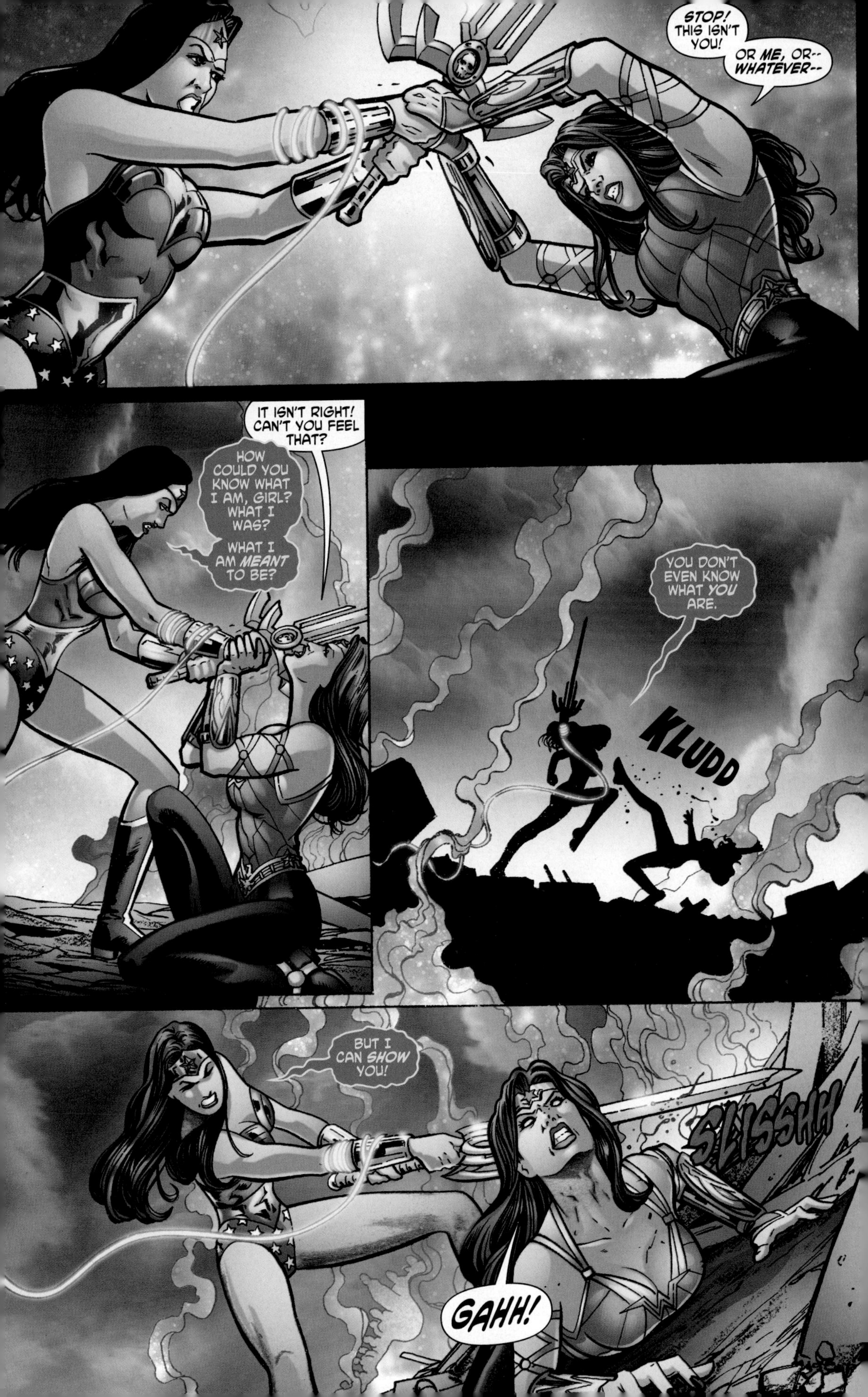
STOP! THIS ISN'T YOU!
OR ME, OR-- WHATEVER--
IT ISN'T RIGHT! CAN'T YOU FEEL THAT?
HOW COULD YOU KNOW WHAT I AM, GIRL? WHAT I WAS?
WHAT I AM MEANT TO BE?
YOU DON'T EVEN KNOW WHAT YOU ARE.
KLUDD
BUT I CAN SHOW YOU!
SLISSHH
GAHH!

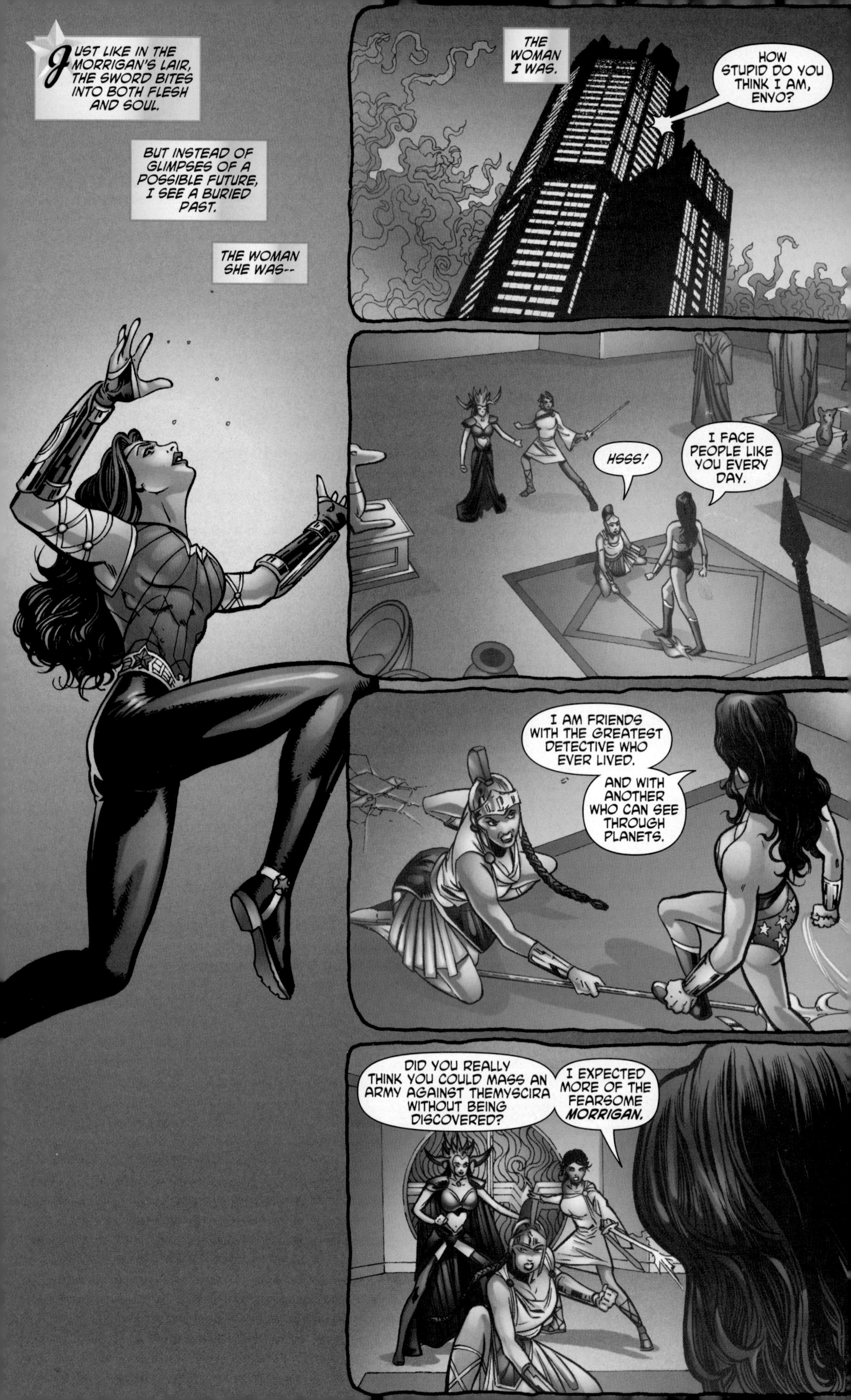
JUST LIKE IN THE MORRIGAN'S LAIR, THE SWORD BITES INTO BOTH FLESH AND SOUL.
BUT INSTEAD OF GLIMPSES OF A POSSIBLE FUTURE, I SEE A BURIED PAST.
THE WOMAN SHE WAS--
THE WOMAN I WAS.
HOW STUPID DO YOU THINK I AM, ENYO?
HSSS!
I FACE PEOPLE LIKE YOU EVERY DAY.
I AM FRIENDS WITH THE GREATEST DETECTIVE WHO EVER LIVED.
AND WITH ANOTHER WHO CAN SEE THROUGH PLANETS.
DID YOU REALLY THINK YOU COULD MASS AN ARMY AGAINST THEMYSCIRA WITHOUT BEING DISCOVERED?
I EXPECTED MORE OF THE FEARSOME MORRIGAN.

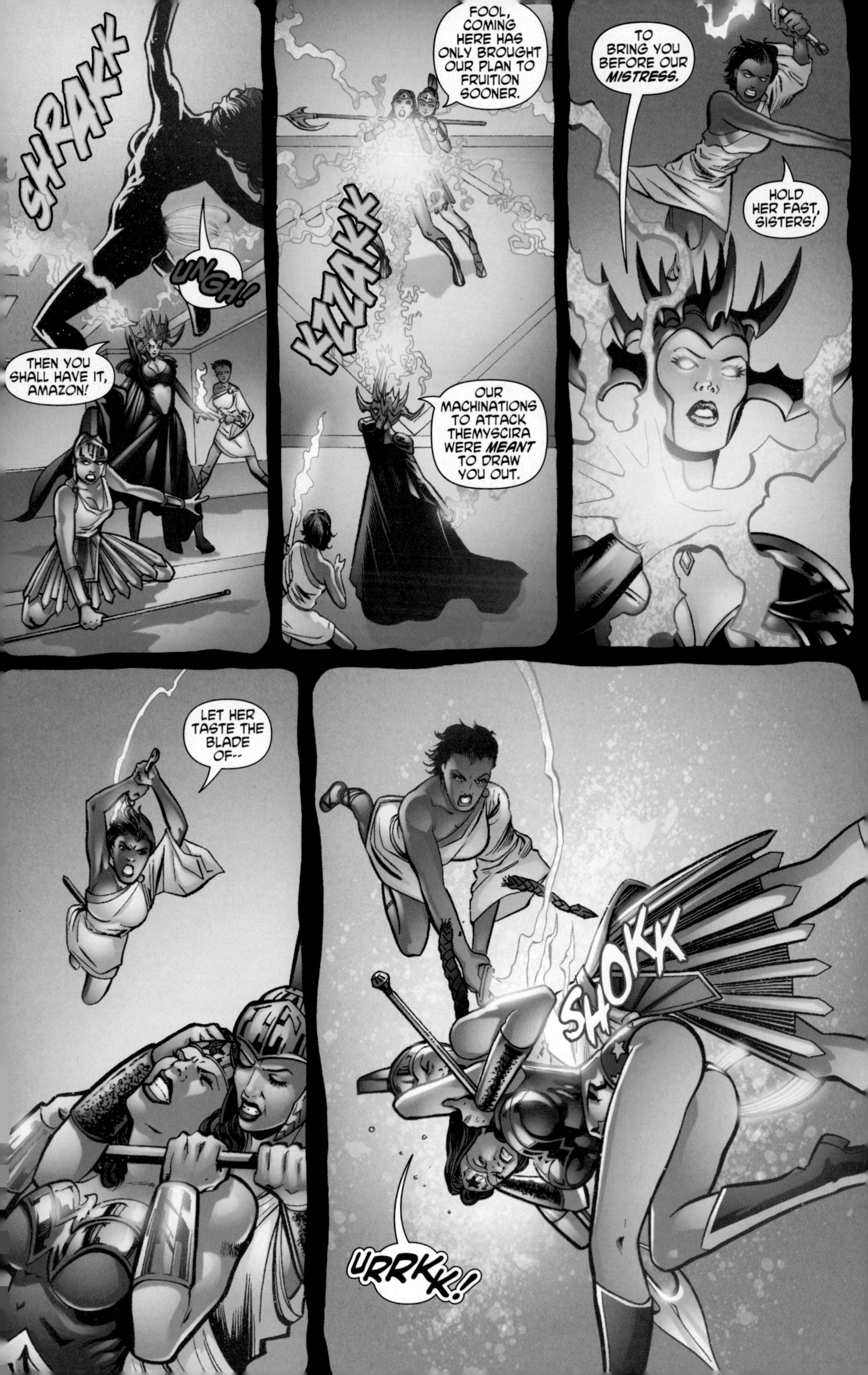
SHRAKK
UNGH!
THEN YOU SHALL HAVE IT, AMAZON!
FOOL, COMING HERE HAS ONLY BROUGHT OUR PLAN TO FRUITION SOONER.
KZZAKK
OUR MACHINATIONS TO ATTACK THEMYSCIRA WERE *MEANT* TO DRAW YOU OUT.
TO BRING YOU BEFORE OUR *MISTRESS.*
HOLD HER FAST, SISTERS!
LET HER TASTE THE BLADE OF--
SHOKK
URRKKK!

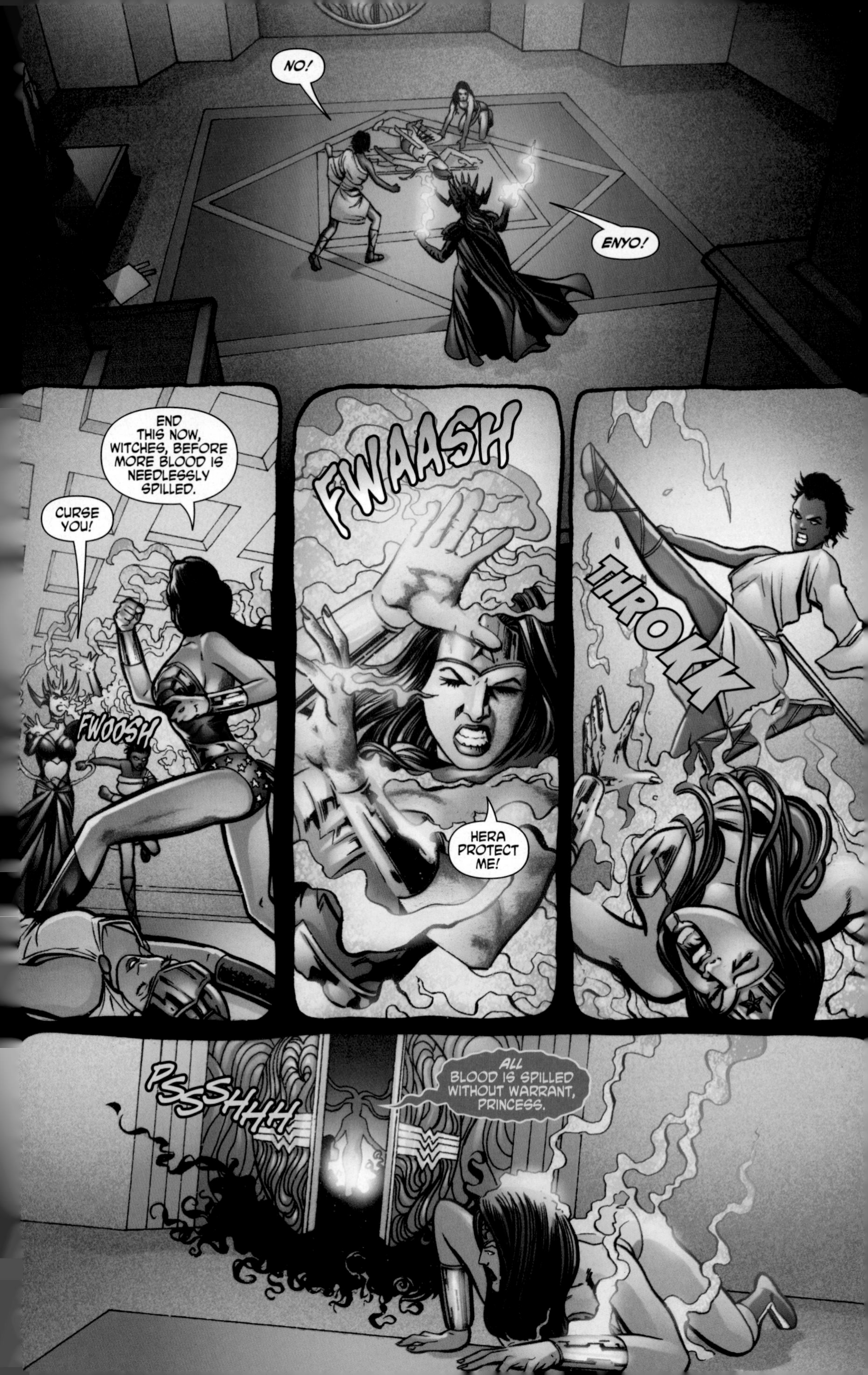
NO!
ENYO!
END THIS NOW, WITCHES, BEFORE MORE BLOOD IS NEEDLESSLY SPILLED.
CURSE YOU!
FWOOSH
FWAASH
HERA PROTECT ME!
THROKK
PSSSHHH
ALL BLOOD IS SPILLED WITHOUT WARRANT, PRINCESS.

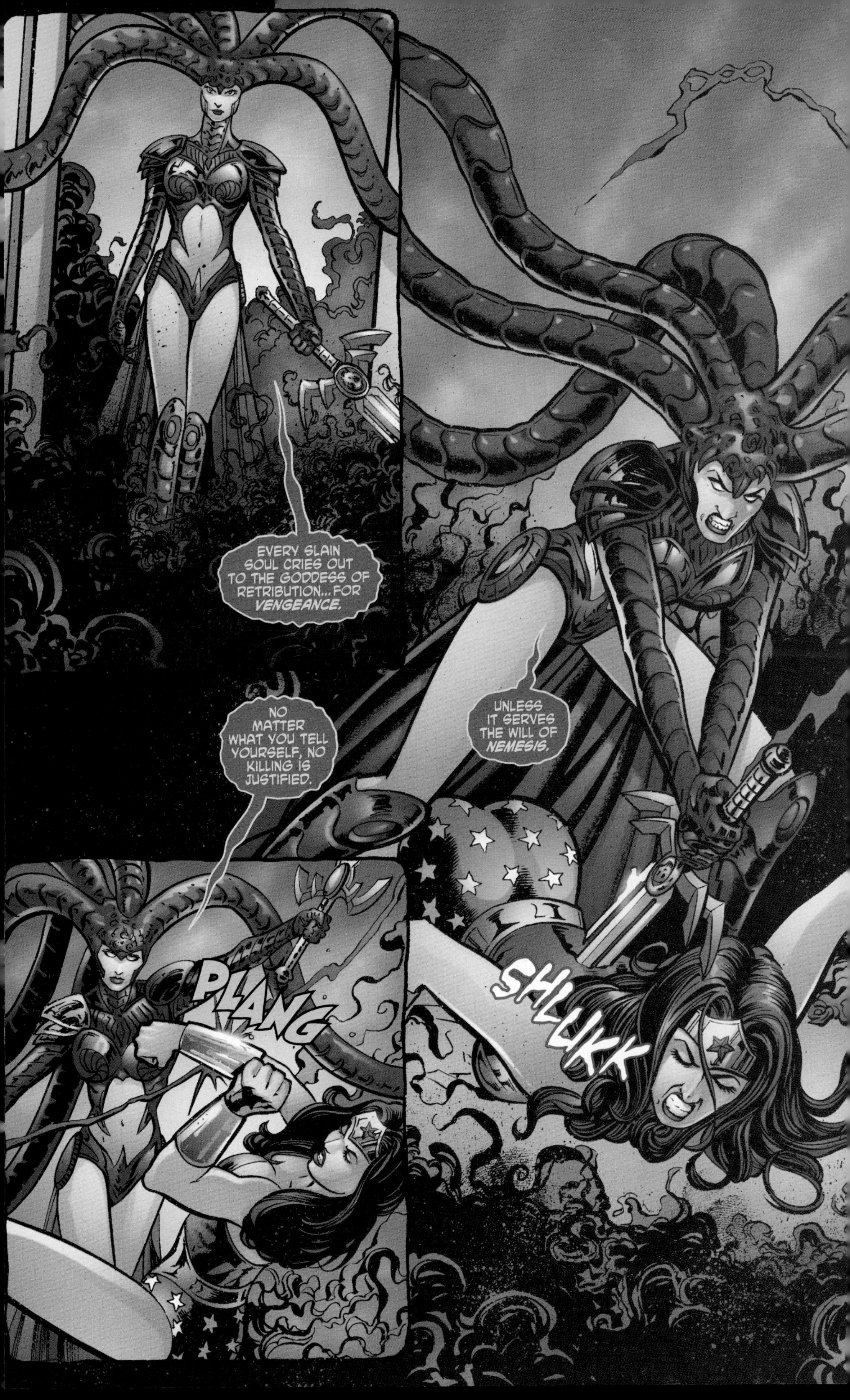
EVERY SLAIN SOUL CRIES OUT TO THE GODDESS OF RETRIBUTION... FOR *VENGEANCE.*
NO MATTER WHAT YOU TELL YOURSELF, NO KILLING IS JUSTIFIED.
PLANG
UNLESS IT SERVES THE WILL OF *NEMESIS.*
SHLUKK

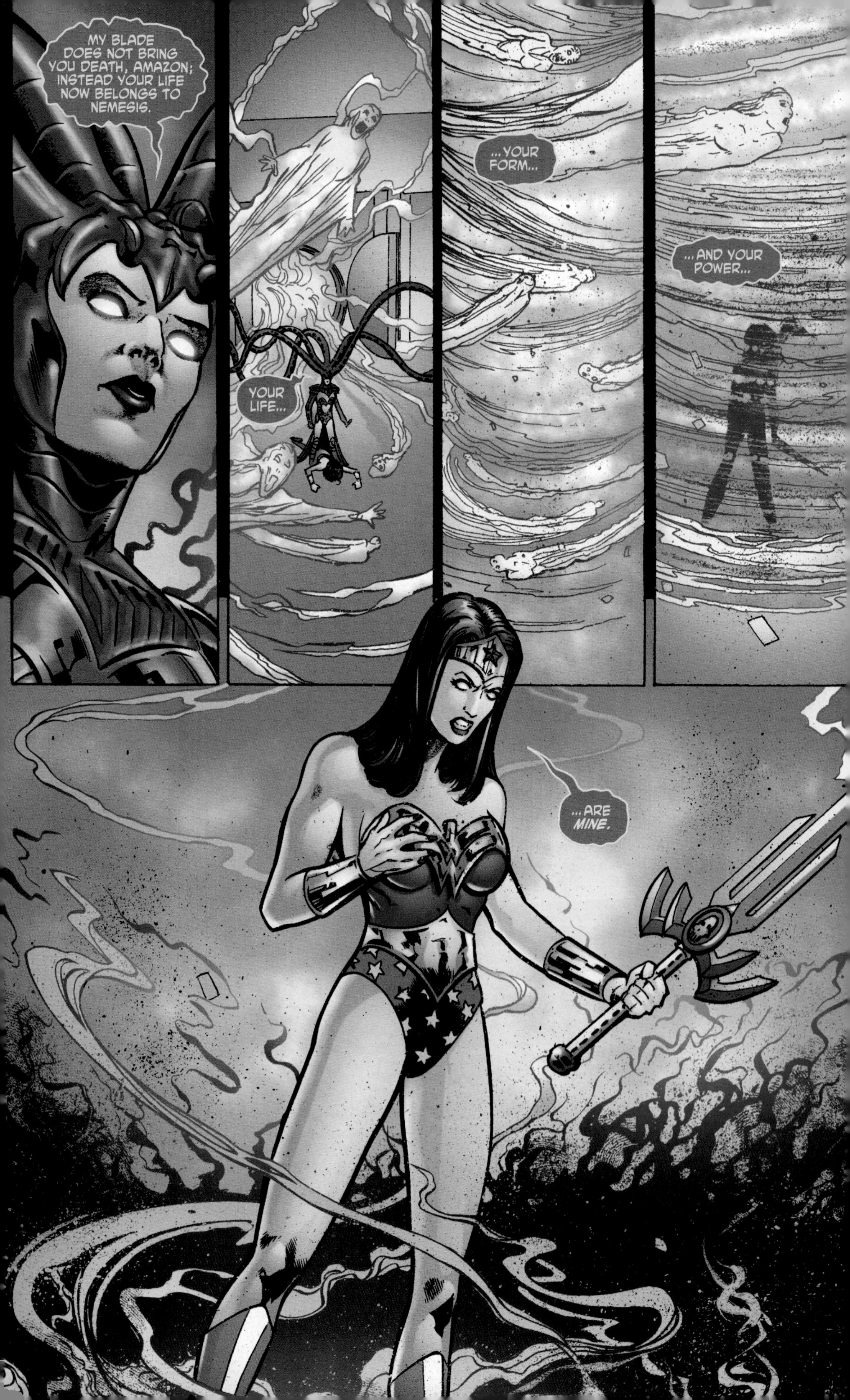
MY BLADE DOES NOT BRING YOU DEATH, AMAZON; INSTEAD YOUR LIFE NOW BELONGS TO NEMESIS.
YOUR LIFE...
...YOUR FORM...
...AND YOUR POWER...
...ARE MINE.

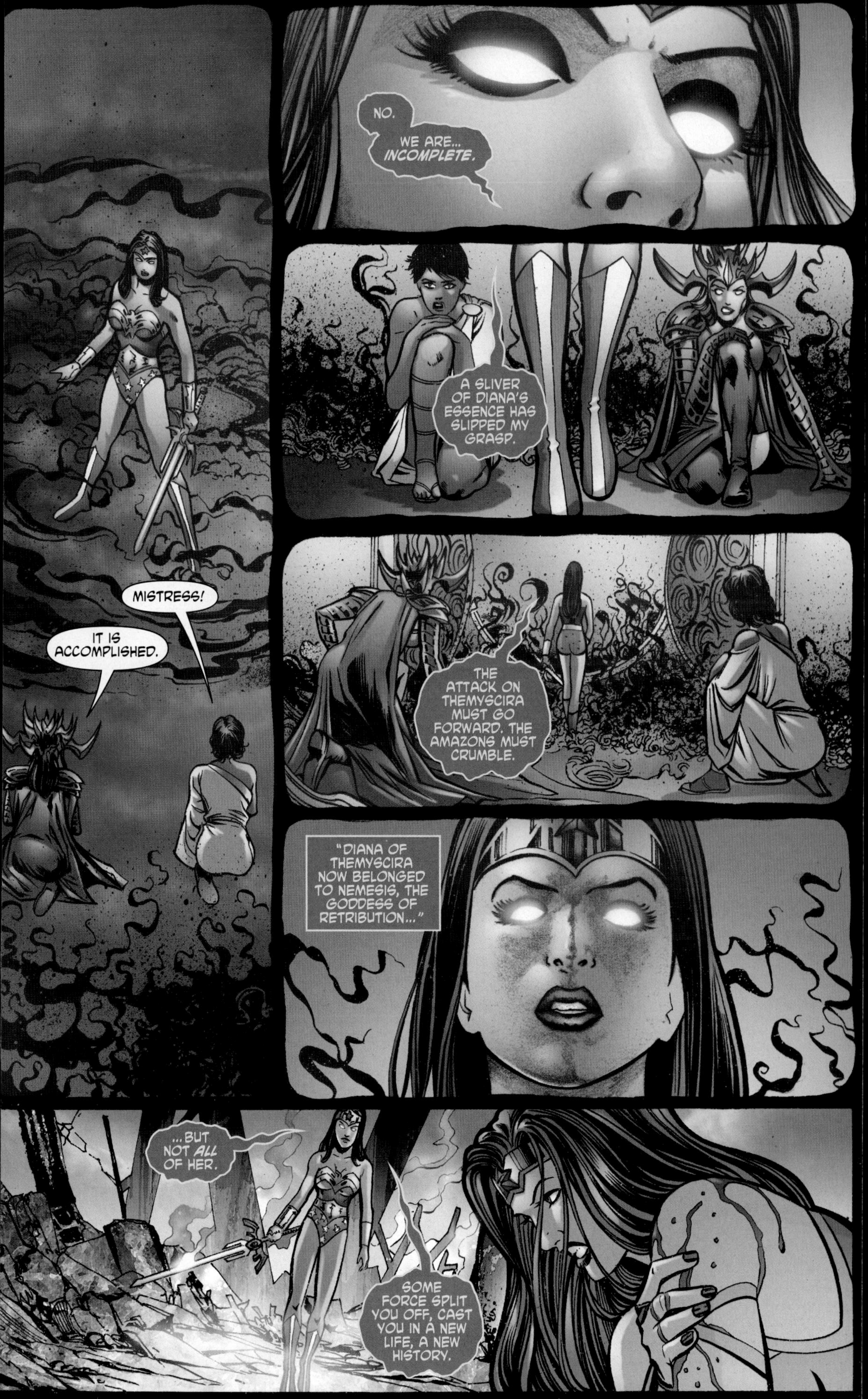
NO.
WE ARE... INCOMPLETE.
MISTRESS!
IT IS ACCOMPLISHED.
A SLIVER OF DIANA'S ESSENCE HAS SLIPPED MY GRASP.
THE ATTACK ON THEMYSCIRA MUST GO FORWARD. THE AMAZONS MUST CRUMBLE.
"DIANA OF THEMYSCIRA NOW BELONGED TO NEMESIS, THE GODDESS OF RETRIBUTION..."
...BUT NOT ALL OF HER.
SOME FORCE SPLIT YOU OFF, CAST YOU IN A NEW LIFE, A NEW HISTORY.

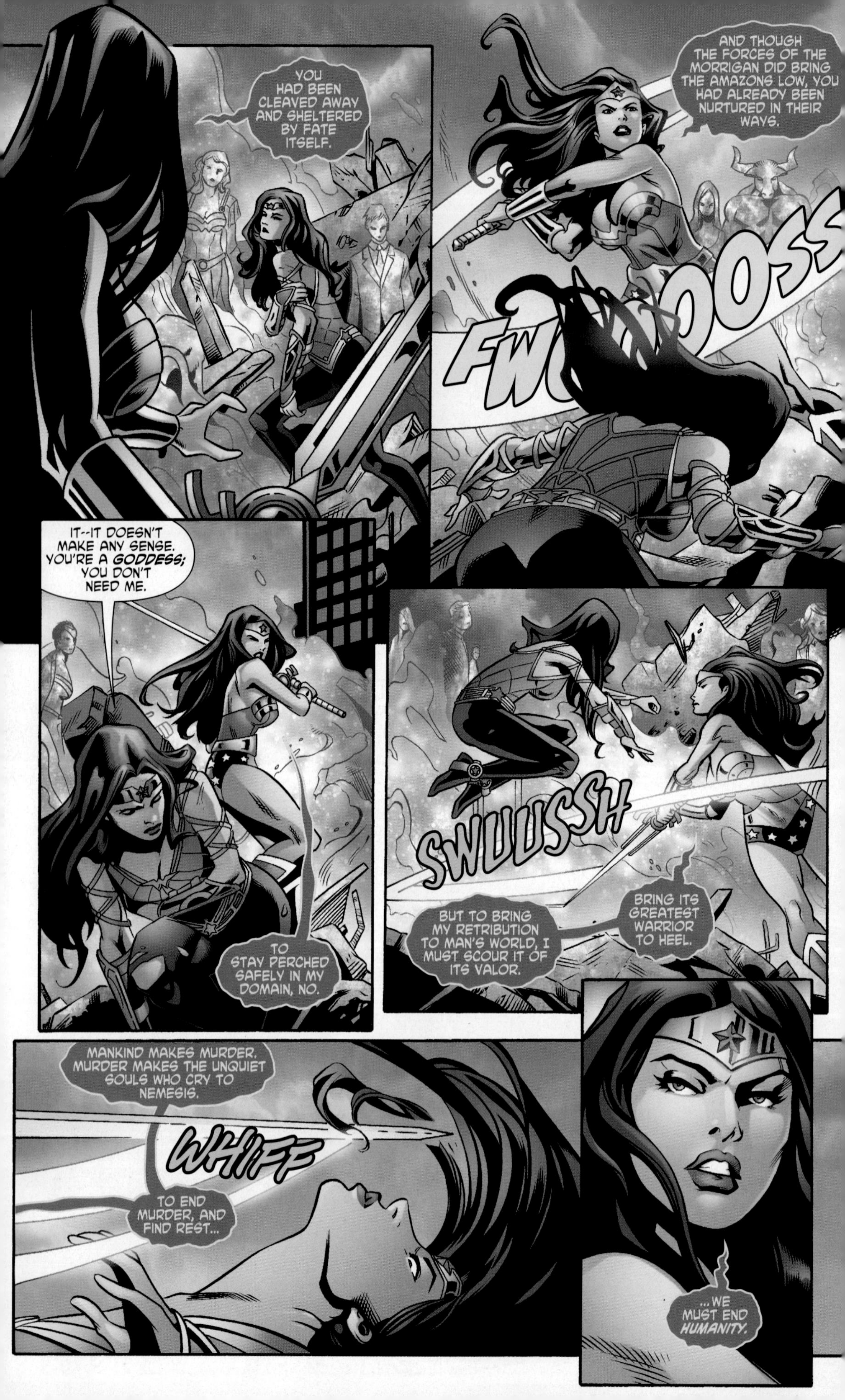
YOU HAD BEEN CLEAVED AWAY AND SHELTERED BY FATE ITSELF.
AND THOUGH THE FORCES OF THE MORRIGAN DID BRING THE AMAZONS LOW, YOU HAD ALREADY BEEN NURTURED IN THEIR WAYS.
IT--IT DOESN'T MAKE ANY SENSE. YOU'RE A *GODDESS;* YOU DON'T NEED ME.
TO STAY PERCHED SAFELY IN MY DOMAIN, NO.
SWUUSSH
BUT TO BRING MY RETRIBUTION TO MAN'S WORLD, I MUST SCOUR IT OF ITS VALOR.
BRING ITS GREATEST WARRIOR TO HEEL.
MANKIND MAKES MURDER. MURDER MAKES THE UNQUIET SOULS WHO CRY TO NEMESIS.
WHIFF
TO END MURDER, AND FIND REST...
...WE MUST END *HUMANITY.*

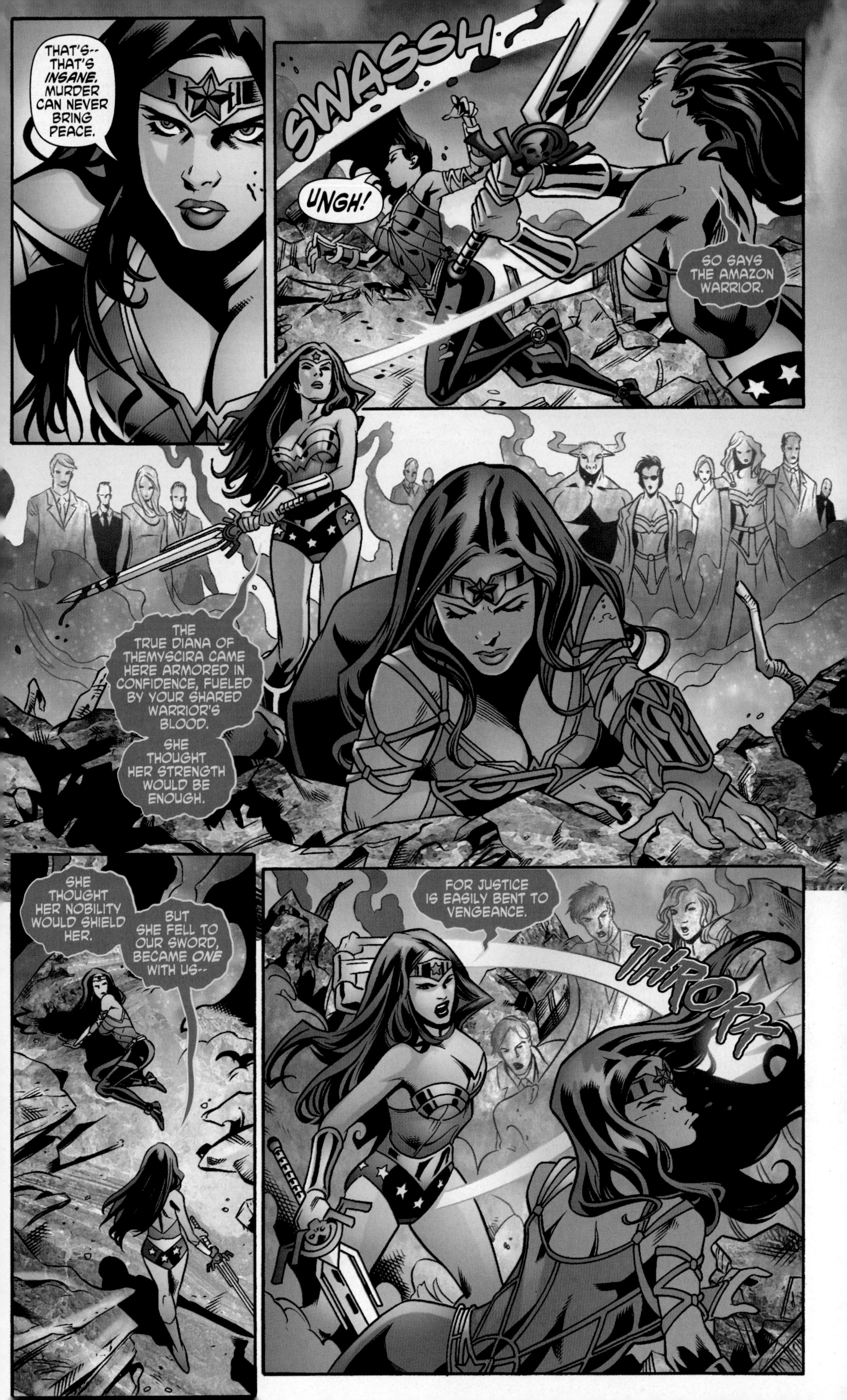
THAT'S-- THAT'S *INSANE.* MURDER CAN NEVER BRING PEACE.
SWASSH
UNGH!
SO SAYS THE AMAZON WARRIOR.
THE TRUE DIANA OF THEMYSCIRA CAME HERE ARMORED IN CONFIDENCE, FUELED BY YOUR SHARED WARRIOR'S BLOOD.
SHE THOUGHT HER STRENGTH WOULD BE ENOUGH.
SHE THOUGHT HER NOBILITY WOULD SHIELD HER.
BUT SHE FELL TO OUR SWORD, BECAME *ONE* WITH US--
FOR JUSTICE IS EASILY BENT TO VENGEANCE.
THROKK

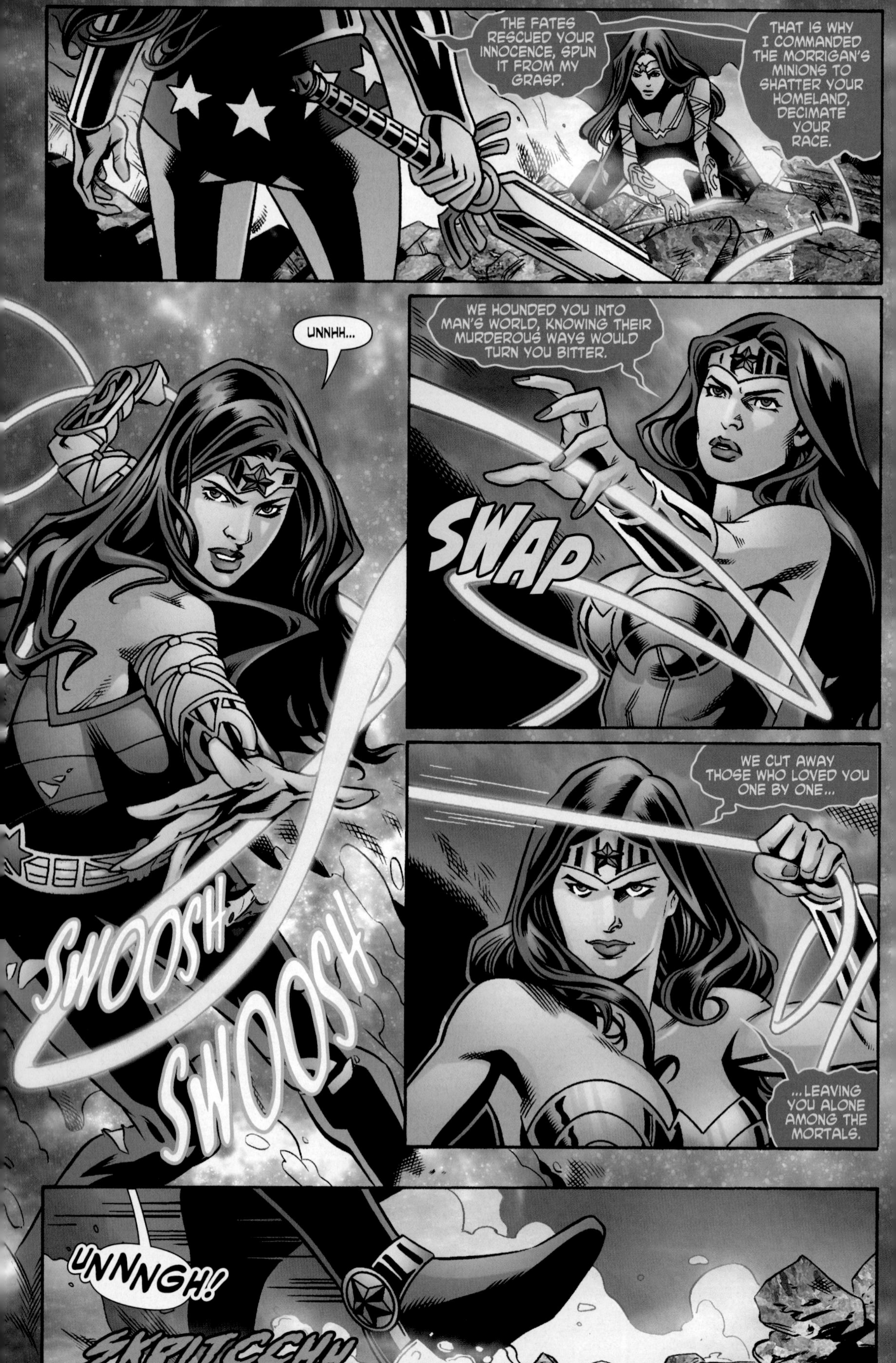
THE FATES RESCUED YOUR INNOCENCE, SPUN IT FROM MY GRASP.
THAT IS WHY I COMMANDED THE MORRIGAN'S MINIONS TO SHATTER YOUR HOMELAND, DECIMATE YOUR RACE.
UNNHH...
WE HOUNDED YOU INTO MAN'S WORLD, KNOWING THEIR MURDEROUS WAYS WOULD TURN YOU BITTER.
SWAP
SWOOSH
SWOOSH
WE CUT AWAY THOSE WHO LOVED YOU ONE BY ONE...
...LEAVING YOU ALONE AMONG THE MORTALS.
UNNNGH!
SKRITCCHH

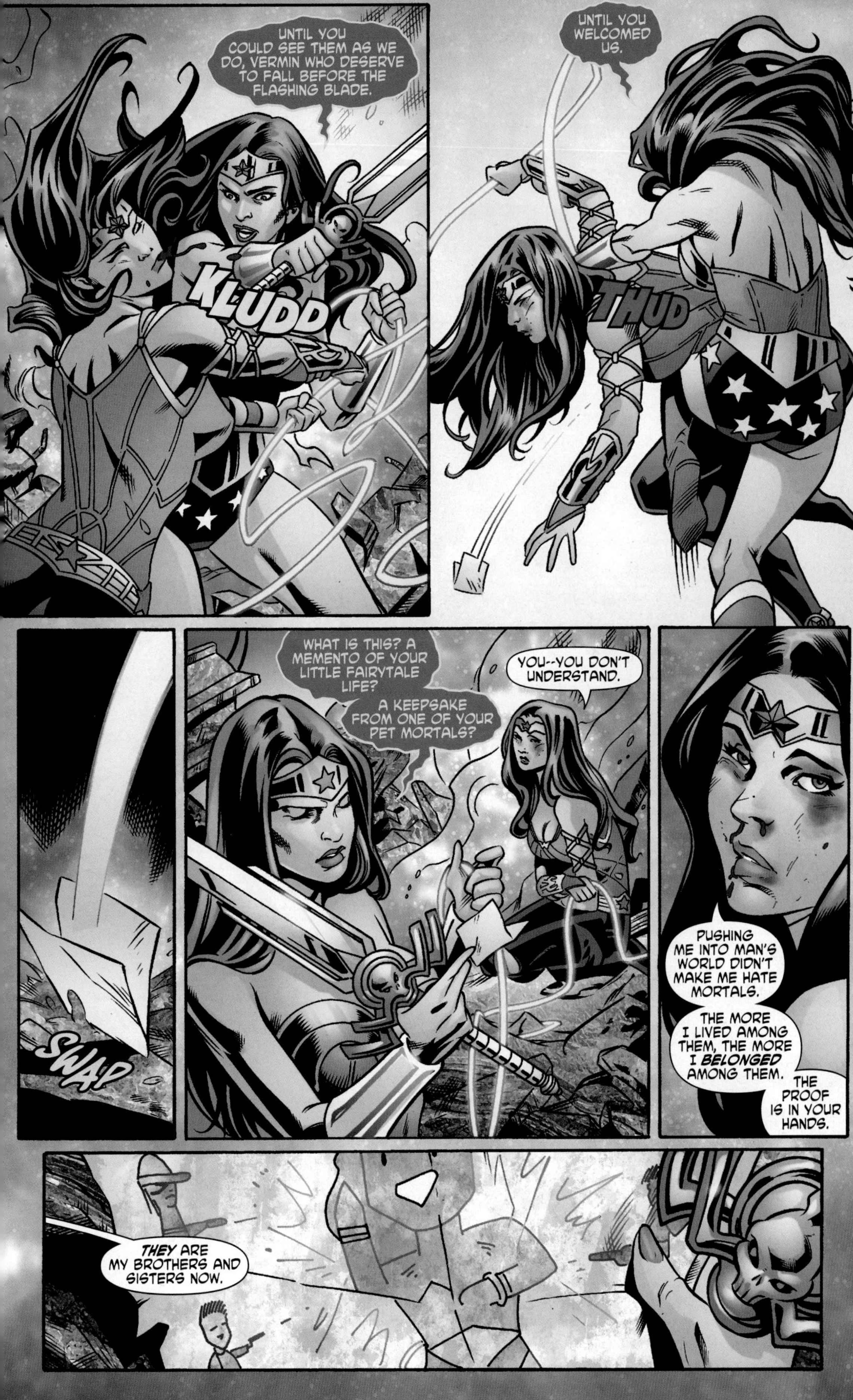

UNTIL YOU COULD SEE THEM AS WE DO, VERMIN WHO DESERVE TO FALL BEFORE THE FLASHING BLADE.
KLUDD
UNTIL YOU WELCOMED US.
THUD
SWAP
WHAT IS THIS? A MEMENTO OF YOUR LITTLE FAIRYTALE LIFE?
A KEEPSAKE FROM ONE OF YOUR PET MORTALS?
YOU--YOU DON'T UNDERSTAND.
PUSHING ME INTO MAN'S WORLD DIDN'T MAKE ME HATE MORTALS.
THE MORE I LIVED AMONG THEM, THE MORE I *BELONGED* AMONG THEM.
THE PROOF IS IN YOUR HANDS.
THEY ARE MY BROTHERS AND SISTERS NOW.

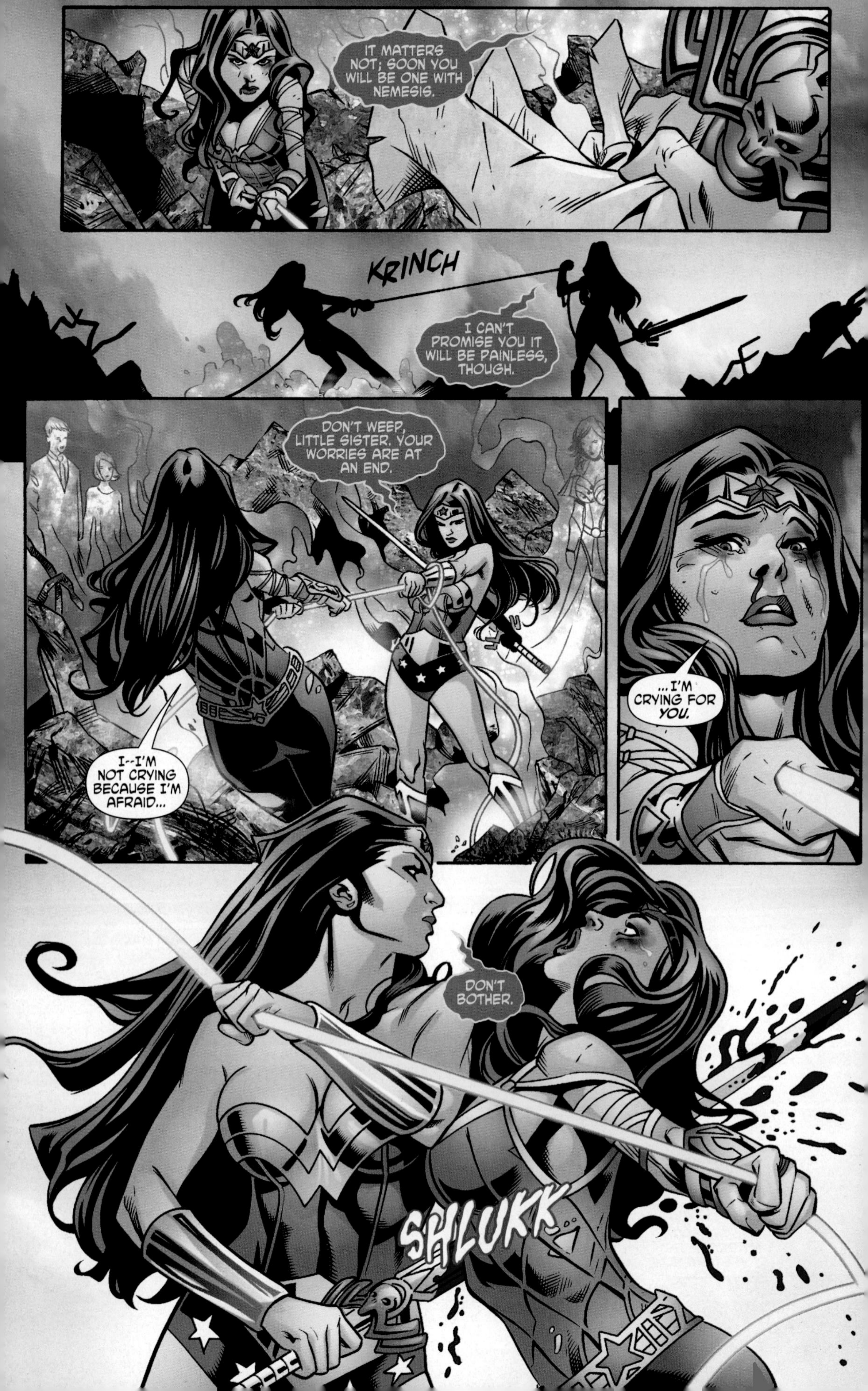
IT MATTERS NOT; SOON YOU WILL BE ONE WITH NEMESIS.
KRINCH
I CAN'T PROMISE YOU IT WILL BE PAINLESS, THOUGH.
DON'T WEEP, LITTLE SISTER. YOUR WORRIES ARE AT AN END.
I--I'M NOT CRYING BECAUSE I'M AFRAID...
...I'M CRYING FOR YOU.
DON'T BOTHER.
SHLUKK

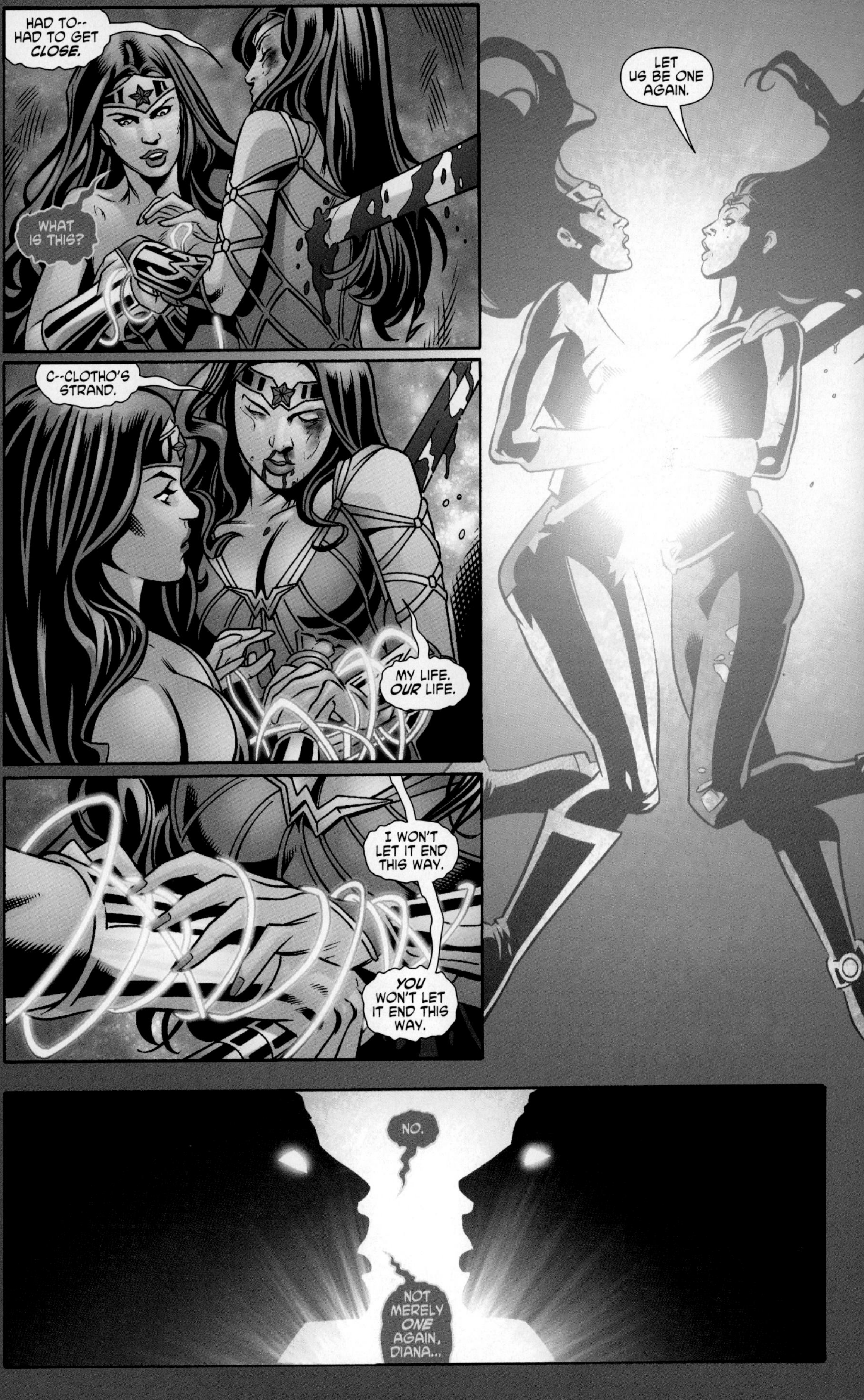
HAD TO-- HAD TO GET *CLOSE.*
WHAT IS THIS?
C--CLOTHO'S STRAND.
MY LIFE. *OUR* LIFE.
I WON'T LET IT END THIS WAY.
YOU WON'T LET IT END THIS WAY.
LET US BE ONE AGAIN.
NO.
NOT MERELY *ONE* AGAIN, DIANA...

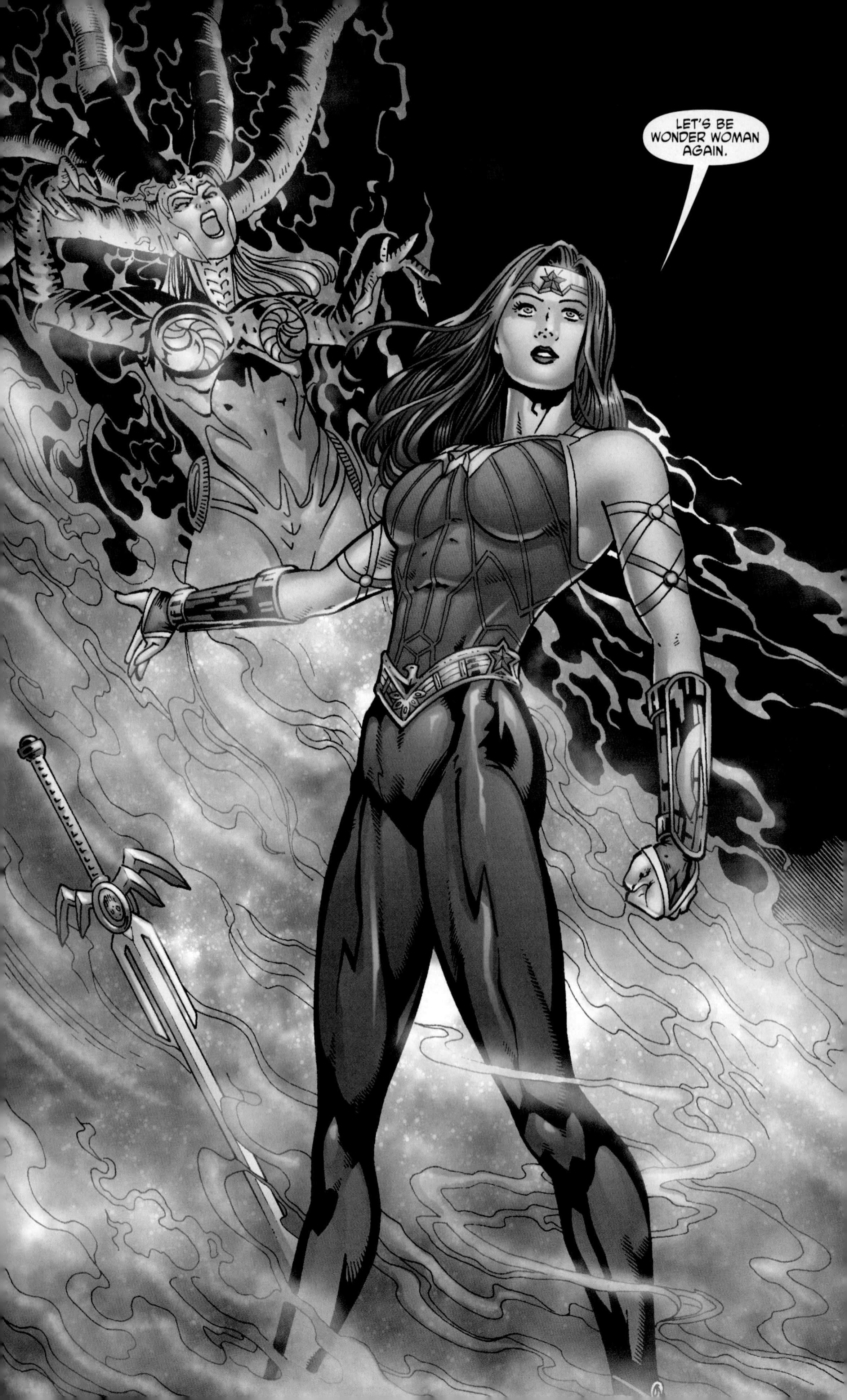
LET'S BE WONDER WOMAN AGAIN.

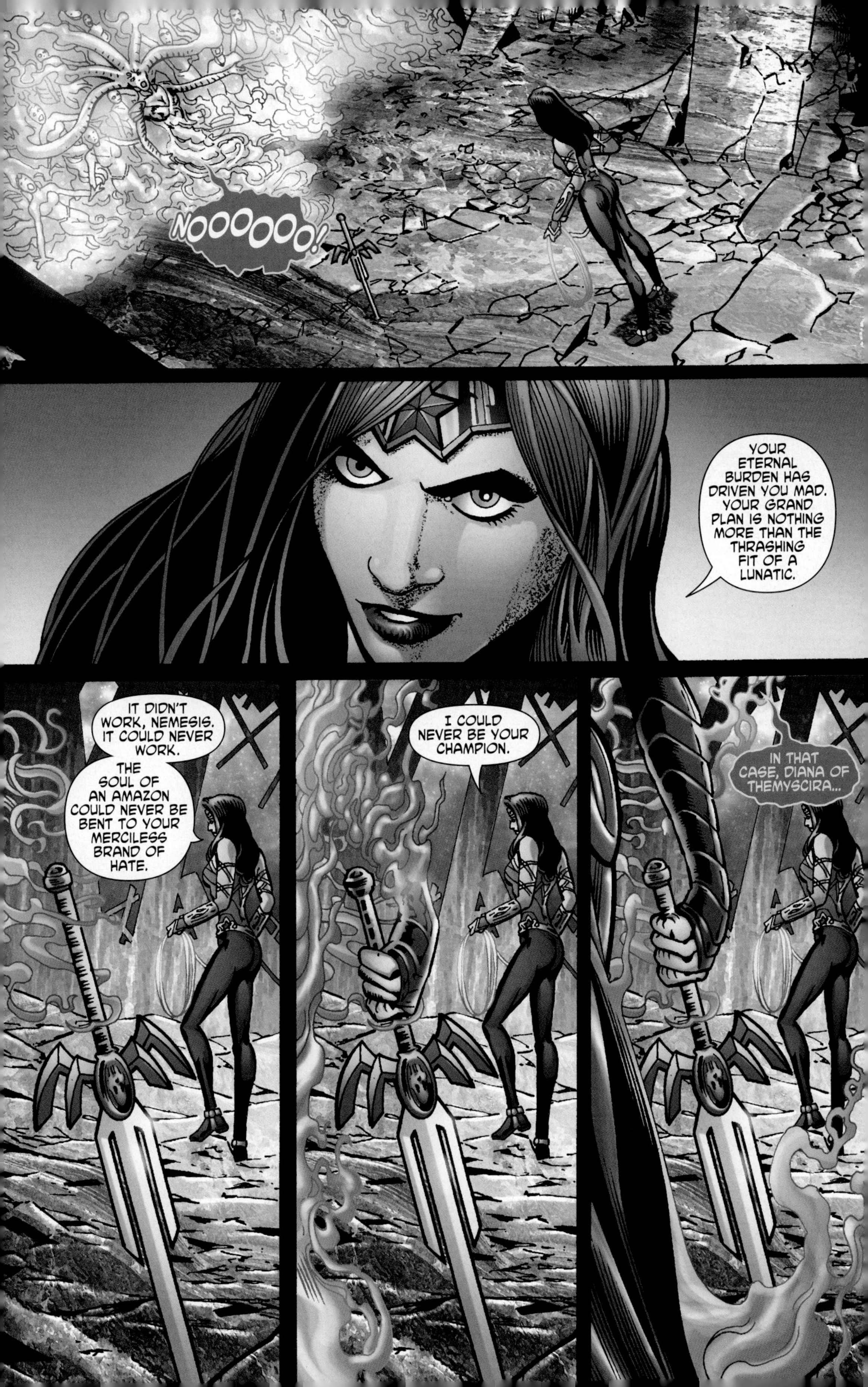
NOOOOOO!
YOUR ETERNAL BURDEN HAS DRIVEN YOU MAD. YOUR GRAND PLAN IS NOTHING MORE THAN THE THRASHING FIT OF A LUNATIC.
IT DIDN'T WORK, NEMESIS. IT COULD NEVER WORK.
THE SOUL OF AN AMAZON COULD NEVER BE BENT TO YOUR MERCILESS BRAND OF HATE.
I COULD NEVER BE YOUR CHAMPION.
IN THAT CASE, DIANA OF THEMYSCIRA...

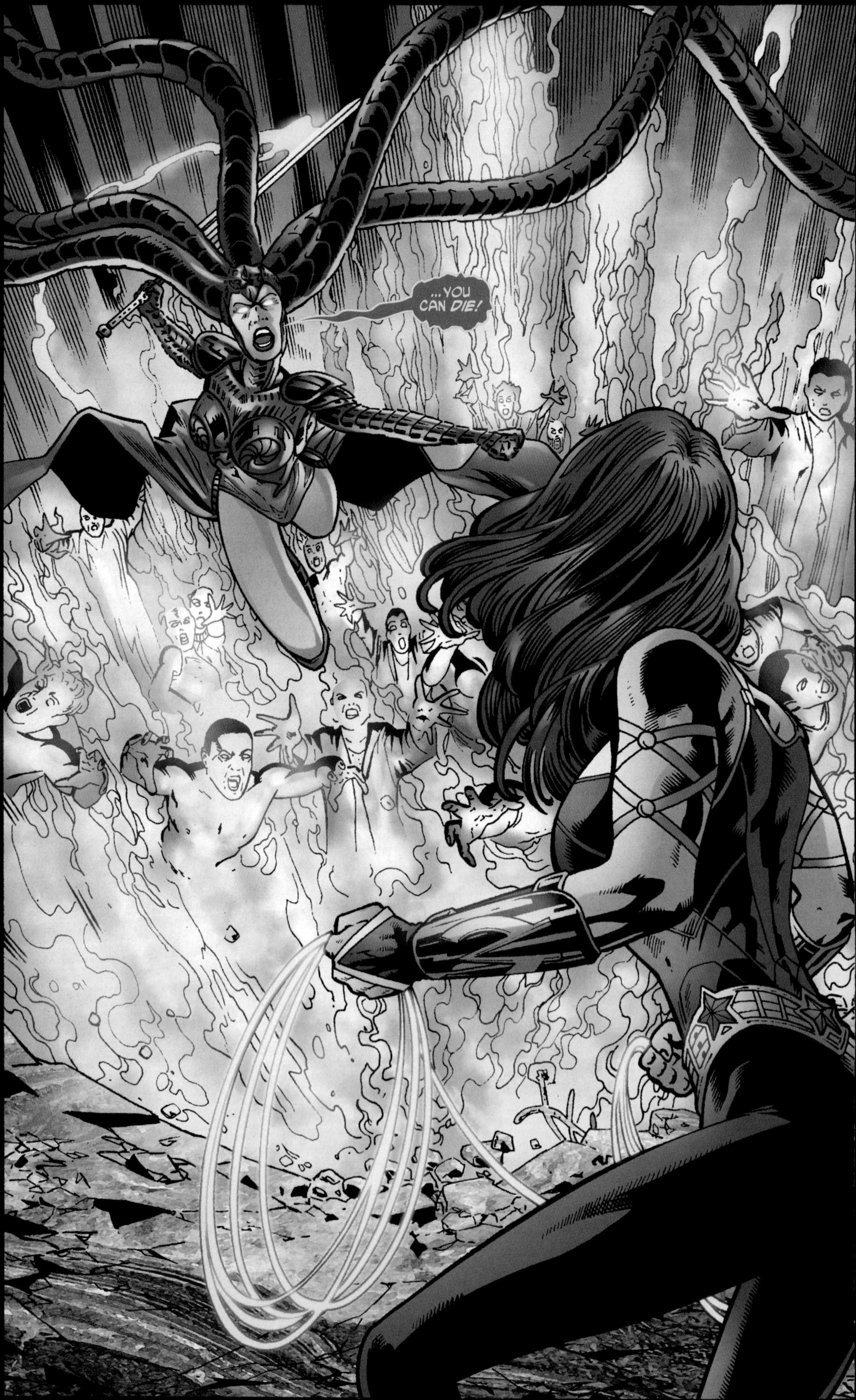
...YOU CAN DIE!

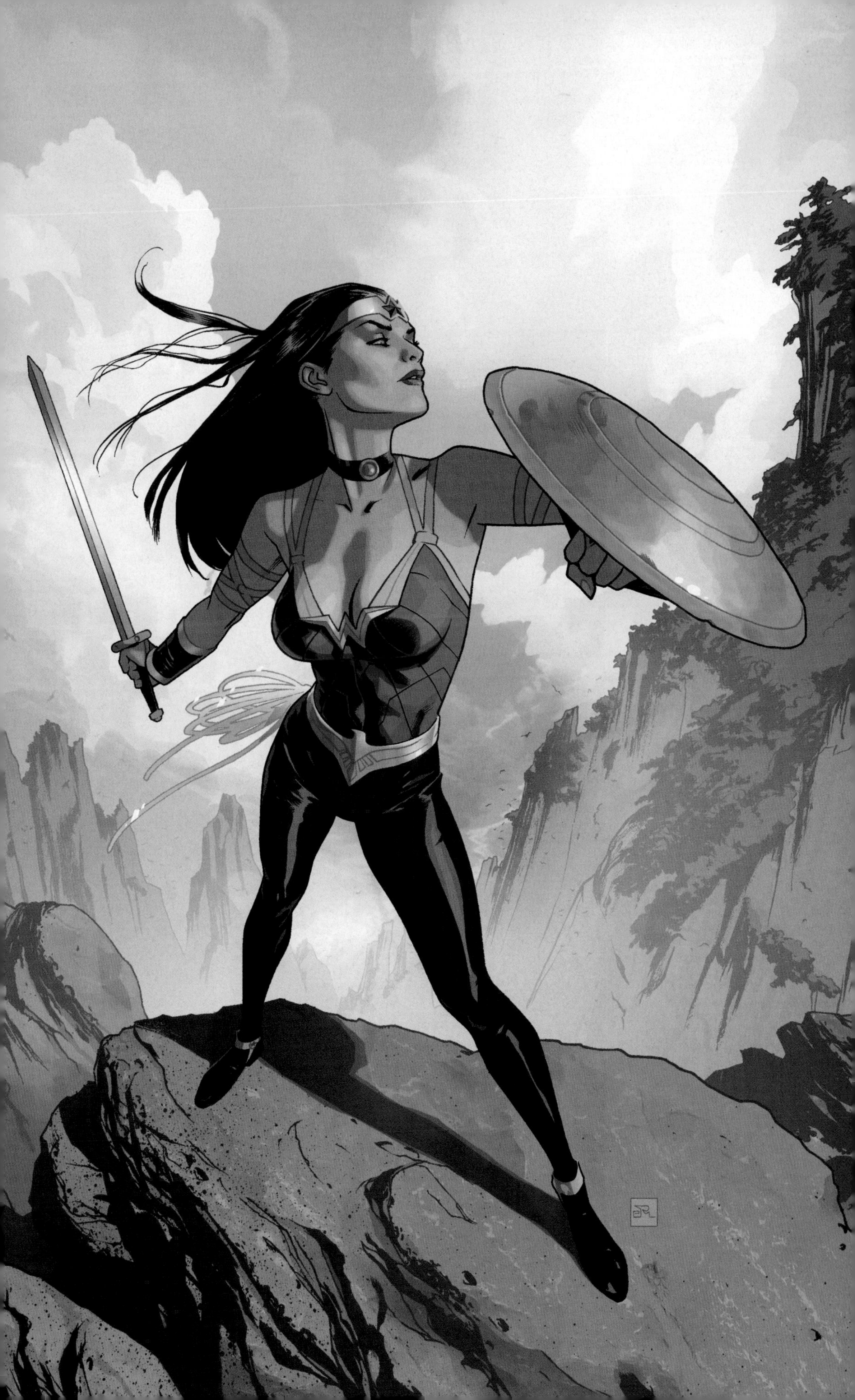

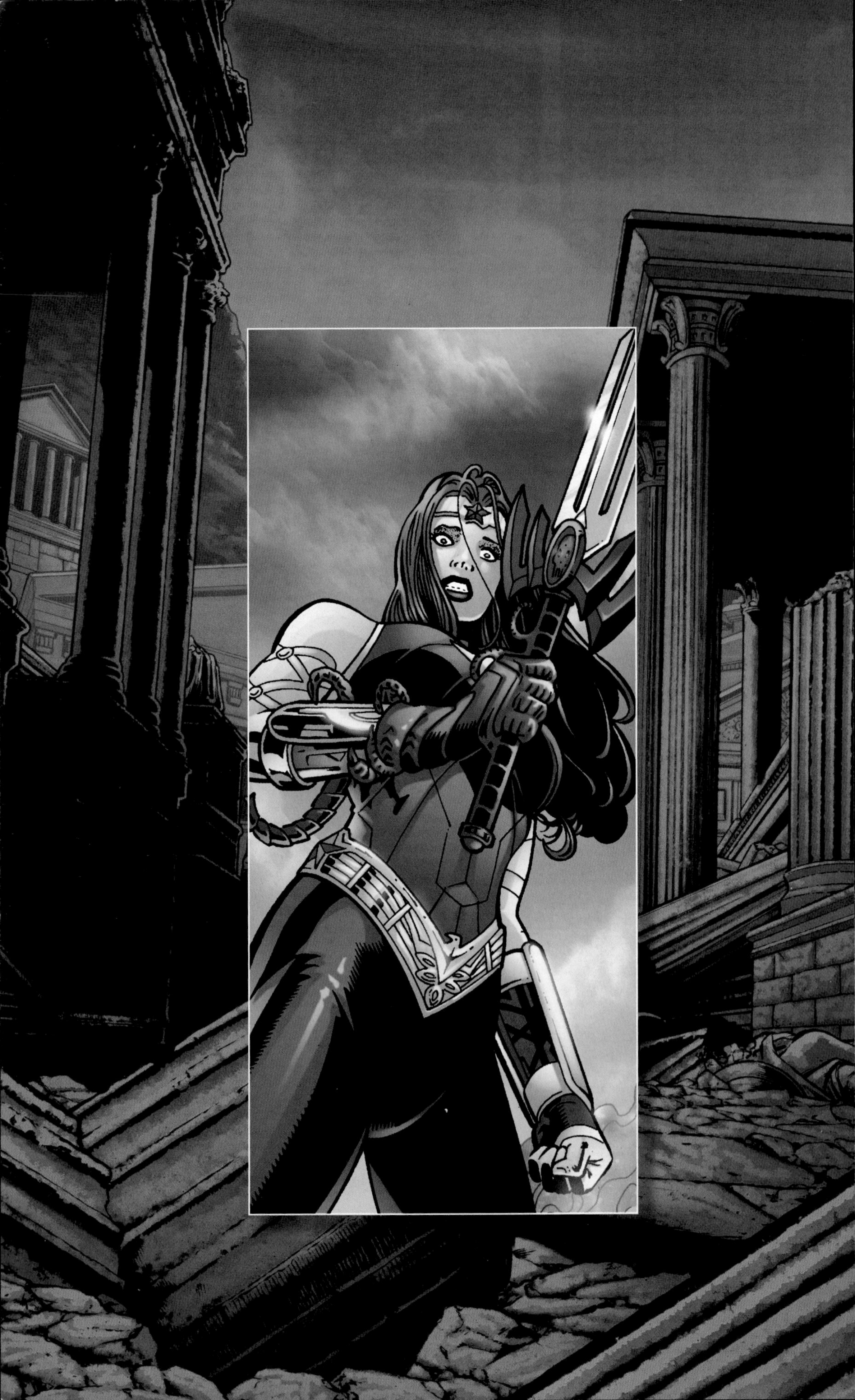

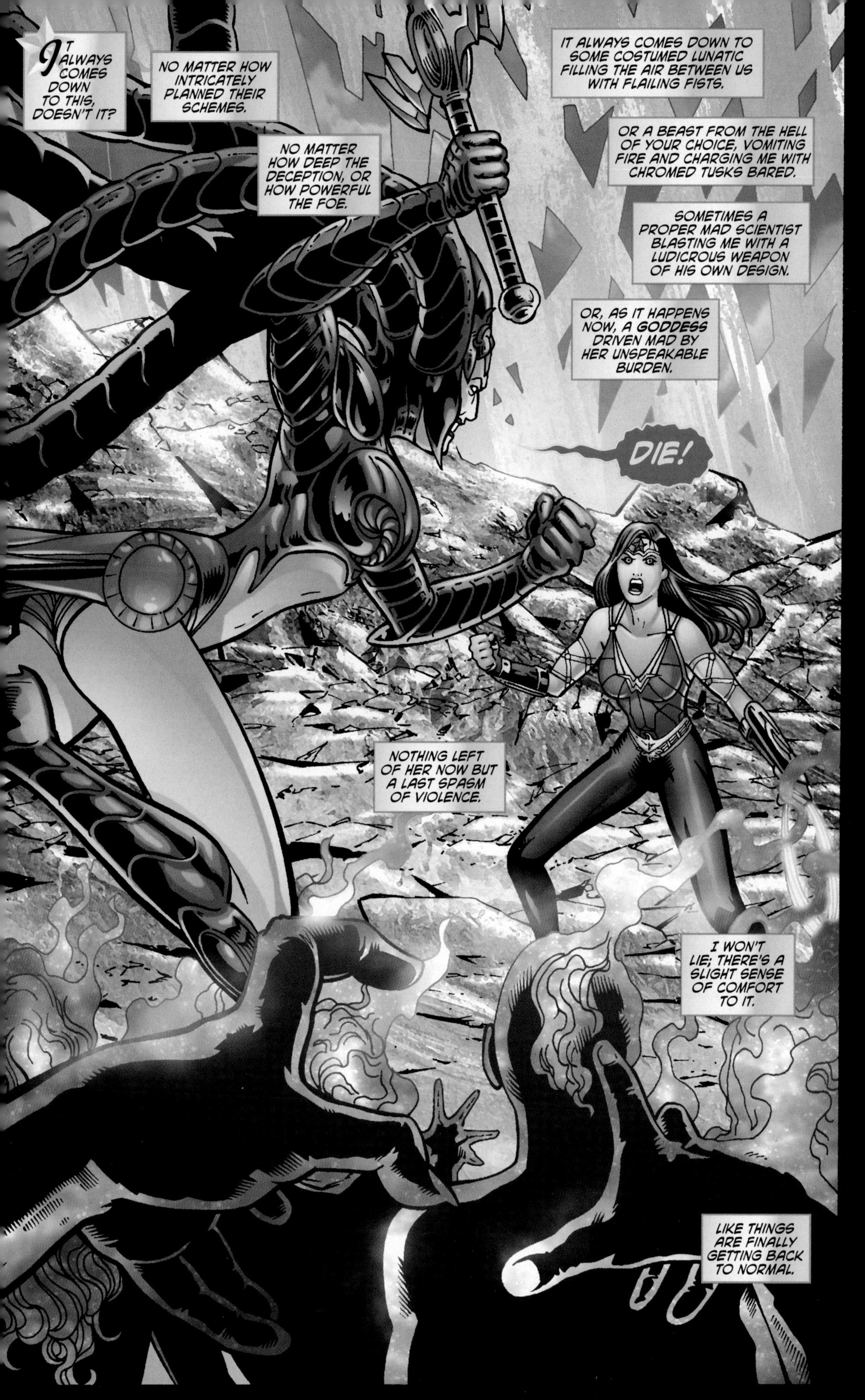
IT ALWAYS COMES DOWN TO THIS, DOESN'T IT?
NO MATTER HOW INTRICATELY PLANNED THEIR SCHEMES.
NO MATTER HOW DEEP THE DECEPTION, OR HOW POWERFUL THE FOE.
IT ALWAYS COMES DOWN TO SOME COSTUMED LUNATIC FILLING THE AIR BETWEEN US WITH FLAILING FISTS.
OR A BEAST FROM THE HELL OF YOUR CHOICE, VOMITING FIRE AND CHARGING ME WITH CHROMED TUSKS BARED.
SOMETIMES A PROPER MAD SCIENTIST BLASTING ME WITH A LUDICROUS WEAPON OF HIS OWN DESIGN.
OR, AS IT HAPPENS NOW, A GODDESS DRIVEN MAD BY HER UNSPEAKABLE BURDEN.
DIE!
NOTHING LEFT OF HER NOW BUT A LAST SPASM OF VIOLENCE.
I WON'T LIE; THERE'S A SLIGHT SENSE OF COMFORT TO IT.
LIKE THINGS ARE FINALLY GETTING BACK TO NORMAL.

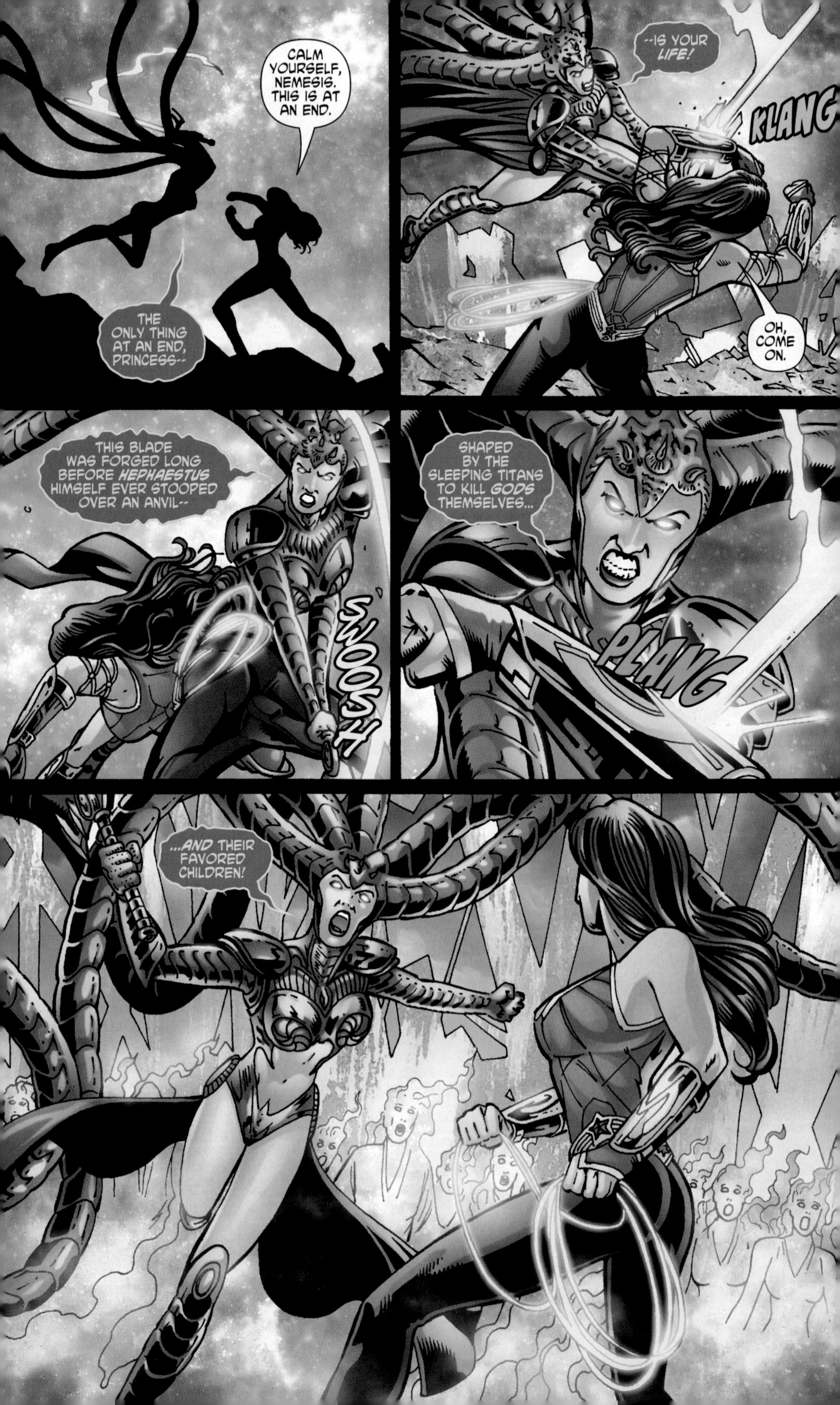
CALM YOURSELF, NEMESIS. THIS IS AT AN END.
THE ONLY THING AT AN END, PRINCESS--
--IS YOUR LIFE!
KLANG
OH, COME ON.
THIS BLADE WAS FORGED LONG BEFORE HEPHAESTUS HIMSELF EVER STOOPED OVER AN ANVIL--
SWOOSH
SHAPED BY THE SLEEPING TITANS TO KILL GODS THEMSELVES...
PLANG
...AND THEIR FAVORED CHILDREN!

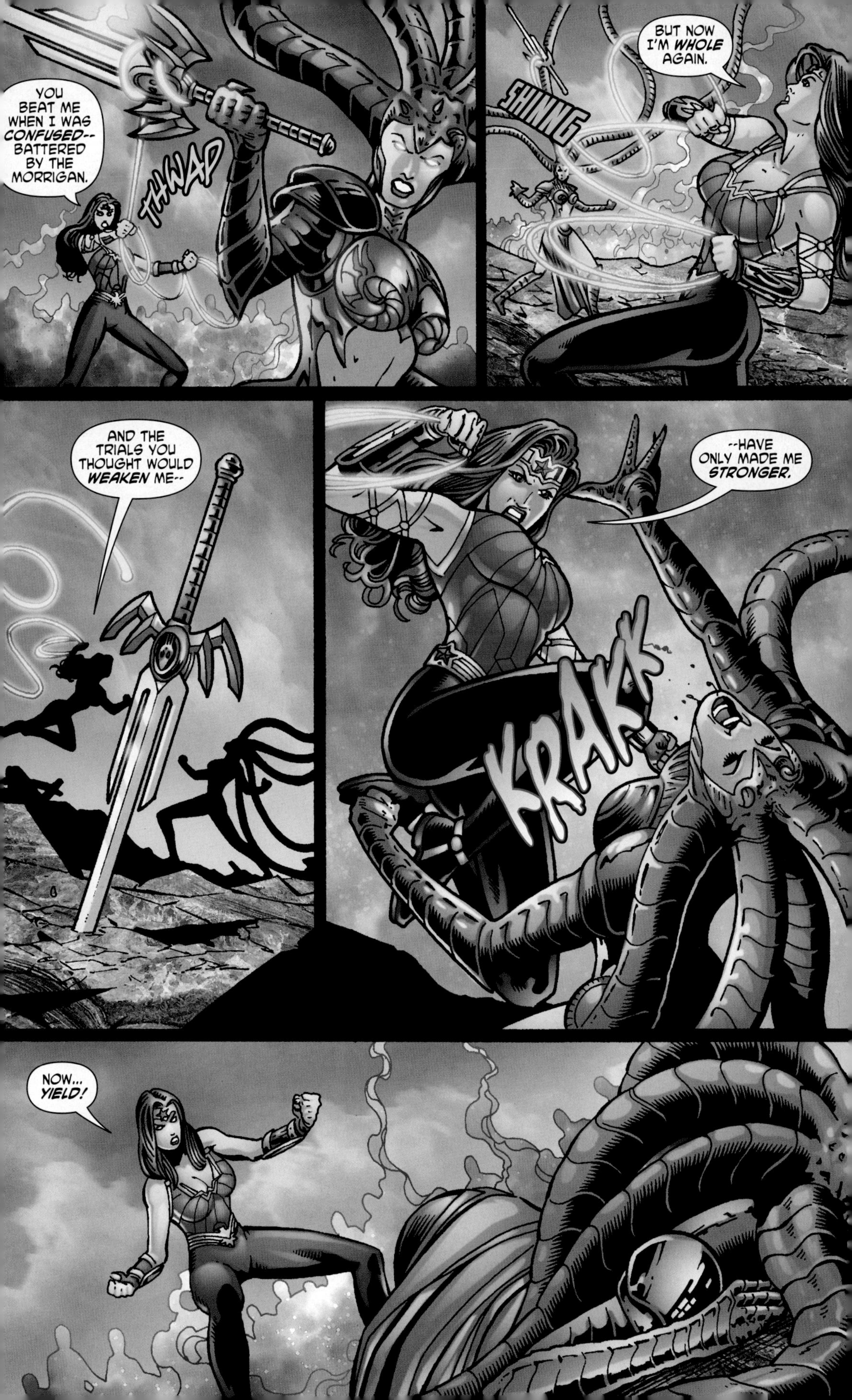
YOU BEAT ME WHEN I WAS CONFUSED-- BATTERED BY THE MORRIGAN.
THWAP
SHING
BUT NOW I'M WHOLE AGAIN.
AND THE TRIALS YOU THOUGHT WOULD WEAKEN ME--
--HAVE ONLY MADE ME STRONGER.
KRAK
NOW... YIELD!

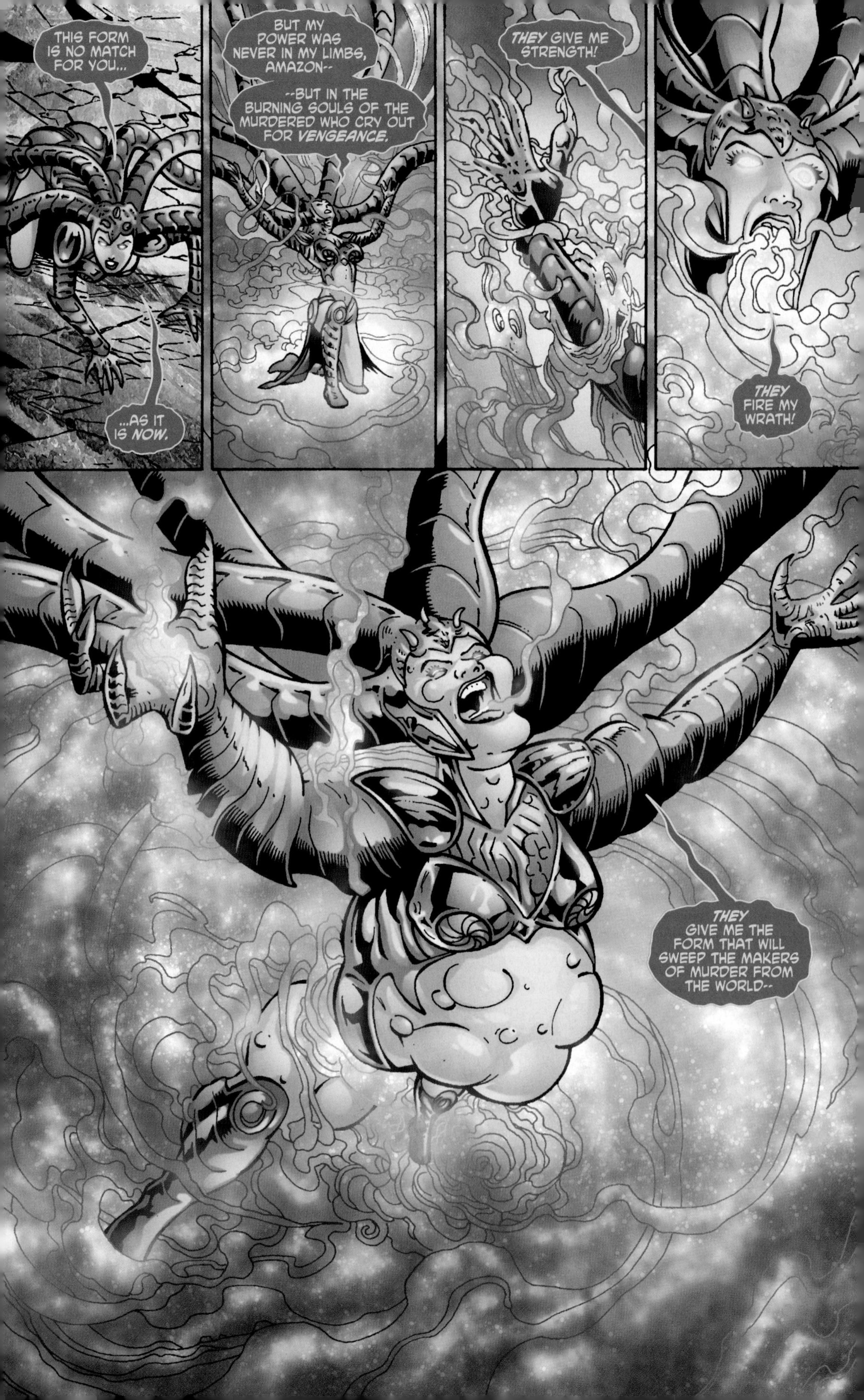
THIS FORM IS NO MATCH FOR YOU...
...AS IT IS *NOW.*
BUT MY POWER WAS NEVER IN MY LIMBS, AMAZON--
--BUT IN THE BURNING SOULS OF THE MURDERED WHO CRY OUT FOR *VENGEANCE.*
THEY GIVE ME STRENGTH!
THEY FIRE MY WRATH!
THEY GIVE ME THE FORM THAT WILL SWEEP THE MAKERS OF MURDER FROM THE WORLD--

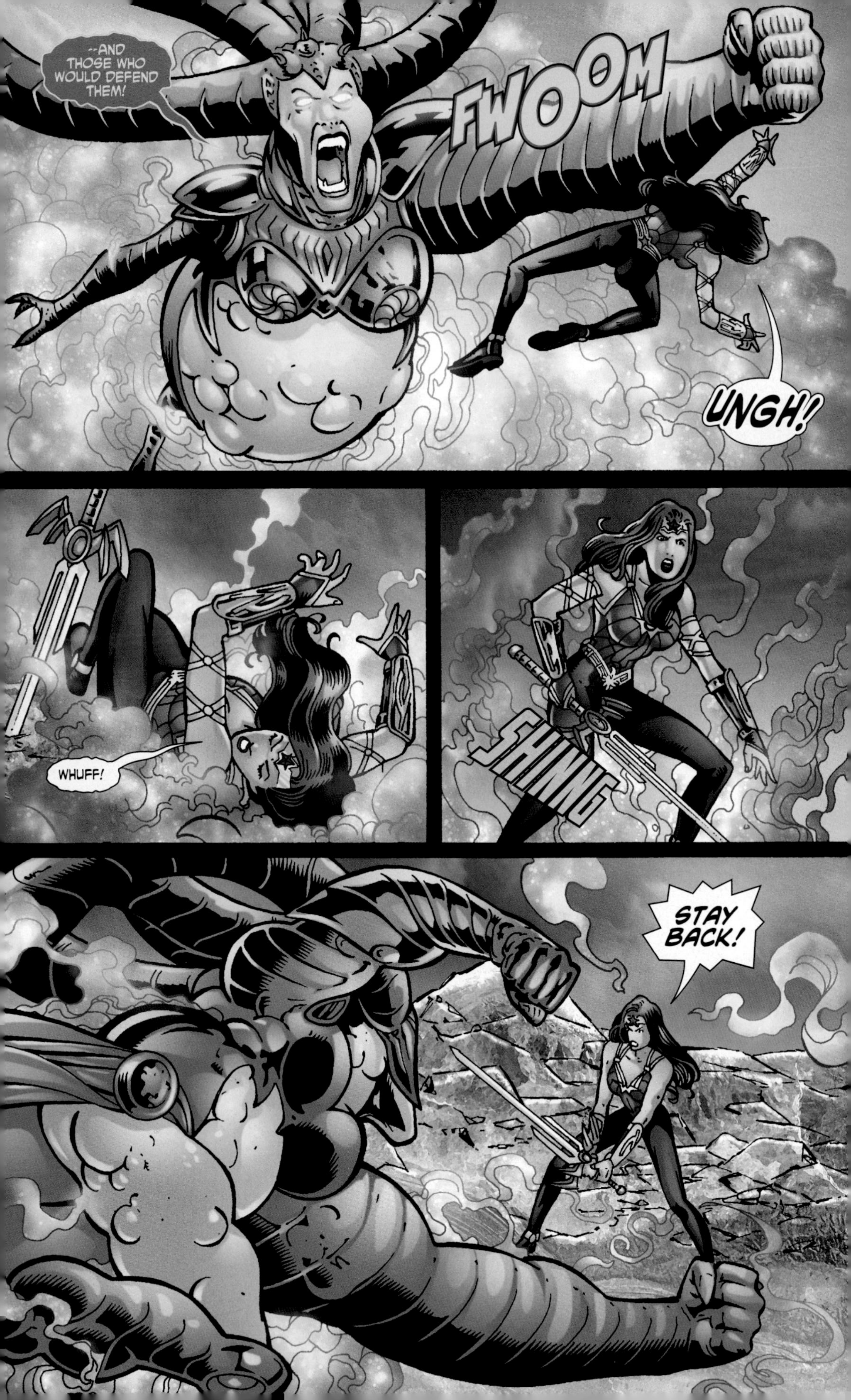
--AND THOSE WHO WOULD DEFEND THEM!
FWOOM
UNGH!
WHUFF!
SHING
STAY BACK!

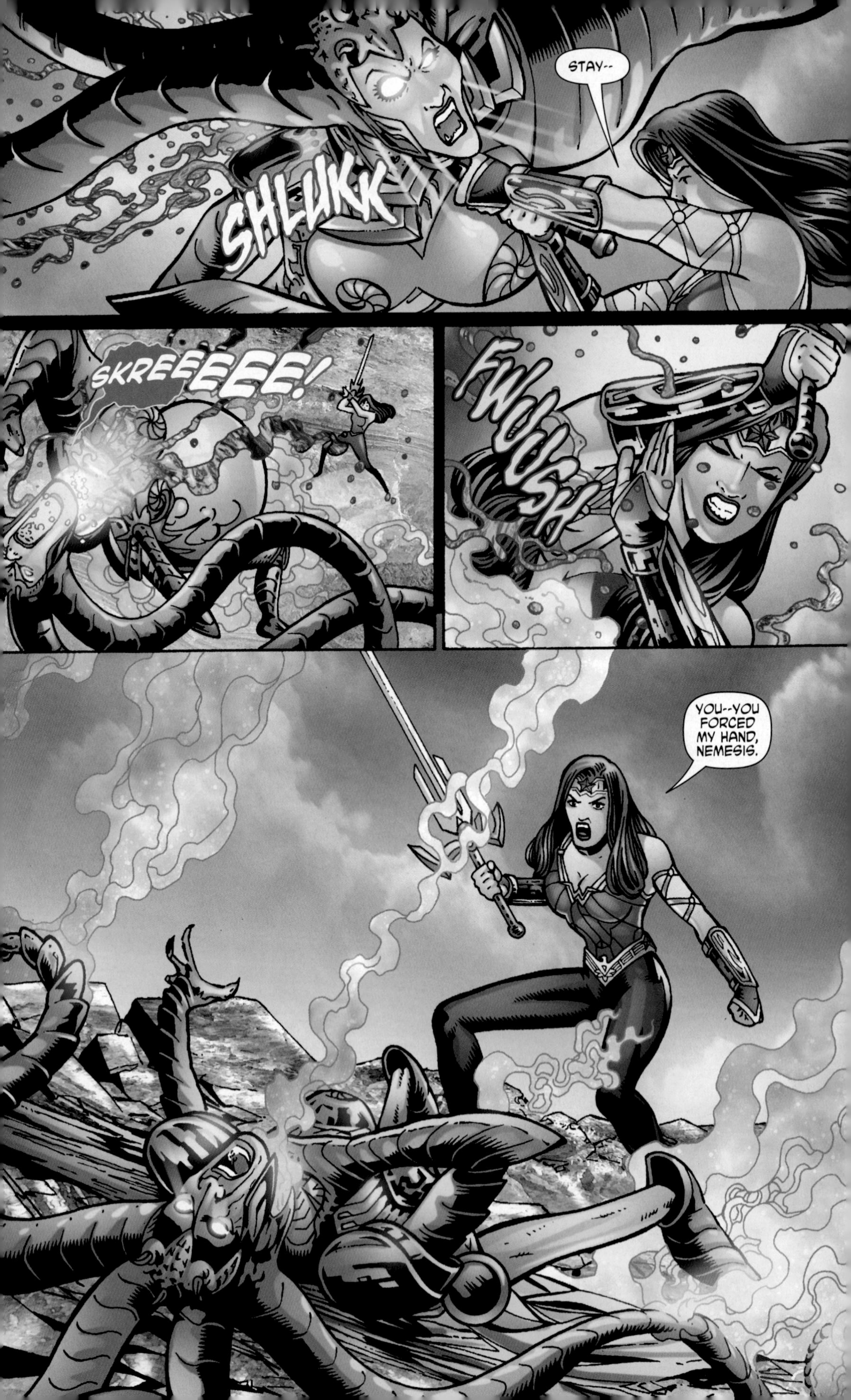
STAY--
SHLUKK
SKREEEEEE!
FWUUSH
YOU--YOU FORCED MY HAND, NEMESIS.

AND *YOU*... PASSED MY FINAL *TEST*.

AT *LAST*.

I WILL BE FREE AT LAST.

I CAN FEEL... DEATH LIFTING MY BURDEN... ALREADY.

THE CRIES OF THE MURDERED... NO LONGER ROAR IN MY EARS.

BUT EVEN WITHOUT ITS OWNER... THE FLASHING BLADE... MUST STILL *PUNISH*, DIANA.

NO! STOP IT! STOP THIS!

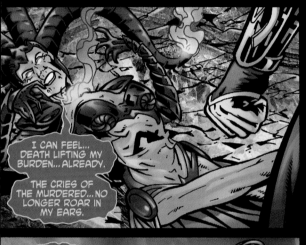

THE URGE TO... PUNISH... FLOWS AWAY WITH MY LIFE...

AND SETS UPON... A NEW CHAMPION.

NEW?

THE SWORD YOU HOLD... WAS MADE TO *KILL GODS*... AFTER ALL.

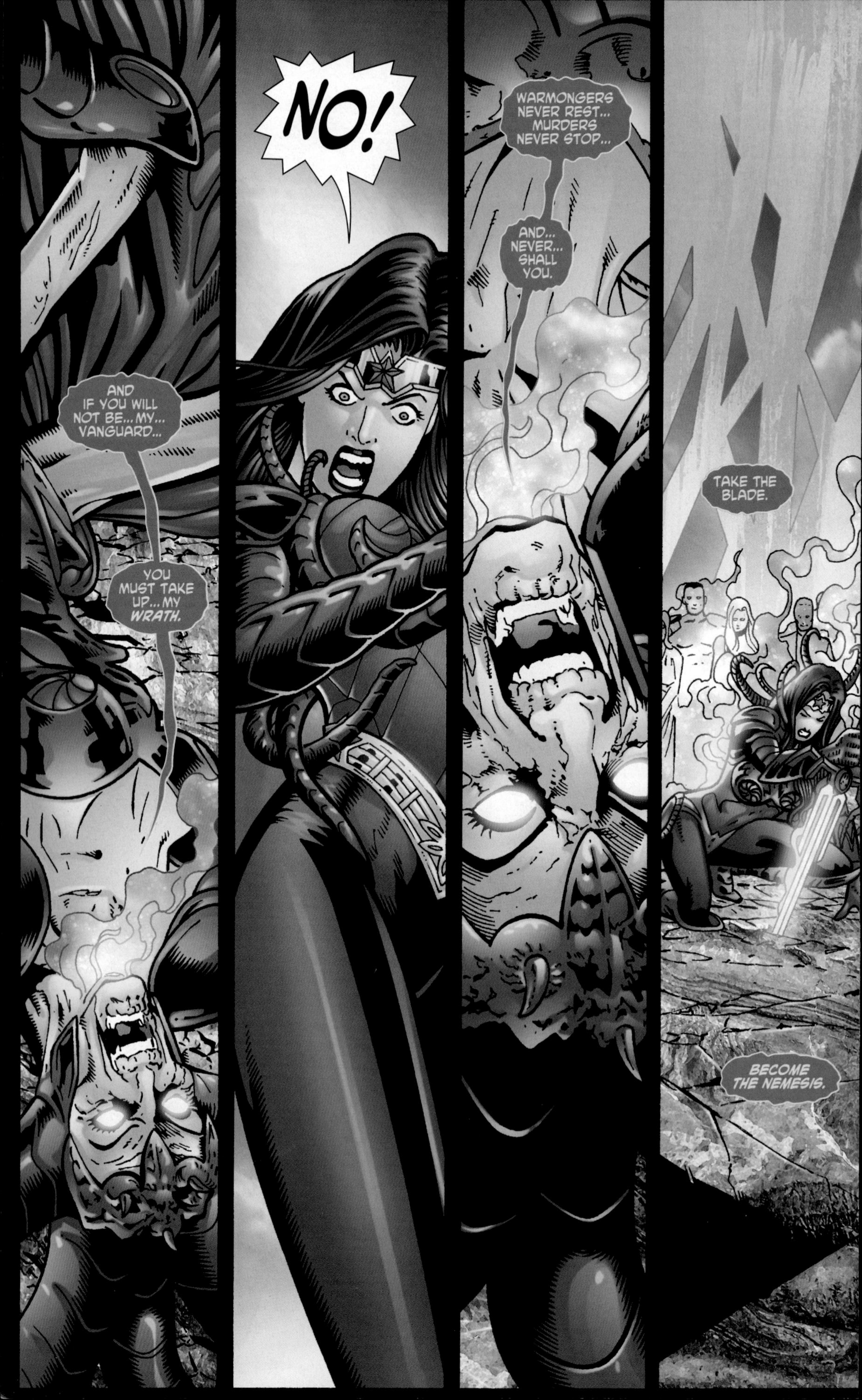
AND IF YOU WILL NOT BE... MY... VANGUARD...
YOU MUST TAKE UP... MY WRATH.
NO!
WARMONGERS NEVER REST... MURDERS NEVER STOP...
AND... NEVER... SHALL YOU.
TAKE THE BLADE.
BECOME THE NEMESIS.

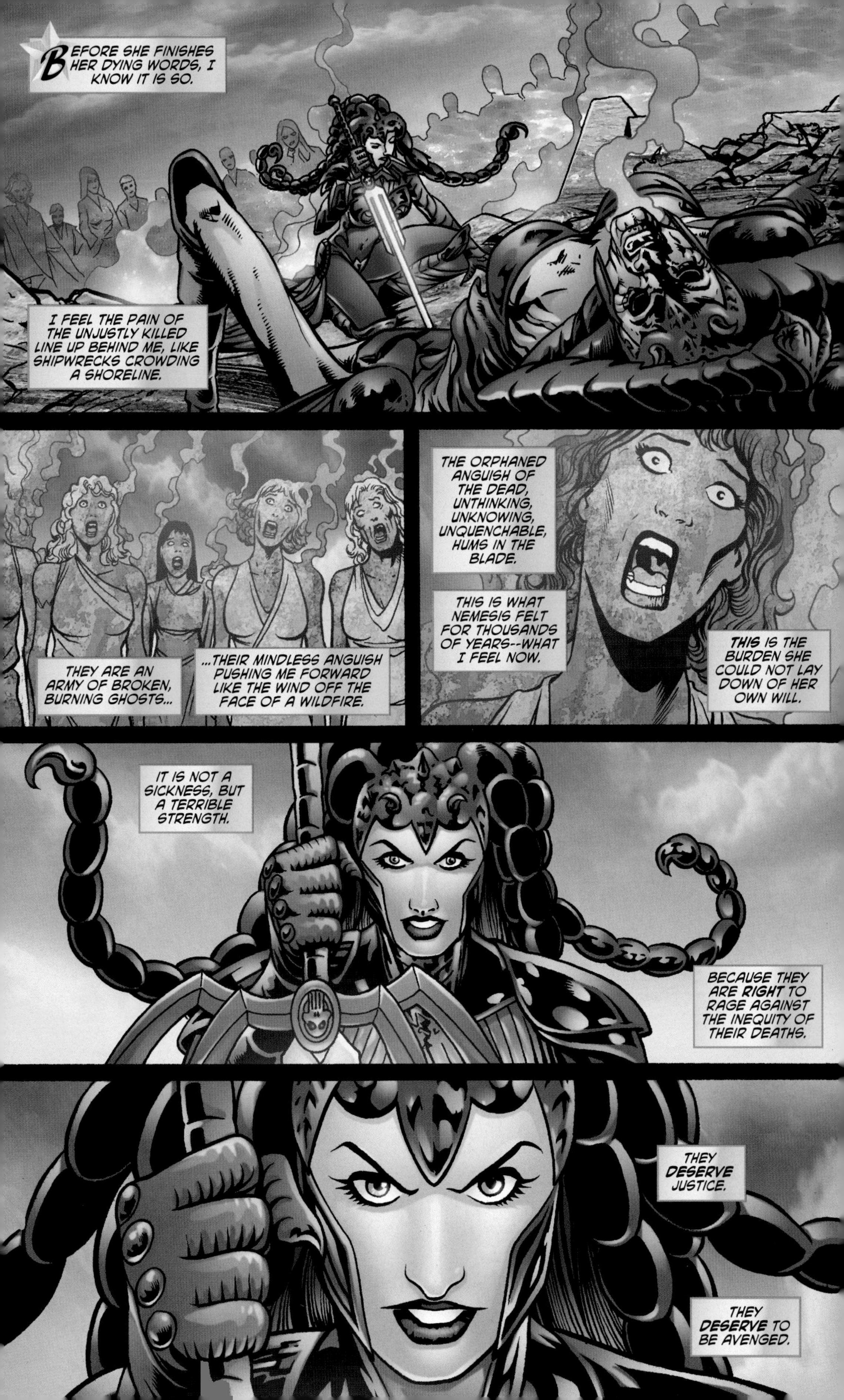
BEFORE SHE FINISHES HER DYING WORDS, I KNOW IT IS SO.
I FEEL THE PAIN OF THE UNJUSTLY KILLED LINE UP BEHIND ME, LIKE SHIPWRECKS CROWDING A SHORELINE.
THEY ARE AN ARMY OF BROKEN, BURNING GHOSTS...
...THEIR MINDLESS ANGUISH PUSHING ME FORWARD LIKE THE WIND OFF THE FACE OF A WILDFIRE.
THE ORPHANED ANGUISH OF THE DEAD, UNTHINKING, UNKNOWING, UNQUENCHABLE, HUMS IN THE BLADE.
THIS IS WHAT NEMESIS FELT FOR THOUSANDS OF YEARS--WHAT I FEEL NOW.
THIS IS THE BURDEN SHE COULD NOT LAY DOWN OF HER OWN WILL.
IT IS NOT A SICKNESS, BUT A TERRIBLE STRENGTH.
BECAUSE THEY ARE RIGHT TO RAGE AGAINST THE INEQUITY OF THEIR DEATHS.
THEY DESERVE JUSTICE.
THEY DESERVE TO BE AVENGED.

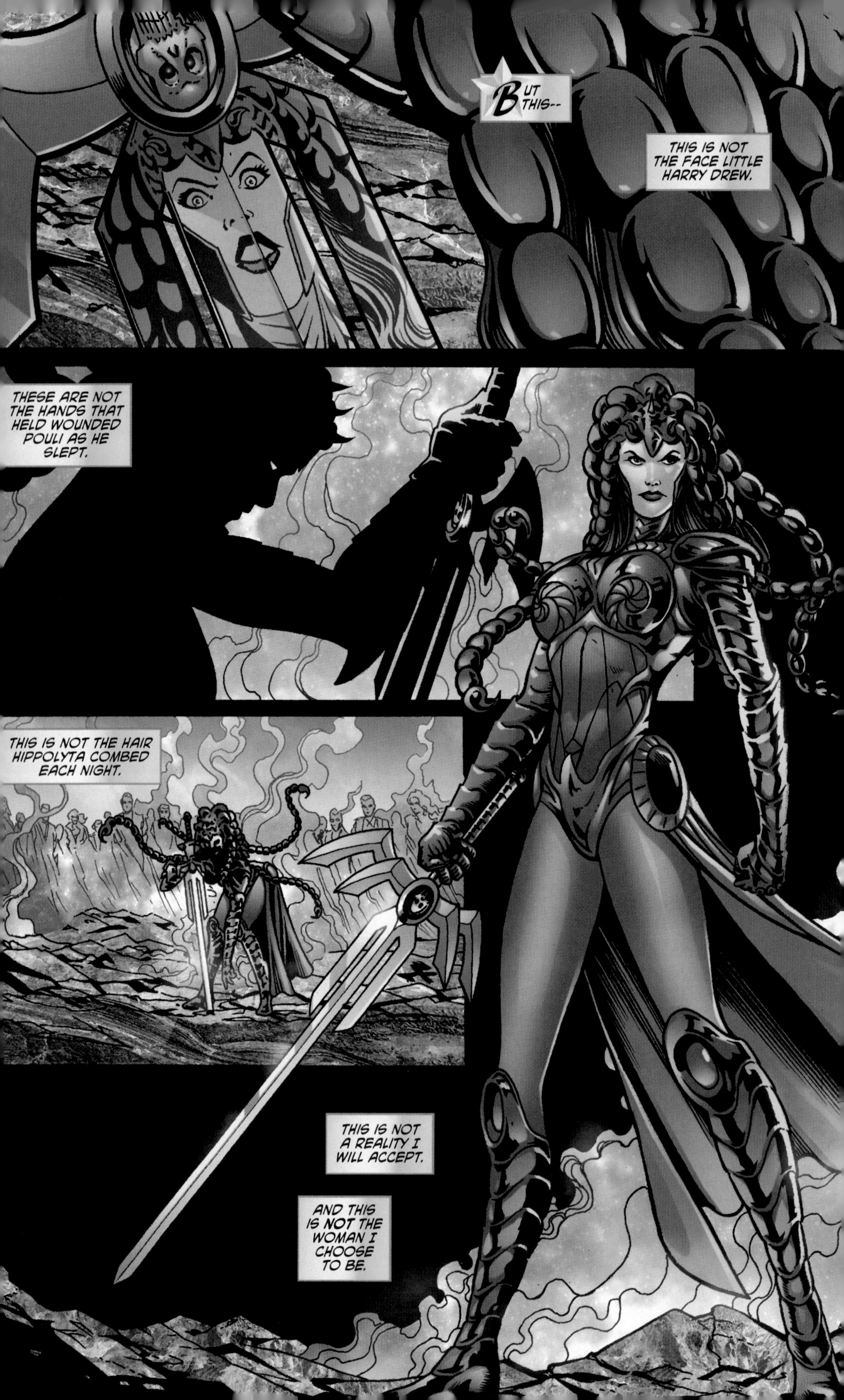
BUT THIS--
THIS IS NOT THE FACE LITTLE HARRY DREW.
THESE ARE NOT THE HANDS THAT HELD WOUNDED POULI AS HE SLEPT.
THIS IS NOT THE HAIR HIPPOLYTA COMBED EACH NIGHT.
THIS IS NOT A REALITY I WILL ACCEPT.
AND THIS IS NOT THE WOMAN I CHOOSE TO BE.

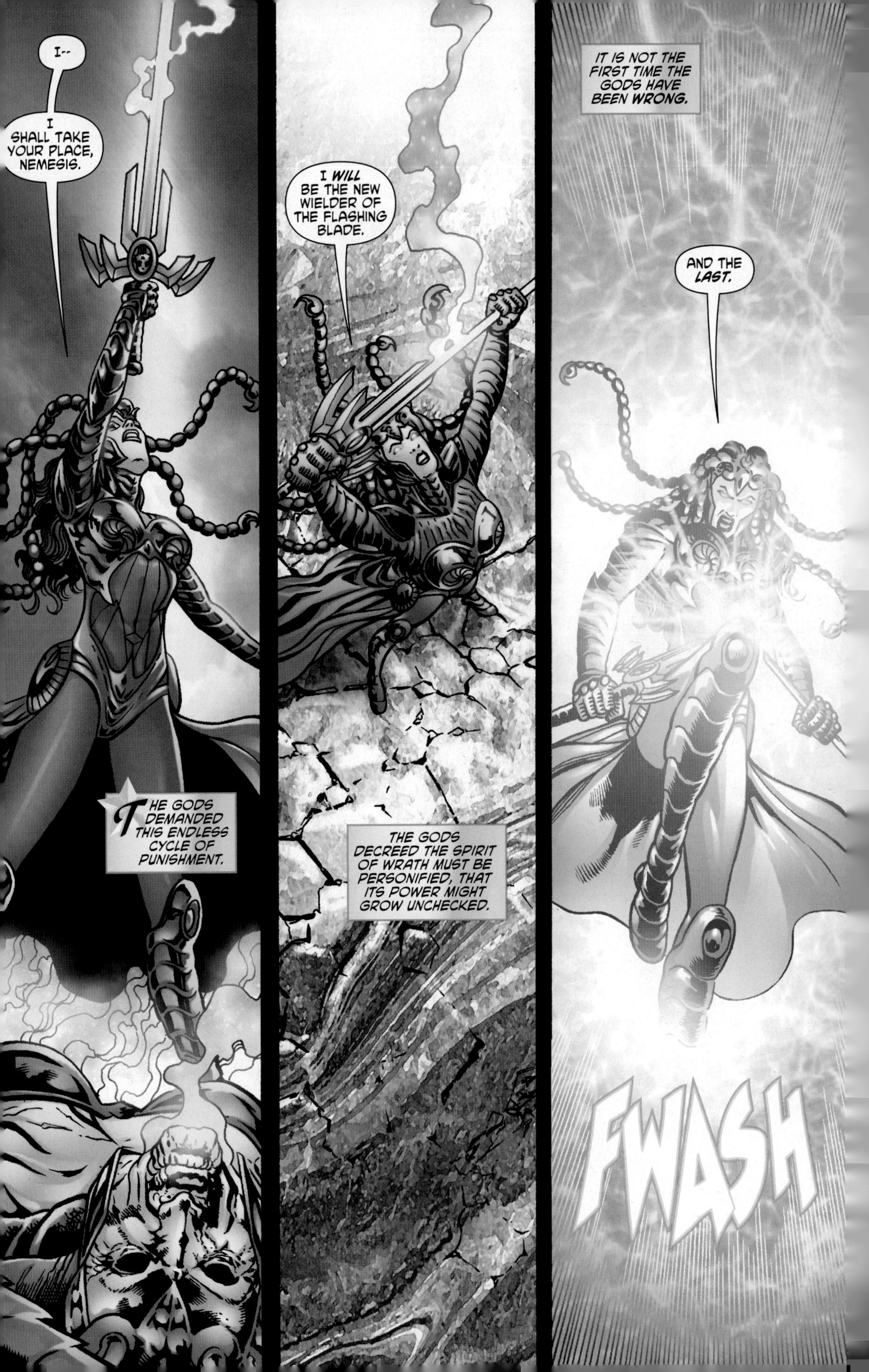
I--
I SHALL TAKE YOUR PLACE, NEMESIS.
THE GODS DEMANDED THIS ENDLESS CYCLE OF PUNISHMENT.
I WILL BE THE NEW WIELDER OF THE FLASHING BLADE.
THE GODS DECREED THE SPIRIT OF WRATH MUST BE PERSONIFIED, THAT ITS POWER MIGHT GROW UNCHECKED.
IT IS NOT THE FIRST TIME THE GODS HAVE BEEN WRONG.
AND THE LAST.
FWASH

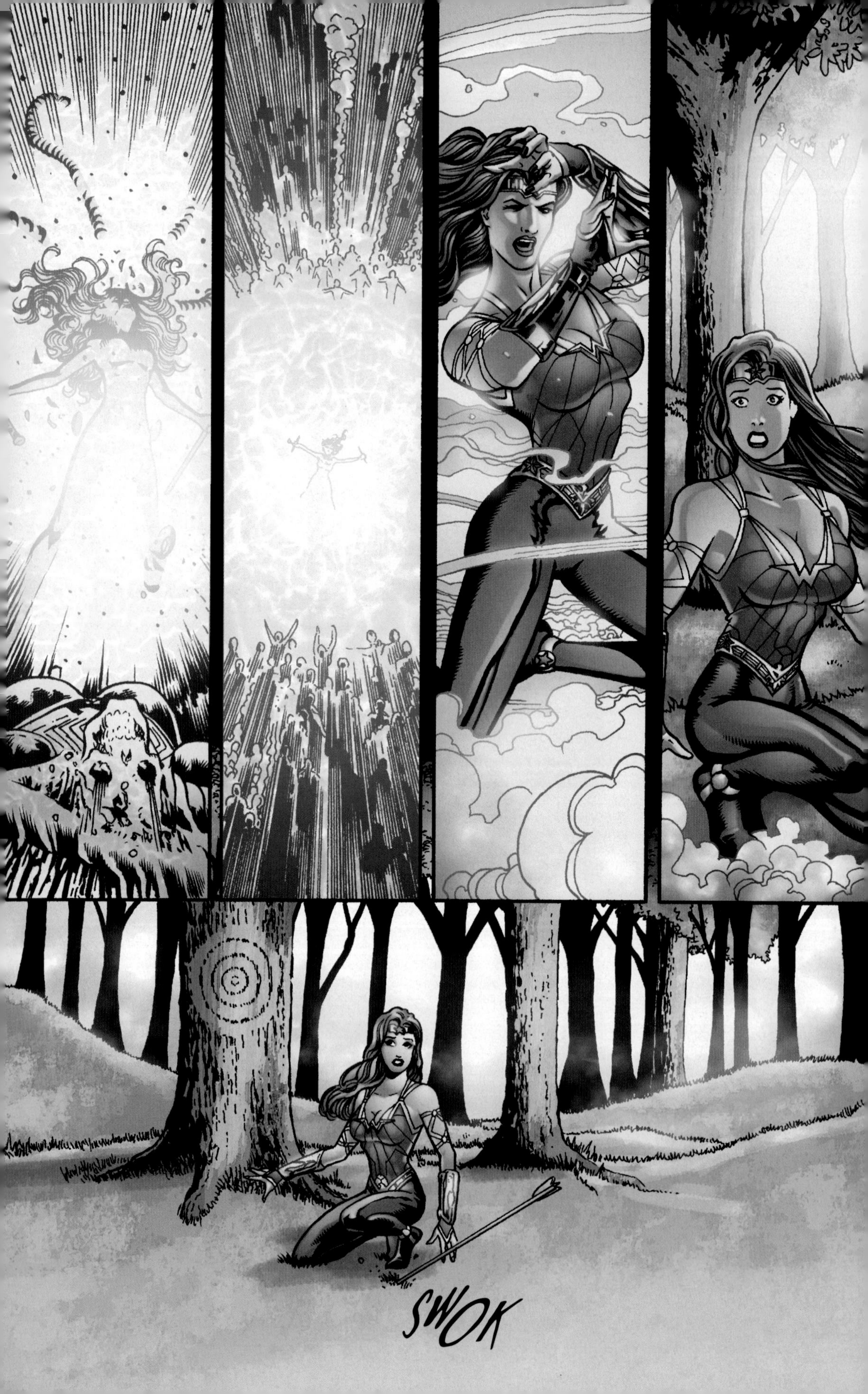
SWOK

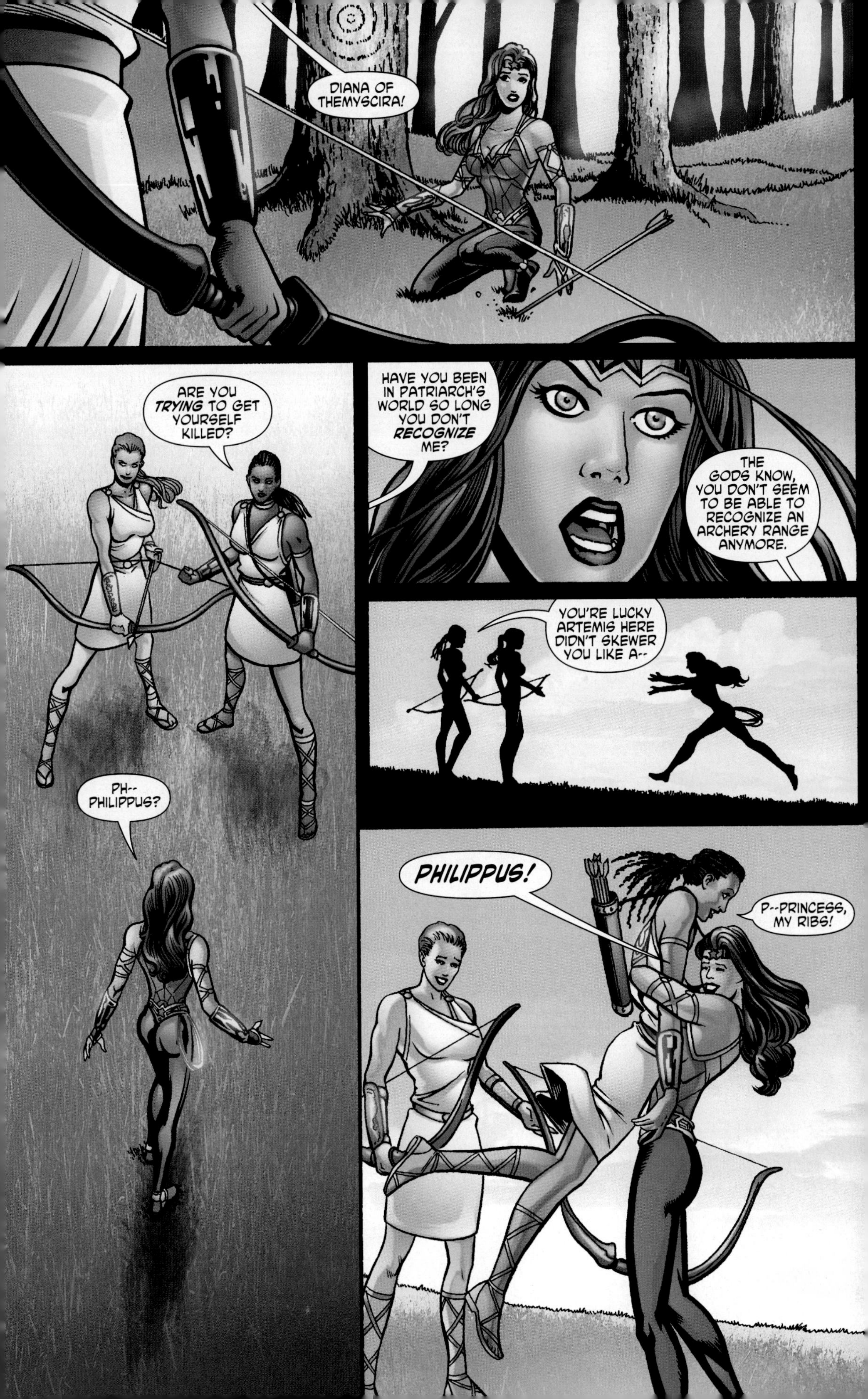
DIANA OF THEMYSCIRA!
ARE YOU *TRYING* TO GET YOURSELF KILLED?
HAVE YOU BEEN IN PATRIARCH'S WORLD SO LONG YOU DON'T *RECOGNIZE* ME?
THE GODS KNOW, YOU DON'T SEEM TO BE ABLE TO RECOGNIZE AN ARCHERY RANGE ANYMORE.
YOU'RE LUCKY ARTEMIS HERE DIDN'T SKEWER YOU LIKE A--
PH-- PHILIPPUS?
PHILIPPUS!
P--PRINCESS, MY RIBS!

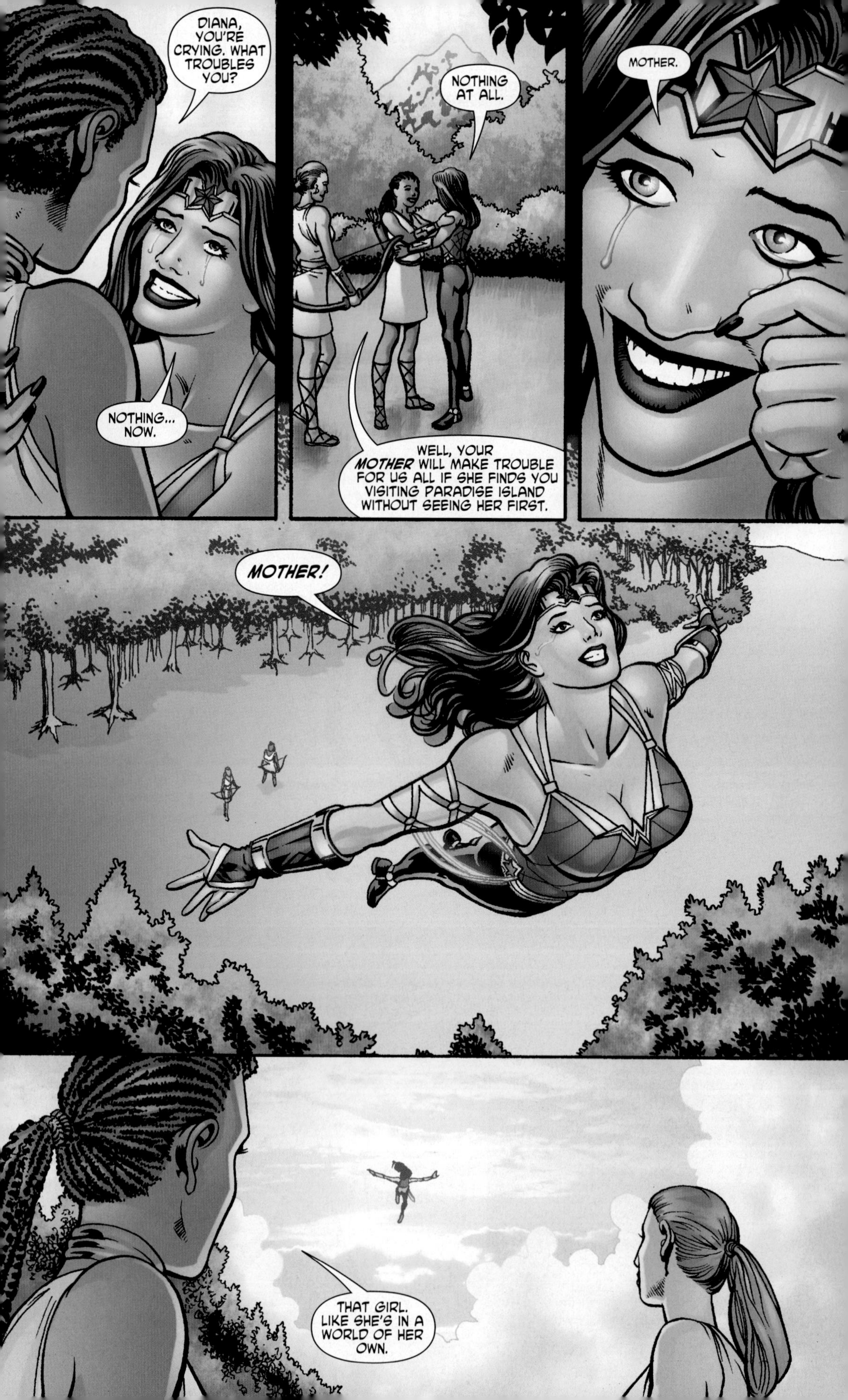
DIANA, YOU'RE CRYING. WHAT TROUBLES YOU?
NOTHING... NOW.
NOTHING AT ALL.
WELL, YOUR MOTHER WILL MAKE TROUBLE FOR US ALL IF SHE FINDS YOU VISITING PARADISE ISLAND WITHOUT SEEING HER FIRST.
MOTHER.
MOTHER!
THAT GIRL. LIKE SHE'S IN A WORLD OF HER OWN.

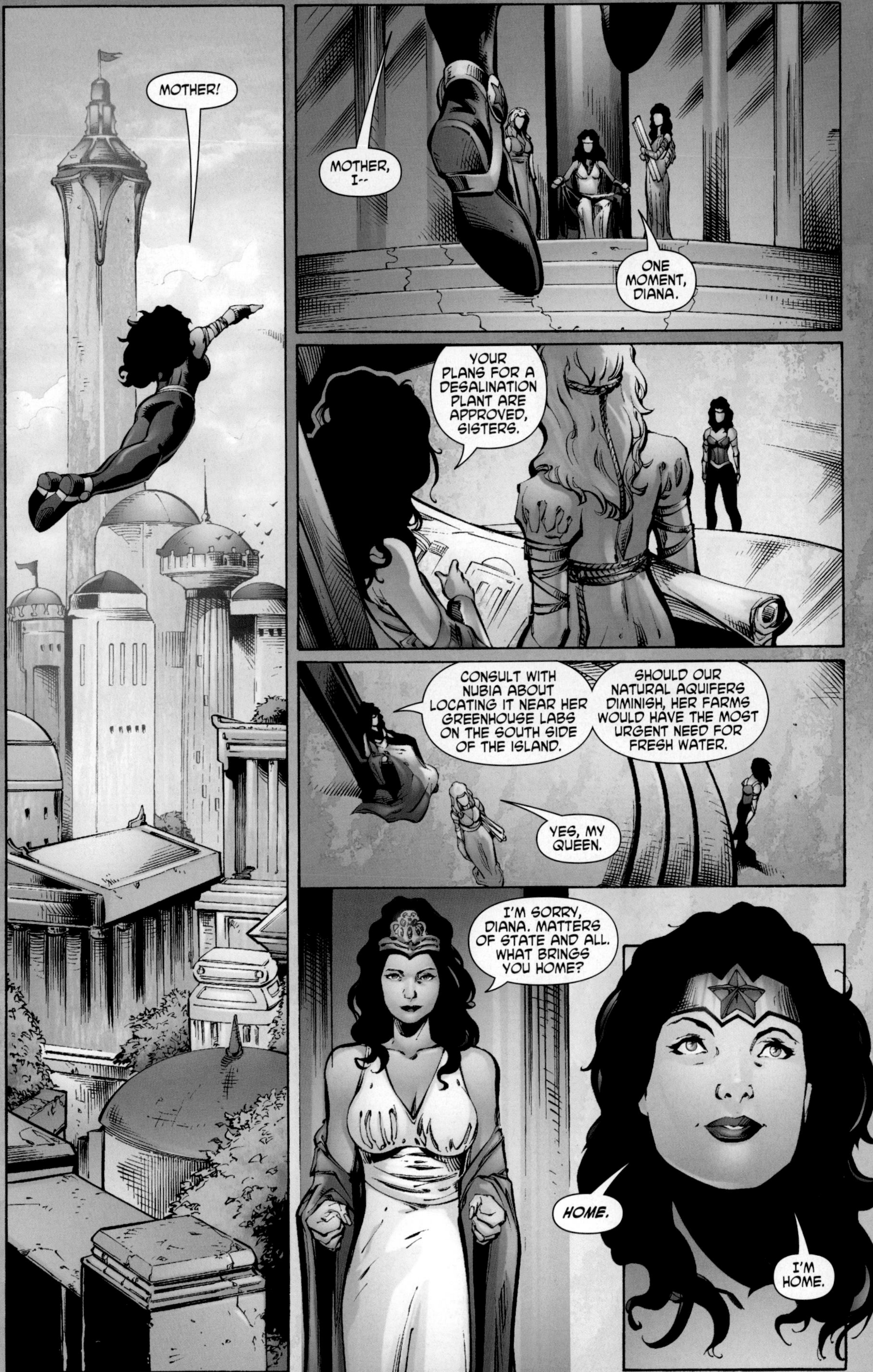
MOTHER!
MOTHER, I--
ONE MOMENT, DIANA.
YOUR PLANS FOR A DESALINATION PLANT ARE APPROVED, SISTERS.
CONSULT WITH NUBIA ABOUT LOCATING IT NEAR HER GREENHOUSE LABS ON THE SOUTH SIDE OF THE ISLAND.
SHOULD OUR NATURAL AQUIFERS DIMINISH, HER FARMS WOULD HAVE THE MOST URGENT NEED FOR FRESH WATER.
YES, MY QUEEN.
I'M SORRY, DIANA. MATTERS OF STATE AND ALL. WHAT BRINGS YOU HOME?
HOME.
I'M HOME.

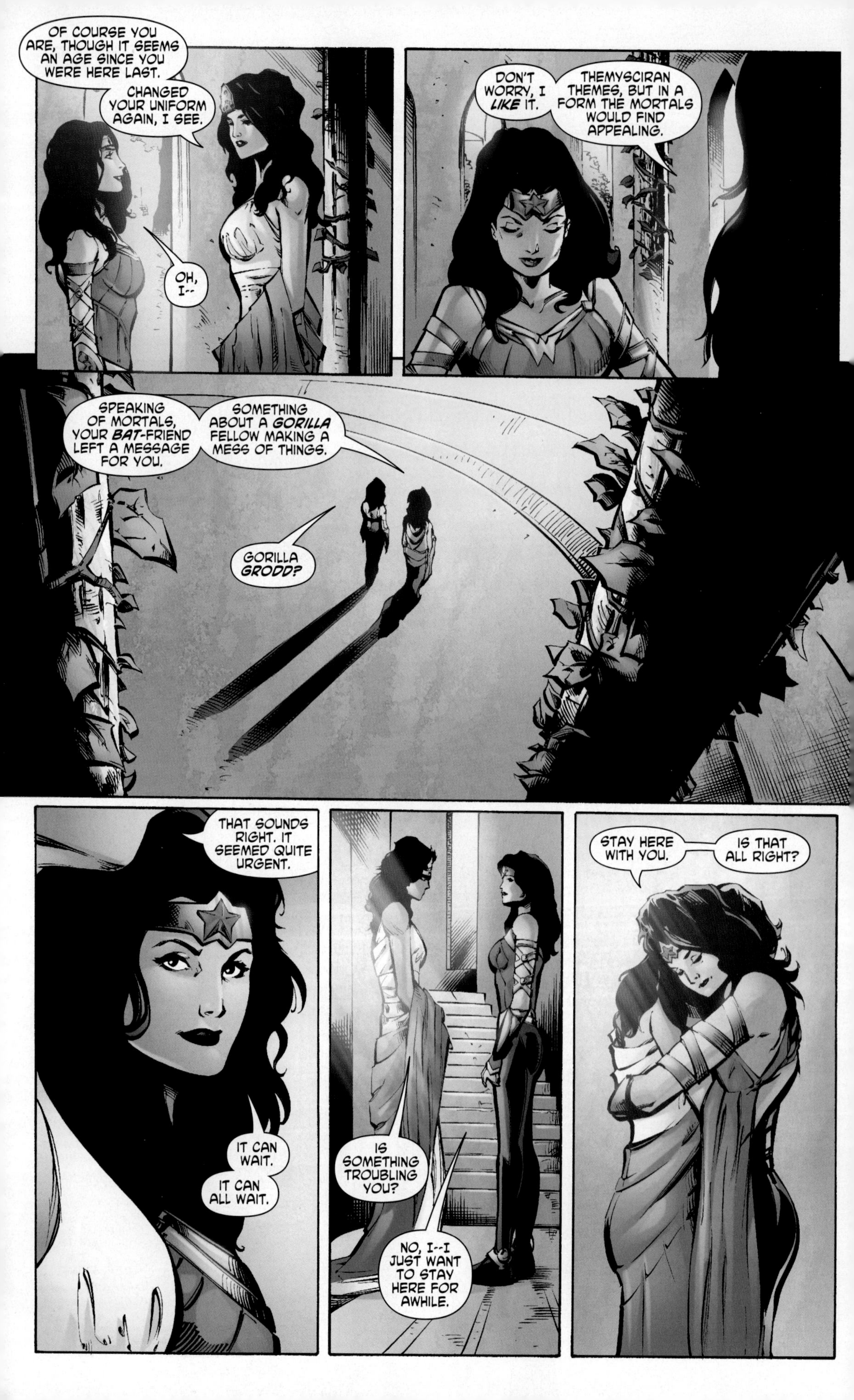
OF COURSE YOU ARE, THOUGH IT SEEMS AN AGE SINCE YOU WERE HERE LAST.
CHANGED YOUR UNIFORM AGAIN, I SEE.
OH, I--
DON'T WORRY, I LIKE IT.
THEMYSCIRAN THEMES, BUT IN A FORM THE MORTALS WOULD FIND APPEALING.
SPEAKING OF MORTALS, YOUR BAT-FRIEND LEFT A MESSAGE FOR YOU.
SOMETHING ABOUT A GORILLA FELLOW MAKING A MESS OF THINGS.
GORILLA GRODD?
THAT SOUNDS RIGHT. IT SEEMED QUITE URGENT.
IT CAN WAIT.
IT CAN ALL WAIT.
IS SOMETHING TROUBLING YOU?
NO, I--I JUST WANT TO STAY HERE FOR AWHILE.
STAY HERE WITH YOU.
IS THAT ALL RIGHT?

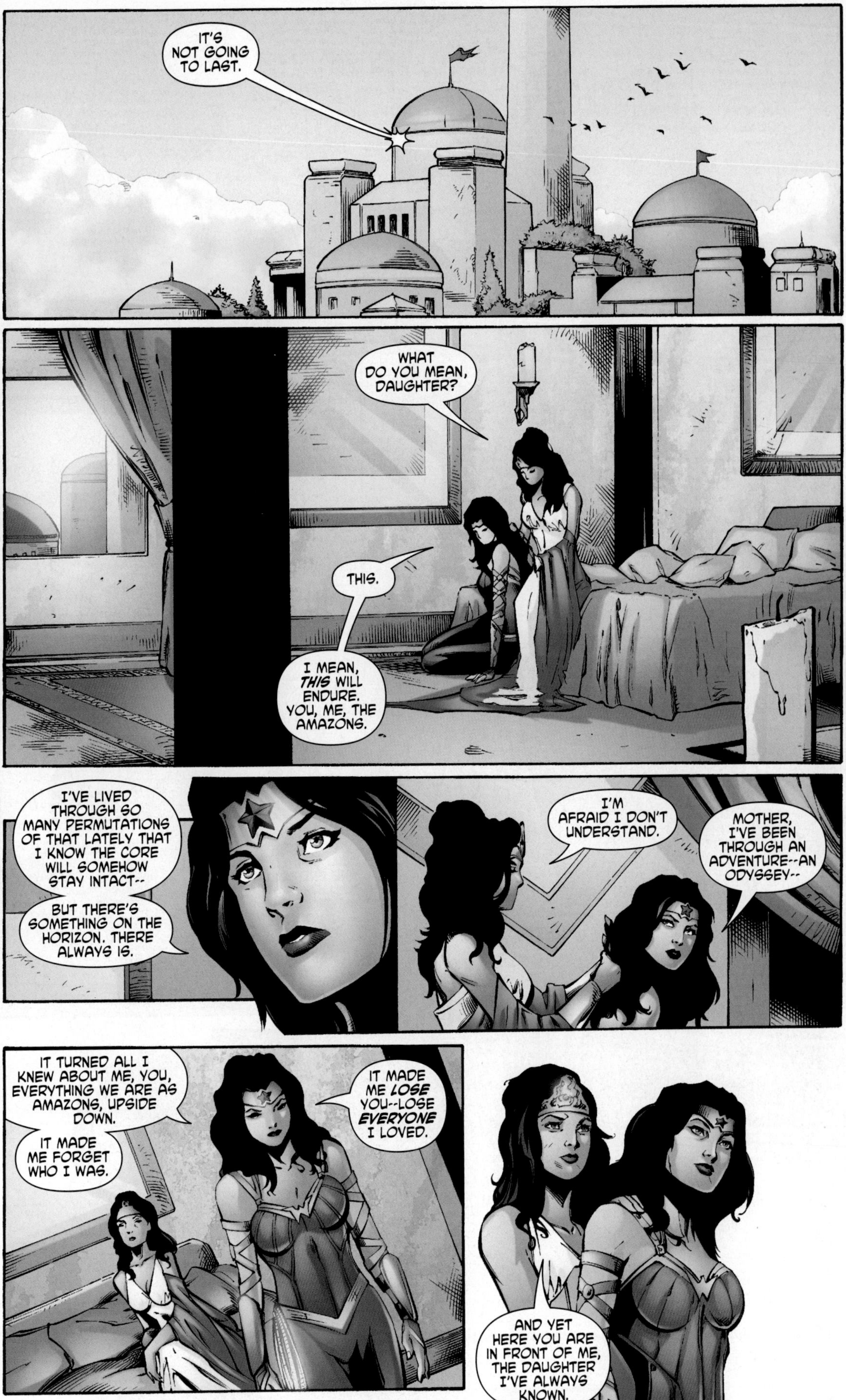
IT'S NOT GOING TO LAST.
WHAT DO YOU MEAN, DAUGHTER?
THIS.
I MEAN, THIS WILL ENDURE. YOU, ME, THE AMAZONS.
I'VE LIVED THROUGH SO MANY PERMUTATIONS OF THAT LATELY THAT I KNOW THE CORE WILL SOMEHOW STAY INTACT--
BUT THERE'S SOMETHING ON THE HORIZON. THERE ALWAYS IS.
I'M AFRAID I DON'T UNDERSTAND.
MOTHER, I'VE BEEN THROUGH AN ADVENTURE--AN ODYSSEY--
IT TURNED ALL I KNEW ABOUT ME, YOU, EVERYTHING WE ARE AS AMAZONS, UPSIDE DOWN.
IT MADE ME FORGET WHO I WAS.
IT MADE ME LOSE YOU--LOSE EVERYONE I LOVED.
AND YET HERE YOU ARE IN FRONT OF ME, THE DAUGHTER I'VE ALWAYS KNOWN.

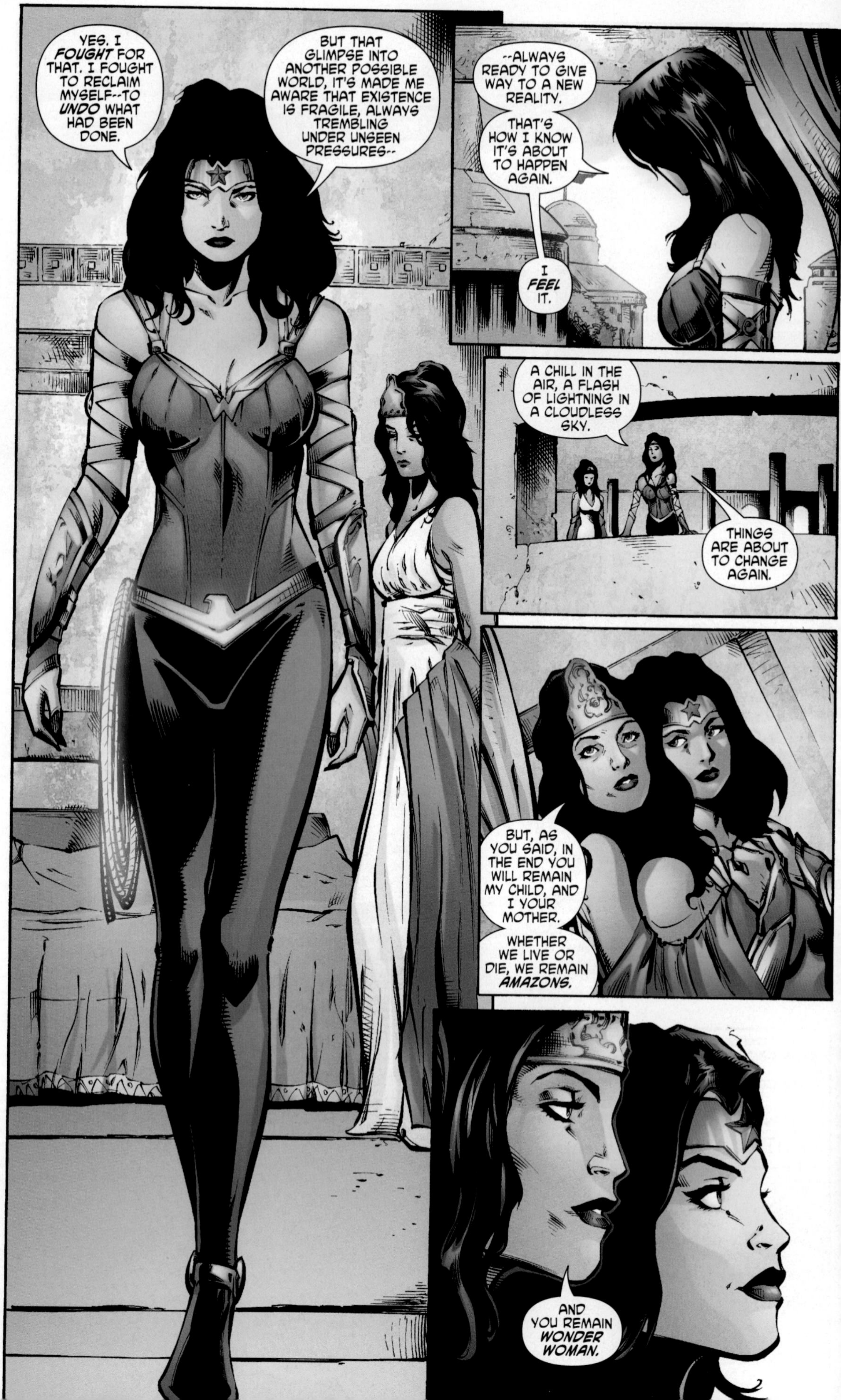
YES. I FOUGHT FOR THAT. I FOUGHT TO RECLAIM MYSELF--TO UNDO WHAT HAD BEEN DONE.
BUT THAT GLIMPSE INTO ANOTHER POSSIBLE WORLD, IT'S MADE ME AWARE THAT EXISTENCE IS FRAGILE, ALWAYS TREMBLING UNDER UNSEEN PRESSURES--
--ALWAYS READY TO GIVE WAY TO A NEW REALITY.
THAT'S HOW I KNOW IT'S ABOUT TO HAPPEN AGAIN.
I FEEL IT.
A CHILL IN THE AIR, A FLASH OF LIGHTNING IN A CLOUDLESS SKY.
THINGS ARE ABOUT TO CHANGE AGAIN.
BUT, AS YOU SAID, IN THE END YOU WILL REMAIN MY CHILD, AND I YOUR MOTHER.
WHETHER WE LIVE OR DIE, WE REMAIN AMAZONS.
AND YOU REMAIN WONDER WOMAN.

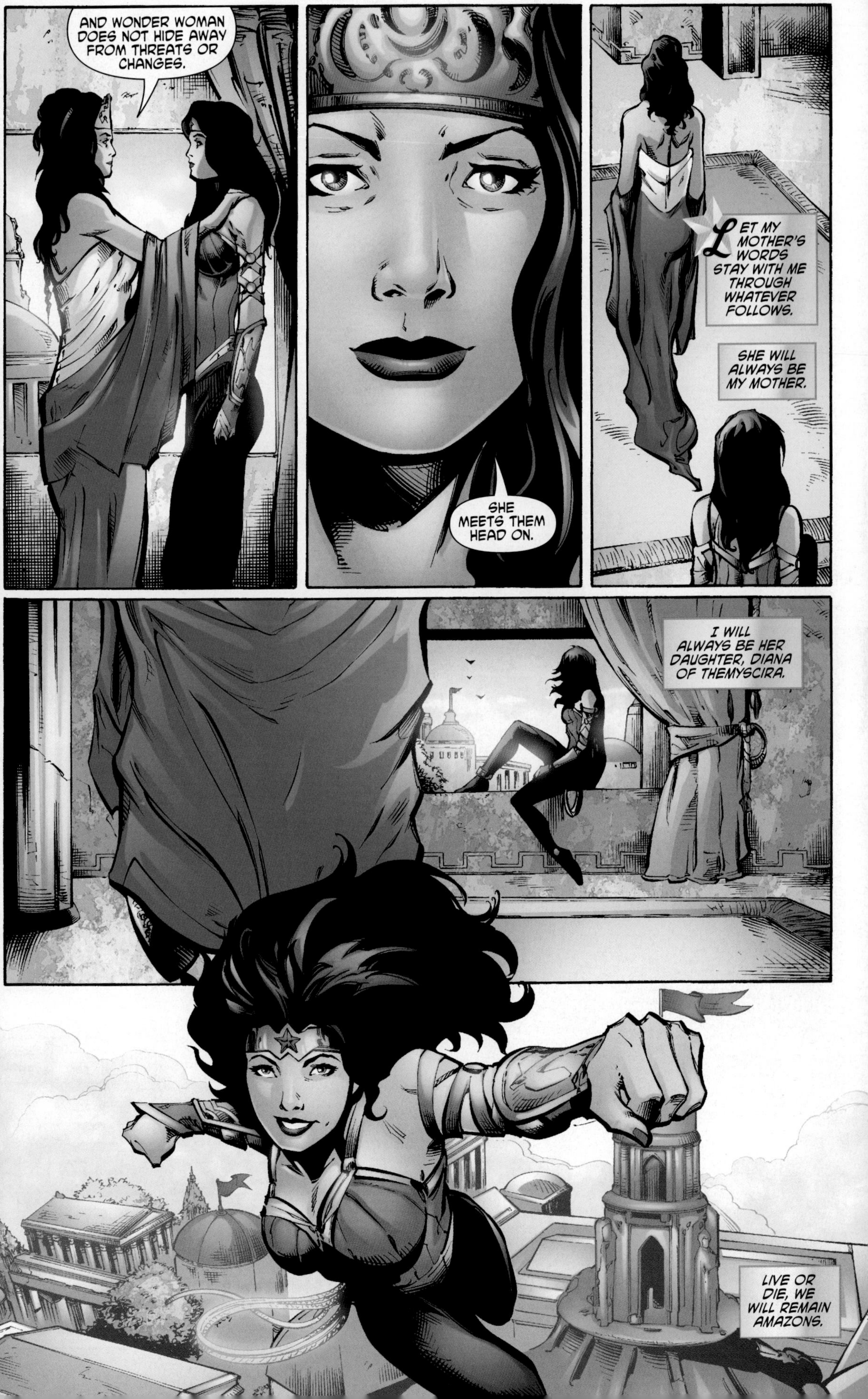
AND WONDER WOMAN DOES NOT HIDE AWAY FROM THREATS OR CHANGES.
SHE MEETS THEM HEAD ON.
LET MY MOTHER'S WORDS STAY WITH ME THROUGH WHATEVER FOLLOWS.
SHE WILL ALWAYS BE MY MOTHER.
I WILL ALWAYS BE HER DAUGHTER, DIANA OF THEMYSCIRA.
LIVE OR DIE, WE WILL REMAIN AMAZONS.

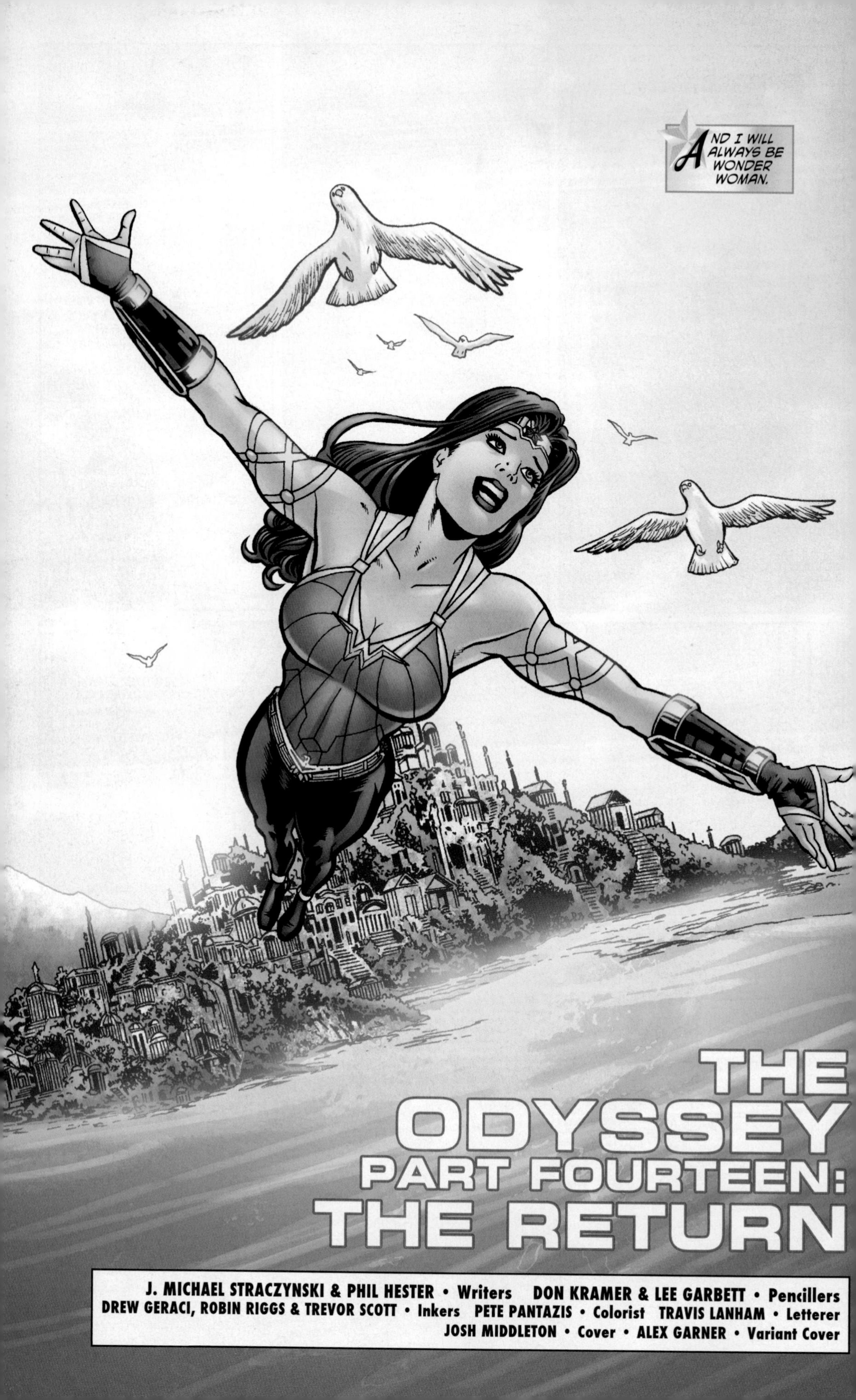
AND I WILL ALWAYS BE WONDER WOMAN.
THE ODYSSEY
PART FOURTEEN:
THE RETURN
J. MICHAEL STRACZYNSKI & PHIL HESTER • Writers DON KRAMER & LEE GARBETT • Pencillers
DREW GERACI, ROBIN RIGGS & TREVOR SCOTT • Inkers PETE PANTAZIS • Colorist TRAVIS LANHAM • Letterer
JOSH MIDDLETON • Cover • ALEX GARNER • Variant Cover

Variant cover gallery

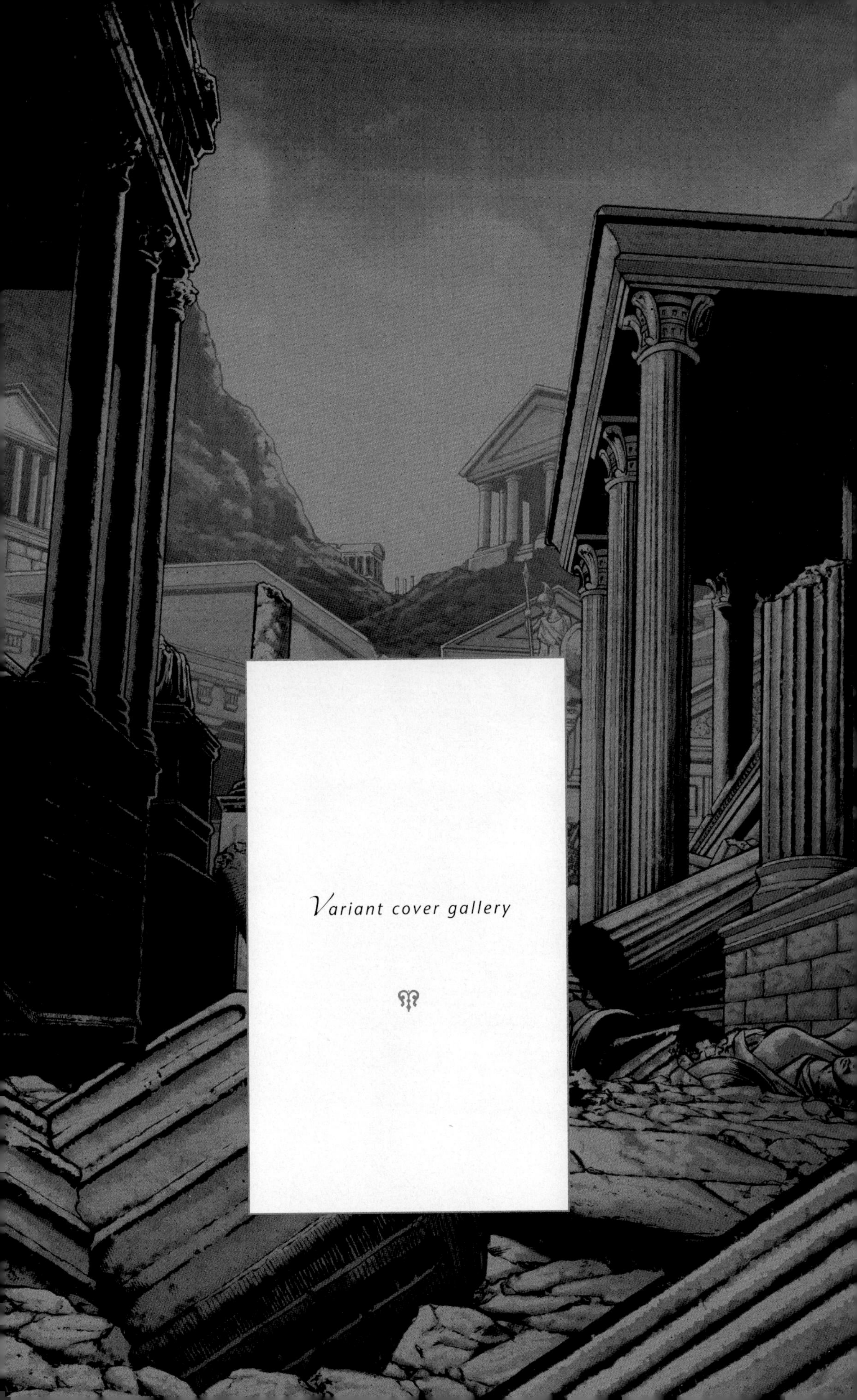

Cover #607 Variant art by Felipe Massafera

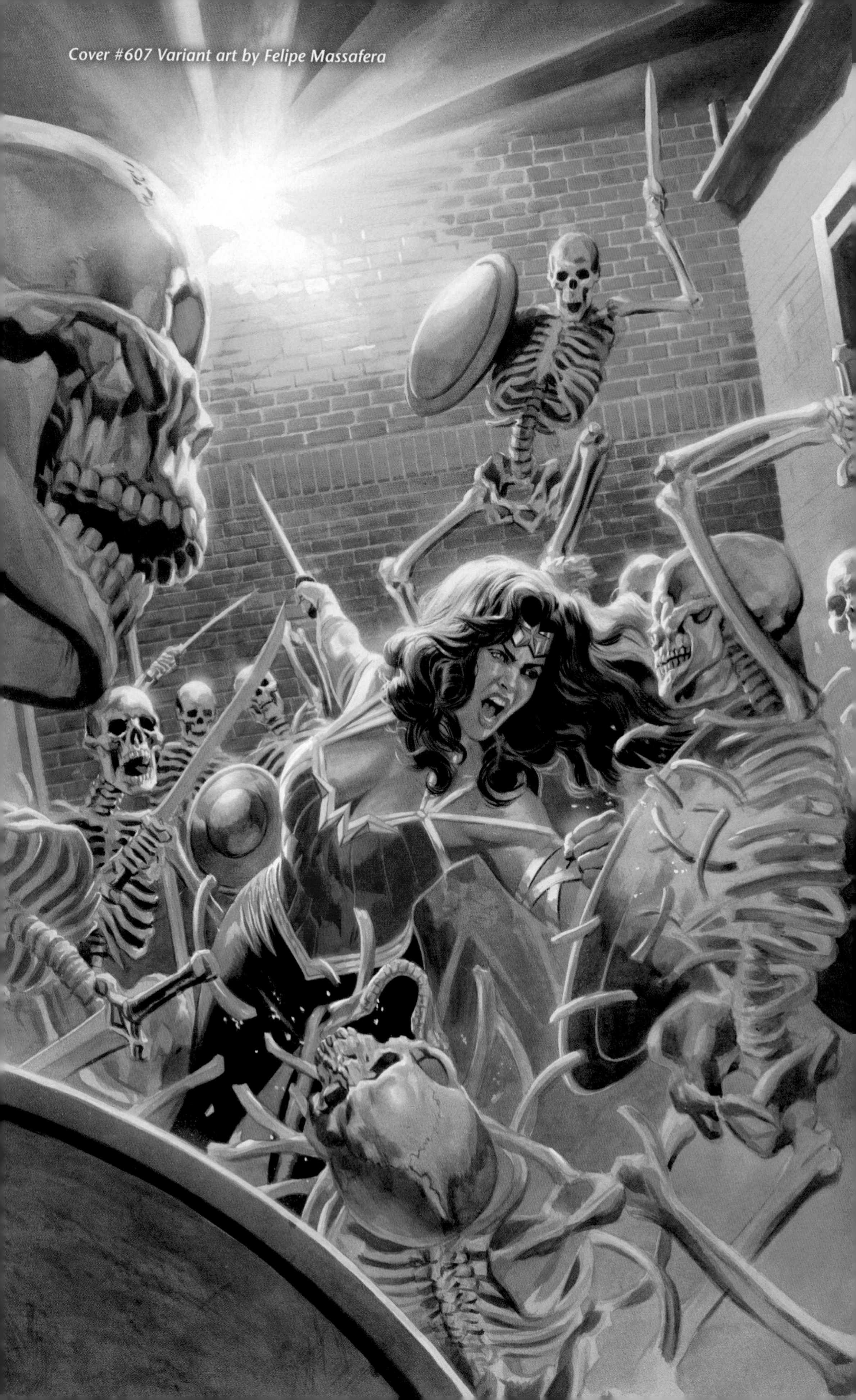

Cover #608 Variant art by Alex Garner

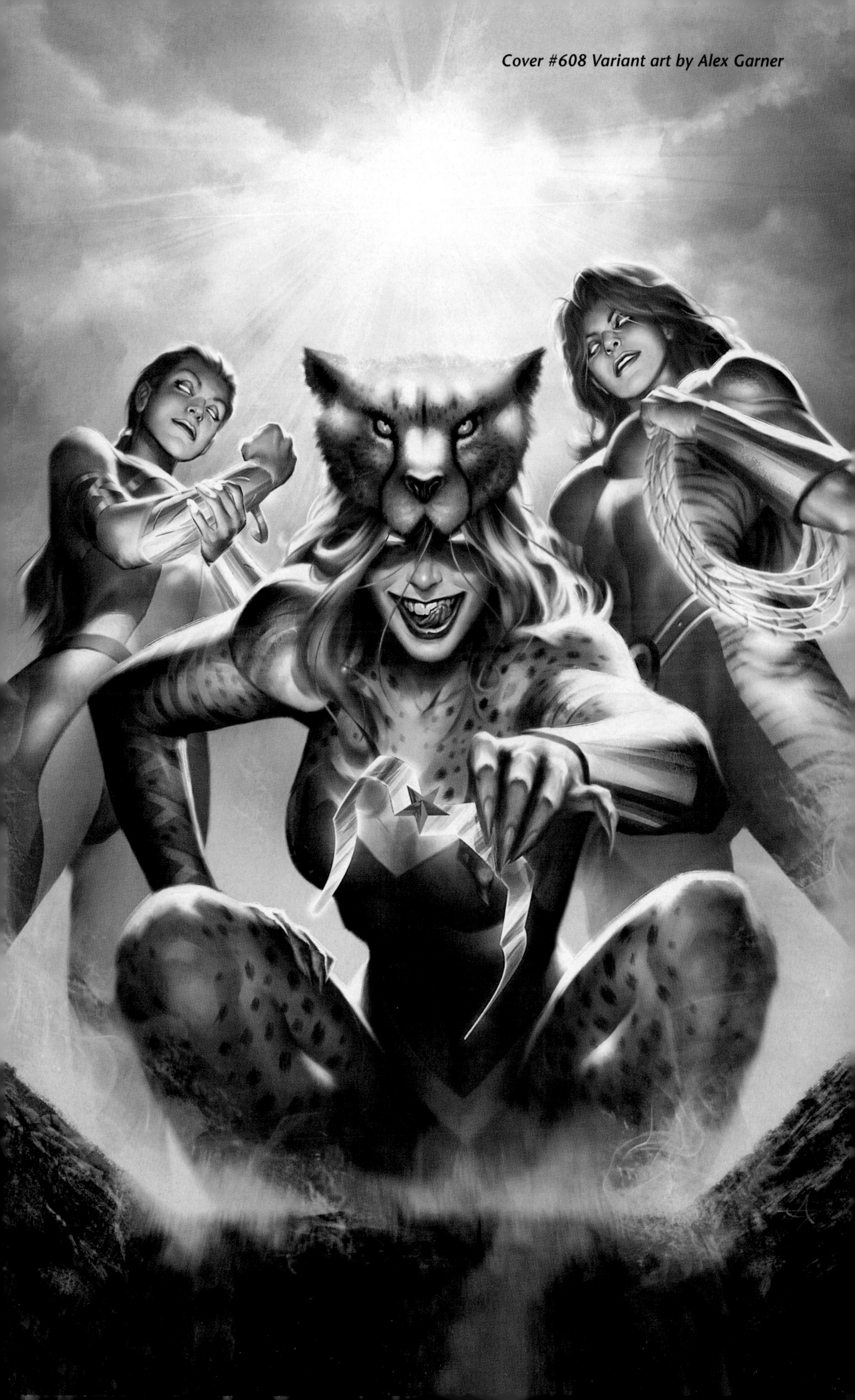

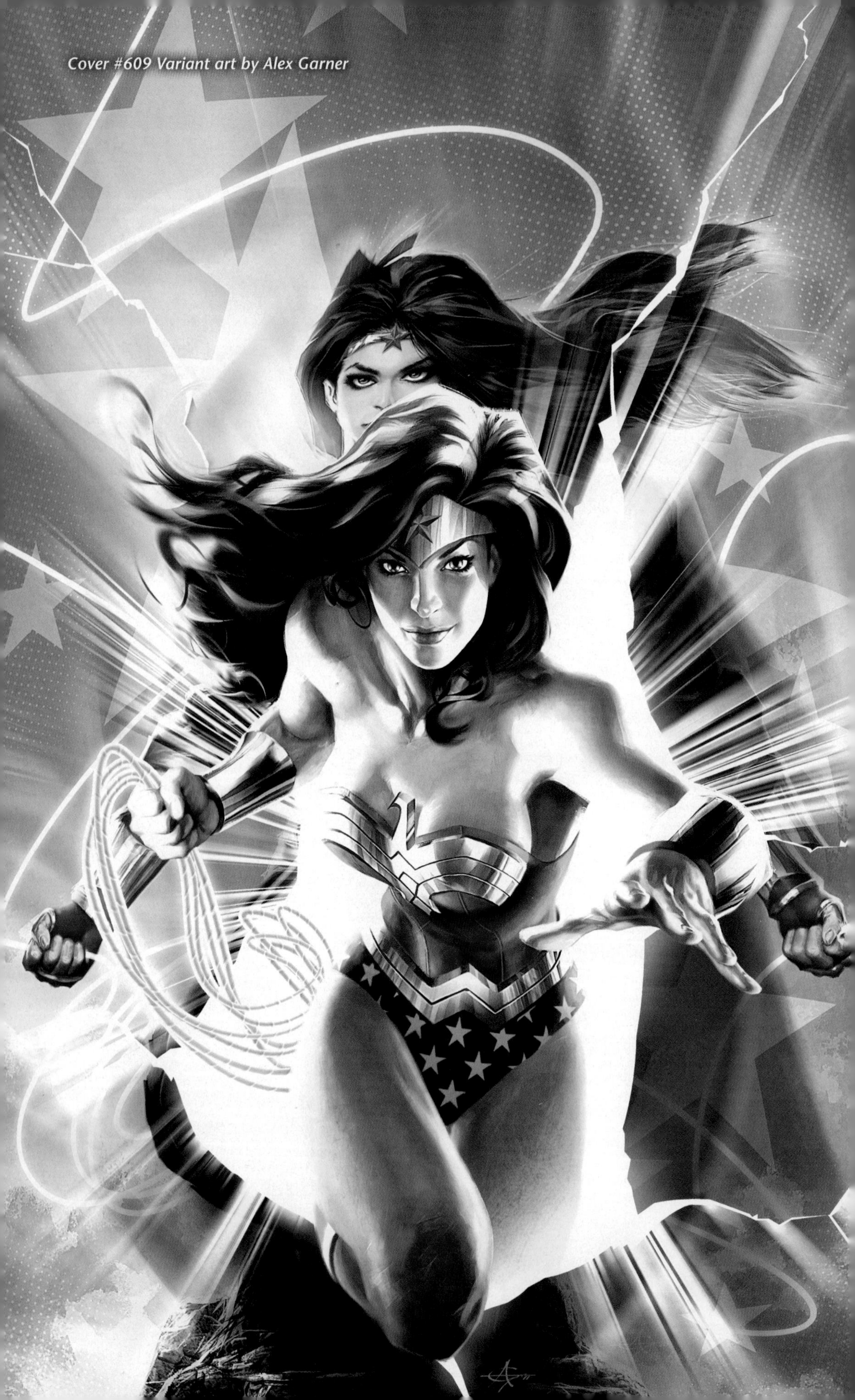

Cover #609 Variant art by Alex Garner

Cover #610 Variant art by Alex Garner

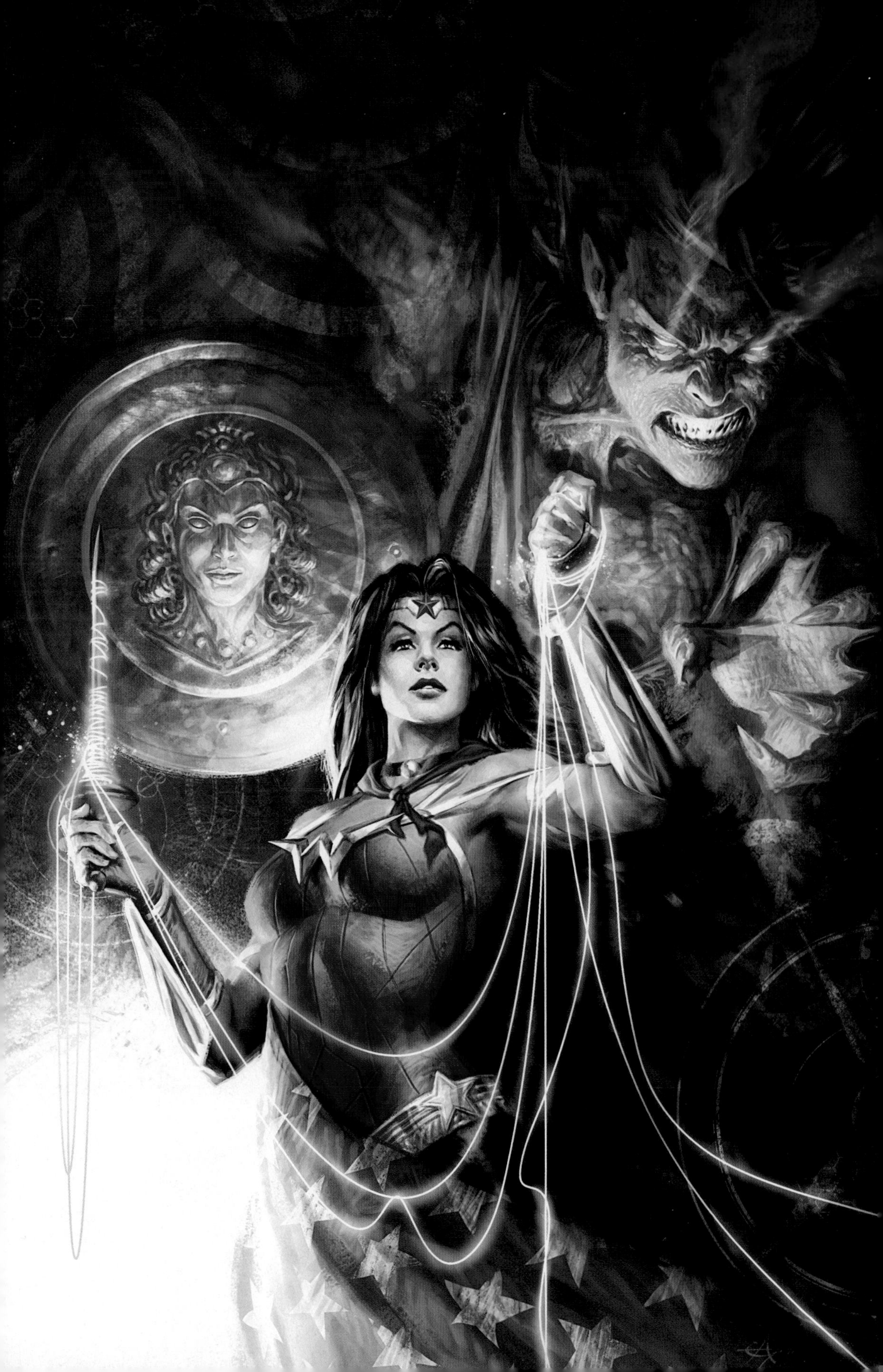

Cover #611 Variant art by Alex Garner

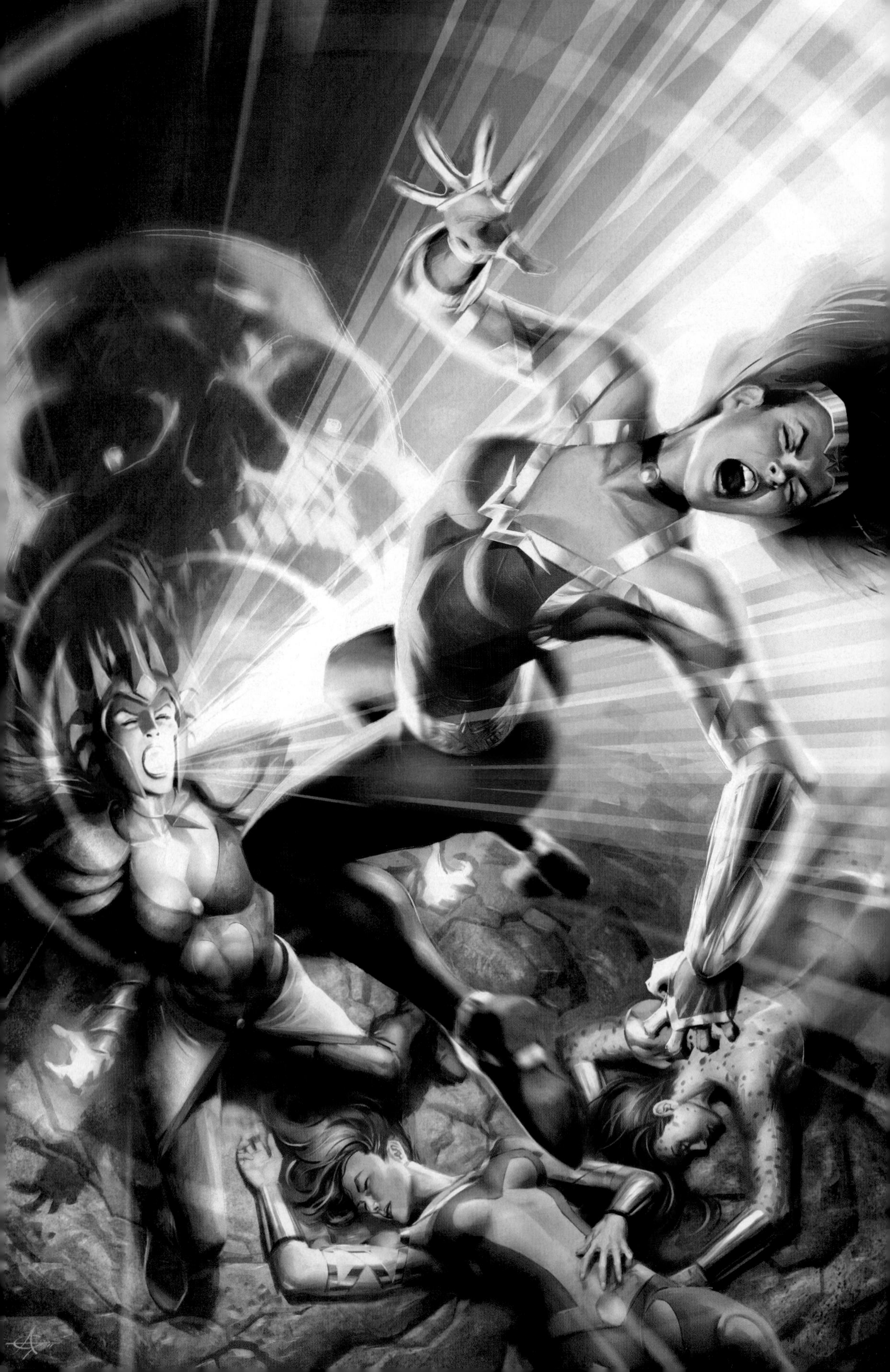

Cover #612 Variant art by Alex Garner

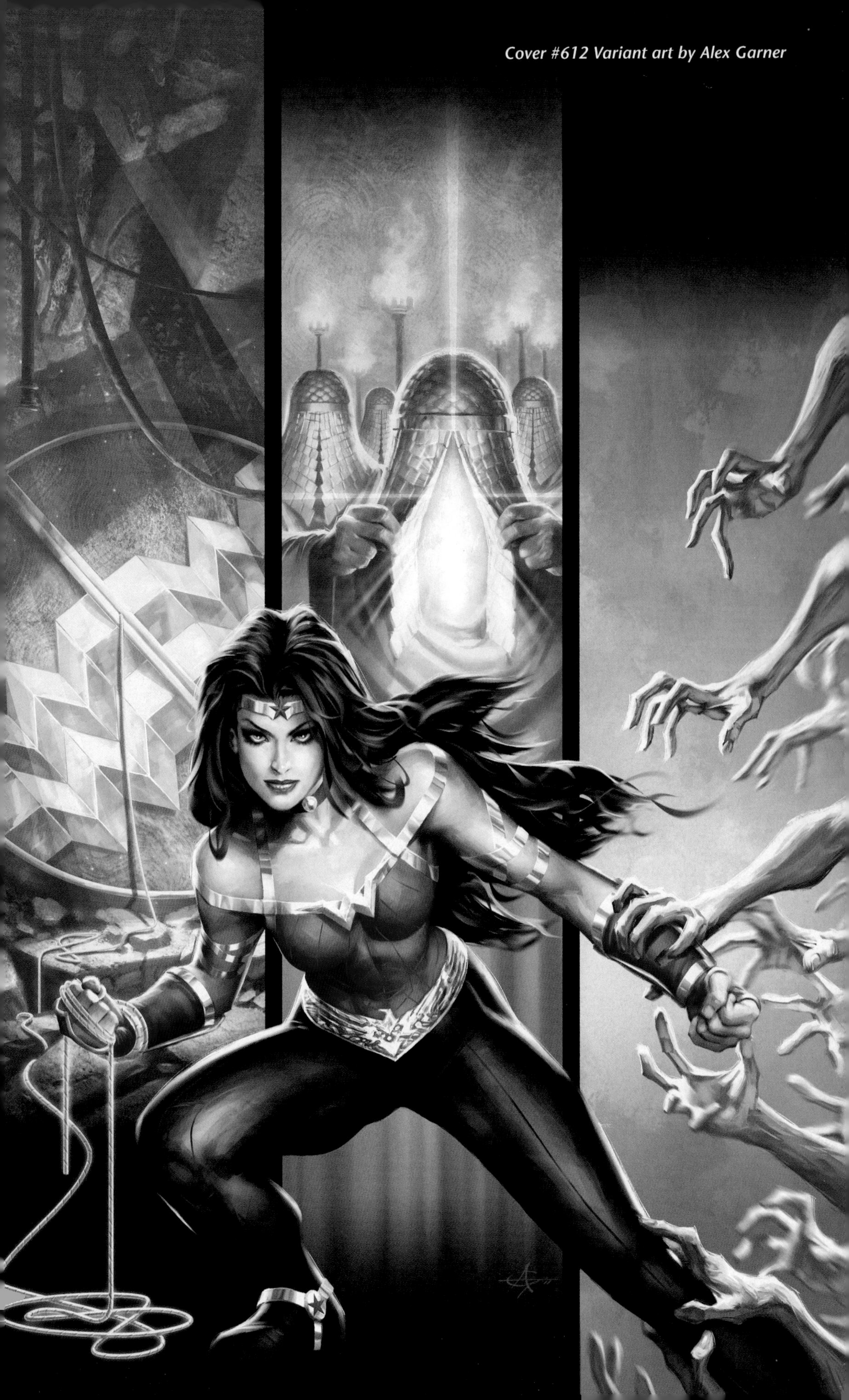

Cover #613 Variant art by Alex Garner

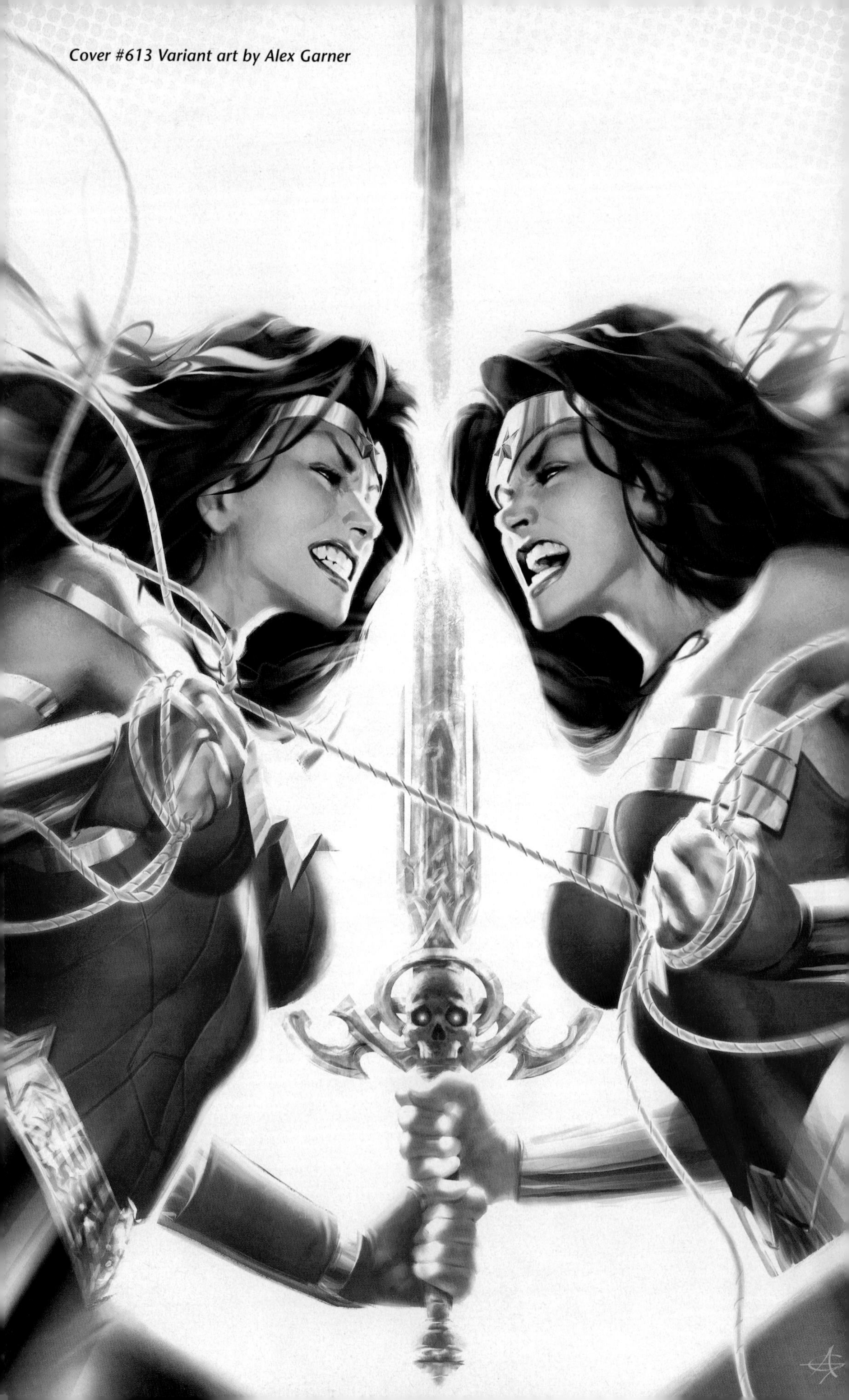

Cover #614 variant art by Alex Garner

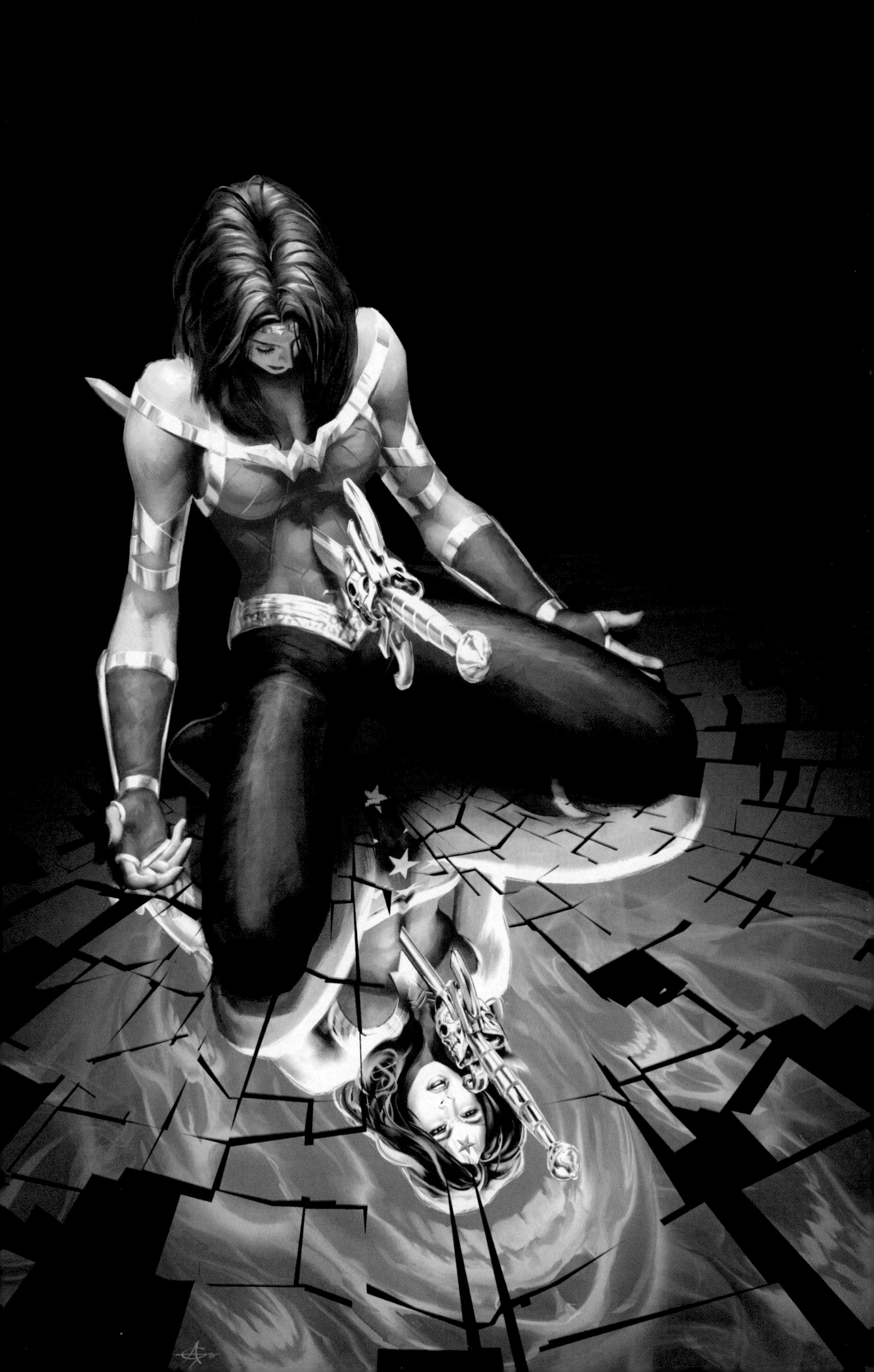

"Clear storytelling at its best. It's an intriguing concept and easy to grasp."
—NEW YORK TIMES

"Azzarello is rebuilding the mythology of Wonder Woman."
-MAXIM

START AT THE BEGINNING!

WONDER WOMAN VOLUME 1: BLOOD

MR. TERRIFIC
VOLUME 1:
MIND GAMES

BLUE BEETLE
VOLUME 1:
METAMORPHOSIS

THE FURY OF FIRESTORM:
THE NUCLEAR MEN
VOLUME 1:
GOD PARTICLE

"Excellent...From its poignant domestic moments, delivered in mostly warm, fuzzy flashbacks, to its blockbuster battles, Straczynski's SUPERMAN: EARTH ONE renders like a feature film just waiting for adaptation."
—WIRED

FROM *THE NEW YORK TIMES* #1 BESTSELLING AUTHOR

J. MICHAEL STRACZYNSKI

with SHANE DAVIS

TEAM-UPS OF THE
BRAVE AND THE BOLD

with JESUS SAIZ

SUPERMAN:
GROUNDED VOLS. 1-2

with EDDY BARROWS

WONDER WOMAN:
ODYSSEY VOLS. 1-2

with DON KRAMER

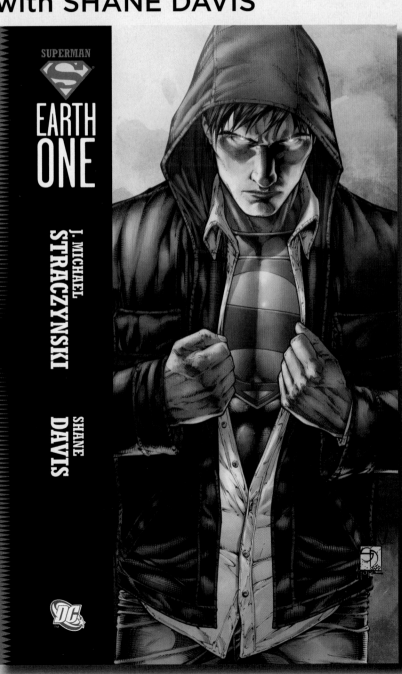